D1230365

A NEAT PLAIN MODERN STILE:

Philip Hooker
and
His Contemporaries
1796–1836

Ph; Hooker Arch!

This exhibition and catalogue were supported in part by a grant from the National Endowment for the Arts, a Federal agency; public funds from the New York State Council on the Arts; donations made by the Hamilton Friends of Art; a grant from the Friends of Hyde Hall, Inc.; and funds donated by the Turpin Bannister Chapter, Society of Architectural Historians.

Exhibition shown at:

Albany Institute of History & Art
Albany, New York
March 28–June 28, 1992

Emerson Gallery, Hamilton College
Clinton, New York
September 25–December 6, 1992

A NEAT PLAIN MODERN STILE:

Philip Hooker and His Contemporaries 1796–1836

Organized by

Emerson Gallery, Hamilton College

William Salzillo, Director

Curators and Contributing Authors

Douglas G. Bucher and W. Richard Wheeler

Edited by Mary Raddant Tomlan
in association with Ruth Osgood Trovato

Preface by Roger G. Kennedy

Distributed by
University of Massachusetts Press

Cover:
North Dutch Reformed Church, Albany, Hooker's sectional elevation, 1797.
Ink and watercolor on paper.
Archives, First Church in Albany, Albany, N.Y.

Back Cover:
St. Peter's Episcopal Church, Sherrill, N.Y., Hooker's framing elevation of the front, 1818.
Ink and wash on paper.
The New-York Historical Society, New York, N.Y.

PHOTOGRAPHIC CREDITS

Edward Pierrepont Beckwith: Figs. 14, 142, 144.
Joseph Levy: Figs. 3, 4, 10, 11, 16, 17, 28, 35, 72, 125, 154, 156, 158.
Harry Lott: Fig. 8.
Allen J. Manning: Fig. 41.
Marianita J. Peaslee: Figs. 2, 19, 20, 21, 24, 26, 53, 64, 65, 66, 169, 176, 181.
Stephen Schreiber: Figs. 77, 78, 140.
David Tewksbury: Figs. 23, 25, 30, 42, 43, 44, 57, 58, 59, 108, 109, 110, 111, 112, 132, 135, 136, 150, 183.
Walter Richard Wheeler: Figs. 27, 39, 145, 146, 147, 148, 149, 174, 175, 186.

ISBN 0-87023-768-3

Library of Congress Catalogue Card Number: 92-080130
Design by Grant Jacks
Printed by Penmor Lithographers, Lewiston, Maine 04240
Distributed by University of Massachusetts Press, Amherst, Mass. 01004

CONTENTS

ACKNOWLEDGEMENTS

The curators, the editor, and I would like to thank the lenders to the exhibition: Albany City School District; Albany County Hall of Records, Albany; Albany Institute of History & Art; Albany Medical College Archives; Frances D. Broderick; Douglas G. Bucher; Don Carpentier; Thomas Clarke; The Clinton Historical Society, Clinton, N.Y.; Cornell University, Department of Manuscripts and University Archives, Olin Library, Ithaca, N.Y.; The Detroit Institute of Arts; First Church in Albany; Friends of Hyde Hall, Inc., Springfield, N.Y.; Hamilton College Archives, Clinton, N.Y.; Thomas S. Kernan; The New-York Historical Society, New York, N.Y.; New York State Archives, Albany; New York State Library, Albany; Rensselaer County Historical Society, Troy, N.Y.; Schenectady County Historical Society, Schenectady; St. Peter's Episcopal Church, Albany; Union College, Schaffer Library, Schenectady; University of Michigan, William L. Clements Library, Ann Arbor; and W. Richard Wheeler, Troy, N.Y.

We would also like to single out the individuals who assisted in research and provided documentation on material in their collections: Albany County Hall of Records, Mary Vines, Executive Director, and Tracy Grimm, Archivist; Albany Institute of History & Art, Tammis Groft, Chief Curator, Wesley Balla, Curator of History, Prudence Backman, Chief Librarian, Cathleen Anderson, Registrar, and Janet Ayers, Public Relations Associate; Boston Public Library, Norma Mosby; Don Carpentier; First Church in Albany, Dr. Robert Alexander, Historian; First Lutheran Church, Albany, Flo Christoph, Historian; Friends of Hyde Hall, Inc., Douglas R. Kent, Curator; Morris Gerber, Albany; Hamilton College, Frank K. Lorenz, Archivist, and Lynn Mayo, Reference Librarian; The Huntington Library, San Marino, Calif., John Rhodehamel, Curator of American History; Lansingburgh Historical Society, Frances D. Broderick; The New-York Historical Society, Holly Hotchner, Director, Mary Ann Monet, Associate Registrar, and Diana Arecco, Photographic Services; New York Public Library, Mary B. Bowling, Curator, Manuscripts and Archives Section, Valerie Wingfield, Manuscripts Specialist, and Rocco Lombardo, Head, Copy Services; New York State Library, Billie Aul, Senior Librarian, James Corsaro, Associate Librarian, Paul Mercer, Archivist, and Kathleen Lawson, Supply Assistant; Oneida County Historical Society, Douglas Preston, Director; Rensselaer County Historical Society, Stacy Pomeroy Draper, Curator/Registrar, and Kathryn Sheehan, Curatorial Assistant.

We share in acknowledging the invaluable contributions of Norman S. Rice, Director Emeritus of the Albany Institute of History & Art. We are also grateful for the encouragement and financial support of the Friends of Hyde Hall, Inc.; special thanks to Douglas R. Kent; the Turpin Bannister Chapter, Society of Architectural Historians; and the Hamilton Friends of Art. For their generous direct support, we acknowledge Mesick · Cohen · Waite · Architects—

John I Mesick, James Cohen, John G. Waite. Thanks also to Regina Kellerman, Michael Lynch, Allen C. Miller, Jr., Jeane Newbold Miller, and Tim Post. Diana S. Waite was very helpful in the initial stages of this project. Roger G. Kennedy, Director, National Museum of American History, Smithsonian Institution, in addition to contributing to this catalogue, provided generous periodic advice.

Douglas G. Bucher would like to thank Charles E. Barth, Jr.; Frederick D. Cawley, Executive Director, Preservation League of New York State; Lynn Dunning Vaughan; Amy Facca; Bill Perrotte; Edward Sullivan; and Dr. Bruce Venter, Albany City School District.

W. Richard Wheeler wishes to acknowledge Jane B. Davies, Elizabeth D. Shaver, and Paul V. Turner.

Mary Raddant Tomlan would like to acknowledge Andrea J. Lazarski, Executive Director, Temporary State Commission on the Restoration of the Capitol, Albany, and extends special thanks to Douglas R. Kent.

I would like to acknowledge with thanks the Trustees and Administration of Hamilton College and the Hamilton Committee on the Visual Arts, William G. Roehrick, chair. Their support has helped establish the third historical link between Philip Hooker and Hamilton College.

I extend thanks to the direct participants in this project. Douglas G. Bucher and W. Richard Wheeler, curators and contributing authors, deserve full credit for excavating Philip Hooker's life and career. I am deeply indebted to Mary Raddant Tomlan, a peerless editor. Thanks also to Michael Tomlan for all his help and especially for introducing us to Mary.

I acknowledge with pleasure the hard work and commitment of our regular team: Grant Jacks, catalogue designer; Benjamin Critton, exhibition designer and fabricator; Marianita Peaslee and David Tewksbury, photographers; and my good friend, Ruth Osgood Trovato, associate editor. Thanks also to Dwight N. Lindley, Professor of English, Emeritus, for help with additional editing and proofreading.

I gratefully acknowledge the staff of the Emerson Gallery: Wanda Denise Jackson and Katherine LeGrand Reittinger as well as our Hamilton College student workers. Wanda and Kathi figuratively, and sometimes literally, glued the pieces together. For their help in typing the catalogue manuscript, thanks go to Sally Carman and Sally Emery.

Final thanks to Marjorie Salzillo for her patience, advice, and support.

William Salzillo, Director
Emerson Gallery, Hamilton College

EDITOR'S FOREWORD

It is particularly appropriate that the Emerson Gallery at Hamilton College in Clinton, New York, is the sponsor of *A Neat Plain Modern Stile: Philip Hooker and His Contemporaries 1796–1836.* The first major study of the Albany architect, published in 1929, was authored by Edward W. Root, a noted art collector and Hamilton faculty member. Indeed, the two venues of this exhibition—Albany and Clinton—were settings for Hooker's work and for Root's research as well.

Although Philip Hooker's practice and most of his buildings were located in Albany, a number of his works were constructed in central New York. The migration of members of his family to Utica about 1797 undoubtedly helped the architect obtain commissions in the vicinity, especially since his father, Samuel, and brother, John, were both carpenters. Among Philip's later designs in the region was the front elevation and steeple for the chapel at Hamilton College, its handsome form surviving to the present day.

Edward W. Root may have been predisposed to the architecture of the late eighteenth and early nineteenth centuries by the Federal-style Root family home in Clinton and by the classically based taste of his own time. It seems likely that he was led to focus on the work of Philip Hooker by his personal ties to the Hamilton College campus and by his wife's Albany origins. Root, a member of the Class of 1905, was a third generation graduate of the college. His grandfather, Oren, had been a Hamilton College professor; his father, Elihu, had become chairman of Hamilton's Board of Trustees in 1909, a post he would hold for nearly thirty years. Edward Root returned to his alma mater in 1920 as Lecturer on Art, several years after his marriage to Grace Cogswell of Albany. In the capital city, his wife's father and brother were officers of the successor institution to the New York State Bank, whose building Hooker had designed in 1803. It may be more than coincidental that, when the bank erected its new quarters in 1927, portions of Hooker's facade would be preserved, removed, and reincorporated as the entrance feature of that sixteen-story structure.

Root implied in the preface to his *Philip Hooker: A Contribution to the Study of the Renaissance in America* that he had begun his investigation of the architect's career about 1919. By that time, Hooker had been the subject of local research that was given national exposure in professional journals. Draftsman John L. Dykeman had studied and produced measured drawings of a half dozen or more Hooker buildings during the teens, presenting some in restored form.

During the more than sixty years since Root's book appeared, Hooker has been recognized primarily in New York State, although his work has received broad publication. The preservation of the 1803 bank facade was described in the *American Architect* in 1930, while photographs of Hooker's residential masterpiece, Hyde Hall, were included in the 1933 publication, *Great Georgian Houses of America.* That superb country house for George Clarke has received by far the greatest amount of published attention of any individual design by the architect, from articles by Henry S. F. Cooper, Jr., and Douglas R. Kent concerning its preservation and restoration, to Diana S. Waite's study of its tin roofing and Henry Wiencek's recounting of myths and family history associated with the building. Hooker's work was discussed by Talbot Hamlin in 1944 within the context of the Greek Revival style, and has been mentioned in subsequent surveys of American architectural history. More recently, Roger G. Kennedy has drawn on Douglas G. Bucher's research and published articles to consider Hooker and his buildings in the light of work by French architects active in the new republic. Finally, Walter Richard Wheeler has provided an up-to-date review of Hooker's *oeuvre* in *Antiques* magazine.

While *A Neat Plain Modern Stile: Philip Hooker and His Contemporaries 1796–1836* is firmly based on past studies, the effort here has gone far beyond those presentations. The exhibition offers nearly two hundred images and objects associated with Hooker's work, including drawings, documents, and even architectural fragments. The grouping of these according to broad function types introduces the viewer to design problems of Hooker's day—problems of planning, expression, and construction—and permits the study of the architect's approaches and solutions to similar projects. The original drawings and documents illustrate contemporary presentation techniques and practice, while the inclusion of material by designers whose work influenced or was simply parallel to Hooker's provides valuable opportunities for comparison.

This catalogue generally follows the format of Root's earlier publication, with its introduction to the Albany setting, review of the architect's career, and listing of his works, all amply illustrated. Yet it takes significant steps forward in the presentation and discussion of a greatly expanded number of commissions, drawings, and construction documents. Furthermore, while the organization of each section is chronological, the reader may replicate the approach of the exhibition by using the Index of Catalogue Raisonné Entries and Attributions, which is arranged according to function types.

In addition, this volume presents a broader view of building in Albany during Hooker's time. The reader will begin to recognize the names of Hooker's various partners and associates—Elisha Putnam, Robert Higham, and James T. Kelly—and of such prominent and successful members of the building trades as carpenter-builder John Boardman, stonemason Peter McNab, and woodcarver Henry Farnham, who contributed much to the buildings he designed and superintended. The catalogue entry for the Albany City Hall presents the mature Hooker alongside other professionals from Boston and New York, as well as some fascinating local architectural criticism. The numerous construction documents transcribed for the catalogue offer readers interested in technique and terminology an opportunity to look more closely at building practice of the time.

Much about Philip Hooker remains unknown, especially about his personal life and early architectural training. Nevertheless, the discovery and publication here of increased visual and written material from the architect's own hand has offered the means of better understanding his abilities and professional activities. Perhaps more importantly, these documents also reveal how Hooker himself approached and characterized his work, from the earlier *neat, plain, modern stile* of the trim in Elsie Fonda's town house to the later *bold* detailing of the Fourth Presbyterian Church.

Mary Raddant Tomlan

PREFACE

Some Thoughts about Philip Hooker

This exhibition is almost as much a work of archaeology as if it were devoted to the Native American architecture of the Ohio Valley of the fourth century. Instead, its subject is the work of the most popular and successful architect of the Hudson Valley in the early nineteenth century.

By archaeology I mean digging into archives as well as earth, and I use the term in contradistinction to the pleasures of judging an architect's work by the scrutiny of existing buildings above ground and in three dimensions. Only a tenth part of Hooker's work remains available to us. Bulldozers, parking lots, imperial governors, and the American embarrassment in the presence of the past have accounted for the rest.

Hooker had the misfortune to lay his work in the path of what was called in the 1930s, at its dispirited conclusion, *a Century of Progress.* He died in 1836, as that century commenced. Progress was often confused with nervous change, each change justified by a disparaging view of the past.

Progress is often bad for architecture, architecture being, by its nature, an obstruction, but for a profoundly conservative architect like Philip Hooker the consequences were disastrous. Nearly all his buildings were obliterated.

Judging from the few which have survived, especially his Hamilton College Chapel, his Albany Academy, and his quirky Hyde Hall near Cooperstown, as well as from the drawings in this exhibition, many of those buildings were very good and have been replaced by worse.

No one was more important than Hooker in creating the environment within which upstate New Yorkers lived. From an architectural point of view, Albany was Hooker's town, as it was, from a political point of view, the town of Erastus Corning and, before him, of Martin Van Buren. The city multiplied itself ten times during his lifetime; he gave it a state capitol, city hall, academy, and the five churches which brought it out of what had been its *gothic* phase into the—what shall we say?—last half of the eighteenth century? All but one of his major works was done in the first third of the nineteenth, but that is merely a chronological fact, not one easily confirmed by the evidence of the eyes.

Hooker was the perfect architect for an elite devoted to a seventeenth and eighteenth century way of life. The Van Rensselaers, and Ten Broecks, and Clarkes were in no hurry to abandon the patroonship system or the architectural forms which expressed it. Like the seigneuries of the French along Lake Champlain (and like the earlier *encomiendas* of the Spanish empire), the patroonships of the Dutch and manor lordships of the British had been a deliberate return to ancient Roman modes of colonization. They gave into the hands of people assumed to have military competence the governance of the people living on their lands. In return for protection within the fortified manor house of the patroon, lord, or seigneur, and his leadership in battle, his tenants would deliver a portion of their crops and labor.

As matters worked out, diamond merchants like the first Van Rensselaer, merchants like the first Livingston, and sugar planters like the first Clarke engrossed these lands and privileges. None of them ever sniffed powder nor heard the clang of arms, but they got the land, the tenants, and the feudal dues. After a time, as so often happens, the forms obliterated the formation; the seigneuries were converted into country estates, and the patroon-lords were able to hold on to their enormous holdings, resisting sale and collecting rents well into the nineteenth century.

Naturally enough, they preferred to think of themselves as country gentlemen descended from country gentlemen, though the inky smell of the counting house did linger. They secured from Philip Hooker, his father, and his brother designs which would serve to reinforce the impression that a happy squirearchy had been long established in the Hudson and Mohawk valleys. Stage sets of a bucolic England ensued, centered upon churches a century late in style with boot-cleaners at the door and a pew for the lord. The state capitol appeared like a county courthouse; there were steepled churches, schools, and neat, tight town houses. Albany assumed the aspect of a market town in, say, Dorset, or the Clarkes' ancestral Wiltshire.

Hooker was a first-rate stage designer for these effects, but he was considerably more. Architecture is not an art of illusion. It has to stand on its own. Tight-fisted clients require that it be well-crafted and constructed to last. It has been difficult to demolish some of Hooker's work; he built not only affectively but effectively as well.

This exhibition provides many insights into the means by which he served the requirements of his clients and his own requirements as an artist. It is not likely that to please them he *had* to draw on as diverse and sophisticated a set of eighteenth-century precedents as, in fact, he did. We may look through these drawings and re-examine his existing buildings, and see that he was familiar with the work of Robert Adam and the *Little Masters* of England. That we might expect. There is, also, a touch of Wyatt in the facade of Hyde Hall, and, if Hooker was responsible for the interior ornament (which seems likely), an interesting merging in the plaster work of the English Baroque with the freer and blockier American vernacular of Asher Benjamin.

There are also hints that he may have known Pierre Pharoux, who brought into his vocabulary something of the neo-classicism of the French Enlightenment. It was not radical by Hooker's time. Hooker's career did not get under way until the late 1790s and lasted until his death in 1836; the 1760s and 1770s were the heyday of French formal experimentation. But until Pharoux appeared in Albany in 1793 and 1794, things were proceeding in an unruffled British country style, roughly a century out of date.

Pharoux, a gentleman-architect whose career I tried to rediscover in *Orders from France*, had less than two years to educate the upstate gentry about the new cosmopolitan style, but educate them he did. He provided city plans and country-house plans and town-house plans, market entries like triumphal arches, cruciform courthouses and temple-form churches and a statehouse which some scholar should review in detail for connections to Hooker's lost State Capitol and Union College building.

The friends and clients of Pharoux included members of the Van Rensselaer clan, Philip Schuyler, and John Porteus. They all turned to Hooker after the death of Pharoux in 1795.

Hooker's North Dutch Reformed Church, built in 1797–99, seems to me to bear the touch of Pharoux's Speranza churches of 1794–95. As this catalogue points out, North Dutch does represent *what may have been the first appearance of a classical portico in the former Dutch colony outside of New York City*, but that is only because the earlier design by Pharoux was not built.

There is no doubt that Hooker was responsive to French ideas; he was explicit in his debt to Joseph Mangin's New York City jail, and another Mangin building, the New York City Hall (in collaboration with John McComb), clearly influenced Hooker's Albany Academy. Hooker's projected house for George Clarke in Albany seems to me to be his most interesting design, and it is derived from Ledoux—or from Pharoux.

I gather that scholars in northern New York are making their way to the Huntington Library, where the sketchbook of Pharoux reposes. It will be interesting to know what they conclude about the French interjections into the artistic life of New York during the lifetime of Philip Hooker. He bridged the gap between the death of Pharoux in 1795 and the appearance of Joseph-Jacques Ramée in 1811–12. Ramée took Hooker's place as the preferred architect for Union College, in Schenectady. Though Ramée had as his sponsor the rich and willful David Parish, he did not, it seems, penetrate very deeply into the squirearchy. He did provide an estate plan and (I believe) barn for another Hooker client, Catherine Duane of Duanesburg, and another for an Ogden island in the St. Lawrence. All the while staid, steady, dependable, and adaptable Philip Hooker went on providing competently for the needs of the gentry until his death.

The Albany Academy and the Hamilton College Chapel are at the highest reach of American craftsmanship of the period in which only the occasional Frenchman, flitting in and out of the scene, gave a sudden dash of elegance to northern New York. Down the Hudson, in the city of New York, the liveliest work of the 1790s through nearly 1820 was largely provided by resident Frenchmen, for, despite the influence of his friend Aaron Burr, Benjamin Henry Latrobe failed to secure clients there. Philadelphia awaited the Greek Revival to rescue it from the conservatism of its Carpenters' Company, while Boston went on with the eighteenth century, manifested with enormous skill in the deliberate derivativeness of Charles Bulfinch.

Prudent, elegant Bulfinch (1763–1844) is an easier analogue to Hooker (1766–1836) than either of their other contemporaries, Latrobe (1764–1820) or George Hadfield (1767–1826). The latter two were cosmopolitans, trained for many years in Italy, Germany, France, and Britain. They were also men of genius. Unlike Hooker, Bulfinch had the benefit of a grand, though brief, tour of England and France, capped by weeks in Rome. Despite this fashionable experience, Bulfinch is much closer to Hooker than to the other two in the breadth and profundity of his architectural training. Indeed, it is absurd to characterize Bulfinch as America's first native-born professionally trained architect, for his training was not superior in any significant way to that of Hooker. It is only that he had richer parents, was able to travel a little more widely both as a youth and as an adult, and received larger commissions.

We simply do not know what Hooker would have done had he been given the opportunities which came crowding to Bulfinch. Probably not quite so well, though the Clarke town house, the Academy, and the Chapel suggest he might.

In any event, this exhibition permits us to dig through the ruins of his career, his plans and letters and proposals, to reconstruct that career as we have never been able to do before. And to ask questions . . . what might have happened? How well did he know Pharoux? They lived in the same city, where the immaculately trained Frenchman held his soirees, amazing the local squires with his skill. The Francophile Livingstons were not alone in rushing to his door. Did the young Philip Hooker follow them, standing in the shadows, taking notes?

Roger G. Kennedy, Director
National Museum of American History
Smithsonian Institution

INTRODUCTORY ESSAY

PART ONE

Trading Post – Capital City

PART TWO

Philip Hooker – Evolution of an Architect

Douglas G. Bucher

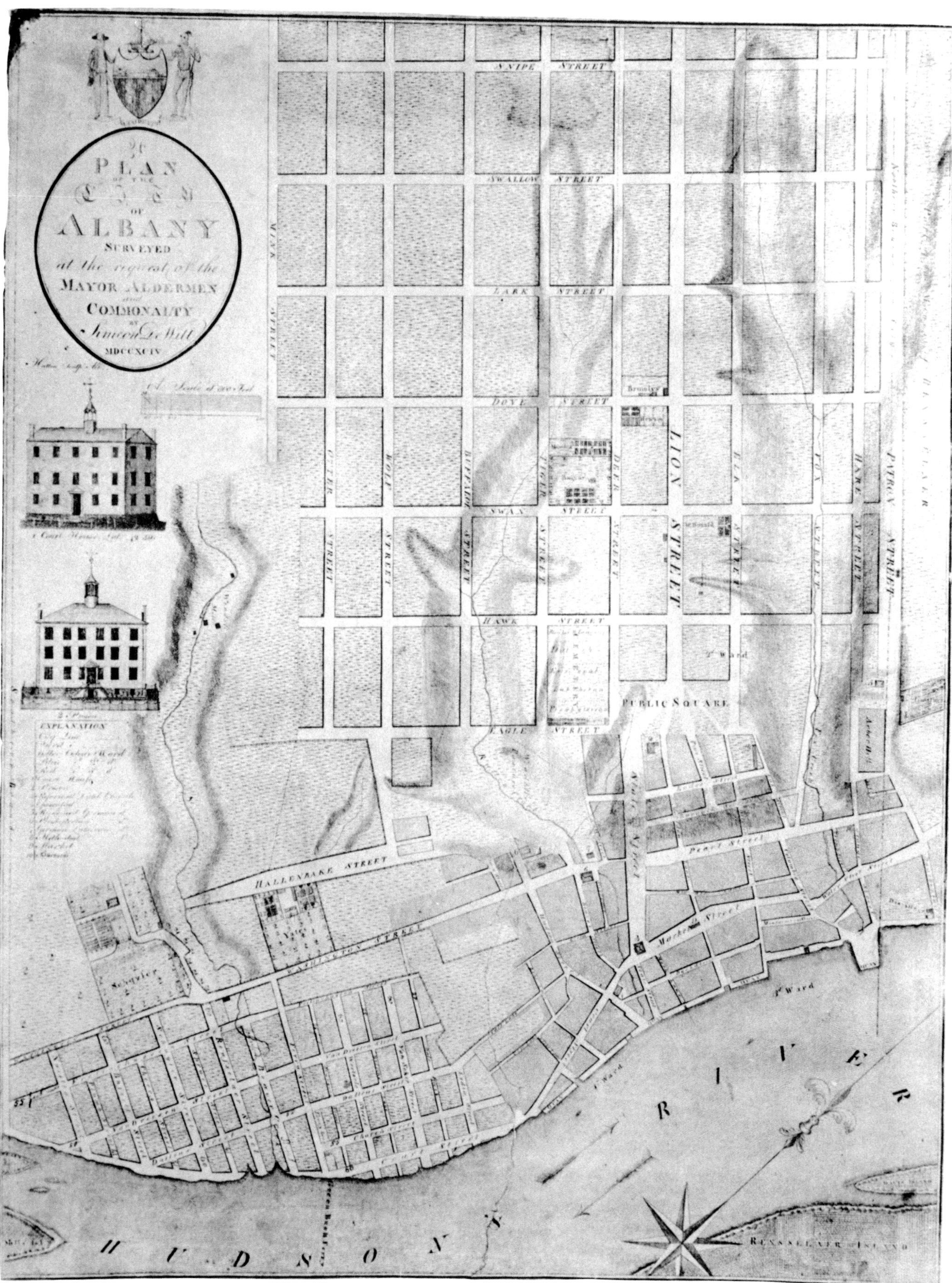
A PLAN OF THE CITY OF ALBANY
SURVEYED
at the request of the
MAYOR ALDERMEN
and
COMMONALTY
BY
Simeon De Witt
MDCCXCIV
SNIPE STREET
SWALLOW STREET
LARK STREET
DOVE STREET
SWAN STREET
HAWK STREET
EAGLE STREET
MINK STREET
OTTER STREET
WOLF STREET
BUFFALO STREET
TIGER STREET
DEER STREET
LION STREET
ELK STREET
FOX STREET
HARE STREET
PATROON STREET
PUBLIC SQUARE
HALLENBAKE STREET
WASHINGTON STREET
Pearl Street
Market Street
RIVER
HUDSON
RENSSELAER ISLAND

PART ONE

Trading Post – Capital City

ARRIVAL: THE HOOKER FAMILY

When Samuel Hooker, his wife Rachel, and their three young children arrived at the banks of the Hudson River opposite Albany some time soon after 1772, they saw before them a unique settlement whose history had already encompassed more than 150 years.[1] Yet their thoughts must have concerned the future rather than the past, and particularly the new opportunities that awaited them as they moved westward from Massachusetts. Whatever their plans and dreams, surely this husband and wife could not have known that their first-born son, Philip, would someday transform this small but vital community into the elegant capital city it was destined to become.

Albany huddled in a compact mass below the one-hundred-year-old Fort Frederick situated near the top of the present State Street hill. At the foot of this unusually wide, unpaved street, near the river, was the impressive form of the Dutch Reformed Church (1715), marked by a tall cupola rising from its high hipped roof. The appearance of this remarkable structure would be recorded later by Philip Hooker (fig. 2).[2] Surrounding the church and extending part way up the hill were the neat, small houses and stores of the diverse but distinctly Dutch inhabitants. These were wooden structures, whose tall narrow facades terminated in high gables; many of them were dressed up with a brick veneer fronting on the street. The medieval style buildings gave the town its peculiarly ancient air.

In contrast to these older structures were several recently constructed mansions. Situated north of the city was the Van Rensselaer Manor House (1765), an impressive brick structure in the modern English Georgian style. Located near the Hudson River, the great mansion dominated the flat plain beyond the town. South of the community, on a rise above the flood plain, was the fine brick mansion house of Philip Schuyler (1761), the first house to be constructed in the English style in the vicinity of Albany (fig. 1).[3] Equally impressive was the elegant brick house of Hendrick Cuyler (1767) which was sited near the river across from Albany, and may have been seen by the young Hooker family as they passed through Greenbush from the east. In contrast was the nearby house known today as Fort Crailo (c. 1704), constructed of brick in a plainer style. Philip Hooker was to be involved with at least two of these important houses in later life.[4]

◀ Fig. 1. *Plan of the City of Albany*, 1794, by Simeon De Witt, including the Schuyler Mansion grounds to the south, the Reformed Dutch and Episcopal churches in State Street, and the Public Square. Albany Institute of History & Art, McKinney Library.

ALBANY: THE EARLY YEARS

The locale that was to evolve into the city of Albany was first seen by Henry Hudson and his crew on 19 September 1609. Their small vessel could sail no farther up the Great River (the Hudson) and dropped anchor near this site. The prospect of a rich trade in beaver pelts provided the impetus for the construction in 1613 of a fort on Castle Island, situated south of the present city. Flooding soon forced the relocation of this Fort Nassau to the west shore of the river, near the mouth of Norman's Kill.[5]

By 1624 the recently chartered Dutch West India Company was settling families on a new site farther north which became known as Fort Orange. In 1629 the Charter of Freedoms and Exemptions divided New Netherland into manors, vast grants of land controlled by private individuals known as patroons. Kiliaen Van Rensselaer, a wealthy Amsterdam diamond merchant, was the most successful of the patroons. Rensselaerswyck, encompassing lands on both sides of the river at Albany, would eventually include some 700,000 acres.[6]

In 1643 the French missionary, Father Jogues, described the colony as "*. . . composed of about a hundred persons, who reside in some twenty-five or thirty houses built along the river. . . . In the principal house lives the Patroon's agent. . . . All their houses are merely of boards and thatched, with no mason work except the chimneys.*"[7] These transitory structures were soon to be replaced by ones which were slightly more substantial.

After Director-General Pieter Stuyvesant's attempts to control development of the community surrounding Fort Orange in 1648, the settlement was moved northward to the present site of downtown Albany. The new settlement was known as Beverwyck. By 1660 a stockade was erected and a church had been constructed in the intersection of what would later be known as State Street and Broadway. Dutch rule ended in 1664 when Charles II of England presented to his brother James, Duke of York and Albany, the *Empire of the Beaver* (the lands of the Dutch West India Company), and the settlement of Beverwyck became Albany. After a brief hiatus in which the Dutch regained control, the English solidly established their rule. By 1676 Fort Frederick was in place above the western edge of the town at the head of Jonckers Street (now State Street).[8]

This dual culture community was described in 1680 by Jasper Danckaerts and Pieter Sluyter, missionaries from Holland.

> *". . . it is nearly square, and lies against a hill with several good streets, on which there may be eighty or ninety houses. Fort Orange . . . lies below on the bank of the river, and is set off with palisades, filled in with earth on the inside. It is now abandoned by the English, who have built a similar one back of the town, high up on the declivity of the hill, from which it commands the place. From the other side of this fort, the inhabitants have brought a spring of water, under the fort and under the ground into the town, where they have in several places fountains always of clear, fresh, cool water.*

▶ Fig. 2. *A View of the Late Protestant Dutch Church in the City of Albany,* the church of 1715 as engraved by Henry W. Snyder from a drawing by Hooker. Engraving. Collection Douglas G. Bucher.

> *The town is surrounded by palisades, and has several gates corresponding to the streets. It has a Dutch Reformed and a Lutheran Church. The Lutheran minister lives up here in the winter and down in New York in the summer. There is no English Church, or place of meeting, to my knowledge. As this is the principal trading fort with the Indians, who come from the far interior to trade, and as the privelege of trading is granted to certain merchants, there are houses or lodges erected on both sides of the town where the Indians live during the time they are here."*[9]

On 22 July 1686, the English Governor Dongan granted Albany its City Charter, and Pieter Schuyler was appointed its first mayor. The city whose physical character Philip Hooker would transform had been given a new political shape.

The predecessors of three of Hooker's commissions were constructed by 1750: the Dutch Reformed Church (1715), superseding the earlier one on the same site at the intersection of the present State Street and Broadway; the Anglican (later Episcopal) Church (1715) midway up the State Street hill; and the simple three-story masonry City Hall or Court House (1741–44; later State House) at what is now Broadway and Hudson Avenue (fig. 1). Peter Kalm, the Swedish naturalist who toured the colonies from 1748 to 1751, described the city as he found it in 1749, with particular attention to its architectural character.

> *"The houses in this town are very neat, and partly built with stones covered with shingles of the White pine. Some are slated with tiles from Holland . . . most of the houses are built the old way, with the gable-end toward the street; a few excepted, which were lately built in the manner now used [the English type of building, fronting the street]. The gutters on the roofs reach almost to the middle of the street. This preserves the walls from being damaged by the rain; but is extremely disagreeable in rainy weather for the people in the streets, there being hardly any means of avoiding the water from the gutters. The street doors are generally in the middle of the houses and on both sides are seats on which, during fair weather, the people spend almost the whole day . . . in the evening these seats are covered with people of both sexes. . . . The streets are broad, and some of them are paved; in some parts they are lined with trees . . . the street which goes between the two churches* [State Street] *is five times broader than the others, and serves as a market place. The streets upon the whole are very dirty, because the people leave their cattle in them during the summer nights. There are two market places in the town, to which the country people resort twice a week."*[10]

Three large stone docks were proposed by the city in 1766.[11] The river front, a continuously evolving area, slowly reached out into the Hudson as the city expanded.

Albany's location made it a crossroads of great activity during the many years of the American Revolution, and there was a great influx of people into the city. In 1780 the State Legislature met for the first time at Albany, in the old City Hall.[12] A respite from the years of war, struggle, and fear came with the 27 June 1782 visit by General George Washington. The General accepted the freedom of the city and was entertained at Hugh Denniston's Tavern at the corner of Green and Beaver streets.[13]

In the years following the Revolution, floods of New Englanders, heading west, literally passed through the center of Albany as if it was a great gateway. State Street was the road westward, and Fort Frederick was getting in the way. No longer deemed necessary by the city fathers, the old fortress was ordered demolished in 1784, its stones to be used for public improvements.[14]

◀ Fig. 3. North Pearl Street, west side from Maiden Lane north, Albany, as it was in 1814, as recalled by James Eights, c. 1850. Watercolor on paper. Albany Institute of History & Art, Bequest of Ledyard Cogswell, Jr.

By 1786, the city had again become prosperous after years of privation during the Revolution. Philip Hooker was 20 years old and Albany, in its centennial year, had a population of over 3,000, and about 550 houses.[15] The fur trade which gave birth to the settlement was no longer the driving force; lumber and grain were the new commodities and government would soon become a major component of the local economy. In 1797, Albany became the permanent seat of state government; 188 years had passed since Henry Hudson and his crew first set eyes on the richly forested site which would evolve into the capital city.

1. The specific circumstances and date of the Hookers' arrival in Albany are not known, but these seem to be the most likely.
2. Henry W. Snyder produced the engraved view of the 1715 Protestant Dutch Church after a drawing by Philip Hooker. The engraving was published by John Low in New York City in 1806. There are two versions of the engraving; the earlier, which is reproduced here, shows no sky or background. A second printing includes a textured sky with clouds, as well as buildings on State Street and Broadway; the towers of Hooker's North Dutch Reformed Church can be seen in the distance. For Snyder, see p. 60, n. 17.
3. For a thorough investigation of this house and a discussion of contemporary building practices in Albany, see New York State, Bureau of Historic Sites, *Schuyler Mansion: A Historic Structure Report* ([Albany]: State of New York, Office of Parks and Recreation, 1977).
4. For his work on the Van Rensselaer and Schuyler mansions, see cat. 44 and A14, respectively. The author had seen documentation of Hooker's association with the remodeling of Fort Crailo, but has not now been able to locate it in the Van Rensselaer Manor Papers, SC 7079, Manuscripts and Special Collections, New York State Library, Albany, N.Y.
5. Codman Hislop, *Albany: Dutch, English, and American* (Albany: The Argus Press, 1936), pp. 24, 30–35.
6. Ibid., p. 56.
7. Ibid., p. 67.
8. Ibid., p. 104.
9. Ibid., pp. 106–7.
10. Ibid., pp. 145–46.
11. Cuyler Reynolds, comp., *Albany Chronicles* (Albany: J. B. Lyon Company, Printers, 1906), p. 263.
12. Ibid., p. 351.
13. Hislop, pp. 204–5. Hugh Denniston's son, Isaac, was later to occupy a house reportedly designed by Philip Hooker (A19).
14. Reynolds, p. 365.
15. Hislop, pp. 209–10.

PART TWO

Philip Hooker – Evolution of an Architect

Philip Hooker was a regional phenomenon, a man of many facets. Through sheer will and a good deal of talent and ability, this tradesman's son, whose personal life and appearance remain unknown, managed to rise to an impressive level in the architectural profession. Over the course of at least forty years, he developed along with Albany in a unique partnership which allowed his visions to become reality and his chosen city to evolve into the splendid metropolis its destiny demanded. The old adage seems most appropriate here: Philip Hooker was the right person in the right city at the right time in its history. As the following story reveals, the results of the fortuitous circumstances were sometimes extraordinary.

GROWING UP

Born in the town of Rutland, Worcester County, Massachusetts, on 28 October 1766, Philip was the first child of Samuel Hooker and Rachel Hinds. Samuel, twenty years old at the time, was a carpenter and builder by trade.[1] Samuel and Rachel's ancestors had been settled in Massachusetts for several generations.[2] Although the earliest known record of Samuel Hooker's presence in Albany is dated 2 November 1787,[3] it was probably some time shortly after 1772 that the young husband and wife migrated with their three children to the city on the Hudson.[4] The reason for this move is not known, but one can speculate that Albany's reputation as a vital and growing community tempted the young craftsman to seek greener pastures. As the face of the city was shifting away from its medieval Dutch personality to one of modern, fashionable English character, the arrival of Samuel Hooker, a carpenter from the New England building tradition, was very fortuitous and in keeping with the city's new cultural direction.

Philip Hooker would have been at least six years old at the time his family moved to Albany, and the journey was probably considered a great adventure by him. The years of his youth were dominated by the American Revolution, and Albany was active with local heroes, distinguished visitors, and others involved with the war. The inquisitive young Philip would have had numerous opportunities to meet people from many walks of life and with diverse talents. Unfortunately, we know nothing of his schooling or apprenticeship during this lively period.

The federal census of 1790 recorded nine persons in the family of Samuel Hooker.[5] Philip, who was then twenty-three or twenty-four years of age, was likely among that number, along with his four brothers—John (1769–1829), James, William, and Samuel—and two sisters—Susannah (1772–18- -) and Sarah, the youngest of the siblings.[6] The family resided in the Second Ward, the newly evolving portion of the city on the flat plain above the river, beyond the site of the old fort.

The best description of Albany during this period is provided by Lt. John Enys of the British army, who visited the city in November 1787:

> *After a good Nights sleep I arose very much refreshed and as we were not to move this day as soon as we had cleaned ourselves a little we went to see the town. This is a very Ancient* [city] *it having been founded before New York. It is very large and Poppolous and appears to carry on a very considerable trade by the number of small sloops & schooners we saw at its Quay's. This place seems to be improving very fast a great many very good new houses having been lately built in a very pretty style, as to the old part of the place it is perfectly german like its inhabitants. It is chiefly built of Brick but the old part looks dreadfully Ill as they only present the Gable end of the house to the street and in general keep all the Doors and windows shutt. I am also informed it is a custom here to make but very little use of the front Door, but keeping that shut to oblige every one to go round by the Back door. The town is situated in a low Spot near the water side surrounded with Hills towards the Land on one of which just out of the town stands the remains of an old fort* [Fort Frederick] *which is at present in ruins. There are here several Churches for the Church of England that of Scotland and a Dutch one togeather with a very handsome Gaol.* [For an illustration of this prison, located on the site of Hooker's and Richardson's city halls, see fig. 1.] *As well as several good houses in the town there are some in the Neighbourhood of Which that of Mr. Van Ranselwark [Stephen* [Van] *Rensselaer] the Patroon as they call him or Lord of the manner situated just as you enter the place from the Northward and those of General Schuyler and a Mr. Yaetes [Peter Waldron Yates] situated on the Rise of a hill to your right hand as you go out of town on the opposite side may be called by far the best. The latter was built by the Late general Broadstreet [John Bradstreet]. Altho this place is 165 Miles from New York yet it has the advantage of a very strong tide which not only comes here but goes up near to the New City* [Lansingburgh]. *When tired of walking we returnd to Dinner after which we crossed the ferry* [the Hudson River] *and Mr. Muirson introduced me to the house of a Mr. [Abraham? Henry?] Cuyler who had formerly been an Officer in the British Army. His house* [Vlie House] *is a very Genteel Building on the east side of the Hudsons River nearly opposite to that of General Schuyler.*[7]

Enys refers to *a great many very good new houses having been lately built in a very pretty style.* These were likely the brick houses in the current English mode that would continue to transform the streets of the city, contrasting with the earlier Dutch dwellings (fig. 3). Among the residences on the outskirts, the mansion of Peter Waldron Yates, later called Ash Grove, was probably the most elegant one constructed in the years immediately following the Revolution.[8] Some of these new structures were undoubtedly the work of Samuel Hooker, perhaps with the assistance of his two eldest sons, Philip and John. Judging from his inclusion as one of five men approved by the city council in November 1787 to appraise a recently constructed building, both Samuel Hooker and his work were respected in the community.[9]

An intriguing bit of ephemeral construction was undertaken by the city in 1788 as part of the celebration of the approval of the Constitution. This elegant structure, called the *Federal Bower,* was erected at the head of State Street. It was an *edifice . . . 154 feet long and 44 feet broad, raised upon four rows of pillars 15 feet high, composing 11 arches wreathed in flowers.*[10] Nothing like it had ever been erected in the city, and it is possible that the Hookers played some part in its design and erection.

1790–1800: THE FIRST YEARS

The beginning of Philip Hooker's involvement in building can be dated approximately to 1790 by a statement he made in 1815 that he had "*. . . an experience of twenty-five years in building and a close application in the research of antient and modern architecture.*"[11] The *building* experience seems most likely to have come about through working with his father, while the *research* component probably resulted from the study of carpenter's manuals and architectural books, as well as the observation of construction. Hooker's work points to a keen eye. Like all good architects, he would have observed, mentally recorded, and perhaps sketched what he saw.

It is not known if Hooker was able to travel to other locales as he began his career. With no documentation of his presence in Albany between his likely enumeration there in 1790 and his first identified design in late 1796, it is possible that he spent time elsewhere during the intervening years, not only viewing buildings but working with others or testing his own skills. He may well have been the *Hooker, Philip* who was listed as a *house-carpenter* in the New York City directories for 1792 and 1793, having gone to seek opportunities in that city of more than 30,000 persons.[12]

Had Hooker remained in Albany through the 1790s, the young designer would have found it an endless living textbook. Although its population in 1790 was only about 3,500,[13] the city served in the decades after the American Revolution as a great portal through which many people of diverse talents passed, sometimes deciding to linger or even to settle. In one three-day period during the winter of 1795, some 1,200 sleighs carrying immigrants to the west passed up the State Street hill.[14]

▶ Fig. 4. East side of Market Street (now Broadway) from Maiden Lane, Albany, 1805, as recalled by James Eights, c. 1850. Watercolor on paper. Albany Institute of History & Art, Bequest of Ledyard Cogswell, Jr.

World events were also to influence the development of the city. The French Revolution brought a great influx of talented and well-educated personalities into New York State and particularly the Hudson River Valley during this period.

Three such men arrived in Albany in the fall of 1793. They were the architect-engineers Pierre Pharoux and Simon Desjardins, commissioners of the Company of New York, and the young novice engineer Marc Isambard Brunel.[15] On behalf of the company and its French investors, Pharoux and Desjardins were engaged to survey its lands—known as Castorland—between the Adirondacks and Lake Ontario. The commissioners kept an extensive journal of their activities, while Pharoux, working for other clients as well, put down elegantly rendered designs in a fifty-nine-page architectural sketchbook.[16] Included among the real and fantastical schemes were at least one and perhaps other designs for Albany. An inquisitive young builder with architectural aspirations seems likely to have learned of and sought out all three men.

Of Pharoux's designs, the most intriguing are the fully delineated plans and elevations for a three-story brick shop, granary, and residence for Jacob Quesnel to be located on the northeast corner of Market (now Broadway) and State streets (fig. 5).[17] Evidence indicating that the Pharoux design may actually have been constructed is found in two of James Eights's watercolor illustrations of Albany as it appeared in 1805.[18] The artist's view of the east side of Market Street looking south (fig. 4) clearly depicts a large three-story structure with a massive central chimney, hipped roof, and a long rear wing, much as Pharoux represented it in his elevation drawings. Another view which looks down State Street toward the east shows the same massive chimney in the distance. The main facade of the Quesnel building features an elegant arcaded first story be-

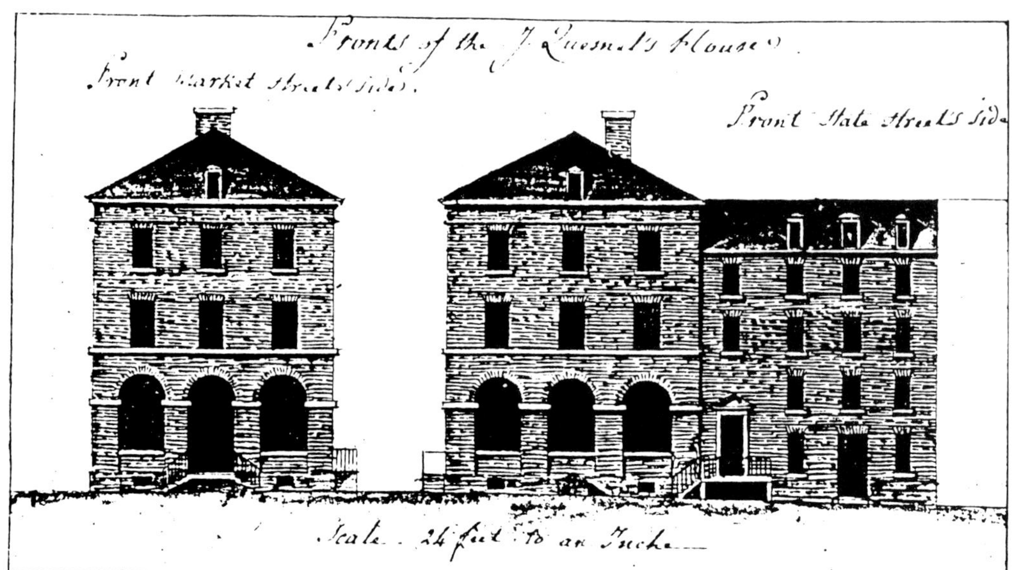

Fig. 5. House and store for Jacob Quesnel, Albany, designed by Pierre Pharoux, elevations, 1795. Ink and wash on paper. The Huntington Library, San Marino, Calif.

low a belt course. This is the first appearance on a facade in Albany of this arched arrangement so prevalent in neoclassical design. Hooker would make use of this motif in his own designs for the Consistory House of the North Dutch Reformed Church (1814–15) and the Gansevoort Town House (c. 1815).[19]

A further indication that Hooker may have been familiar with Pharoux's work is found in that architect's scheme for a large country house for M. Chorand at Coxsackie (fig. 6), a design that was unique at the time for the region. The main elevation of this house, with its hipped roof and wrap-around single-story covered piazza, brings to mind Hooker's later rendering of George Clarke's *cottage* in Otsego County, which depicts a facade of similarly austere character behind an extended piazza.

There is evidence of Pharoux's contact with Albany's professional community during the two years before his death in the fall of 1795. Prior to embarking on their first journey to Castorland in October 1793, he and Desjardins consulted with Simeon De Witt, the state's surveyor-general. In March 1795, Pharoux wrote to De Witt from New York City, describing in technical detail . . . *the manner of Calcining Gypsum, as practised near Paris,* and expressing a desire to continue communicating with De Witt, through correspondence, on matters of observation or experience.[20]

Whether or not Hooker, the young Albany architect, learned from these French visitors, his education would have also followed a more traditional path. Hooker's reference to *a close application in the research of antient and modern architecture* suggests his use of architectural books. The eighteenth century was the great age for the publication of books dealing with architecture by and for architectural professionals and amateurs. Many of the ideas made into reality by contractors, gentlemen builders, and architects, had English, French, and later, American pattern books and how-to manuals as their sources.

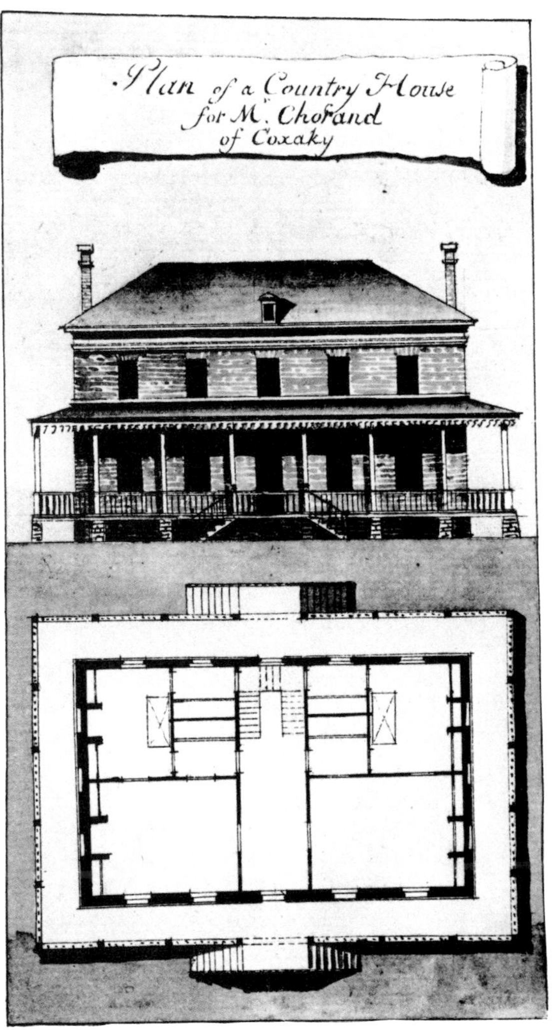

▶
Fig. 6. Country house for M. Chorand, Coxsackie, N.Y., designed by Pierre Pharoux, elevation and plan, 1795. Ink and wash on paper. The Huntington Library, San Marino, Calif.

Until recently, one of the few clues to books that may have been used or owned by Hooker was in the comparison of his designs with those found in published sources. For example, the triple arches on the first floor of Hooker's Consistory House for the North Dutch Reformed Church are reminiscent not only of Pharoux's earlier use of this detail for the Quesnel house but also of the town house illustrated in Plate 33 of Asher Benjamin's *The American Builder's Companion* (Boston, 1806). The facades of his Pearl Street Theatre (1824–25) and Albany City Hall (1829–32) resemble the compositional scheme illustrated by the courthouse design in Plate 42 of that work.[21]

While Hooker's familiarity with Benjamin's publication and similar sources must remain open to speculation, his ownership of one such volume is clear. A copy of Abraham Swan's *The Carpenters Complete Instructor* (London, 1768) is inscribed *Phil, Hooker 1797* in ink on the fly leaf.[22] The fifty-five finely engraved plates in this publication are primarily designs for roof trusses and framing but also include designs for cupolas, towers, domes, and curiously, a whole series of bridges ornamented with delicate Chinese fretwork railings. The last-named features are reminiscent of the balustrades at the Ten Broeck and Schuyler mansions, in whose design Hooker may have had a hand. Plate 1 is a section cut through the vast dome of St. Paul's Church in London, a building of such scale that few American architects of the time could ever hope to emulate it.

Unfortunately there are no personal annotations in the small volume, although there are a few pencilled lines inserted in some of the truss elevations. Certain plates relate to designs produced by Hooker. Plate 9 illustrates the roof structure for a three-aisled church similar to that delineated by Hooker for the North Dutch Reformed Church (1797–99). The interior dome shown in Plate 5 can be compared to the dome of the

▶ Fig. 7. State Hall, Albany (1797), designed by William Sanders. Courtesy Douglas G. Bucher.

Supreme Court Room (later Senate Chamber) located on the second floor of the New York State Capitol (1806–9).

How Philip Hooker acquired the twenty-nine-year-old volume is not known. No bookseller's label is to be found in the book, although at least three American dealers offered this edition for sale in the eighteenth century.[23] Nor do any documentary clues shed light on a possible previous owner. One wonders whether this copy of Swan's publication might have been a prized possession of Philip's father, presented as a gift to his talented first son.[24] The discovery of this single volume suggests that Hooker maintained some sort of an architectural library. Regardless of the extent of his personal collection, it is likely that he made use of books available in the libraries of wealthy clients such as the Van Rensselaers, Gansevoorts, and George Clarke.

The year 1797 was a significant one for Albany, as the city was named the permanent seat of government in New York State and the cornerstone was laid for the first purpose-built state office building (fig. 7). That structure, which was situated at the southwest corner of State and Lodge streets, was designed by one William Sanders, who had probably been trained in his native England. Sanders had also provided a design for a state prison, but its construction was halted before its completion.[25] It was also in 1797, on 4 August, that a great fire destroyed fifty houses in the old portion of the city, including Montgomery, Dock, Steuben, North Market, Columbia, and James streets.[26] This tragedy likely provided oppor-

▶ Fig. 8. Whitestown Court House, Whitesboro, N.Y. (1807), design provided by John Hooker. Oneida County Historical Society, Utica.

tunities for Hooker and others to make use of their design and building skills in the reconstruction of the devastated area.

The prospects for Albany's growth must have given Philip Hooker ample reason to remain in the city. His father and brother, John, however, were engaged by agents of the Holland Land Company to construct a large brick hotel at Old Fort Schuyler, about one hundred miles westward. It was apparently in 1797 that Samuel and Rachel Hooker, with John and others of Philip's siblings, left Albany for the settlement that would soon be incorporated as Utica.[27] The new hotel there, *a square, three storied structure, with a four-sided roof*, would be noteworthy for its great size, its masonry construction, and its foundations of hemlock logs placed lengthwise.[28] Philip Hooker would later employ a variation of that type of foundation for his St. Peter's Episcopal Church in Albany (1802–3).

While apparently keeping in close touch with Philip, the Hookers remained in Utica and were active in its development.[29] The impressive new hotel undoubtedly acted as an advertisement for Samuel and John's carpentry and building skills, and they obtained work in the village and surrounding region. John Hooker, for example, would be associated with the construction of the Whitestown Court House at Whitesboro (1807), a building whose forms echoed those being used by his architect-brother in Albany (fig. 8).[30]

It was in 1797 that construction began on the North Dutch Reformed Church in Albany, the first design known to have been from

▶
Fig. 9. North Dutch Reformed Church, Albany (1797–99), view before remodeling of 1857–59. Lithograph. New York State Library, Albany.

Philip Hooker's hand (fig. 9). This church was erected at the edge of the old urban center, in a newly developing area, and it dominated the surrounding neighborhood. Its twin-towered form was unique in the region at that time, and seems to have been directly inspired by Charles Bulfinch's Hollis Street Church, constructed in Boston about ten years earlier. Hooker could have visited that church, or seen it published in the April 1788 *Columbian Magazine* or the December 1793 *Massachusetts Magazine.* Although his initial concept for the Albany church followed closely the Bulfinch prototype, Hooker's original drawings of 1796 exhibit an assured competence beyond the work of a novice and the church as

▲
Fig. 10. Southeast View of Union College, Schenectady, drawn by Hooker, c. 1807–8. Ink and wash on paper. Albany Institute of History & Art.

built is solely his creation. In the wake of the August 1797 fire in the city, Hooker specified the use of tin plates to roof the new building. Unfortunately, this early experiment in tinplate roofing in the United States was unsuccessful, and the metal roof had to be covered with a sanded paint in 1798 to curtail the problem of leakage.[31]

Hooker's partner in erecting the North Dutch Reformed Church was Elisha Putnam, who had recently built the First Presbyterian Church (1795–96) in Albany. While nothing is known of the origins of their association, Putnam's subsequent career as a builder and as superintendent of the Albany Water Works suggests that his practical skills and expertise were of especial value to Hooker.[32] The two men would work together on at least four additional projects before the dissolution of their partnership.

By the end of the 1790s, Philip Hooker had received two other major commissions—for the second building of Union College (1797–1804) in Schenectady (fig. 10) and the New York State Arsenal (c. 1799) in Albany. This early stage of his career thus featured impressive projects that ordinarily might not appear in an architect's *oeuvre* until later in life. As the nineteenth century began, the thirty-four-year-old architect seemed well positioned to continue his active involvement in shaping the rapidly expanding capital city.

1800–1810: DECADE OF SUCCESS

A rapid succession of important public projects in this first decade of the new century would attest to Hooker's growing stature and ability. Of perhaps equal significance is the fact that the nature of his involvement with his projects changed, possibly effected or at least hastened by the dissolution of his partnership with builder Elisha Putnam in 1803.[33] Hooker, who was an organizer of the Mechanics' Society, incorporated in 1801,[34] would turn from actually erecting the buildings he designed to superintending their construction by others, moving from the role of a carpenter-designer to one of a more specialized professional.

It was also during this period that Hooker developed a regional clientele, undoubtedly as an outgrowth of his family's move to Utica. The reputations and associations established by Samuel and John Hooker in that village and area almost certainly led to Hooker's designs for Trinity Episcopal Church (1803–10) in Utica and the First Presbyterian Church (1804–6) in Cazenovia. The latter work seems likely to have been related to a non-architectural project, in which Philip Hooker put his drawing skills to work for Jedediah T. Turner, a member of the Cazenovia congregation (fig. 11).[35]

Hooker was responsible for the design of several other churches in this first decade, including the impressive St. Peter's Episcopal Church (1802–3) and South Dutch Reformed Church (1805–11), both in Albany, and, on the east side of the Hudson River, St. Paul's Episcopal Church (1804–5) in Troy and Trinity Episcopal Church (c. 1804–5) in Lansingburgh. Credit for at least a portion of the elegant design of the South Dutch Reformed Church must be shared with Elisha Putnam, who was engaged as superintendent for this project. Putnam was responsible for the concept of full length windows which greatly enhanced the beauty of the church. Unfortunately, the upper stages of its steeple were never constructed.

This was also the decade of Hooker's politically, if not architecturally, most important commission, the New York State Capitol (1806–9), which for so long was to dominate the city from its dramatic site at the head of the State Street hill (fig. 12). Edward W. Root has pointed out the possible inspiration for the capitol building's facade from various plates in Colen Campbell's five-volume *Vitruvius Britannicus* (London, 1715–71).[36] One of these volumes could have been in Hooker's library.

In connection with the construction of the capitol, Hooker traveled to Stockbridge, Massachusetts, and to New Jersey.[37] Both journeys would have afforded Hooker with excellent opportunities to study architecture beyond his own region. Perhaps he saw Bulfinch's Congregational Church (1790–93) in Pittsfield, Massachusetts.[38] The route of travel southward to New Jersey would have taken the architect along the east side of the Hudson River, where a considerable amount of new construction was to be seen in the many prosperous communities between Albany

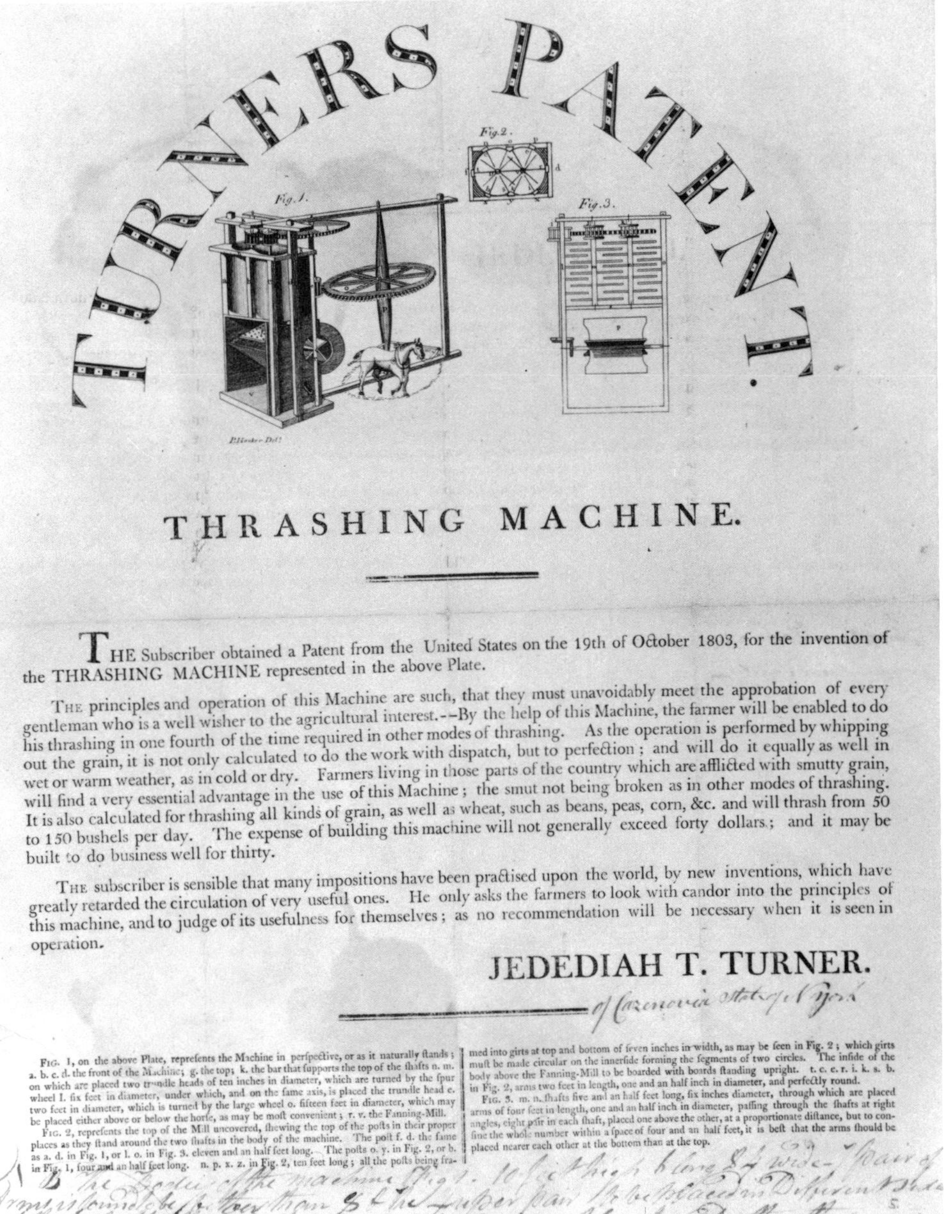

TURNERS PATENT.

Fig. 1. Fig. 2. Fig. 3.

THRASHING MACHINE.

THE Subscriber obtained a Patent from the United States on the 19th of October 1803, for the invention of the THRASHING MACHINE represented in the above Plate.

THE principles and operation of this Machine are such, that they must unavoidably meet the approbation of every gentleman who is a well wisher to the agricultural interest.--By the help of this Machine, the farmer will be enabled to do his thrashing in one fourth of the time required in other modes of thrashing. As the operation is performed by whipping out the grain, it is not only calculated to do the work with dispatch, but to perfection; and will do it equally as well in wet or warm weather, as in cold or dry. Farmers living in those parts of the country which are afflicted with smutty grain, will find a very essential advantage in the use of this Machine; the smut not being broken as in other modes of thrashing. It is also calculated for thrashing all kinds of grain, as well as wheat, such as beans, peas, corn, &c. and will thrash from 50 to 150 bushels per day. The expense of building this machine will not generally exceed forty dollars; and it may be built to do business well for thirty.

THE subscriber is sensible that many impositions have been practised upon the world, by new inventions, which have greatly retarded the circulation of very useful ones. He only asks the farmers to look with candor into the principles of this machine, and to judge of its usefulness for themselves; as no recommendation will be necessary when it is seen in operation.

JEDEDIAH T. TURNER.

FIG. 1, on the above Plate, repreſents the Machine in perſpective, or as it naturally ſtands; a. b. c. d. the front of the Machine; g. the top; k. the bar that ſupports the top of the ſhafts n. m. on which are placed two trundle heads of ten inches in diameter, which are turned by the ſpur wheel l. ſix feet in diameter, under which, and on the ſame axis, is placed the trundle head e. two feet in diameter, which is turned by the large wheel o. fifteen feet in diameter, which may be placed either above or below the horſe, as may be moſt convenient; r. v. the Fanning-Mill.

FIG. 2, repreſents the top of the Mill uncovered, ſhewing the top of the poſts in their proper places as they ſtand around the two ſhafts in the body of the machine. The poſt f. d. the ſame as a. d. in Fig. 1, or l. o. in Fig. 3. eleven and an half feet long. The poſts o. y. in Fig. 2, or b. in Fig. 1, four and an half feet long. n. p. x. z. in Fig. 2, ten feet long; all the poſts being framed into girts at top and bottom of ſeven inches in width, as may be ſeen in Fig. 2; which girts muſt be made circular on the innerſide forming the ſegments of two circles. The inſide of the body above the Fanning-Mill to be boarded with boards ſtanding upright. t. c. e. r. i. k. s. b. in Fig. 2, arms two feet in length, one and an half inch in diameter, and perfectly round.

FIG. 3. m. n. ſhafts five and an half feet long, ſix inches diameter, through which are placed arms of four feet in length, one and an half inch in diameter, paſſing through the ſhafts at right angles, eight pair in each ſhaft, placed one above the other, at a proportionate diſtance, but to confine the whole number within a ſpace of four and an half feet, it is beſt that the arms ſhould be placed nearer each other at the bottom than at the top.

5.

▶
Fig. 11. Plate showing Jedediah T. Turner's Thrashing Machine, patented 1803, from a drawing by Hooker, date unknown. Engraving. Albany Institute of History & Art, McKinney Library, Broadside Collection.

and New York City, as well as on the large estates, particularly those belonging to the Livingstons. In the years between 1790 and 1800, an extraordinary series of elegant and unusual country houses were constructed, including Arryl House (1792–93) for Robert R. Livingston, Masséna (1795–97) for John R. Livingston, and Linlithgo (1796–99) for Henry Walter Livingston. The designs for these fine houses have been attributed to the French architect Pierre Pharoux. It was during this same brief period that Pharoux produced the remarkable plan for the town of Esperanza on the west side of the river (also called Speranza, and now Athens) for the Livingston family.[39]

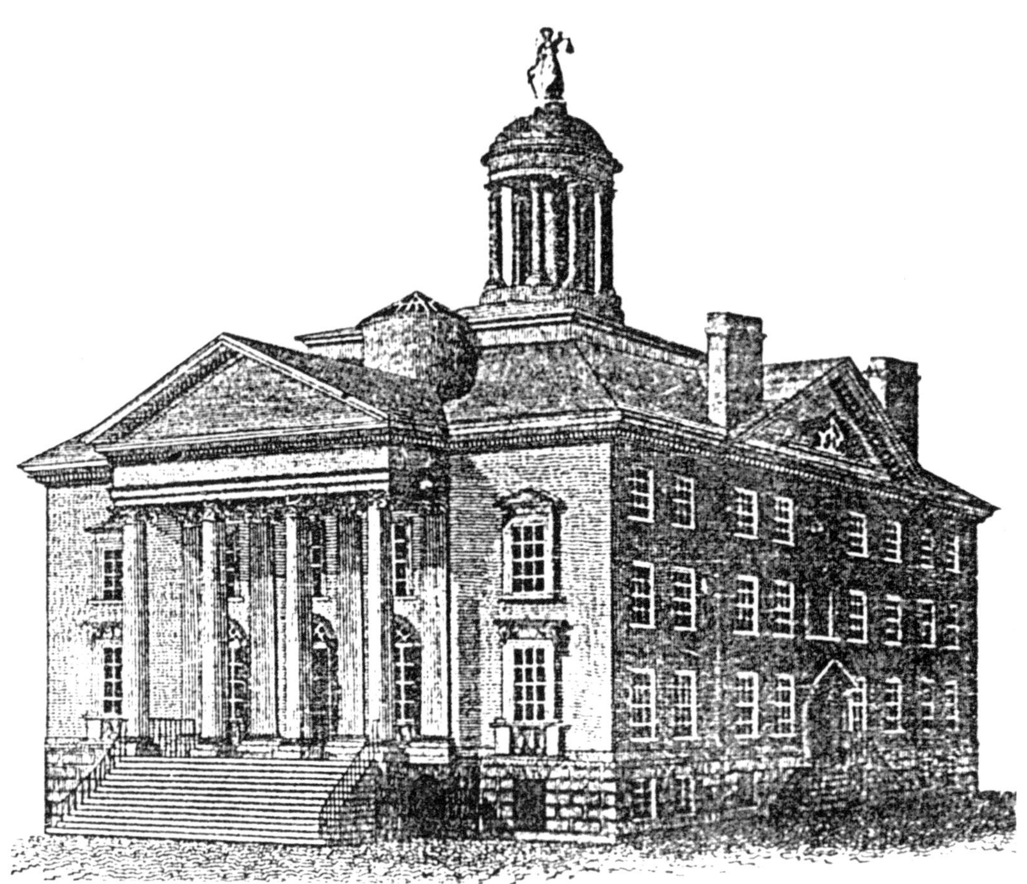

▶ Fig. 12. New York State Capitol, Albany (1806–9), detail from Evert Van Alen map, 1832 (fig. 17). Albany Institute of History & Art, McKinney Library, Map Collection.

Hooker was also designing elegant homes for Albany's wealthy families, including a town house for Elsie Fonda (1802–3) and perhaps a handsome villa for the merchant Samuel Hill (c. 1810). While Hooker's architectural design work for Stephen Van Rensselaer III evidently did not begin until the following decade, bills identify the architect's professional contact with the patroon as early as 1802.[40] His earliest documented country house on a grand scale was the 140-foot-long mansion designed for George W. Featherstonhaugh (c. 1809) at Mariaville, west of Schenectady. There is only one known illustration of the house, which was destroyed by fire in 1828. Featherstonhaugh had the young artist Thomas Cole, a fellow Englishman, execute a large painting which records the house in its landscape setting, a minor element in the overall composition.

Additional projects during this period include banks, town houses, and a stable designed for Richard Lush (1803), whose town house was located on Market Street (now Broadway). The small jewel-like building for the New York State Bank on State Street was designed and constructed in 1803. The delicately detailed brick and brownstone facade was probably inspired by Robert Adam's building for the Society for the Encouragement of Arts, Manufactures & Commerce in London, published in the first volume of the Adam brothers' *Works in Architecture* in 1778. On the front elevation of the Adam design, the two circular plaques which flank the large Palladian window feature groupings of classical figures. For the State Bank building, the clever Hooker transformed the stone roundels into replicas (obverse and reverse) of the 1803 American silver dollar.

By the end of the decade, Albany had begun to acquire a new, more sophisticated character as the capital city of the Empire State, and its population had nearly doubled to 9,356 citizens.[41]

1810–1820: CONTINUED SUCCESS

The second decade of the new century was a period of change in Hooker's personal life. Mary Hooker, Philip's first wife, died on 26 September 1812, at the age of thirty-nine. Nothing is known of this marriage, but apparently the couple was childless. On 2 January 1814, Hooker married Sarah Monk, the daughter of a local cartman.[42] In the architect's will, dated 19 January 1836, he stated that Sarah "... *has by her industry and frugality assisted me in an essential manner to acquire what I possess.*"[43] A daguerreotype of Sarah Hooker in her old age was seen by Root, who surmised that she ... *was a woman of austere and resolute character.*[44] Hooker left no children from his second marriage, and his widow passed away in New Bedford, Massachusetts, about 1858.[45]

During this period Hooker took steps to broaden his contacts and knowledge. It is possible that he crossed paths with Joseph-Jacques Ramée, the talented French architect who provided handsome and sophisticated designs for the campus and buildings of Union College in Schenectady beginning in 1813 (fig. 13). Ramée is known to have made brief visits to Albany in that year and was evidently paid $200 by Stephen Van Rensselaer III for unidentified plans.[46]

In 1814, Hooker was elected to membership in the Society for the Promotion of Useful Arts, in the State of New-York.[47] While the Albany Mechanics' Society had been formed largely to provide its members and their families with social benefits,[48] the Society for the Useful Arts was ... *calculated to promote, collect and preserve the knowledge of useful arts.*[49] Members had access to a modest but growing library, and could learn from their colleagues' presentations on a wide range of subjects. Many of the papers concerned agriculture, but there were also those like Edmond C. Genet's "Remarks and Notes on Colours" and Simeon De Witt's "Drawing in Perspective Mechanically."[50]

The statewide charter and membership of the Society for the Promotion of Useful Arts gave Hooker opportunities for contact with a broad range of individuals. Among the members of the society at the time Hooker joined in 1814 were clients Stephen Van Rensselaer III and George W. Featherstonhaugh, and two men for whom he would subsequently provide designs—Englishman George Clarke, then an Albany resident, and Judge Morris S. Miller of Utica.[51] In the year of his election to membership, Hooker is known to have served on the society's Committee of Fine Arts with three other resident members—portrait painter Ezra Ames, who chaired the committee, the Reverend

▶
Fig. 13. President's House, Union College, Schenectady, one of the many drawings submitted by Joseph-Jacques Ramée in connection with his plans for the campus, c. 1814.
Ink and watercolor on paper. Union College, Schenectady, Schaffer Library.

Timothy Clowes, Rector of St. Peter's Episcopal Church, and goldbeater Louis Lemet.[52]

It was at the end of this decade that Hooker became politically active. He was elected in 1818 and again in 1819 as assistant alderman to represent the Fourth Ward, and in 1820 to the position of full alderman. In these offices, he served on various council committees including those for the Academy, the Lancaster School, Lands, the Ferry, Flagging and Paving, and the Engine.[53] On 25 January 1819, Hooker was appointed City Surveyor.[54] He was fifty-two years old, and new responsibilities and opportunities were soon to come. In the following year, Hooker was chosen as chairman of the Night Watch Committee; even then architects seem to have been notorious for burning the midnight oil.[55]

Even before he entered the political arena, Hooker was well known to those in local government. His three major works from the first half of this decade were designed for municipal clients. The Albany Jail, with its innovative plan, was completed in 1811.[56] This building featured a prominent cupola which provided natural light for the three-story interior well around which the various rooms were arranged. The handsome edifice of the Albany Academy (1815–16) was constructed to house the boys' school that had been chartered by the state in 1813. With its richly detailed brownstone facades, the academy building became the centerpiece of the northern portion of the Public Square, much as Hooker's state capitol dominated the southern part. The second-story chapel and assembly room remains as one of the finest late Federal period public interiors in the country, with its boldly ornamented ceiling so characteristic of Hooker's work and its recently restored color scheme. In 1815 Hooker provided the Albany Common Council with plans for the Lancaster School. Though not as impressively sited as the Albany Academy, this sizable structure with its distinctive cupola became another landmark in the architect's evolving city.

Hooker designed at least two churches during this period. The Lutheran Ebenezer Church (1816–18) was constructed in Albany at a time when Hooker's father-in-law, Christopher Monk, was a trustee of the church.[57] Work apparently began in 1818 on St. Peter's Episcopal Church in Sherrill, New York, a frame mission church erected to serve the Oneidas. Hooker may also have provided plans for Albany's Second Presbyterian Church (1813), constructed by his former partner, Elisha Putnam. In addition, Hooker continued to perform design work for the North Dutch Reformed Church, his projects including alterations to the apse of the church and plans for a consistory house.

In this second decade of the century, Hooker designed at least one bank building. The facade of his Ontario Branch Bank (1815) in Utica resembled that of the earlier New York State Bank in Albany. Stylistic similarities suggest that two contemporary bank buildings may also have been from his hand. The Mechanics and Farmers Bank, completed in Albany about 1812, was a small, pavilion-like building with a curious glass dome.[58] Portions of each street facade recalled that of Hooker's earlier bank in Albany, as did the decorative coin roundels on the Bank of Utica, constructed in that city in 1813.

Hooker's most important domestic commissions were undertaken during this period. In 1816 he provided wealthy landowner George Clarke with drawings for a large house for his recently purchased property in Albany. This extraordinary but never-constructed design is elegantly delineated in plans and elevations rendered with watercolor washes. The drawings and related descriptions are bound together in a marbleized cover and form a small book. Hooker used this technique frequently, including his presentations for the William Alexander house, the house and store for Josephus Bradner Stuart, Clarke's country seat of Hyde Hall, and the church in Sherrill. If built, the Clarke house, designed as an English Regency villa particularly suited to its English client, would have been a unique architectural statement in the area, unsurpassed for its time.

Although George Clarke's Albany house remained unbuilt, in the following year he commissioned what was to become an even more ambitious scheme for his extensive property bordering Otsego Lake (fig. 14). This grand country house was constructed over a period of eighteen years, beginning in 1817. In the words of Douglas R. Kent, who has long been involved in the efforts to preserve this important architectural masterpiece, *Hyde Hall was one of the nation's major private architectural undertakings in the years between the Revolution and the Civil War. Its size (190' x 90'), its cost (over $85,000 spent on building alone), its scale and accommodations . . . all attest to this.*[59] Underlining the elegance of the building itself were its furnishings, including the handsome pieces produced by John Meads, Albany's noted cabinetmaker and contemporary of Hooker.[60] Following a three-day visit in 1835, Tyrone Power, the famous Irish comedian, wrote that *when the spirited proprietor's tasteful plans shall be completed, the mansion will have no equal in this country.*[61] It still has no equal of its period.

▲
Fig. 14. Hyde Hall, Springfield, N.Y., view from the south with the *cottage* in the foreground, 1932. Collection Friends of Hyde Hall, Inc.

It was during this decade that Hooker provided Stephen Van Rensselaer III with a number of designs for his manor house property. Three proposals for a garden pavilion date from 1811, while Hooker was given the commission to alter and enlarge the Van Rensselaer Manor House in 1819. Considered large at the time of its construction in 1765, the brick mansion was transformed by Hooker into a veritable palace. Large wings featuring formal entertaining rooms were constructed at each end of the house. A long, covered piazza was created against the north elevation to take advantage of the extensive garden view beyond the mansion. The appearance of the house after these alterations is documented in an 1839–40 drawing by Thomas Cole, while a series of later nineteenth century photographs attest to the extraordinary richness of the interiors.

Hooker may also have been the architect of a large and refined town house built for the patroon's eldest son, Stephen Van Rensselaer IV (1816–18). The three-story brick and limestone house was located in the fashionable section of North Market Street (now Broadway), immediately south of the entrance to the manor house grounds. Although nothing is known of the interior appearance of this house, it must have been quite splendid with its rich furnishings provided by the French émigré cabinetmaker, Charles-Honoré Lannuier of New York City.[62]

In the ten years from 1810 to 1820, the growth of Albany was far less dramatic than it had been in the previous decade and than it would be in the next, the city's population increasing only to 12,630 persons.[63] This was, however, a significant decade for Hooker, with the construction of highly visible structures in Albany, commissions from several prominent clients, and important new cultural and political endeavors.

1820–1830: NEW RESPONSIBILITIES

The third decade of the century was, for Hooker, a period largely given over to the responsibilities of his public offices, with their resultant provision of a steady income. His Boston contemporary, Charles Bulfinch, had become a public office-holder early in his career due to the financial hardship of supporting his family solely by his architectural endeavors.[64] The importance of such financial stability to Hooker may be understood by reference to two earlier circumstances. In the year after the dissolution of his partnership with Elisha Putnam, Hooker suffered financial embarrassment, a situation that likely developed out of his construction rather than his architectural work. A published notice dated 15 November 1804 named Putnam, a stonemason who had worked with the partners on St. Peter's Church, and a third man as assignees of Hooker's estate under legislation intended to provide relief in cases of insolvency.[65] A few years later, when Hooker's work consisted mostly of design and superintendence, a series of letters written to client George W. Featherstonhaugh points to the architect's erratic and occasionally insufficient income. Having previously declined payment for his services, Hooker in November 1809 wrote that . . . *having been disappointed in some money which I ought to have received ere now, your profer will be very acceptable.* His charge to Featherstonhaugh for a design for a villa, consultation with a builder, and travel expenses was $60.00.[66]

Hooker had been appointed City Surveyor in January 1819.[67] In that post, his work ranged from mapping and laying out vast portions of the rapidly growing city, including lands to the north, south, and west of the original Dutch town (fig. 15), to finding levels and drawing profiles for its streets. (See Appendix.) His familiarity with these newly planned neighborhoods, coupled with his surveying and design skills, brought him new public and private commissions.

On 2 April 1821, at the age of fifty-four, Hooker resigned from his position as Alderman, having added the City Superintendency to his official posts on the preceding 29 January.[68] This was the period that saw extensive growth and development in Albany, brought about in part by the opening of the Erie Canal. Between 1820 and 1830 the population of the city nearly doubled.[69] The list of responsibilities of his new position was quite lengthy, and included providing estimates, soliciting proposals, and letting contracts for new municipal construction. He also supervised the construction and repair of city structures, including the municipal ferry boat. Additional duties included street paving, laying of sidewalks, grading of lots and streets, and the installation of street lamps.[70] A more mundane duty involved the letting of contracts for the collection and disposal of street manure. In addition to Hooker's public as well as private responsibilities, he served as Assessor for the Fourth Ward, having been elected in the years 1824–26, 1828–29, 1832, and 1833.[71]

Like Bulfinch, Hooker still managed to undertake many private design projects during this period. His local work ranged from the design of two pavilions (1824) for the Van Rensselaer Manor House garden to the impressive Pearl Street Theatre (1824–25) and two large adjoining warehouses for Henry Van Schaick and John Holme (1826). Hooker's commissions in other locales included a church in St. Lawrence County (1820), the house in Utica initiated for Judge Morris S. Miller and completed by his widow and son, Rutger B. Miller (c. 1823–30), the Lowville Academy (1825–26), and the First Presbyterian Church (1826–27) in Utica. It was also during this busy period that the handsome Hamilton College Chapel (1825–27) at Clinton was constructed. There is no documentary evidence that the architect traveled to any of these sites.

Hooker declined re-election to the City Superintendency in 1827, having sought to resign twice before.[72] The last years of the decade witnessed an increase in his private architectural practice, with the construction of some of the architect's most impressive creations. Although Elkanah Watson, a long-time acquaintance and possibly a friend, took credit for the design of his country house at Port Kent (1826–28), Hooker was consulted about and provided drawings for at least a portion and likely all of the structure. The uniquely planned stone house was built into a hillside, and featured an elegant second floor *saloon* which opened onto a two-tiered portico and a view of Lake Champlain. It was in this room that Watson kept the full-length portrait of himself that had been painted by Boston artist John Singleton Copley in 1782.[73]

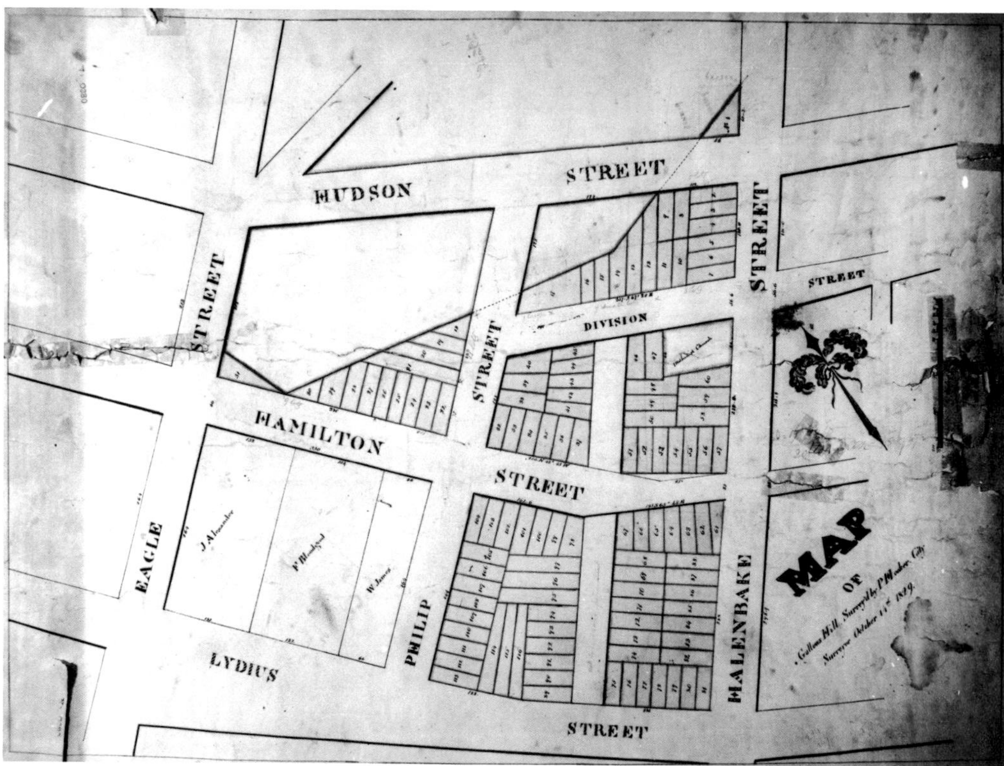

▶ Fig. 15. Map of Gallows Hill, Albany, 1829, drawn by Hooker in his role as City Surveyor. Ink and watercolor on paper mounted on canvas. Albany County Hall of Records, Albany.

▶ Fig. 16. Albany City Hall (1829–32), view from southwest, with Henry Rector's State Hall (1835–42) beyond. Albany Institute of History & Art, McKinney Library, Photograph Collection.

By 1827 Hooker had produced the final design for the *Great House* at George Clarke's estate of Hyde Hall. The bold stone facade of this building was unique in Hooker's work up to this time. Aspects of its design would appear soon thereafter in his first project for the Washington, or Centre, Market (1828) and in the Fourth Presbyterian Church (1829–30), both in Albany. The latter work, termed by a contemporary writer as being *in the most simple style of Grecian architecture,* would have a distinctive coffered ceiling.[74] John Meads, the Albany cabinetmaker whose clients included George Clarke and Stephen Van Rensselaer, constructed a town house which was probably designed by Hooker. Its austere facade featured an elegant and unusual incurvate entrance which formed an inviting niche at the head of the front steps. Two city markets, along with an addition to a third (1829–30) and three other churches—the Dutch Reformed Church (1828–29) in Niskayuna, and St. Paul's Episcopal Church (1828–29) and St. Mary's Roman Catholic Church (1829–30) in Albany—also date from this period. St. Paul's Church constituted a rare attempt by Hooker at design in the Gothic Revival mode. The awkwardly proportioned stone structure was Gothic in its surface ornament only, suggesting that the architect was not comfortable with this style.

This active decade ended with the important opportunity to design Albany's new City Hall (1829–32), resulting from a competition that drew not only local entrants but also architects from Boston, New York, and even Montreal. The lively debates concerning the design of the building prior to its construction provide a fascinating view of contemporary architectural criticism. As built, this monumental white marble civic palace with a bright gold-leafed dome would dominate the community for fifty years from its site overlooking the city and the Hudson River. This was the first large dome to enhance the city's skyline, and it would soon be followed by domes from the hands of other architects (fig. 16).

1830–1836: THE FINAL YEARS

By 1830 virtually all of the important public buildings and residences in the city of Albany were from Hooker's talented and evidently tireless hand. From the state capitol and city hall to the churches whose spires enlivened the skyline and the elegant residences which lined its streets, much of the impressive architecture in the now-mature city was Mr. Hooker's creation (fig. 17).

The last six years of the architect's life witnessed a decrease in his professional activities, although he maintained his position as City Surveyor until 1832.[75] His architectural work consisted primarily of residential structures and other, smaller-scale work for former clients. It is possible that Hooker designed the large wood frame residence of Robert Dunlop (c. 1831–32), facing the Albany-Troy Road in what is now Menands. The facade of this house with its high Doric portico, tall narrow entrance door, and balancing tripartite windows, brings to mind the main elevation of the recently designed *Great House* at Hyde Hall. In 1831 Hooker sketched a proposal for the Gansevoort property in Albany and provided a fence design and site plan for Academy Park. In 1833 he designed a cottage, farmhouse, barn, and country house for property owned by manufacturer Erastus Corning I south of the city; only two of these structures might have been erected from his plans. He designed speculative town houses for property owned by the Lutheran Ebenezer Church in 1834, and a consistory room and dwelling for the same body in the following year.

During this late period, Hooker shared his practice with other professionals. Architect Robert Higham, who may have worked as a draftsman in Hooker's office in 1828 and who had submitted an entry in the city hall competition in 1829, evidently became a junior partner sometime thereafter.[76] In addition to handling various survey projects, the partnership of Hooker & Higham provided a New York State legislative committee with proposals for asylums in 1831. These schemes, none of which was ever built, reflected Hooker's institutional planning ideas found in the Albany Jail.[77]

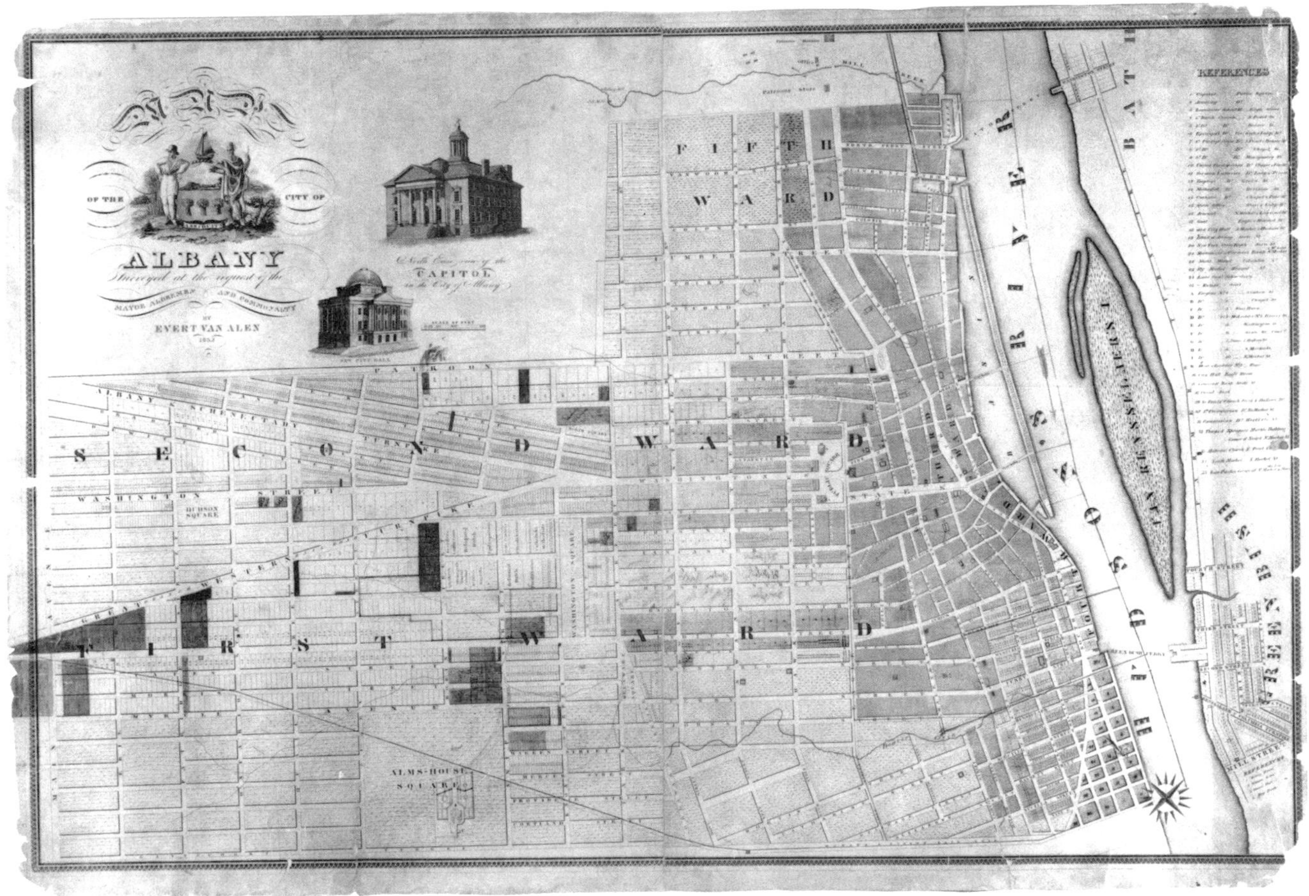

▲
Fig. 17. *Map of the City of Albany*, 1832, by Evert Van Alen, with illustrations of two Hooker-designed buildings and references to others. Engraving. Albany Institute of History & Art, McKinney Library, Map Collection.

Hooker resigned from his position as City Surveyor in January 1832, although he continued to survey privately until the end of 1835.[78] These last surveys represent some of the final work undertaken by the aging architect. An 1835 map of lands belonging to Abraham Varick of New York City is signed by Hooker and Kelly.[79] James T. Kelly, who identified himself as a surveyor in the city directories published in 1834 and 1835, worked in Hooker's office throughout most of 1835, and perhaps in the previous year as well. Kelly also helped with the designs for the Lutheran Ebenezer Church consistory room and dwelling and the unbuilt cottage for Ruell Clapp.[80]

During most of his career, Hooker had little local architectural competition. The English-born William Sanders, who had designed the State Hall, died in the summer of 1797.[81] Richard Allanson is known to have written specifications for a fireproof store in 1800 and provided plans for a market in 1807, and he was listed as an architect through the 1827 city directory. Miscellaneous records also indicate, however, that Allanson continued in actual construction work during this period.[82] Among the local entrants to the city hall competition was one George Vernon, an actor and singer who had emigrated from England and turned to architectural practice when illness forced him to retire from theatre work. In May 1829 Vernon advertised himself in the *Microscope*

▶ Fig. 18. View northward at State Street and Broadway, Albany, 1846, including, from the left, Thorp and Sprague's Marble Building, the dome of Stanwix Hall, the Mechanics and Farmers Bank, and the Exchange Building. Lithograph. New York State Library, Albany.

as an architect and surveyor and also as a *Professor of Perspective Painting and Architecture, pupil of Smirke & Northcote, and Associate of the Royal Academy, London.* Aside from his city hall entry and design of the pulpit and altar for Hooker's St. Paul's Episcopal Church, nothing else is known of Vernon's architectural work prior to his death in 1830.[83]

As Hooker approached his seventieth year, a young builder emerged who would soon replace the older master as the city's preeminent architect. Henry Rector had been born about the time that Hooker was starting out in his chosen profession. Prior to his first known architectural endeavor, an entry in the Albany City Hall competition, Rector's occupation was variously listed in city directories as a carpenter, builder, and carver. Perhaps he had obtained some architectural training in Hooker's office before establishing his own practice, evidently about 1830.[84]

By 1833 it was Rector who was shaping the face of Albany in the newly fashionable Greek style, a style his predecessor had introduced to the city but never fully developed. The changes were evident in the city's skyline and on its streets—the generous dome of Rector's Pearl Street Baptist Church (c. 1833–34) contrasting with the slender steeples of Hooker's churches, and the broadly proportioned State Hall (1835–42) with the earlier city hall (fig. 16). At the corner of State Street and Broadway, the grand, five-story stone mass of Rector's Albany Exchange (c. 1836) dwarfed the adjacent Mechanics and Farmers Bank building, attributed to Hooker (fig. 18).[85] The shadow that the new building cast over its older neighbor was to portend an Albany grander in scale, if not always as elegant, as Hooker's vision.

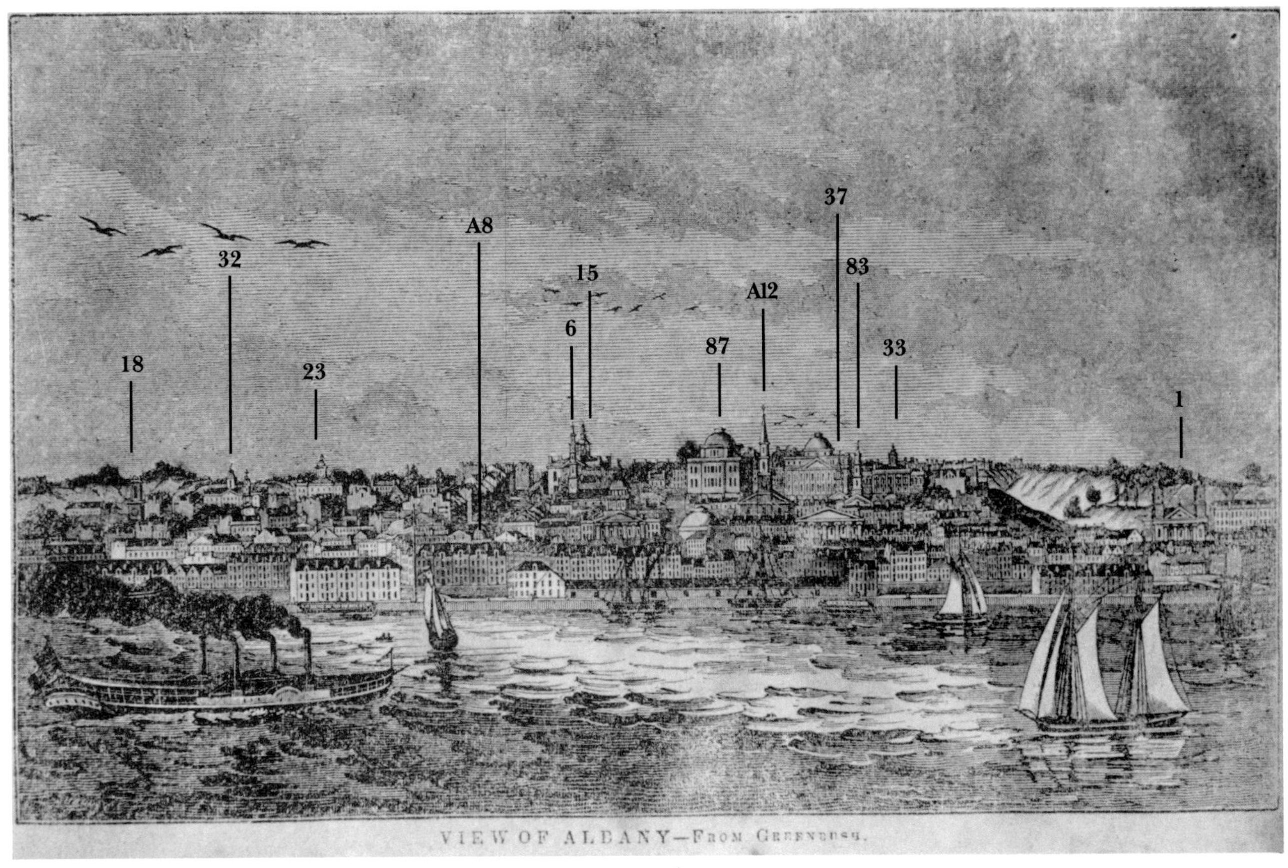

18. *South Dutch Reformed Church*
32. *Lancaster School*
23. *Albany Jail*
A8. *Mechanics and Farmers Bank*

6. *St. Peter's Episcopal Church*
15. *New York State Capitol*
87. *Albany City Hall*
A12. *Second Presbyterian Church*

37. *Lutheran Ebenezer Church*
83. *St. Mary's Roman Catholic Church*
33. *Albany Academy*
1. *North Dutch Reformed Church*

▲
Fig. 19. Mid-nineteenth century view of Albany from the east side of the Hudson River, with catalogue numbers of some of Hooker's major documented and attributed works. Woodcut. Collection Douglas G. Bucher.

Philip Hooker passed away on 31 January 1836 at his residence at 130 Green Street.[86] The modest two-story brick house was one of six matching row houses which the architect probably designed for William James around 1829. Albany would continue to grow and develop, with several architects soon required to satisfy the demand for construction in the burgeoning city. Yet above all the new buildings, the city's mid-nineteenth century skyline would remain a clear witness to Philip Hooker's enterprise, taste, and influence (fig. 19).

---

1. Edward W. Root, *Philip Hooker: A Contribution to the Study of the Renaissance in America* (New York: Charles Scribner's Sons, 1929), pp. 23–24.
2. Root, pp. 215–25.
3. [Joel Munsell, comp.], *Collections on the History of Albany*, Vol. II (Albany: J. Munsell, 1867), pp. 302–3. In addition, Samuel Hooker was likely one of *the carpenters Backer and Hooker*

who proposed in 1786 to remodel the former Lutheran Church building in Albany into a residence for the pastor; Henry H. Heins, *Swan of Albany: A History of the Oldest Congregation of the Lutheran Church in America* (Albany: First Lutheran Church, 1976), p. 56.

4. Of the couple's seven children, the last to have its birth recorded in Rutland was Susannah, who was born 19 April 1772; Root, p. 23. Root surmised that the four younger children were born in Albany.
5. *Heads of Families at the First Census of the United States Taken in the Year 1790: New York* (1908; Baltimore: Genealogical Publishing Company, 1966), p. 13.
6. Root, p. 219. For John Hooker's death date, see M. M. Bagg, *The Pioneers of Utica* (Utica, N.Y.: Curtiss & Childs, 1877), p. 76.
7. John Enys, *The American Journals of Lt. John Enys,* ed. Elizabeth Cometti (Syracuse: Syracuse University Press, and [Blue Mountain Lake, N.Y.]: Adirondack Museum, 1976), pp. 185–86.
8. Philip Hooker may have designed the flanking wings added to this house about 1815 (A15).
9. [Munsell], *Collections,* Vol. II, pp. 302–3.
10. Cuyler Reynolds, comp., *Albany Chronicles* (Albany: J. B. Lyon Company, Printers, 1906), p. 373.
11. Root, p. 134, from a letter dated 20 June 1815.
12. William Duncan, [ed.], *The New-York Directory, and Register, for 1792* (New-York: Printed for the editor, 1792), p. 65; William Duncan, *The New-York Directory, and Register, for 1792* [sic; i.e., 1793] (New-York, 1793), p. 72. For the population of New York City, or Manhattan, see John L. Andriot, comp. and ed., *Population Abstract of the United States,* Vol. I: *Tables* (McLean, Va.: Andriot Associates, 1983), p. 549.
13. Andriot, p. 547.
14. Reynolds, pp. 386–87.
15. The architectural exploits of these Frenchmen in New York State have been eloquently described by Roger G. Kennedy, in *Orders from France: The Americans and the French in a Revolutionary World, 1780–1820* (New York: Alfred A. Knopf, 1989) and *Rediscovering America* (Boston: Houghton Mifflin Company, 1990).
16. For the recent discovery of Pharoux's architectural sketchbook in the collections of the Huntington Library, San Marino, Calif., see Roger G. Kennedy, "A New Discovery Enhances the Architectural Legacy of Pierre Pharoux," *Architectural Digest,* CXXXIX, 2 (February 1991), pp. 27, 30, 34, 38, 40.
17. For the site, see fig. 1. The block was bounded by Market, State, and Dock streets, and Mark Lane.
18. Eights's views of Albany are discussed in Tammis Kane Groft, *The Folk Spirit of Albany* (Albany: Albany Institute of History and Art, 1978), pp. 46–49.
19. Several buildings in Troy, New York, also make use of this design motif, including the John Dickenson house (c. 1807) and the General John E. Wool house (c. 1812) (A9).
20. Edith Pilcher, *Castorland: French Refugees in the Western Adirondacks, 1793–1814* (Harrison, N.Y.: Harbor Hill Books, 1985), p. 40. "Communication," *Transactions of the Society for the Promotion of Useful Arts, in the State of New-York,* Vol. IV, pt. 1 (Albany: Printed by Websters and Skinners, 1816), pp. 142–44. De Witt apparently worked in and out of Albany, although the city had not yet been designated the state capital.
21. The latter scheme was also exemplified by the central pavilion of Charles Bulfinch's State House (1793–96) in Hartford, Connecticut, likely influenced by English sources; Harold Kirker, *The Architecture of Charles Bulfinch* (Cambridge, Mass.: Harvard University Press, 1969), pp. 54–60.
22. This publication was a retitled edition of Swan's *Designs in Carpentry* (London, 1759); Eileen Harris, *British Architectural Books and Writers 1556–1785* (Cambridge, Eng.: Cambridge University Press, 1990), pp. 453–54.
23. It was included in catalogues issued in New York City in 1771 and 1787 and in Boston in 1798; Janice G. Schimmelman, *Architectural Treatises and Building Handbooks available in American Libraries and Bookstores through 1800* (Worcester, Mass.: American Antiquarian Society, 1986), p. 452.
24. This scenario seems particularly plausible given Samuel Hooker's departure from Albany, apparently in 1797.
25. Docs. 14394 and 1199, Manuscripts and Special Collections, New York State Library, Albany, N.Y.
26. Reynolds, p. 355.
27. Bagg, pp. 75, 86–87.

28. Ibid., p. 87. The hotel, located on Whitesboro Street, was known for many years as the York House; the building burned in 1966. Pomroy Jones, *Annals and Recollections of Oneida County* (Rome, N.Y.: Pomroy Jones, 1851), p. 503; *The History of Oneida County* ([Utica, N. Y.]: Oneida County, 1977), p. 242.
29. Bagg, pp. 75–77.
30. The framing contract for the Whitestown Court House refers to a draft or plan furnished by John Hooker; Lincklaen/Ledyard Papers, New York State Office of Parks, Recreation and Historic Preservation, Lorenzo State Historic Site, Cazenovia, N.Y. Typescript on file at the Oneida County Historical Society, Utica, N.Y.
31. Thomas Jefferson was later to make use of this material at Monticello and the pavilions at the University of Virginia; see Mesick · Cohen ·Waite ·Architects, *Monticello Roof Historic Structure Report* (Albany: Mesick · Cohen ·Waite ·Architects, 1990) and *Pavilion VI, University of Virginia Historic Structure Report* (Albany: Mesick · Cohen ·Waite ·Architects, 1991), pp. 141–44.
32. Putnam was a resident of nearby Lansingburgh in the mid-1790s; Minutes, Archives, First Presbyterian Church, Albany, N.Y. For his subsequent roles as builder and waterworks superintendent, see, e.g., Albany city directories, 1813–15; Patent for conduit pipe, Uncatalogued receipt, Van Rensselaer Manor Papers, SC 7079, Manuscripts and Special Collections, New York State Library.
33. For the dissolution of the partnership, see cat. 6.
34. Root, p. 46. At the time of the society's incorporation, Hooker was second vice president; J. Munsell, *Annals of Albany*, Vol. VII (Albany: J. Munsell, 1856), p. 241.
35. Information on Turner's membership provided by New York State Office of Parks, Recreation and Historic Preservation, Lorenzo State Historic Site, Cazenovia, N.Y.
36. Root, p. 120 and figs. 7, 8.
37. Ibid., p. 111.
38. Kirker, pp. 25–27.
39. Kennedy, *Orders from France*, pp. 59–78.
40. Van Rensselaer Manor Papers.
41. Horatio Gates Spafford, *A Gazetteer of the State of New-York* (Albany: H. C. Southwick, 1813), p. 117. Andriot, p. 547, has combined this figure with that for the town of Colonie.
42. Root, p. 44. For Christopher Monk, see J. Fry, comp., *Albany Directory, for the Year 1814* (Albany: Printed by H. C. Southwick, and Packard & Van Benthuysen, 1814), p. 44.
43. Root, pp. 46–47, from the will.
44. Root, p. 44.
45. Ibid., p. 45.
46. Codman Hislop and Harold A. Larrabee, *Joseph Jacques Ramée and the Building of North and South Colleges*, reprinted from *Union Alumni Monthly*, XXVII, 4 ([Schenectady, 1937]).
47. "Catalogue of the Members of the Albany Institute from its Organization in 1824, with the Dates of their Election," in *Transactions of the Albany Institute*, Vol. VI (Albany: J. Munsell, 1870), p. 334.
48. Munsell, *Annals of Albany*, Vol. VII, pp. 240–41.
49. "An Act to Incorporate a Society for the Promotion of Useful Arts," *Transactions of the Society for the Promotion of Useful Arts, in the State of New-York*, [Vol. II] (Albany: Printed by John Barber, 1807), p. 233.
50. "Papers from E. C. Genet, Esq.," *Transactions of the Society for the Promotion of Useful Arts, in the State of New-York*, Vol. III (Albany: Printed by Websters and Skinners, 1814), pp. 146–52; "Selected Papers," *Transactions of the Society for the Promotion of Useful Arts, in the State of New-York*, Vol. IV, pt. 2 (Albany: Printed by Websters and Skinners, 1819), pp. 153–58.
51. "Catalogue of the Members of the Albany Institute," pp. 324–25, 328, 336.
52. *Transactions of the Society for the Promotion of Useful Arts*, Vol. III, p. 258.
53. Root, pp. 25–26.
54. Ibid., p. 34.
55. Ibid., p. 26.
56. The city and county of Albany apparently shared in this project. Hooker stated that this was for the County of Albany, while the Albany Common Council Minutes also refer to this jail (cats. 22–23).
57. Root, p. 149; Heins, p. 76.
58. A finely executed painting of the bank by Albany artist Walter Launt Palmer (1883) is in the collection of the Albany Institute of History & Art, Albany, N.Y.

59. Mendel·Mesick·Cohen·Waite·Hall·Architects, *Hyde Hall: A Restoration Feasibility Study and Master Plan* (Albany: Prepared for the Friends of Hyde Hall, Inc., 1986), p. 18.
60. For Meads, see A31.
61. Mendel·Mesick·Cohen·Waite·Hall·Architects, *Hyde Hall*, p. 18.
62. Norman S. Rice, *New York Furniture Before 1840 in the Collection of the Albany Institute of History and Art* (Albany: Albany Institute of History and Art, 1962), pp. 31–36. The furnishings include card tables, corner tables, and the extraordinary Van Rensselaer bedstead.
63. Andriot, p. 547.
64. Kirker, pp. 14–15.
65. *Albany Register*, 23 November 1804. This reference was pointed out by Wesley Balla, Curator of History, Albany Institute of History & Art.
66. George W. Featherstonhaugh Papers, 1771–1856, McKinney Library, Albany Institute of History & Art.
67. Root, p. 34.
68. Ibid., p. 28.
69. Andriot, p. 547.
70. Root, pp. 28–29.
71. Ibid., p. 43.
72. Ibid., pp. 30–32. He had requested, and obtained, the services of an assistant in 1825.
73. Albany artist Ezra Ames produced a copy of this elegant portrait (c. 1810) which is now in the collection of the Albany Institute of History & Art.
74. Joel Munsell, *Annals of Albany*, Vol. IX (Albany: Munsell & Rowland, Printers, 1858), p. 210.
75. Root, p. 43.
76. An inscription on a map of lots surveyed in 1828 by Hooker and Evert Van Alen notes that the map was copied by *R. Higham*. The Albany city directories of 1829–30 and 1830–31 list Higham as an architect located, respectively, at *60 s. Pearl* and *Law Buildings, s. Market*. This and additional information on Higham has been provided by Regina Kellerman.
77. Hooker may have had a particular personal interest in the design of the asylums, for his brother John reportedly suffered from *occasional attacks of insanity*, even to the extent of at least temporary institutionalization; Bagg, p. 76.
78. Root, p. 43.
79. Ibid.
80. G. J. Loomis and T. G. Wait, comps., *Albany Citizens' Advertiser and General Directory, for 1834–5* (Albany: G. J. Loomis, 1834), p. 278; Edmund B. Child, comp., *Child's Albany Directory, and City Register, for the years 1835–6* (Albany: Printed by E. B. Child, 1835), p. 91.
81. Doc. 14394, Manuscripts and Special Collections, New York State Library.
82. Albany city directories, 1813–27. For the store and market plans, see, respectively, McKinney Library, Albany Institute of History & Art; and Albany City Records, Box 33, SARA, Albany County Hall of Records, Albany, N.Y. For his construction work, note, e.g., his mention as a laborer in building Hooker's Lutheran Ebenezer Church; Archives, First Lutheran Church, Albany, N.Y.
83. H. P. Phelps, *Players of the Century* (Albany: Joseph McDonough, 1880), pp. 112, 120, 122, 125–26, 142–43; *Microscope*, various dates May 1829.
84. Norman S. Rice wrote the first serious study of Rector, published in Cornelia Brooke Gilder, ed., *Albany Architects. The Present Looks at the Past* (Albany: Historic Albany Foundation, 1978), pp. 3–4.
85. Although S. Wilson, comp., *Albany City Guide, 1844* (Albany: Printed by C. Wendell, 1844), p. 32, identifies Rector as the architect of the Exchange building, documentation connected with the New York City firm of Town & Davis indicates that Ithiel Town produced a design for the Albany Exchange about 1835; information provided by Walter Richard Wheeler, from a conversation with Jane B. Davies, November 1990.
86. Hooker resided at many addresses during his career but apparently never owned a home. Among his residences were 165 Court Street (now Broadway) in 1813; 611 South Market Street (now Broadway) in 1818; 29 Church Street (in the newly developed south end of the city) in 1819; 76 Green Street in 1823, 1825–27; 675 South Market Street in 1828–32; Root, pp. 45–46. The Court Street and South Market Street locations were destroyed later in the nineteenth century when that area became heavily industrialized. All of these locations were the sites of three-bay brick town houses of modest scale. ✥

Key to collections, repositories, and sources frequently cited in the notes:

ACHR	Albany County Hall of Records, Albany, N.Y.
A FCA	Archives, First Church in Albany, Albany, N.Y.
MK AIHA	McKinney Library, Albany Institute of History & Art, Albany, N.Y.
MSC NYSL	Manuscripts and Special Collections, New York State Library, Albany, N.Y.
NYHS	The New-York Historical Society, New York, N.Y.
NYPL	New York Public Library, New York, N.Y.
NYSL	New York State Library, Albany, N.Y.
Root	Root, Edward W. *Philip Hooker: A Contribution to the Study of the Renaissance in America.* New York: Charles Scribner's Sons, 1929.
SARA	State Archives Records Administration.

CATALOGUE RAISONNÉ

W. Richard Wheeler

About the Catalogue Raisonné:

In transcribing early documents, we have retained the errors and eccentricities of spelling used by Hooker and his contemporaries. On occasion, however, we have corrected the spelling of a word whose meaning would otherwise be unintelligible. Very occasionally, because of the condition of the manuscript, we have been forced to guess as to the word itself. Capitalization and punctuation, frequently indeterminate, have been changed only as necessary for ease and clarity of reading.

In quoting early documents from secondary sources (e.g., Root), the published version has been employed. All such material quoted from secondary sources has been identified with quotation marks. Ed.

East Elevation 70 feet

North Elevation 98 feet

P. Hooker del.

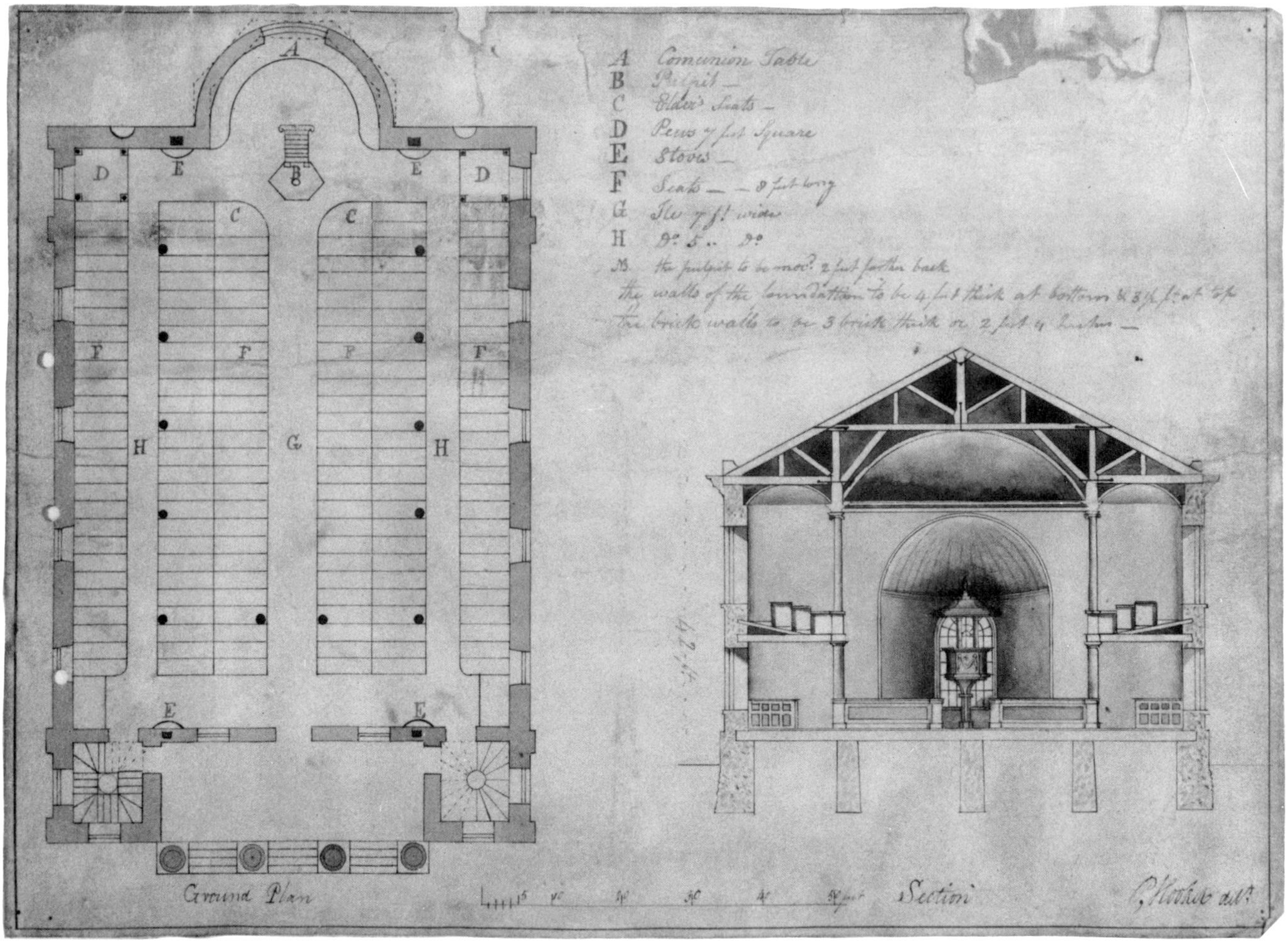

A Comunion Table
B Pulpit —
C Elder's Seats —
D Pews 7 feet Square
E Stoves —
F Seats — — 8 feet long
G Ile 7 f.t wide
H D.o 5 .. D.o

N.B. the pulpit to be mov.d 2 feet farther back
the walls of the foundation to be 4 feet thick at bottom & 3 1/2 f.t at top
the brick walls to be 3 brick thick or 2 feet 4 Inches —

Ground Plan

Section

P. Hooker del.

1. NORTH DUTCH REFORMED CHURCH

North Pearl Street at Clinton Square, Albany, N.Y.
First design before 20 December 1796.
Second design summer 1797; towers designed spring 1798.
Built 1797–99; altered 1813, c. 1820, and 1857–59; extant.
Builders: Philip Hooker and Elisha Putnam.

▶
Fig. 22. Hollis Street Church, Boston (1788), designed by Charles Bulfinch and illustrated in the *Massachusetts Magazine*, 1793. Courtesy Massachusetts Historical Society, Boston.

◀
Fig. 20. North Dutch Reformed Church, Albany, one of Hooker's competition drawings, showing two versions of the towers, 1796. Ink and wash on paper mounted on linen. Archives, First Church in Albany.

◀
Fig. 21. North Dutch Reformed Church, Albany, Hooker's original plan and transverse section, submitted in competition, 1796. Ink and wash on paper. Archives, First Church in Albany.

The Dutch Reformed Church, now known as First Church in Albany, was the cultural backbone of the settlement which became Albany. From its establishment in 1642 the church occupied a prominent location in the community, first near the walls of Fort Orange and by 1656 at the intersection of Jonckers and Handlaars streets (now State Street and Broadway). By the 1790s, the church building that had been erected on the latter site in 1715 was beginning to be an impediment to travel in and through the city (figs. 1, 2). As a means of resolving the question of where to build a new church, it was determined to organize Albany's Dutch Church on the *collegiate* plan, in which a single governing body would oversee several houses of worship dispersed throughout the growing community.[1] The first of three projected churches was to be erected in the northern part of the city, and on 14 November 1796, John Jacob Beeckman was authorized to advertise on behalf of the consistory *to receive proposals for building* [a] *new church and for the delivery of 150 loads of burnt lime stone.*[2] The proposals were *to be delivered in writing on or before the 20th day of December next.*[3]

Hooker completed his first design (figs. 20, 21) in the days between 26 November 1796, when the advertisement appeared, and the 20 December deadline. With its pedimented portico and flanking bell towers, the scheme owes much to Charles Bulfinch's Hollis Street Church, erected in Boston in 1788 and illustrated in the *Columbian Magazine* that same year and in the *Massachusetts Magazine* in 1793 (fig. 22).[4] In his drawings, Hooker offered the church consistory alternative treatments of the towers, the stairs, and the apse. Hooker's handwritten contract was signed the following spring.

> *Articles of agreement indented made and contracted upon this seventeenth day of March, one thousand seven hundred and ninety seven, between the Minister, Elders and Deacons of the Reformed Protestant Dutch Church in the city of Albany of the first part and Philip Hooker and Elisha Putnam of the said city of the second part, and Barent G. Staats, Gerrit W. V. Schaick & Jeremiah Van Rensselaer of the said city of the third part in form following, to wit:*
>
> *Imprimis, the said parties of the 2nd part for themselves, their executors administrators and assigns, covenant and agree, with said parties of the first part and their successors in manner & form following: That is to say that they or one of them, their or some or one of their executors, administrators, workmen, servants or assigns for the consideration hereinafter mentioned shall and will at their own proper costs and charges make and erect build set up or finish one new brick church on the lot of ground belonging to the said parties of the first part in the second ward of the city of Albany now in the occupation of Rensselaer Schuyler and Cornelius Groesbeck, according to the plan or draught thereof hereunto annexed and of the dimensions following, to wit.*
>
> *Seventy feet wide, including the walls, and ninety eight feet long, including the walls.*
>
> *The side walls to be thirty eight feet high from the watertables; and* [the builders of] *the same church shall do, compleat and finish or cause to be done compleated and finished according to the said plans or draught, in a good, elegant, strong and workmanlike manner and with good hard bricks of nine inches long, and good strong and sound mortar timber and other materials, with all the masons and bricklayers work, carpenters work, smiths work, plumbers work, plaisterers work, glaziers work, painters work, joiners work, diggers and clearers work what soever, that is or shall be needful and convenient for the building and compleating of the said church in manner aforesaid; and also that the said church shall be built under the inspection of a superintendant, to be appointed and paid by the said parties of the first part and their successors, whose duty it shall be to exammine the materials and work applied thereto, & to judge of the sufficiency thereof on the part of the said parties of the first part and their successors. And also that the said parties of the second part, their executors, administrators or assigns, shall and will sink the foundation of the said church so far below the surface of the ground as in the judgement of the said superintendant shall bring it at least below the common depth of frost in the winter season and that the foundation wall of the said church shall be four feet in thickness at the bottom, and not less than three feet six inches at the extreme heighth thereof, and the inside walls for the better support of the said church and pillars to be not less than eighteen inches and more proportionately, where in the judgement of the said superintendant it shall be required, and the side walls from the watertables up to the gallery shall be three and a half bricks in thickness, and from the gallery upwards, three bricks in thickness, and thirty eight feet high above the water tables and that the west wall shall be three bricks in thickness up to the plates, and the east wall two and a half bricks in thickness up to the gallery, and both to be two bricks in thickness, upwards above the plates and gallery, the whole length of the gables; and that the octagon shall be two and a half bricks in thickness the whole heighth thereof, and the towers three and a half bricks in thickness in the piers and upwards to the*

1. Robert S. Alexander, *Albany's First Church and its Role in the Growth of the City, 1642–1942* (Albany: First Church in Albany, 1988), pp. 161–62.
2. Dutch Reformed Church (hereafter DRC) Consistory Minutes, 14 November 1796, A FCA.
3. Ibid.
4. *Columbian Magazine* (Philadelphia), II (April 1788), 178, reference from Harold Kirker, *The Architecture of Charles Bulfinch* (Cambridge, Mass.: Harvard University Press, 1969), p. 19; and "Meeting House in Hollis Street," *Massachusetts Magazine*, V (December 1793), 707. Hooker's design was not the first to reflect the influence of the exterior of this Bulfinch church. For earlier examples in Baltimore and Providence, see Sterling Boyd, *The Adam Style in America, 1770–1820*, 2 vols. in 1, Outstanding Dissertations in the Fine Arts (New York and London: Garland Publishing, Inc., 1985), I: 291; II: 172.

heighth of forty feet, and above the height of forty feet to the height of fifty six feet two bricks in thickness and also shall and will cover the roof of the said church with good merchantable shingles and make the window frames of well dressed free stone with arches and keys, and the watertables of free stone, and also shall lath and plaister the ceilings and other walls with as many coats as shall be necessary, but not less than two coats, and oil paint and pencil all the brick walls, and put in three large iron hooks, and as many small ones to hang chandeliers and lights on in such places within the said church as the said parties of the first part and their successors, or their superintendent, shall deign requisite and appoint; but the whole not to exceed the number of thirty six and to be suspended within stocco ovals, or circles in the ceiling. And also shall glaze all the windows, with good clear glass of eleven by fifteen inches, and hang the sashes with good and sufficient weights and brass pullies and shall lay all the floors with and make the steps of the stairs, of good merchantable pitch pine plank, free from sap; and run a handsome stocco cornish all round the ceiling and other places, where cornishes will tend to ornament the said building and be required by the said parties of the first part, and according to the models to be provided by the said parties of the first part; and render and whiten all the inside walls and furnish and put in four handsome stoves and an elegant plain mahogany pulpit, according to the plan or draught thereof also annexed; and also shall face the foundation of the east front with free stone, and make free stone steps and plinths to the collums, and flag the platform of the portico with free stone, first providing good and sufficient foundation to the said steps, plinths and flagging; and also shall do all the inside and outside painting, including the roof twice in oil, with such colours as the said parties of the first part or their successors shall require; and also shall put on good locks and keys to each outside door and hang all the inner doors, including those of the pews with good iron hinges, and put on good and sufficient iron clasps wherever it shall be necessary for the strength and security of any part of the work to the said church; and shall make and compleat in a plain but elegant manner a communion table and seats and ballustrade—with doors in front of the recess according to the said plan annexed and cover the said table and seats with green cloth; and also shall and will in all respects, do perform finish and complete, all the work of the said church and everything appertaining to the completion and finishing thereof, in a good, substantial, modern, elegant and workmanlike manner, according to the true intent and meaning of the said plan or draught annexed not withstanding any ambiguities or omissions in these presents or in the said plans or draught, and also shall and will put up two lightning rods or conductors to be provided by the said parties of the first part or their successors. . . .

. . . [The building is to be] *finished . . . on or before the first day of December in the year one thousand seven hundred and ninety eight and . . . the said parties of the second part, their executors, administrators and assigns shall & will finish the said church so far as to bring it under Roof on or before the 1st day of Dec. ensuing. . . .*

. . . *In consideration . . .* [they will receive] . . . *25,000.*[5]

Prior to this time, Hooker had probably worked with his father, Samuel.[6] That the elder Hooker left Albany for Utica in this year[7] and that Philip entered into a partnership with Elisha Putnam, apparently for the purpose of constructing the Dutch church, may well be related developments. Putnam was roughly the same age as Hooker and seems to have had the benefit of greater experience, including responsibility for the construction of the First Presbyterian Church in Albany, 1795–96 (A5).[8]

5. Doc. 79-1, Dutch Reformed Church Collection, A FCA.
6. For a project that evidently involved one or more of the Hookers, see Henry H. Heins, *Swan of Albany: A History of the Oldest Congregation of the Lutheran Church in America* (Albany: First Lutheran Church, 1976), p. 56.
7. See p. 31.
8. Archives, First Presbyterian Church, Albany, N.Y.

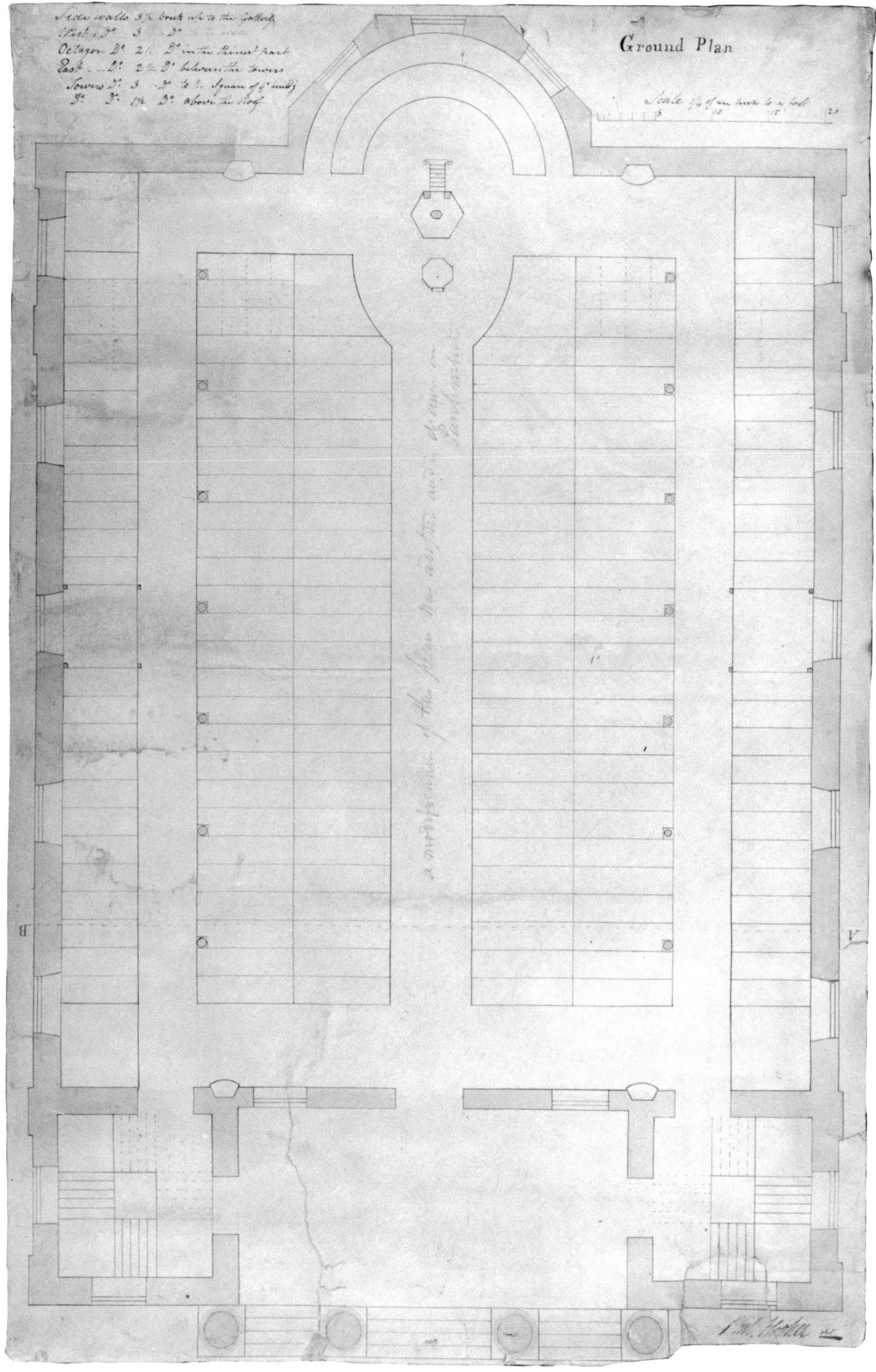

▶
Fig. 23. North Dutch Reformed Church, Albany, Hooker's definitive plan, 1797. Ink and wash on paper. Archives, First Church in Albany.

9. These four drawings and the two earlier ones (figs. 20, 21) bear signs of having been bound to the contract.
10. DRC Consistory Minutes, 24 March 1797.
11. Root, p. 58.
12. Cuyler Reynolds, comp., *Albany Chronicles* (Albany: J. B. Lyon Company, Printers, 1906), p. 355.

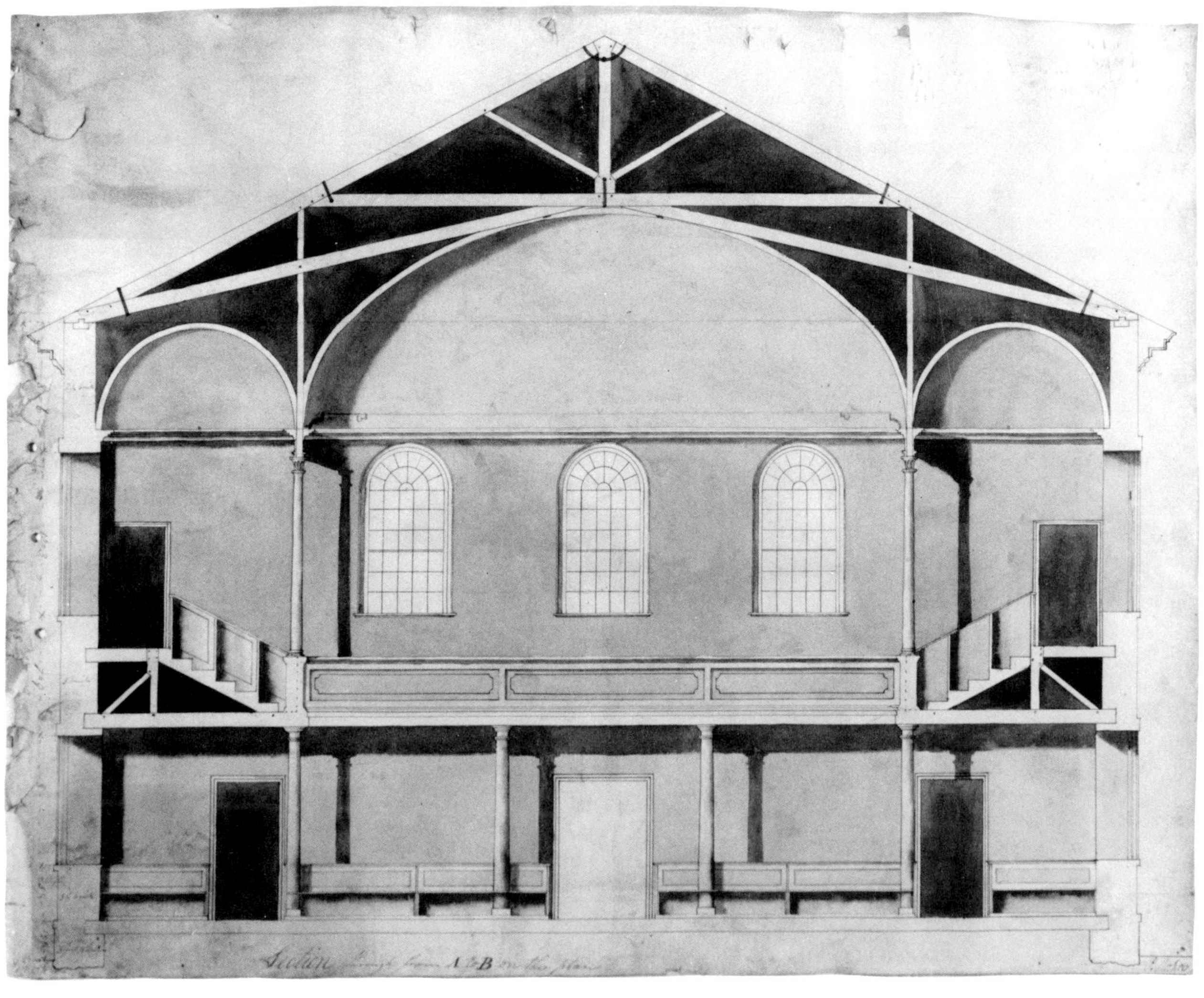

▲ Fig. 24. North Dutch Reformed Church, Albany, Hooker's definitive transverse section, 1797. Ink and wash on paper. Archives, First Church in Albany.

At the time the contract was signed, Hooker submitted a large plan, a section, and a sectional elevation (figs. 23–25), along with a drawing by Putnam for a pulpit (fig. 26). These appear to be part of the set of working drawings, and in their scale are unique among Hooker's surviving drafts.[9] With the exception of the design of the towers they represent the building as executed.

By 24 March 1797 the church leaders were busy making *the necessary arrangements* to pay the installments on the contract.[10] Hooker and Putnam received their first payment on 1 June and the cornerstone of the building was laid on 12 June.[11] On 17 August the consistory concurred with Hooker and Putnam's proposal to roof the church with tin instead of with the wooden shingles previously agreed to. The impetus for this change is clear: the destruction by fire of fifty houses in the city less than two weeks before.[12] On 22 August Hooker and Putnam calculated the roof areas to be covered. Their estimate provides important information regarding the original design of the church.

▶ Fig. 25. North Dutch Reformed Church, Albany, Hooker's sectional elevation, 1797. Ink and watercolor on paper. Archives, First Church in Albany.

An exact measurement of the several roofs of the new Dutch church is to [be] *covered with tin—The main roof is 82 feet long by 42 feet rafter.*

The superficial content of the two sides is	*6888 feet*
the pedement 22 feet projection & 22 feet rafter	*968*
the octagon 44 feet in circumference contains	*616*
the dome of each cupola is 34 feet in circumference	*374*
	8846 feet
which will take 49 boxes [of] *tin at £5 per box*	*£245*
the difference between laying shingles and tin	*20*
the extra expense of timber, iron work, brick, mortar & workmanship &c, to detach the cornice from any of the inside timber	*£40*
	£305
Deduction for shingles [not used]	*70*
The additional sum required	*£235* [13]

13. DRC Consistory Minutes, 22 August 1797.
14. Ibid., 21 March 1798.
15. Ibid., 10 March 1798.
16. For an illustration of the church in Amsterdam, New York, see Jadviga M. da Costa Nunes, *Baroness Hyde de Neuville: Sketches of America, 1807–1822* (New Brunswick, N. J.: Jane Voorhees Zimmerli Art Museum, Rutgers, The State University of New Jersey, and New York: The New-York Historical Society, 1984), p. 7.
17. For Benjamin's *Rudiments of Architecture*, see Boyd, *The Adam Style in America*, I: 307; II: 191. See also Asher Benjamin, *The American Builder's Companion*, 6th ed. (1827; reprint ed., New York: Dover Publications, Inc., 1969), pls. K, L. Snyder, an engraver, had had work published in Boston in 1807 and 1811, and he made a number of line illustrations for the 1816 edition of *The American Builder's Companion*; Glenn B. Opitz, ed., *Mantle Fielding's Dictionary of American Painters, Sculptors & Engravers*, 2d ed., rev. and enl. (Poughkeepsie: Apollo Book, 1986), p. 875.

It is probable that neither Hooker nor Putnam had previously dealt with metal roofing, and problems developed almost immediately because of faulty installation. The consistory minutes indicate, however, that Putnam had provided a solution.

> *It is represented to the board that the roof of our new church is not sufficiently tight, and an experiment . . . made by Mr Putnam of paint and sand . . . appears to have the desired effect. Whereupon* [it is] *resolved that the said roof be painted and sanded as often as is the judgement of this board will be thought sufficient to prevent it from leaking.*[14]

The design of the towers was finalized sometime before 10 March 1798. According to a note in the consistory book from that date, Hooker and Putnam were to have been paid $700 by January 1799 for the completion of *the Cupolo's of our new Church, agreeably to the last design.*[15] This scheme (fig. 27) proved highly influential in the design of various churches across New York State including the Dutch Church in Amsterdam.[16] It was also copied in two of Asher Benjamin's handbooks—*The Rudiments of Architecture* (1820) and *The American Builder's Companion* (1827). Benjamin might have become familiar with Hooker's design through a mutual friend, the Albany engraver, Henry W. Snyder.[17]

▶ Fig. 26. North Dutch Reformed Church, Albany, Elisha Putnam's pulpit drawing, 1797. Ink and wash on paper mounted on linen. Archives, First Church in Albany.

On 26 March 1798 the consistory resolved *to have the outside brick work of* . . . [the] *church oiled, without any mixture of paint.*[18] Since at that time regionally produced brick was soft and porous, the clear oil would protect it from water and act as a stain, bringing out the salmon-red color of the brick. Construction proceeded, and on 3 October 1798 an Albany newspaper announced: "*The new Dutch church in this city is completed. It is a superb and elegant building, furnished in the most modern style. . . .* "[19]

▶
Fig. 27. North Dutch Reformed Church, Albany (1797–99), view of south tower, 1991.

The building opened for worship in January 1799,[20] but finishing touches were executed during the following spring. They included the construction of fences (cat. 3)[21] and redesign of the clerk's desk,[22] both supervised by Hooker and Putnam. In May 1799 the consistory resolved to *cause another coat of paint to be given to the outer wooden work and roof of the . . . church* and to

> *cause the free-stone arches round the windows . . . to be painted white and an oblong square piece of free stone to be prepared to fill the vacancy in the front wall of the . . . church under the portico, with a curtain to be carved thereon, and an oval in the center and the following inscription therein— Glory to God in the highest the dutch church erected in the year 1798* [and to] *cause the pannel*[ing] *of the fence around the . . . church to be painted Spanish brown.*[23]

Hooker's North Dutch Reformed Church featured what may have been the first appearance of a classical portico in the former Dutch colony outside of New York City. The building's completion heralded a new era of architectural sophistication in Albany. For the next thirty-five years, Philip Hooker's interpretation of Federal design was synonymous with *taste* and *modernity* to the people of the Upper Hudson and Mohawk valleys (fig. 9).

The building was altered in 1813 (cat. 27), around 1820, and in 1857–59, when the interior was entirely remodeled and the portico removed and replaced.[24] The structure is still used by the same congregation. ✣

18. DRC Consistory Minutes, 26 March 1798.
19. Root, p. 60, from J. Munsell, comp., *Annals of Albany*, Vol. III (Albany: Joel Munsell, 1852), pp. 188–89.
20. Root, p. 61.
21. DRC Consistory Minutes, 22 January 1799.
22. Ibid., 15 February 1799.
23. Ibid., 14 May 1799.
24. Ibid., various dates, 1856–60; Root, pp. 63–64. Root includes a description of the *Romanesque style* remodeling, taken from Joel Munsell, ed., *Annals of Albany*, Vol. X (Albany: Munsell & Rowland, Printers, 1859), pp. 422–23.

2. UNION COLLEGE

College Street, Schenectady, N.Y.
Designed before 2 May 1797.
Built 1797–1804; razed 1890.
Builder unknown.

▶
Fig. 28. *A South-East View of Union College in the City of Schenectady,* published by Henry W. Snyder, July 27, 1808, from a drawing by Hooker. Engraving. Albany Institute of History & Art, Gift of William Caldwell.

Philip Hooker is named as the architect of Union College's second building in a history of that institution, written by one of its former presidents, Andrew V. Raymond, and published in 1907.[1] Although Raymond does not identify his source, Hooker's recently discovered drawing of the building (fig. 10) and Henry W. Snyder's engraving of that draft (fig. 28) give credence to the statement of the Albany architect's involvement in the design.[2]

The Union building had been proposed as early as 23 June 1796,[3] and by 2 May 1797 the college's Board of Trustees had resolved to

> *"proceed to erect a college building of Brick underpin*[n]*ed with stone and of the following dimensions. To wit—one hundred and thirty-two feet in length, 50 feet in breadth, a projection in the middle 32 feet in front, 12 feet projected from the main body of the house towards the South and 10 feet projected towards the North, 3 stories high, with a cupola. . . .* "[4]

Later descriptions give the plan dimensions as 150 by 60 feet.[5] It is unclear when the decision to increase the size was made.

Construction of the college building must have begun in 1797, based on the progress recorded in the following year by Timothy Dwight, who later became the president of Yale University.

1. Root, pp. 69–70, 71 n. 5.
2. For Hooker's drawing, see Collection, AIHA.
3. Root, p. 66.
4. Ibid., p. 67, from Manuscript Minutes of the Trustees of Union College, 2 May 1797.
5. Root, p. 68.

▲
Fig. 29. Union College, Schenectady, second building (1797–1804), exterior. Schenectady County Historical Society, Schenectady.

> "[The building] *was at the time of our journey* [1798], *raised to the base of the third story. It is built of leaden-coloured stone, dug up in the neighborhood, and fortunately discovered since the edifice was projected. The windows are arched with a brown free-stone, and based with a dark-coloured marble of a fine texture, lately found here also. It is intended to contain a hall, library, a public room for the Commencement exhibitions* [also used as a chapel], *recitation rooms, a philosophical chamber, and rooms for the residence of the Faculty, and their families. The students are to board, and lodge, in the city.*"[6]

The structure, which was completed in 1804 at a cost of about $56,000, was owned by Union College until 1815, when it was sold to the city and county of Schenectady for governmental uses. The college repurchased the building in 1831 and used it until 1854. Thereafter it served the city as a public school until it was razed in 1890 (fig. 29).[7]

Hooker's design of the Union College structure relies heavily upon seventeenth and early eighteenth century collegiate building traditions. The arrangement of the roof, balustrade, and cupola owe much to late English Renaissance design, aspects of which Hooker employed at various points in his long career. ✣

6. Ibid., p. 70, from Timothy Dwight, *Travels in New England and New York*, Vol. II (New Haven: Timothy Dwight, 1821), p. 486.
7. Root, pp. 68–70.

3. FENCES FOR NORTH DUTCH REFORMED CHURCH

North Pearl Street at Clinton Square, Albany, N.Y.
Designed before 22 January 1799.
Built 1799; razed c. 1830.
Builders: Philip Hooker and Elisha Putnam.

Not long after the completion of the North Dutch Reformed Church (cat. 1), Hooker and Putnam were retained

> *. . . to construct a fence on the sides and rear of the . . . church of the kind designated on the draft presented to the consistory by Messrs. Hooker & Putnam by N°. 1 and also to construct a fence of the kind designated on the said draft by N°. 2 to be erected on a wall in front of the . . . church to be built for that purpose.*[1]

Later records, which make no distinction between the front fence and that on the sides and rear, indicate that *the fence* was constructed of wood and that its *pannel*[ing] was to have been painted *Spanish brown.*[2]

Through a comparison of watermarks in types of papers used by Hooker at this time, an unsigned and undated drawing (fig. 30) in the Archives of the First Church in Albany can be attributed to him. While it cannot be definitely related to this project, it may contain similar elements. The drawing shows a wrought iron lamp standard and its attachment to the top of a fence post that features an urn finial. The classically inspired design of the ironwork owes much to the Adam brothers. A diagram for a *throw-over* light appears in the upper right margin of the sheet. Such an arrangement would have been used in connection with gates in the fence that faced North Pearl Street. ✤

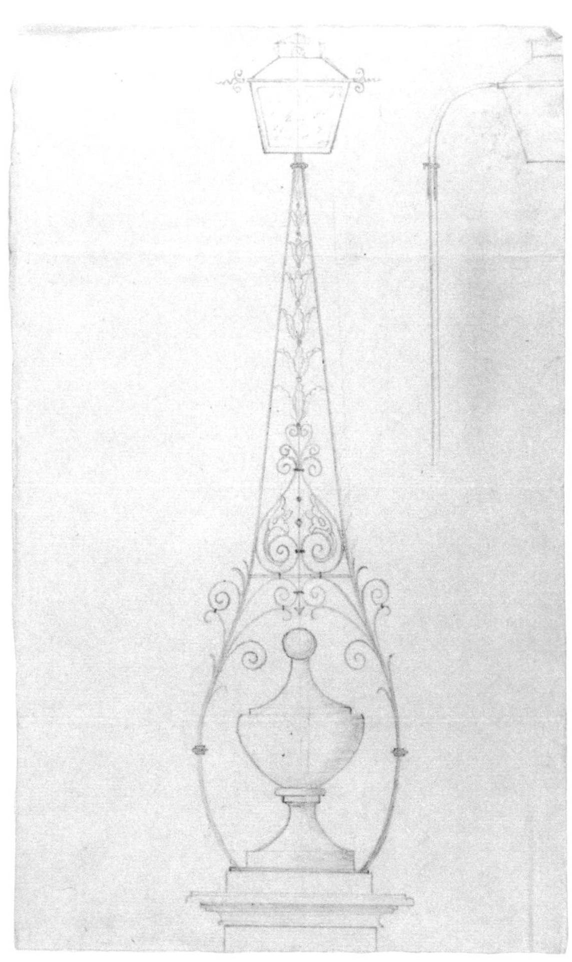

▶ Fig. 30. Drawing of light fixtures for a fence, attributed to Hooker, probably for North Dutch Reformed Church, Albany. Pencil on paper. Archives, First Church in Albany.

1. Dutch Reformed Church Consistory Minutes, 22 January 1799, A FCA.
2. Ibid., 14 May 1799.

4. PROPOSAL FOR SOUTH DUTCH REFORMED CHURCH

Albany, N.Y.
Designed before 26 April 1799.
Unbuilt.

In keeping with its plans to have several *collegiate* churches,[1] the consistory of the Dutch Reformed Church on 12 April 1799 *resolved that a new church be built & that the same be erected on the old burying ground and that the length thereof be 70 feet, by 40* [feet] *in the clear & with one steeple.*[2] Gerrit Groesbeeck, John D. P. Douw, and Jacob Bleecker, Jr., were appointed to *procure a draft or plan of a Church of the above dimensions.*[3] After 12 April Hooker was contacted and by 26 April *a plan of a church drawn by Mr. Hooker was laid before the board for their approbation.* The consistory approved of the design *so far as respects the size and dimensions.*[4]

Church records contain no further mention of this project, which was intended to replace the old building of 1715 on a different site. When a new church was finally constructed (cat. 18), its design differed significantly from this initial proposal. ✤

1. Robert S. Alexander, *Albany's First Church and its Role in the Growth of the City, 1642–1942* (Albany: First Church in Albany, 1988), pp. 162, 165.
2. Dutch Reformed Church (hereafter DRC) Consistory Minutes, 12 April 1799, A FCA.
3. Ibid.
4. DRC Consistory Minutes, 26 April 1799.

5. NEW YORK STATE ARSENAL

Lawrence Street and Water Vliet Street (now Broadway), Albany, N.Y.
Designed before 29 April 1799.
Built c. 1799; altered c. 1857; razed c. 1960.
Builders: Philip Hooker and Elisha Putnam.

An Act of the New York State Legislature, passed on 17 August 1798, provided for the construction of an arsenal *for the further defence of* [the] *State.* On 29 April 1799,[1] Governor John Jay signed the contract for the project along with Hooker and Putnam. Documentation of this commission includes a sheet of drawings (fig. 31) and the contract, which reads in part:

> *Philip Hooker and Elisha Putnam do covenant and agree to build and erect an arsenal on the land belonging to this state fronting on Water Vliet Street* [now Broadway] *in the town of Water Vliet in the county of Albany, according to the annexed plan, with the addition of two windows in each story in the east and west ends of the building, and to compleat the same in the manner herein after mentioned on or before the first day of December next. The said building to be one hundred feet in length from Water Vliet Street eastward toward Hudson's River and fifty feet in breadth at each end on the outside and that the said Philip Hooker and Elisha Putnam shall provide and furnish at their own expence all the requisit materials of every kind such as stone, brick, lime, sand, water for making the mortar, timber, boards, planks, nail, iron locks, hinges, hooks for keeping open the*

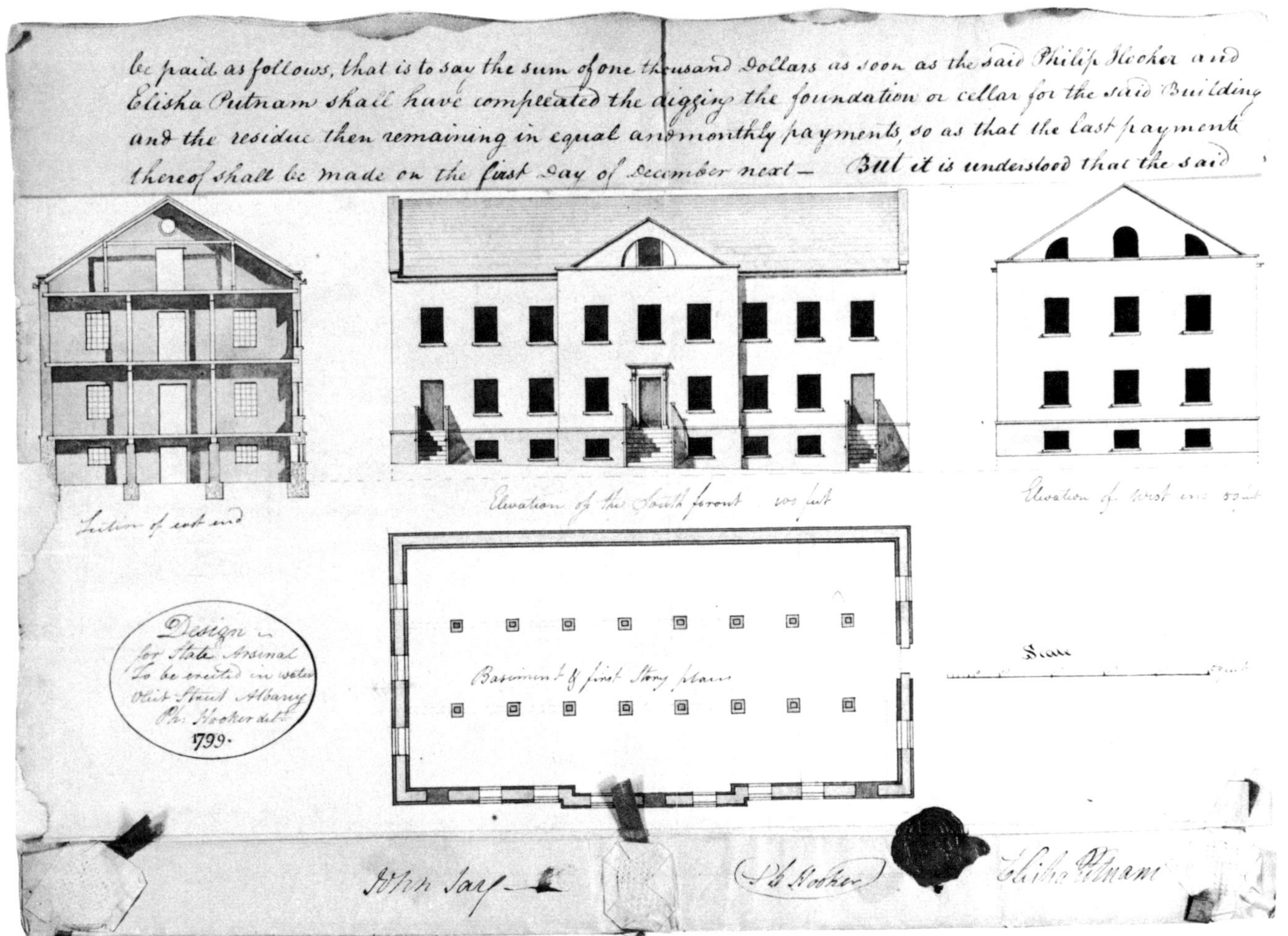

▲
Fig. 31. New York State Arsenal, Albany, Hooker's elevations, plan, and section, 1799. Ink and wash on paper. New York State Archives, Albany, Freedom Train Collection.

window shutters, tin water leaders from the gutters, bolts for doors and windows, such iron hooks for suspending the arms and accoutrements as shall be directed by the public agent herein after mentioned, iron grates to the windows of the basement story, with a cross bar in each window frame three inches broad and one inch thick and the upright bars to be one inch square to pass thro the horizontal bars and the bars to be four inches asunder; iron grates to the windows of the first story, with three cross bars of half an inch thickness, with upright bars of one inch square passing thro the horizontal bars and to be set four inches asunder, sash-weights, pullies, cords, glass of ten by twelve inches for all the windows, door and window-frames, doors, shutters, and sashes, tile for the roof, and as many racks for suspending the arms and accoutrements as shall be directed by the public agent, together with every other non enumerated material and article requisite, necessary and appurtenant perfectly to compleat the building for the purposes for which it is intended both outside and inside. That the walls of the basement story shall be made of stone and shall be three feet thick and eight feet and an half in heighth above the surface of the ground at the east end of the building. And the cellar-door in the east end shall be eight feet and an half wide in the clear when finished. That the first story shall be thirteen feet high in the clear from the floor to the under side of the beams next above; and the walls shall be of brick and from the stone walls to the upper side of the beams above. The first story shall be in thickness equal to the length of two bricks and an half with a hewn free-stone water-table between the stone and brick work. That the second story shall be twelve feet in the clear from the floor to the underside of the beams next above; and the walls shall be of brick and be continued from the brick wall of the first story fourteen feet nine inches to the wall-plate and of the thickness of the length of two bricks and the gabel-ends of the thickness of a brick and a half and covered with a coping of hewn free stone. That the cellar or basement-story wall shall be well pointed and all the brick walls shall be fair and pencilled on the outside and fair but not pencilled on the inside, which shall be whitewashed but not plaistered. That the gutters shall be neat and proper for such a building. That the mortar for the stone work shall be made of one third lime and two thirds real sand, and for brick work of at least one third lime and two thirds real sand. That the beams of the first floor shall be supported by strong bearers running parallel to the north and south walls and resting on brick pillars or piers of three bricks in length square as designated in the annexed plan. That the beams of the second and third floor shall be supported in the same manner, but by strong wooden posts directly over the brick piers, with intermediate posts of joists of three inches square, that they may serve as one of the ranges of rackes for suspending arms and accoutrements. That the beams of the first floor shall be fairly hewn. Those for the second and third floors shall be planed on the sides in sight; and the second and third floors shall be planed on the under side; and all the posts to support the beams and all the joists for the racks shall also be planed. That the floors shall be of plank, two inches thick and well grooved and tenanted into each other and joints broke in laying; that the staircases shall be plain and seven feet wide with a plain square railing; and the steps shall be broad and not exceeding seven inches in rise, and shall be made of plank of two inches thick; that the stoops shall be made neat with a plain railing; that the rafters shall be supported by posts and plates to supercede the necessity of collar-beams; that there shall be four beams to every fourteen feet in length for laying the floors on; that there shall be as many doors and windows as are designated in the annexed plan, with the addition of two windows in each story in both the east and west ends of the building as above mentioned.

. . . for completing the whole building on or before the first day of December next in a good substantial and workmanlike manner the said Philip Hooker and Elisha Putnam shall be allowed nine thousand eight hundred dollars. . . . [2]

The contract describes a building constructed chiefly for utilitarian purposes—the storage of arms. The exterior, however, was to be given a formal treatment, its Flemish bond brick walls *pencilled* and trimmed with cut stone.[3] During this period exterior brickwork was typically stained with linseed oil and red pigment to protect against moisture and unify surface appearance. Pencilling, or the application of white paint to the joints of the brickwork, served to highlight the bond pattern formed by the bricks. The contract's reference to tile for the roof of the building marks the only documented use by Hooker of this material in new construction. Thereafter slate would be the preferred roofing material, especially for urban buildings (cats. 7, 59, 60), although wood shingles also remained in use (cats. 15, 22).

In a later view of Hooker's state arsenal, which shows it radically altered for use as a school, the original outline and massing are still discernible.[4] ✥

1. State Comptroller Building Contract for State Arsenal between Governor John Jay and Philip Hooker & Elisha Putnam, Builders, 29 April 1799, with design by Philip Hooker, Archives, Office of the State Comptroller, New York State Archives, NYSL.
2. Ibid.
3. The Flemish bond of the exterior walls of the arsenal is visible in the photograph noted below, n. 4.
4. The author has seen such a photograph in an early twentieth century yearbook of the Albany school district, Collection, AIHA.

6. ST. PETER'S EPISCOPAL CHURCH

State and Lodge streets, Albany, N.Y.
Designed before 12 October 1801.
Built 1802–3; razed 1859.
Builders: Philip Hooker and Elisha Putnam with Samuel Hooker.
Masons: Abraham Kark, John Turner, and Caleb Russell.
Stonemasons: James Hodge and William Hannagan.

The Anglican, later St. Peter's Episcopal, Church building was constructed on a site in the middle of State Street near Fort Frederick in 1715. By 1800, however, after the destruction of the fort and subsequent expansion of the city westward it had become a traffic obstruction (fig. 1). In 1801 the Albany Common Council acted to facilitate the removal of the building by directing that the congregation be paid $2,500 for the land.[1] A draft of Hooker's handwritten contract records the congregation's interest in the fate of the early structure and the construction of a new church.

> *Articles of agreement and Contract entered into this 12th day of October 1801 between Philip Hooker, Elisha Putnam of the first part and the Rector and Inhabitants of the City of Albany in Communion of the protestant Episcopal Church of the State of New York of the Second part, as follows—*
>
> *The said party of the first part Contract and agree with the said party of the Second part, to errect the Walls for the foundation of a Church on the Corner of State and Lodge Streets in the City of Albany, of the following Dimentions and agreeably to a plan, hereunto annexed, to dig a trench for the Same and to find the Stone, Mortar, Workmanship, labour &c. The Walls to be on a level and to average six feet in height all round three feet in thickness and of such extent as to admit the Walls of the Church to be Sixty two feet on State Street and ninety feet on Lodge Street to be built of Stone laid on Timber and without mortar two feet and a half from the foundation the remainder to be laid in mortar Containing a due proportion of lime,—the foundation wall to be faced on the east side on Lodge Street the lenght of ninety feet with hewn Stone and on the South side on State Street three feet in height all round except the entrance door in the Tower with a range of plain Water Table of hewn Stone eight inches in height and of a proper depth to Crown the Wall of the foundation on the four Sides except at the entrance Door in the Tower, which is to project six feet on State Street. Eighteen piers to be sunk three feet deep within the walls of the said foundation to be two feet Square built of Stone and laid in Mortar at such places as will be Conveniant for laying the Timbers for the floor and for supporting the Galleries—*
>
> *The whole to be executed and Compleated in a proper and workman like manner and subjected during the prossess of the work to the occasional inspection of such person or persons, as the said party of the second part may thing* [i.e., think] *proper to employ for that purpose—*
>
> *The said party of the second part, do Contract on their part, to have the Ground on which the said foundation is to be erected, dug down to a proper level, and the earth removed at their own expence, and to pay to the said party of the first part the sum of fourteen hundred and eighty four Dollars fifty cents, in the following payments to wit—*
>
> *The State Tower of Saint Peters Church as it now Stands on State Street to be taken down and removed by the said party of the first part at their own expence— and received in lieu of a payment of 311 Dollars 50 Cts—the Sum of 300 Dollars to be paid, in Cash on the executing of these presents, a further Sum of 250*

Dollars to be paid during the progress of the work of laying the Dry Stone at such period as it may be required by the said party of the first part—

A further sum of 300 Dollars on the day that, that part of the work of the Stone to be laid in Mortar is commenced and the remaining sum of 210 Dollars & 50 Cents on the day the work of the said foundation is compleated.—

For the true and faithfull performance of each and every part of these presents, the parties mutually agree to bind themselves each to the other in the penal Sum of two thousand Dollars and have hereunto interchangably set their hands and Seals the day and date first above mentioned—provided the Ground be properly levelled by the party of the Second part, and the Season will admit, the work to be Commenced this fall and that part of the Stone work directed to be laid without Mortar Compleated and the remaining part of the work to be Commenced and Compleated without any unnecessary delay as early in the Spring as the wheather will admit of mason work being performed.— [2]

At this point Hooker and Putnam were to be employed to build only the foundation. During the eighteenth and nineteenth centuries it was common for a client to postpone entering into a building contract until a foundation was in place and had had time to settle. The proposal to construct the new foundation using the stone from only the tower of the original church would have enabled the congregation to continue to use the old sanctuary during the beginning stage of the building process. After the completion of the foundation, the remainder of the earlier structure would be demolished.

This original contract was never signed and three months later it was superseded by another.

Articles of agreement and Contract, Indented and made this Twenty Sixth day of January in the year one Thousand, eight hundred and two, between the Rector and Inhabitants of the City of Albany in communion of the protestant Episcopal Church of the State of New York of the first part, and Philip Hooker, Elisha Putnam, Gerret W. Van Schaick and Samuel Hill of the second part as follows.

That for and in Consideration of the Covenants herein specified to be performed by and on the part of the said party of the first part or their successors in office, they the said party of the second part, do for themselves, their heirs executors, administrators, and assigns, Covenant promise and agree to, and with the said party of the first part and their successors in office, that they the said party of the second part will erect, build and Compleat a Stone Church, on a Lot of Ground the property of the said party of the first part, situate in the first ward of the City of Albany, at the intersection of State and Lodge Street, and adjoining to the Rectory House and Lot, occupied by the Reverend Thomas Ellison, according to the two several plans and drafts, hereunto annexed, marked with the letters A. and B. and distinguished by the figures 1. 2. 3. 4. and 5, and shall at their own proper Cost and Charges, furnish all and singular, the necessary, and proper Materials, including all the Stone, free Stone, Lime, Sand, water, Slate, Timber, Plank, Boards, Lead, Ironmongery, Nails, Locks, Hinges, Bolts, Paint, Crown Glass, and evry other Article that may be requisite and necessary for the Compleating and finishing the aforesaid Church, according to the aforementioned plans or drafts hereunto annexed, and shall and will do or cause to be done, all and singular the Masons, Stone Cutters, Carpenters, Slaters, Plaisterers, Plumbers, Glaziers, Painters, Turners, Smiths, Cartmen and Labourers, work, with all and singular, the workmanship, labour and materials of evry kind, and description necessary to finish and Compleat the aforesaid Church, . . . (the Steeple and the Seating of the

Galleries excepted,) which are not meant or intended to be included in this Contract, the aforesaid Church to be Compleatly under Cover, and inclosed, and the Scratch Coating finished in the inside, on or before, the tenth day of November ensuing; and the whole to be finished and Compleated in all its parts, (the said Steeple, and Seating of the Galleries excepted) in the neatest, best, and most substantial manner, and of the best, and most durable Materials of evry kind, on or before the fifteenth day of June, in the Year of our Lord, one Thousand, Eight hundred and three.—

The said party of the second part, further agree, to receive the Episcopal Stone Church now standing in State Street in the City of Albany, as a payment for twelve hundred, and fifty Dollars in these presents, with all its appendages, (the Bell, Clock, and other moveable furniture excepted) and to be taken down, and removed, at the expence of them the said party of the second part, and the Street cleaned and leveled to the satisfaction of the Corporation of the City of Albany, on or before the first day of September ensuing the date hereof, the Stone thereof to be used in erecting the new Church, so far as they may be found to answer.—

Payment for the contracted work was to be $17,000, broken down into thirteen payments of $1,000 or $2,000 each, scheduled monthly, except less frequently during the winter. Figured into these payments was the *aforementioned Stone Church in State Street,* valued at $1,250. The contracting parties further agreed

. . . that the said party of the Second part, their executors, administrators or assigns, shall not become liable to any penalty, by virtue of these presents, in case of any injury, the said intended building may sustain, by fire communicated thereto, from any House, or building in its vicinity, and not connected with the building, or Church, to be erected, or not under the immediate charge, or direction, of the said party of the second part, or any of their agents, workmen, labourers, or dependants: but in case of any accident by fire, or otherwise, happening to the said intended building, from causes originating in the interior thereof, or from any of the Houses, or sheds, connected in any manner with the said building, or the erecting thereof, such damages, or injury, with all its consequences, to be at the sole risque, and expence, of the said party of the second part, their heirs, executors, and administrators;—

It is also agreed, between the aforesaid Contracting parties, that in case any dispute shall arise, respecting the true and faithfull performance, of any, or either, of the foregoing articles, on the part of either of the said Contracting parties, the same shall be forthwith submitted, to the investigation, and decision of three indifferent persons, one to be chosen by the party of the first part, one other to be chosen by the party of the second part, and a third, to be named by the two so chosen, and the award or decision, made by such three persons, or by a majority of them, and given in writing, under their hands, within thirty days of their being so chosen, to be final and conclusive.

It is also agreed by the two aforesaid Contracting parties, that the ground, on which the said Church is to be erected, shall be dug down, leveled and cleared, proper for the digging of the Trenches for laying the foundation, by and at the expence of the said party of the first part, and in proper Season, for the commencement of the erecting of the intended building, the Trenches for laying the foundation to be dug, and prepared at the expence of the said party, of the second part.

For the true, and faithfull performance of all, and singular, the Covenants, and agreements herein stipulated and contained, each of the aforementioned contracting parties, do respectively bind themselves to the other, in the penal sum of five Thousand Dollars, the party of the first part, have affixed their Common

Seal, and the party of the second part, have subscribed their Names, and affixed their Seals, the day and date, first above written.[3]

The methods of payment and arbitration recorded in this second agreement are typical of Hooker's contracts and of building practice in Albany at the time.

Foundations were constructed in the spring and the cornerstone was laid on 7 May 1802.[4] On 27 May Hooker and Putnam billed for services not covered by the contract up to that point.

Church Wardens & Vestrymen of St. Peters
to Hooker & Putnam D[r]

1802		
May 27th	*Carting 3353 loads Clay from the Foundation of the Church @ 2c pr*	*$67— 6*
	103 Days Labour at Diging Clay Loose 7/ *31* [Days Labour at Diging Clay Loose] *6/6* }	*115—31*
	4 Days Cartmen [Picking] *bank and Necessary* [i.e., privy] *that fell Down 16/pr Day* }	*8— ~*
		$190. . 37
	8 prCent Commissions	*15—*
	2 Days Carting as above Omitted 14/ *72 Loads Clay* [as above Omitted] *2 cents* }	*4—94*
	Albany 10th *Sept. 1802 Rec*[d] *payment*	*$210. 31*

Hooker & Putnam[5]

Work was halted after the completion of the foundations, and in December 1802 Hooker presented the drawings for the church. All but one of the drawings referred to in the text below have been lost. The one drawing known to have survived (fig. 32) bears the heading *fig: 1.B* and the following text:

References, to the ground plan, elevation, profile, & sections, of a design, for the intended Church of S[t.] *Peter, in the City of Albany.*
fig: 1. *A Section of one of the side walls drawn to a Scale of 3/8 of an inch to a foot, shewing the different thicknesses & heights of the walls, the Colour'd parts, are to be of hewn Stone, the Ashlar* a.a. *is not to be Continued all round the building, but upon State & Lodge Streets only, & crowned with a water table* bb. *which is to be Continued all round the building & forming the window Cells* [i.e., sills] *in the same range, from thence rise the Pillasters* c. *(four on Lodge & four on State Streets, as Represented in the elevation* fig[s]. 3 & 5 *) two feet six inches in breadth, & five inches in thickness, with their bases & capitals neatly moulded agreeable to the doric orders which support the entablature* d. *Constructed of wood & detached from the internal timbers, by the wall* e. *the whole to be Crowned with a ballustrade as Represented in* fig: 3. *the 10 real windows & the 4 Blank windows as represented in the ground plan* fig: 2, *are to have free stone frames* f. fig: 1. *8 inches in width & 4 inches in thickness with Keys to Close the arches, & to Contain 84 lights of Crown Glass 15 by 11 inches exclusive the semi-Circular tops, two Sashes in each window, hung with proper pullies & weights, all the walls in said Church to be constructed of good rough Stone, except the walls Mark'd* g g. *in* fig: 2, *which may either be built of brick 14 inches in thickness or stone 18 inches in thickness, all the exterior wall above the watertable to be covered*

1. Root, p. 71.
2. Archives, St. Peter's Church, Albany, N.Y. (hereafter A SPC). The author is aware that the sum of payments listed does not equal the total specified.
3. Ibid.
4. Root, p. 81.
5. A SPC.
6. Ibid. Based on this description, the five drawings would have been as follows: 1. Wall section, 2. Ground plan and gallery plan, 3. Lodge Street elevation, 4. Longitudinal section, and 5. Front, or State Street, elevation.
7. A SPC.

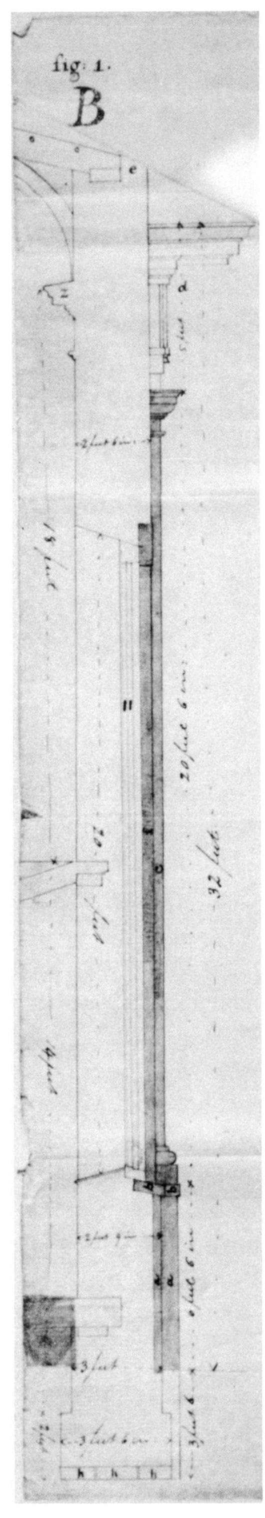

▲
Fig. 32. St. Peter's Episcopal Church, Albany, Hooker's section through one of the side walls, 1802.
Ink and wash on paper.
Archives, St. Peter's Episcopal Church, Albany.

with a coat of rough casting, Composed of Materials that will withstand the weather, & all the interior walls & Ceilings plaistered in the best manner. all the floor, Gallery Roof & other timbers of the best kind and framed in the most substantial manner, the roof to be Covered with Slate well Laid in Morter & nailed upon 1 1/4 Inch planks, the walls of the foundation of the tower to be four feet in thickness 2 feet in height & from thence upward to the height of 33 feet, 3 feet in thickness, & from thence to the top (which is 40 feet above the surface of the street) 2 1/2 feet in thickness the angles of which are to be rusticated as also the entrance with free stone 2. *See* fig. 5. *free stone steps to the entrance, see* fig: 2. & 5. *the floors Seats* a. a. a. a. *&c. & Pulpit* b, *reading desk* c, *clerk desk* d, *communion* [table] e, *& font* f, *to geather with the pillasters, gallery fronts,— Collumns & stocco Cornices* z *that Support the Ceiling see* fig: 4. *to be executed in the most substantial manner and of the best Materials, & according to the plan* fig: 2 *& Section* fig: 4.— *and the walls of the foundation to be laid on 3 inch planks* hh *and all & Singular the work & materials of every Kind to be of the first rate, according to the plans* [word or words crossed out] *and discription herein specified—* o. o. o. o. [are] *flues to be carried up to the top of the Ballustrade.*

Ph. Hooker Arch

Albany December 15th 1802[6]

During the summer of 1803, when the church was nearly complete, Hooker and Putnam dissolved their partnership. Subsequent bills submitted by Hooker indicate that he enlisted his father's help to finish the building,[7] drawing on the elder man's greater experience in construction.

Later that year Hooker submitted an account of expenses, which is valuable for its description of services and costs and for information on the former *copartnership.*

Albany 16th Decem[be]*r 1803*

Gentm

The Statement accompanying this of the actual expences of St. Peters Church Is as accurate as the nature & circumstances of the case will admit of, not having the Least Idea at the Commencement of the Business that we should ever have occasion to make such a Statement, the Accounts of the Church have in many Instances, (with respect to workmanship & Materials,) been Conected & Blended, with other concerns, Consequently no other mode of ascertaining the expence of many Parts of the building could be adopted, but by Calculation. altho: we have Bills of considerable amount, both for Materials, & work, which was applied wholly to the Church, yet many Items of the Same Part, are Charged on book as the work Progressed. The Within Statement is therefore necessarily founded upon, & drawn from, three Sources, to Witt: from bills, from our books & from calculations, & we verily believe upon the whole that altho: some articles may be charged too high, that some also may be charged too low, but the result is rather if any way against our selves—

You will observe the Statement goes to the disolution of the copartnership and amts [to] *$13,496..90 1/2— Since which time the Business has been wholly Conducted by Philip Hooker.*

Yrs Respectfully
Ph: Hooker
Elisha Putnam

Expenditures on St. Peters Church		
Amt Allowed for old Church	*$1250..*	
Ab[raha]*m Karks Bill of Masons & Labour*	*1832..48*	
Turner & Russels [Bill of Masons & Labour]	*453..93*	
James Hodge Bill of Cut Stone	*2075..*	
W[illia]*m Hannagan* [Bill of Cut Stone]	*170..*	*5781..41*
Allens Bill of Slate	*805..75*	
Sundry [Bill of] *Stone*	*644..95*	
[Sundry] *Charges p*[er] *Book*	*240..89*	
Lime as p[er] *Bills & Book*	*819..32*	
Tho[ma]*s Shepherds bill of Smiths work*	*170..—*	
Spencer Staffords bill of Tin	*57..*	
John Brinkerhoff Sheet Lead	*79..50*	
Samuel Hill. bill of Lead & Pullies	*121..87*	
Rich[ar]*d Allansons* [bill of Lead & Pullies] *& Davids Sh*[ee]*t Lead*	*25..—*	
15 M [i.e., thousand] *Bricks @ 56/*	*105..—*	*3070..22*
24 M [i.e., thousand] *Splitt Lath 9/*	*27..—*	
21 Loads Stone p[aid] *D. Waters*	*17.. 6*	
Sundry Cartmen's acc[oun]*ts*	*1029..—*	
Use & wasteage of Scaffold[in]*g Horses boxes nails gangways &c*	*150..—*	
Taking down old Church, digging Sand Bank, Slacking lime &c	*124.. 7*	
Paid for dressing & Slating	*158..—*	*1505..13*
10 Bbls boil[e]*d Plaister*	*40..*	
digging foundation & carting g[roun]*d*	*65..*	
12,354 feet Timber, & workmansh[i]*p By Calculation @ 7 d p*[er] *foot*	*900..81*	
66 1/2 Squares of Planking on roof Tongued & grooved, good Plank 34/	*282..62 1/2*	
		1288..43 1/2
Carried forward		*$11,645..19 1/2*

[The *Amt Brot forward* is repeated on the following page of the document.]

Plank workmanship nails &c for Arching Ceilings	*148..22*	
10 window frames & Sashes Materials & work	*275..*	
Cornice & Pediments including Timber, Plank, boards, Scantling work &c By Calculation	*1172..70*	
54 M [i.e., thousand] *Lath nails 4/*	*28..25*	
Centres &c for doors & windows	*40..—*	
452 Plank for floors & stairs 2/2	*122..41*	
Russils bill for Paint'g & Putty	*32..63*	
Roofing Tower	*22..50*	
		1841..71
Ph. Hooker & Elisha Putnam		*13,496..90 1/2* [sic]

The above was previous to the dissolution of the Copartnership of Hooker & Putnam,

Since which time I have kept an accurate acc[t] to a cent, as will appear by my Book, which am[ts] to	*4499..21*
actual expence	*$17,986..11 1/2* [sic]
As nothing has been allowed in the above am[t] as a Compensation for the Contractors we trust that 8 p[er] *C*[en]*t Commission will not be deemed unreasonable, that being a Customary allowance on such occasions—which am*[oun]*ts to—*	*$1438..88*
expences including Commission	*$19,424..99* [sic]
Albany 16th Decem[be]*r 1803*[8]	

The church was consecrated on 4 October 1803,[9] with the altering of seats, construction of the communion table, hanging of doors, and making of a table for the baptismal font completed by mid-December.[10] The galleries were not completed until 1815, when John Boardman agreed to erect and finish *a gallery . . . aggreeable to the plan* for $400 and to create *a door through the tower wall & stairs ascending to the gallery.*[11]

▶ Fig. 33. St. Peter's Episcopal Church, Albany (1802–3), interior looking south at the organ loft, c. 1858. Archives, St. Peter's Episcopal Church, Albany.

▶
Fig. 34. St. Peter's Episcopal Church, Albany (1802–3), interior looking northeast toward the pulpit, c. 1858. Archives, St. Peter's Episcopal Church, Albany.

Edward W. Root quotes from the draft of a letter, apparently written in 1802, which describes the building as proposed in Hooker's original contract.

> *"The Church, which promises to be strong and durable, is built of rough stone, to be finished on the exterior with a rough cast of proper cement, and situated on the north side of State street at the intersection with Lodge street. The walls are two feet six inches in thickness, sixty-two feet wide on State street and ninety feet long on Lodge street, ornamented with freestone in a manner to render it neat and respectable, and covered with the best Welsh slate. The interior of the Building is fifty-seven feet wide, and seventy-two feet long in the clear, the tower projecting six feet in front on State street and forms a base of twenty-two feet square The whole is contracted to be finished with pews, Galleries on their sides, Pulpit, reading desk, clerk's desk, Communion Table, Font, etc, in a complete and workmanlike manner, with materials of the best, . . ."*[12]

Recently discovered photographs (figs. 33, 34)[13] show the austere interior in which there is little decorative treatment aside from the curiously reeded columns, the paneling on the face of the galleries, and the consoles used to punctuate the junctures between the three arched ceilings. The ceilings over the galleries were almost semicircular in section; that of the sanctuary appears to have been elliptical.

8. Ibid.
9. Root, p. 81.
10. A SPC.
11. St. Peter's Episcopal Church Papers, Albany, N.Y., Records, 1790–1900, SC 19680, MSC NYSL.
12. Root, p. 78, from Joseph Hooper, *A History of Saint Peter's Church in the City of Albany* (Albany: Fort Orange Press, 1900).
13. A SPC. There is a third interior photograph, looking northwest.
14. Root, pp. 81–82.

▶ Fig. 35. St. Peter's Episcopal Church, Albany (1802–3, steeple 1822), exterior, c. 1858. Albany Institute of History & Art, McKinney Library, Photograph Collection.

On the exterior of St. Peter's Church (fig. 35), Hooker articulated the end bays of the side elevations, as he had done in the design of the North Dutch Reformed Church (fig. 20). Here, however, each is treated as a tall, pedimented pavilion containing a blind arch, its overall form echoing the entrance facade of the tower. The well-proportioned and finely detailed steeple was constructed in 1822 (cat. 51). Hooker's building was demolished in February and March of 1859.[14]

7. TOWN HOUSE FOR ELSIE FONDA

North Market Street (now Broadway), Albany, N.Y.
Designed before 12 June 1802.
Built 1802–3; razed.
Builders: Philip Hooker and Elisha Putnam.

Elsie Fonda, born in 1783, was the daughter of Lyntje Fonda and Richard Lush, a prominent Albany lawyer. In using her mother's surname she followed an ancient Dutch tradition. The 12 June 1802 contract and specifications for her town house, reprinted below, provide detailed information on the construction of a significant upper class house of the period.

> *Articles of agreement . . . between Elsie Fonda . . . and Elisha Putnam & Philip Hooker . . . that* [Hooker and Putnam] *will erect and completely finish one dwelling house (on a lot of ground, situate between Market & Montgomery Streets, and bounded on the north, by a lot of ground owned by Peter Gansevoort, and on the south by the lot of James Fonda) of the following dimensions: thirty feet seven inches front and rear, and fifty two feet deep from front to rear and thirty five feet in height, from the water table to the wall plates thereof, and to be divided according to the several plans hereunto annexed. The front and rear walls of the foundation to be two feet, six inches in thickness at the top, and the flank walls twenty inches at the top. Partition walls of brick nine inches in thickness. All the walls of the foundation to be eight feet in height. The front wall above the surface of the street to the under side of the water table to be constructed of good free stone, laid in regular courses. The whole to be laid in good morter, except eighteen inches of the bottom, which will be made a dry wall. The superstructure is to be built with good merchantable hard burnt brick. All the brick that are to* [be] *used in the said building are to be of the best hard burnt brick and laid in morter, composed of good lime and coarse sand, taken from the Patroon's* [land] *or from the island below the city* [south of Albany]. *The front and rear walls are to be eighteen inches in thickness, the flank walls fourteen inches in thickness, and the gable walls nine inches in thickness. Partitions to be framed of pitch pine scantling 3 by 5 inches, and 12 inches from center to center. Floor timber of the first and second stories to be 11 1/2 inches deep and 2 3/4 inches thick, and to be laid twelve inches from center to center. Floor joists of third story 11 by 4 inches, laid twenty four inches from center to center. Joists of the gerrat floor 10 by 4, laid three feet from center to center, all of good sound timber and well framed. Roof to be constructed of good proportionable timber, & constructed in the best manner for slate, and covered with plank, and well slated, with best sort of Welsh slate, nailed with two nails each, at least of the same quality and size of those lately laid on the house of John van Schaick in Market Street in this city, and gable walls and chimneys coped with free stone. The floor on the first storey to be laid with the best yellow pine, narrow battins.* [In the floor of the] *second* [story], *best white pine, narrow battins, tongued and grooved in the heading joints and matched. Third story laid with good white pine plank, full width, neatly planed, tongued and grooved together. Gerrat and cellar floors to be laid with good sound plank and the cellar floors to be of yellow pine, tongued and grooved, but not planed, except the cellar kitchen, which is to be yellow pine and to be planed. The doors in the first and second stories to be one inch and three fourths in thickness, faced on both sides and neatly trimmed with mortice locks of the best kind; doors in the third story, one and one fourth inches thick, to have iron rim*[me]*d locks, also those in the cellar kitchen &c.*

The windows in the first and second stories to be glazed with glass of 12 by 18 Inches and to contain twelve panes each. Third story windows to contain twelve panes of glass 12 by 16 [inches] *all of the best London crown glass; all of the front windows, eight in number, except the two in the lower story which are to have outside shutters, to be trimmed in the best manner with inside folding shutters; the back windows being eight in number, & to be glazed with the same size and quality of glass aforesaid, to have out side shutters lined with tin, and to be trimmed on the inside with framed backs and elbows, jambs, & soffitt. Front and back rooms in first story, and front room in second story to have Philadelphia marble hearths, and facings to fire places and cast iron backs & jambs. The fire places in the lower rooms to be four feet six inches wide, and* [those in the] *second story to be four feet six inches wide, and the hearth stones to be five feet six inches long and one foot and ten inches broad in one piece. Fire places in the third story and back room in the second story to have free stone hearths and facings. All the bases, surbases, architraves, chimney pieces, and trimmings of every kind to be done in a neat, plain, modern stile, and made of the best materials and executed in a workmanlike and most approved manner. Stair case to be executed in a masterly manner, with a continued mahogany hand rail, from the first to the third story. All the principle rooms and halls to have stoco cornices and ceilings finished with putty. All the walls of the first, second, & third stories to be finished for painting or papering as* [Elsie Fonda] *shall direct; all the windows to have free Stone Arches and Cells* [i.e., sills], *and free stone cells to all the back windows, and free stone cells to front or hall door. Front stoop to be made in a light handsome form of wood, red cedar posts, pitch pine steps and platform, unless* [Elsie Fonda] *shall chuse to have a stone stoop, in which case* [she] *shall pay the difference between the price of a stone and a wooden stoop. Cellar steps, front and rear, of blue stone, in one piece. . . . The front cornice to be made of wood and lined with sheet copper & disconnected with the interior timbers by a brick wall carried up to the under side of the slate & supported with gutter irons, and the gutter in the rear to be of sheet iron well supported, and tin gutter to back building; and the conductors to all the gutters to be large & made of the best double tin. The front and rear walls to be neatly oiled and pencilled. All the wood work inside and out to have two coats of paint of such colours as* [Elsie Fonda] *shall direct; Prussian blue and green excepted; and* [Hooker and Putnam] *further agree to erect a back building adjoining the aforesaid dwelling house as represented in plan N*[umber] *1 to consist of a cellar, and one upper story; the stone walls of which shall be sixteen inches in thickness, and eight feet high, and the brick walls thereof shall be nine inches in thickness. Roof to be covered with slate in* [the] *same manner and size as the dwelling house aforesaid, inside well finished, and according to the plan above mentioned; and it is expressly understood between the respective parties that* [Hooker and Putnam are] *to furnish all and singular the materials of every kind, that shall be required (of the best quality) for completing the aforesaid dwelling house, including stone, brick, lime, sand, slate, iron, timber, plank, boards, paints, glass, pullies, weights, locks, hinges, nails, screws, brads, glue, and every other article that shall be found requisite for finishing & completing the aforesaid building according to the several plans, hereunto annexed, and in a neat, substantial & workmanlike manner, and according to the true intents and meaning of these presents and that* [Hooker and Putnam] *shall and will at* [their] *own proper costs and charges employ & pay, or cause to be employed and paid, all and singular, the carpenters, masons, stone cutters, smiths, painters, glaziers, plumbers, plaisterers, cartmen and labourers of every kind, that may be required for carrying the aforesaid work into execution. . . .*[1]

Hooker and Putnam agreed to finish the house and outbuilding by 15 June 1803 for a sum of $6,500. In addition, the contract provided for the settling of disputes between the two parties and included a performance bond for $7,000 to protect Elsie Fonda from loss.[2]

In December of 1803 final expenses totaled $7,346.90.[3] The additional charges were due to changes requested by the client: the addition of seven inches to the width of the house ($50.00); *for the consideration of using all hard brick* ($84.00); and *building stable, erecting fence etc* ($712.90). This last item appears to refer to a structure not originally contemplated (cat. 12), and could account for the extension of payments through October 1803.[4]

Not included in the account of construction costs is the amount of $100 (£40) receipted by Hooker and Putnam *for extra work in raising* [i.e., adding] *one foot to the house . . . & also for free stone arches & imposts to the 2nd story in front . . . according to mutual aggreement . . . in July last.*[5]

Since the specifications do not indicate room heights, a section and/or an elevation might have accompanied the plans in the original set of drawings. Even without the existence of these documents today, it is clear from the contract specifications and the building costs that Elsie Fonda's town house was one of the finer Albany residences of its time. ✥

1. Philip Hooker Papers, MK AIHA.
2. Ibid.
3. Lush Family Papers, MK AIHA.
4. Philip Hooker Papers.
5. Ibid.

8. PROPOSAL FOR THE NEW YORK STATE CAPITOL

Albany, N.Y.
Designed between 28 February and 7 March 1803.
Unbuilt.

The Albany Common Council Minutes for 28 February 1803 recorded the following resolution: . . . *that Mr. Cuyler, Mr. Cooper,* [and] *Mr. Yates be a committee . . . to cause a map to be made of the ground in the* [Public] *Square sufficiently spacious and suitable for the construction of a State and Court House* and to submit an estimate of its cost.[1] They presented their estimate of $30,000 on 7 March 1803, together with a *plan of the building made by Mr. Hooker, Architect.*[2] This plan was superseded by another prepared by Hooker at the request of the state legislature the following year (cat. 15).

It is important to note that Hooker had been proposed to submit plans for a new state house as early as 11 March 1802, when the common council first considered its construction. Although that resolution was not passed, it is indicative of Hooker's professional standing at the time.[3] ✥

1. Albany Common Council Minutes, 28 February 1803, ACHR.
2. Ibid., 7 March 1803.
3. Ibid., 11 March 1802.

9. RENOVATIONS TO ST. PETER'S EPISCOPAL CHURCH PARSONAGE

Maiden Lane and Lodge Street, Albany, N.Y.
Designed c. March 1803.
Built 1803–4; razed.
Builders: Philip Hooker, Caleb Russell, and John Turner.

As a result of the construction of the new church for St. Peter's congregation (cat. 6), the parsonage of 1792 required modifications to restore its usefulness. The proximity of the church to the house made access to its outbuildings difficult. In a letter written sometime in March 1803, Hooker submitted an initial proposal accompanied by a sketch (fig. 36).

> *Gentlemen*
> *I beg leave to suggest the propriety of moving the parsonage house, back in a line with the west side of the Church, which will leave a Court yard in front of 29 feet in* [from the street] *& will give a yard* [in] *back of 40 feet. Take 12 feet of that for Stable, Chair house &c. There will remain 28 feet for* [a] *wood yard. The probable expence of moving, taking down & rebuilding Chimneys & doing the*
>
> | | |
> |---|---|
> | *necessary repairs will be about* | *$200* |
> | *new foundation* | *350* |
> | *digging & carting away ground* | *100* |
> | | *$650* |
> | *deduct for Stone in old walls* | *164* |
> | *probable expence* | *$486* |
>
> *with Respect*
> *Ph: Hooker*[1]

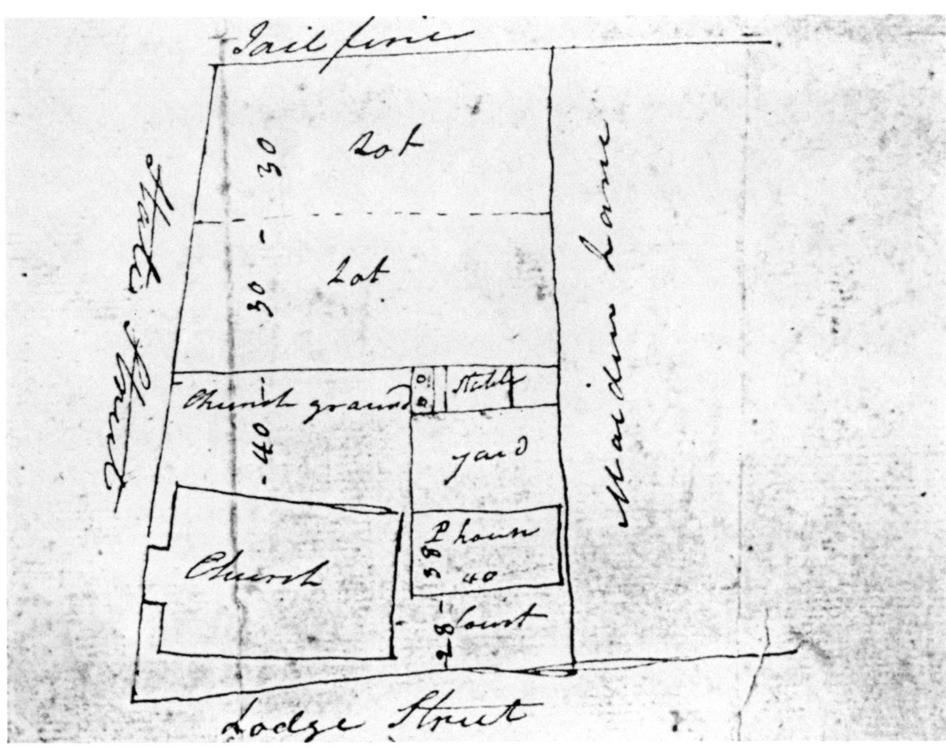

▶ Fig. 36. St. Peter's Episcopal Church, Albany, Hooker's sketch of the site, showing proposed relocation of the parsonage house, 1803. Ink on paper. Archives, St. Peter's Episcopal Church, Albany.

Hooker kept separate accounts for this project. They indicate that the work, done between April and December 1803, cost a total of $876.35.[2] Invoices indicate that Philip had enlisted the help of his brother, James, in the completion of this work.[3]

Perhaps due in part to stresses put on the building during its move, the parsonage required repairs in 1804. The scope of this work is documented by Hooker's handwritten contract.

> *Articles of agreement and contract entered into this 24th day of August in the year one thousand eight hundred and four. between Caleb Russell and John Turner of the city of Albany, bricklayers of the first part— and Samuel Hill and Daniel Hale for and in behalf of the Vestry of Saint Peters Church in said city of the second part as follows.*
>
> *That the party of the first part do undertake and engage to repair the dwelling house situated on the corner of Lodge street and Maiden Lane adjoining to Saint Peters Church the property of the Corporation of the said church in the following manner, to wit:*
>
> *1st To erect a wall thro the cellar in the place and of the extent of the former one of a brick and a half in thickness on a proper foundation and laid in good and sufficient mortar and to finish the same, with the other walls of the kitchen apartment, with two coats of proper and sufficient brown mortar. To lath plaister and properly finish in the same way the partitions to be erected by a carpenter to be employed at the expence of the party of the second part in the same place in the cellar apartment where they have formerly stood previous to the situation of the house having been altered. To take down rebuild and properly finish the oven in the form it now stands, and to take down such parts of the lower parts of the kitchen chimney as may be defective by setling, cracking or unsound bricks. To repair and s*[t]*rengthen the same so as to render it sufficiently strong and durable, and to lay the cellar steps with stone and mortar and complete and finish the necessary mason work for the passage or door way.*
>
> *2nd To repair the rear foundation wall by replacing the stone*[s] *thereof as far as possible in their original position with the necessary pointing and repairing of defects. And to repair such parts of the front foundation wall as have become injured by the weather. The placing of the building thereon or in any other way and putting the whole as far as possible in a proper state of repair.*
>
> *3rd To carry up and completely finish the two stacks of chimneys with proper and sufficient hard brick well laid and in good mortar. To lay and complete all the hearths and fire places, in the kitchen, and in every room requiring the same and to place such free stone slabs around the fire places as may be furnished by the party of the second part.*
>
> *4th To take down all such parts of the plastering of the first and second stories of the buildings as are cracked, defective and insufficient, leaving none but what adheres solidly to its wall or cieling and will remain firm and durable and then to give the whole and every part of the said two stories that may now be defficient either from not having been plastered or from the plastering having become defective three sufficient coats of plastering. The last coat to be of white and what is commonly called a hard*

finish to fill up and neatly finish all opening, cracks or fissures that there may appear in any part therof, so as to leave the whole and every part of the plastering in the said two stories in a proper, finished, complete and durable state. Replacing and repairing the brick filling in every part where it may be found defficient or out of order.

5th To find and furnish all the brick, stone, lime, lath, nails, hair, sand, water and every other necessary material and labour, service and workmanship of every description at the cost and expence of them, the party of the first part, necessary to finish and complete the said undertaking. The whole of which is to be done in a strong durable neat and workmanlike manner without any slight, hurry or irregularity of any description and without any unavoidable or unnecessary delay.

The party of the second part for and in behalf of the Vestry of Saint Peters Church do engage:
That the brick and stone the property of the said Church Vestry now laying in the vicinity of the said building shall be furnished [to] *the said party of the first part free of any charge and they do promise and engage to pay to them . . . for the finishing the aforementioned work in a neat sufficient complete and workmanlike manner, the sum of five hundred & seventy dollars.*

For the true and faithfull performance of all and every part of the foregoing contract, the parties do hereby obligate and bind themselves each to the other in the penal sum of five hundred dollars, and have hereunto interchangeably set their hands and seals the day and year first above written. It is further agreed by the parties of the 2nd part to finish the passage way into the garrett.[4]

Accounts from 24 August 1804 to January 1805 indicate that the repair costs totaled £363.1.2 or $907.64, far exceeding the contract sum of $570.00.[5] ✥

1. Archives, St. Peter's Church, Albany, N.Y.
2. Ibid.
3. St. Peter's Episcopal Church Papers, Albany, N.Y., Records, 1790–1900, SC 19680, MSC NYSL.
4. Ibid.
5. Ibid.

10. NEW YORK STATE BANK

State Street, Albany, N.Y.
Designed before 6 April 1803.
Built 1803; altered 1860, 1890s, and c. 1914; razed 1927; fragments survive.
Builder: Philip Hooker.

The New York State Bank was chartered by the legislature on 19 March 1803,[1] the earliest possible date for Hooker's work on this project. On 6 April the bank's Board of Directors appointed

> "*Mr. Mather* [later replaced by Mr. Lansing] *Mr.* [Elkanah] *Watson & Mr. Stewart . . . a Committee with Power to purchase the Lot of Isaiah Townsend in State Street for such sum as they shall deem reasonable—and that they be also empowered to contract with Smith and* [John] *Boardman for such Sum and on such terms as they shall approve for building a Banking house on the said Lot agreeably to the Plan thereof submitted to this Board by Philip Hooker.*"[2]

▶
Fig. 37. Robert and James Adam, Society for the Encouragement of Arts, Manufactures & Commerce, London, elevation, published in the first volume of their *Works in Architecture*, 1778.
Courtesy New York State Library, Albany.

▶ Fig. 38. New York State Bank, Albany (1803), State Street facade, c. 1865. Albany Public Library.

Subsequent minutes of the board indicate that the directors did not engage Smith and Boardman to erect the structure but rather, at their 11 May meeting, approved *"a contract made with Philip Hooker for the building of a Banking house."* [3]

The contract, reported to the bank's board on 11 May 1803 and referred to by Root in his monograph on Hooker, provides details of the proposed building's design and construction. [T]*he contract provides for a window of 28 panes, 18 x 12 inches* [located between the doors on the first floor. T]*he contract also provides for the use of freestone between the "porches,"* [probably indicating the use of this stone from the level of the top of the stairs down to grade level between the stairs]. *Two air holes . . . were to be placed between the water table and the sidewalk.* Root also recorded that the *original entrance doors were of solid wood.*[4] In addition, he reconstructed the original arrangement of the rooms.

> *If we read the contract carefully we can arrive at some idea of the size and interior arrangement of the original structure. It was designed with a height of 28 feet between the water table and the wall plates, a width of 37 feet 6 inches, front and rear, and a total depth of 52 feet. At some intermediate point a transverse stone partition extended from wall to wall and from below the floor of the cellar to a foot or more above the roof. The interior was thus divided into two distinct parts. The cellars of these two parts did not communicate and were put to widely different uses. That in front contained a vault and a staircase to the banking room and that in the rear a store room, bed room, kitchen and kitchen staircase. On the ground floor, in front, the right hand doorway led from State Street into the banking room, and the doorway on the left opened into a hall containing the stairs to the second floor. As one entered this hall from the street a door on the right led into the bank room and another door in the partition wall at the end of the hall led into one of the rooms in the rear half of the building. This room was possibly the apartment designated in the contract as the "back parler." If so it had a marble hearth and mantel and a fireplace with cast iron back and jambs. In all probability the adjoining and communicating room was the cashier's office. At any rate the contract indicates quite positively that the cashier's office was somewhere in the rear on the ground floor. Upstairs, in front and reckoning from east to west, were the "directors' room," the "drawing room" and the upper hall, and communicating with the latter, in the rear, several apartments with freestone fireplaces. Like the "back parler," the bank room, directors' room and drawing room had marble hearths and mantels and iron fireplaces, and somewhere in the second story a closed staircase led up to the garret.*[5]

Elkanah Watson, who some twenty years later was to work with Hooker on his house in Port Kent (cat. 62), took credit for the design of the bank.[6] While Watson may well have offered suggestions, the documentation refutes his claim, as does the cornerstone of the building which reads simply: *Philip Hooker, Architect, 1803.*

The composition of the bank's facade and some of its motifs (fig. 38) would be recalled in Hooker's subsequent designs. The broken entablature may be found in the Ontario Branch Bank at Utica (fig. 80) and St. Peter's Church at Sherrill, New York (fig. 115), while the Palladian opening set into a blind arch reappeared in the South Dutch Reformed Church (fig. 59) and the Dutch Reformed Church at Niskayuna (fig. 145). The latter element and indeed the general organization of the State Street facade of the bank owed a considerable debt to an elevation published in the Adam brothers' *Works in Architecture* about a quarter of a century earlier (fig. 37).[7] Hooker incorporated a witty twist in his interpretation of that prototype, which features classical scenes in the roundels. By substituting the obverse and reverse of an 1803 silver dollar he made specific reference in the decorative scheme to the building's use as a bank.

Root discussed at some length the probable fenestration of the State Street elevation, illustrated in part by John L. Dykeman's 1916 restoration drawing.[8] The earliest photograph of the building (fig. 38), dating from about 1865, may well represent the facade as constructed, with the

1. Root, p. 86.
2. Ibid., from New York State Bank, Manuscript Minutes of the Board of Directors, 6 April 1803. Smith and Boardman had previously been engaged by Isaiah Townsend to erect a building on what had then been his property.
3. Root, p. 87, from New York State Bank, Manuscript Minutes, 11 May 1803.
4. Root, p. 92. This contract is now lost.
5. Ibid., pp. 92–93.
6. Ibid., pp. 88–89.
7. The elevation of the House of the Society for the Encouragement of Arts, Manufactures & Commerce, later the Royal Society of Arts building, was published in 1778 as Plate IV of Vol. I, No. IV of the *Works*; No. IV had been published individually in 1776; Robert Adam, *The Works in Architecture of Robert and James Adam*, ed. Robert Oresko (London: Academy Editions, and New York: St. Martin's Press, 1975), pp. 7, 147.
8. Root, pp. 90–92, fig. 47.
9. Ibid., p. 94; Henry Ives Cobb, Jr., "1803 Facade moved as a Unit," *American Architect*, CXXXVII, 2580 (February 1930), 60–61, 84.

▶
Fig. 39. New York State Bank, Albany, a portion of the 1803 facade incorporated into the bank's sixteen-story office building of 1927; photograph 1991.

exception of the window sashes which were probably replaced in the 1860 renovations. The carving of rosettes and swags above the first floor window is thought to be original, based on a comparison with similar detailing in other Hooker designs.

The New York State Bank was remodeled extensively in 1860, the 1890s, and around 1914. In 1927 the building was razed and the State Street facade was reused, with modifications, as the entrance to the bank's new sixteen-story office building designed by Henry Ives Cobb (fig. 39).[9] ✤

11. TRINITY EPISCOPAL CHURCH

Broad and First streets, Utica, N.Y.
Designed 1803.
Built 1803–10; altered before 1828; enlarged 1833; razed c. 1927.
Builders: Samuel and John Hooker.

In 1803 Philip Hooker provided the plans for Trinity Episcopal Church in Utica,[1] a wooden structure with a tower reminiscent of the cupola designed for Union College (cat. 2). Samuel and John Hooker, the architect's father and brother, were among the original subscribers for the building, and they received the contract to construct it. Although the church was consecrated in September 1806, it was not completed until 1810.[2]

▶
Fig. 40. Trinity Episcopal Church, Utica (1803–10), sketch by Baroness Hyde de Neuville, 1807. Watercolor on paper. The New-York Historical Society, New York, N.Y.

An 1807 watercolor shows the exterior of the building as originally completed (fig. 40). Details regarding its interior arrangement are provided in a letter written by Robert J. Hubbard around 1898.

> [T]*he glass* [of the windows] *was clear and in square panes. . . . The gallery . . . at that time extended to the rear wall of the building. . . . The color of the walls and wood work of the church was white. . . .* [and] *there was no chancel. The South wall of the church was strikingly effective. . . . The pulpit, of the "candle-stick" order, stood against the wall so high up that the preacher could cast his eyes along the occupants of the galleries. This pulpit was entered by a small door through the rear wall, the stairs being concealed. . . . Below the pulpit was the reading desk, formed in a semi-circle around its base, and below was the communion table, surrounded by the chancel rail.*[3]

1. Root, p. 95.
2. Pomroy Jones, *Annals and Recollections of Oneida County* (Rome, N.Y.: Pomroy Jones, 1851), pp. 570–72; Root, p. 95.
3. John R. Harding, ed., *One Hundred Years of Trinity Church, Utica, N.Y.* (Utica, N.Y.: Thomas J. Griffiths, 1898), pp. 85–87.

▶ Fig. 41. Trinity Episcopal Church, Utica (1803–10), as remodeled in the *Gothick* style and enlarged; photograph c. 1910. Oneida County Historical Society, Utica.

4. *The Utica Directory* (Utica, N.Y.: Elisha Harrington, 1828), p. 93. The remodeling might have been as early as 1818, for the contract written by one of the builders of Hooker's St. Peter's Episcopal Church in Sherrill (cat. 43) refers to the *gothic* windows in the Episcopal Church, Utica.

5. Elisha Harrington, *The Utica Directory. No. 5 –1834* (Utica, N.Y.: E. A. Maynard, Printer, 1834), p. 54.

6. Root, p. 95.

By 1828 Trinity Church had been remodeled in the *Gothick* style,[4] and in the summer of 1833 it was enlarged by adding twenty feet to the front of the structure and *rebuilding the steeple* (fig. 41).[5] The church was razed about 1927.[6]

12. STABLE FOR RICHARD LUSH

North Market Street (now Broadway), Albany, N.Y.
Designed before 2 July 1803.
Built 1803; razed.
Builder unknown.

1. Lush Family Papers, MK AIHA. The cost of this stable was included in the total of expenses for the town house of Elsie Fonda, the daughter of Richard Lush (cat. 7).

Hooker's financial accounts for the Lush stable indicate that construction took place between 2 July and 28 September 1803. The building, of which there is no surviving visual record, cost Lush $712.90, which included Hooker's fee of $48.00 for superintendence of construction.[1] ✜

13. TOWN HOUSE FOR WILLIAM ALEXANDER

South Ann Street, Little Falls, N.Y.
Designed c. 1803–4.
Built 1804; razed 1874.
Builder unknown.

William Alexander was born in Schenectady, New York, in 1779. He moved to Little Falls in 1796 and served as that town's second postmaster from 1803 until his death in 1816.[1] He married Catherine Porteus, the daughter of John Porteus, a major landowner in Little Falls whose business contacts had included architect-engineer Pierre Pharoux.[2]

In late 1803 or early 1804 Alexander commissioned Hooker to design a house. Hooker sent a small book of plans bound with a letter:

> *Plan's & Elevation of A Design, for William Alexander at the little falls*
>
> *The following Plans are an imperfect Scetch of a design for a dwelling house. Should it coincide with Mr. Alexander's Ideas, I will draw proper plans which will be accurate for the workman to work by, & give the necessary dimentions. I Could wish to know of what Materials the Building is to be Constructed, . . . wheather of wood, Brick, or Stone & what aspect it will have.*[3]

The sketches contained in the book (figs. 42–44) were intended only to give a general sense of the design. The working plans to which Hooker referred would have been much more detailed and on a larger scale than these, which were drawn at fifteen feet to the inch.

Hooker included keys to the drawings and a brief statement about the design.

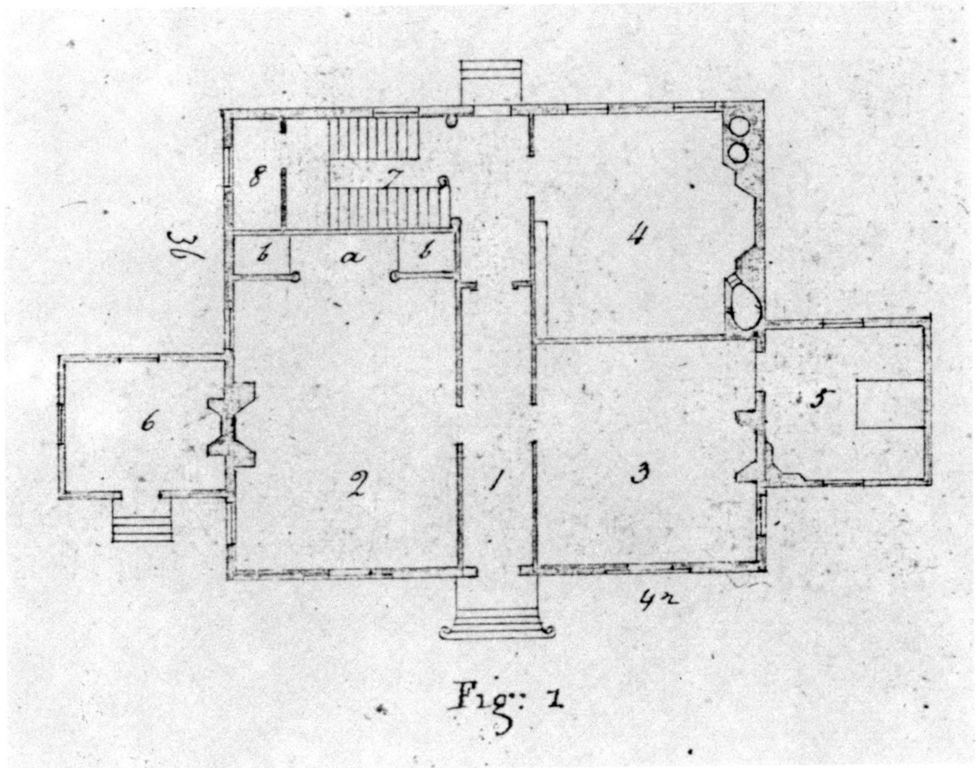

▶
Fig. 42. William Alexander Town House, Little Falls, N.Y., Hooker's plan of the principal, or first, floor, c. 1803–4. Ink and wash on paper. Herkimer County Historical Society, Herkimer, N.Y.

Fig. 1 Plan of the Principal floor [fig. 42]

N° 1 Hall 6 feet wide
2 Dining Room 24 by 19 [feet]
a alcove for Side Board
bb China & Glass Clossetts
3 Parlour 19 by 18 [feet]
4 Kitchen 18 by 17 [feet]
5 Bed room 14 by 14 [feet]
6 Office 14 by 12 [feet]
7 Stair Case
8 Pantry

By having the office & bed room in wings (which rooms are absolutely necessary on the first floor), the dimentions of the building is Considerably Contracted, & perhaps afford as many rooms in the 2^d Story as may be required—

Fig: 2 Plan of 2nd floor [fig. 43]

1 well hole for Stair Case
2 Landing of [Stair Case]
3 Ladies dressing Room 17 by 18 [feet]
4 Nursery 17 by 18 [feet]
5 Nurse's Bed room 12 [by] *7* [feet]
6 Spare Bed Room 18 by 16 [feet]
7 Bed room for Servant 18 [by] *9* [feet]
8 Steps to Scuttle in Roof

Fig: 3 Elevation of the Front drawn to a Scale of 15 feet to an Inch [fig. 44]

By

Ph: Hooker[4]

1. Susan R. Perkins to the author, 3 August 1988.
2. Porteus is mentioned in Pharoux's "Journal of Castorland," English translation, MSC NYSL.
3. Collection, Herkimer County Historical Society, Herkimer, N.Y.
4. Ibid.
5. Susan R. Perkins to the author, 3 August 1988.

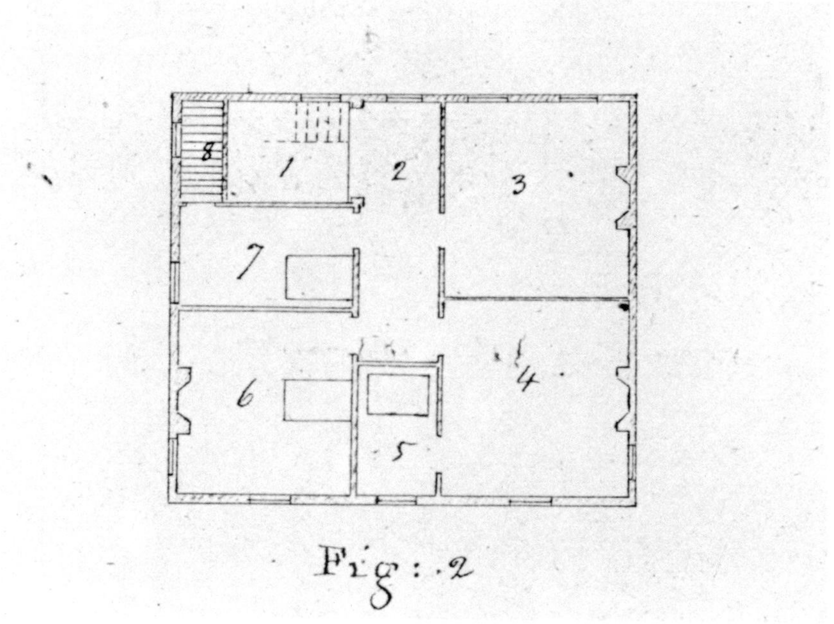

▶
Fig. 43. William Alexander Town House, Little Falls, N.Y., Hooker's plan of the second floor, c. 1803–4.

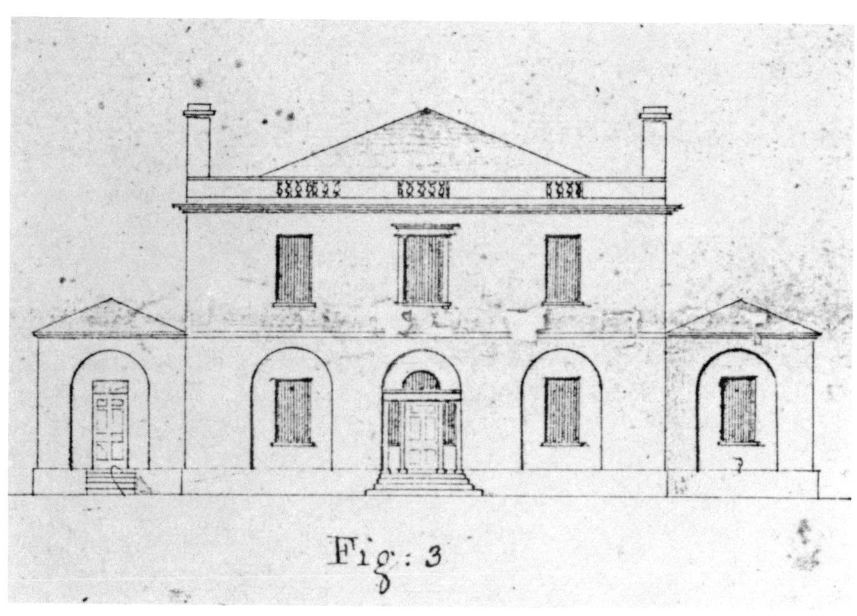

▶
Fig. 44. Hooker's front elevation, c. 1803–4. Ink and wash on paper. Herkimer County Historical Society, Herkimer, N.Y.

The plan of the Alexander house is a straightforward and well thought out adaptation of the center-hall type. On the first floor (fig. 42), columns frame the opening at the base of the staircase. In the dining room, an alcove for a sideboard is flanked by closets for china and glass. On the exterior (fig. 44), the front elevation features a neoclassical blind arch, which is repeated five times. As the frame for the Palladian doorway, it generally echoes the central motif of the contemporary New York State Bank in Albany (fig. 38).

The Alexander town house was razed in 1874 as a result of the expansion of the New York Central Railroad.[5]

14. FIRST PRESBYTERIAN CHURCH

Originally at the head of Church (now Hurd) Street;
moved to Albany Street, Cazenovia, N.Y.
Designed before 29 February 1804.
Built 1804–6; moved 1828; altered 1869; extant.
Builder: Nathan Smith.

An entry in John Lincklaen's personal account book documents Hooker's connection with this project: *The meeting house at Cazenovia: 1804. Feb. 29 To cash for a plan of the house pd Hooker of Albany $10.00.*[1] Lincklaen was one of three men elected by the congregation to contract and superintend the construction of a new church. He was probably familiar with Hooker through the architect's father, Samuel, and brother, John, who had previously worked for the Holland Land Company, for which Lincklaen acted as agent.[2]

The contract, which was signed on 30 April 1804, guaranteed the builder, Nathan Smith, a payment of $5,000 upon completion.[3] Hooker's handwritten agreement indicates the original appearance of the building (fig. 45).

> . . . [Nathan Smith] *shall and will in a workman like manner erect and build on lot No. 10 of the town plot of Cazenovia, being that part lately surveyed into lots by E. Johnson, a church or meeting house for the* [Presbyterian] *congregation of the size of fifty feet by sixty four feet, and agreeably in all respects to the plans thereof agreed with the name of the said party of the first part and numbered* **one** *(1)— except the alteration in the gallery hereafter mentioned— and place the same in such position as the said parties of the second part* [the congregation] *may elect.* **And also** *shall and will by the first day of December next make or cause to be made a good substantial foundation of stone laid in good lime morter on which to erect the said church. Which foundation shall be eighteen inches thick, eighteen inches above ground, where the ground is highest, and be so far under ground as to rest on the hard pan and be below the reach of the frost,* **and** . . . *cut, hew, draw and frame (of such good substantial hard wood as the said parties of the second part may or shall approve of) a large substantial frame for the said church and the steeple thereof. Each timber to be of such size as the parties of the second part may or shall approve of. The sills, posts and lower ties of studs to be of white elm, cherry or red beech— and the said frame to be composed of as great a quantity of timber as the said parties of the second part may judge necessary for making the same strong and durable.* **And also** *shall and will at his own expence raise the said frame by the time aforesaid,* **and also** *shall* . . . *board up the sides and ends of the said church and steeple in the time aforesaid with rough boards three quarters of an inch thick and nail the same with ten penny wrought nails and then cover the same with clapboards of good sound clear stuff six inches to the weather and lap*[pe]*d not less than an inch and a quarter, and nailed to the studs with wrought ten penny nails.* **And** . . . *board the roof of the said church with hemlock inch* [thick] *boards, as tight as straight edged boards will admit of. Nail the same boards with wrought ten penny nails and cover the same with a roof of good eighteen inch shingles clear of shakes and splits.* **And** . . . *by the first day of December eighteen hundred and five will* . . . *make all the windows of the said church and steple, frame the sashes and glaze the same; the frames of the said windows to be made of pine slit work clear of knots and to be spiked upon the studs with large wrought spikes. The lower tier of windows to contain forty panes of glass, 10 by 8* [inches], *five panes wide and eight high. The upper tier of windows to be the same as the lower, except that semi-circular heads are to be*

1. Lincklaen/Ledyard Papers, New York State Office of Parks, Recreation and Historic Preservation, Lorenzo State Historic Site, Cazenovia, N.Y.
2. For the Hookers' work, see p. 31. For Lincklaen, see, e.g., Russell A. Grills, *Cazenovia: The Story of an Upland Community* (Cazenovia, N.Y.: Cazenovia Preservation Foundation, Inc., 1977), pp. 9–22. Whether before or after Hooker provided a design for the church, he had business contact with another member of its congregation. Hooker provided a drawing of *Turners Patent Thrashing Machine* (fig. 11) for Jedediah T. Turner, whose patent was obtained 19 October 1803. The date of Hooker's drawing is not known.
3. Construction contract between John Lincklaen, Church Representative, and Nathan Smith, Builder, Archives, First Presbyterian Church, Cazenovia, N.Y.

added. The semicircular window in front of the tower to contain seventy panes of 10 by 8 [inch] *glass, to be seven panes wide and ten high exclusive of the circular head, and also will put . . . in the north end of said church as many windows and of the same dimensions, as are to be in the south end thereof; The whole of the said windows to be handsomly cased and finished. . . .* [He will] *make three large strong, handsome, panneled outside doors for the said church.* [He] *will hang the same with large, strong iron hinges. All the said doors to have good iron latches; two of these to have staples and bars to fasten them, and the other of these (at the election of the parties of the second part) to have a large lock, key & good bolt to fasten the same—* ***and*** *. . .* [he will] *cause a large, strong iron lightning rod to be made for the said church, and will fix the same to the top of the spire in the usual manner, and will extend the same down the side of the tower into the ground at least six feet. . . .* [He will] *lay the floor of the said church, first lining the same with half inch boards, and then laying thereon good seasoned inch* [thick] *pine boards, as clear of knots as possible. The said boards not to be more than eight inches wide, to be nailed with wrought spikes, double tens; and will raise the floor of the wall pews eight inches above the level of the main floor of the church,* ***and*** *. . . make in the lower story of the said church <u>sixty six</u> pews, the out sides of which* [are] *to be panneled with wainscoat work and the partitions to be panneled above the seats. The whole of the pews to be handsomly cap*[pe]*d. The wall pews to have seats on three sides, and the other pews a seat on one side and one end. And* [he] *will make to each pew in said church a neat panneled door, hang the same with good wrought iron hinges put on with screws and will put on each pew door a hook or bolt to fasten the same. Each pew to be of the dimensions & in all aspects agreeably to the plans aforesaid.* ***And*** *. . .* [he will] *make in the said church a handsome gallery agreeably to the plans aforesaid and will support the same on handsome turned pillars of the Tuscan order and will pannel & finish the front of the said gallery in the best manner, and will put and finish therein wall pews (instead of rear seats) and will make one seat in front of said gallery with an alley between that and the wall pews. The said wall pews to be panneled, & to have doors, hinges &* [to be] *similar to the wall pews below. . . .* [He will] *make one pair of large stairs in said church of the size & agreeably to the plans aforesaid, and will put on the outer edge of the said stairs a handsome cherry balustrade,* ***and*** *. . . erect in the north end of the said church a handsome pulpit, conformably to the plans aforesaid, with stairs to ascend it on each side with a handsome cherry balustade to each stairs—* ***and*** *. . . seal the walls of the said church with boards up to the lower edge of the windows, both in the first & second story; and the remainder of the said wall, both in the first & second story,* [he] *will lath in the best manner and plaister the same with at least two good coats of morter and afterwards white wash the same at least two times over. . . .* [He] *will make the sealing* [i.e., ceiling] *of the said church agreeably to the plans aforesaid and will lath, both plaister & whitewash the same as aforesaid. . . .* [He will] *paint the roof of the . . . church with three good coats of spanish brown & linseed oil and will paint the remainder of the outside of said church and steeple with three good coats of white lead & linseed oil. . . .* [He] *will paint the pulpit & stairs, all the windows & casings pillars that support the gallery & the front of the s*[ai]*d gallery in the best manner, and of such a colour as the said parties of the second part may elect.* [He] ***also*** *shall . . . make to each of the outside doors of the said church, good, neat substantial plank steps. . . .* [He] *also shall . . . number the pews of the said church by painting with white lead the numbers of each pew, on a black ground first painted on the door of each pew, in an oval form. . . .* [He] *shall . . . in all other respects not particularly mentioned above build, erect, and finish the said church so as that the same shall be made of good material, be well substantially & handsomly built, and be in every way well proportioned and agreeably to the rules of architecture. . . .* [4]

4. Ibid.
5. Conversation with Dr. Mark Campbell Ioset, August 1991.
6. Ibid. For a photograph of the remodeled structure, see Grills, p. 17.

▶
Fig. 45. First Presbyterian Church, Cazenovia, N.Y. (1804–6), before its remodeling in 1869. Courtesy W. R. Wheeler, Troy, N.Y.

The church was dedicated on 13 February 1806.[5] It was moved in 1828 to a location closer to the emerging town center, and was extensively remodeled in 1869.[6] The existing rear elevation preserves elements of the original fenestration, and by envisioning the remainder of the exterior without its heavy brackets and window surrounds, one may gain some idea of Hooker's design. None of the original interior details has survived. ✤

15. NEW YORK STATE CAPITOL

State Street at Public Square (now Capitol Park), Albany, N.Y.
Designed between 6 April 1804 and 4 April 1806.
Built 1806–9; altered c. 1818 and 1853; razed fall 1883; fragments survive.
Builder unknown.
Stonemason: Peter McNab.

On 6 April 1804 the New York State Legislature passed a law facilitating the erection of a capitol building in Albany. A commission of five was appointed and charged with procuring drawings "*upon such construction and plan as by them shall be judged proper.*"[1] The structure was to provide spaces for state as well as city government, and in effect it served as a capitol and city hall until the city offices were moved in 1831.

Construction was under way by 4 April 1806, according to evidence in a later bill submitted and receipted by Hooker.

"*The Commissioners for erecting the new State House to Philip Hooker—Dr.*

To sundry services performed as per agreement in drawing plan & superintending etc. up to the 4th day of April 1806— which was the time the foundation was laid out	*$250. .*
Expences to New Jersey & Stockbridge [Massachusetts] *as per bills*	*26. .59*
from the 4th April up to the 18th June is 65 working days; which @ $4. per day is	*260. .*
	$536. .59
Cr[edit] *By cash on acct at Sundry times*	*375. .*
Ballance due P. H	*161. .59*
If my wages did not commence until the cornerstone was laid, then must be deducted 16 days which @ $4 . . p[e]*r* [day] *is*	*64. .*
	$97. .59

"*As I have not a coppy of the agreement I am at a loss to determine at what Period, the Commissioners would consider my wages to commence—I wish them to determine this period.*

"*My time has been nearly all employed in the business of the Commissioners service [from] the 4th of April as above stated. Whatever the result of this conclusion shall be, I shall be satisfied, as I wish to do Justice, to my employers, & I have the fullest confidence that they will do Justice to me.*"[2]

Hooker continued to superintend the construction of the capitol, receiving $24.00 a week from 21 June to 29 November 1806, from 4 May 1807 to 2 January 1808, and from 23 April 1808 to 21 January 1809, and $12.00 weekly from 15 April to 2 October 1809.[3] The gaps in Hooker's activities correspond to the winter months during which construction would have been suspended. In 1808 Hooker was also paid $30.00 for "*drawing a perspective view of the State House,*" and $15.00 for a second copy of this

▶
Fig. 46. New York State Capitol, Albany (1806–9), view from the southeast, prior to 1880.
Albany Institute of History & Art, McKinney Library.

drawing.[4] It is possible that Hooker's view of the building is the same as that published by Evert Van Alen on his maps of the city in 1818 and 1832 (fig. 12).

The building was partly occupied in the summer of 1809 and completed by the end of that year (fig. 46).[5] A contemporary description, probably derived from information provided by Hooker, was published by Horatio Gates Spafford in his *Gazetteer of the State of New-York* in 1813.

> *Among the public buildings, the* Capitol *challenges distinguished attention. This building stands at the head of State-Street, adjoining the public square, and on an elevation of 130 feet above the level of the Hudson. It is a substantial stone building, faced with free-stone taken from the brown sand-stone quarries on the Hudson below the Highlands. The east front, facing State-Street, is 90 feet in length; the north, 115 feet; the walls are 50 feet high, consisting of 2 stories, and a basement story of 10 feet. The east front is adorned with a portico of the Ionic order, tetrastyle; the columns, 4 in number, are each 3 feet 8 inches in diameter, 33 feet in height, exclusive of the entablature which supports an angular pediment, in the tympanum of which is to be placed the Arms of the State. The columns, pilasters, and decorations of the door and windows, are of white or grey*

1. Root, p. 110, from *Laws of the State of New York,* Vol. III, 1804, p. 482.
2. Root, pp. 111–12, from a receipted bill in the State Comptroller's office.
3. Root, pp. 112–13. It may be inferred that he continued to earn $4.00 a day, working six days a week in the earlier period and three days a week in the latter.
4. Ibid., p. 112.
5. Ibid., pp. 113–14.

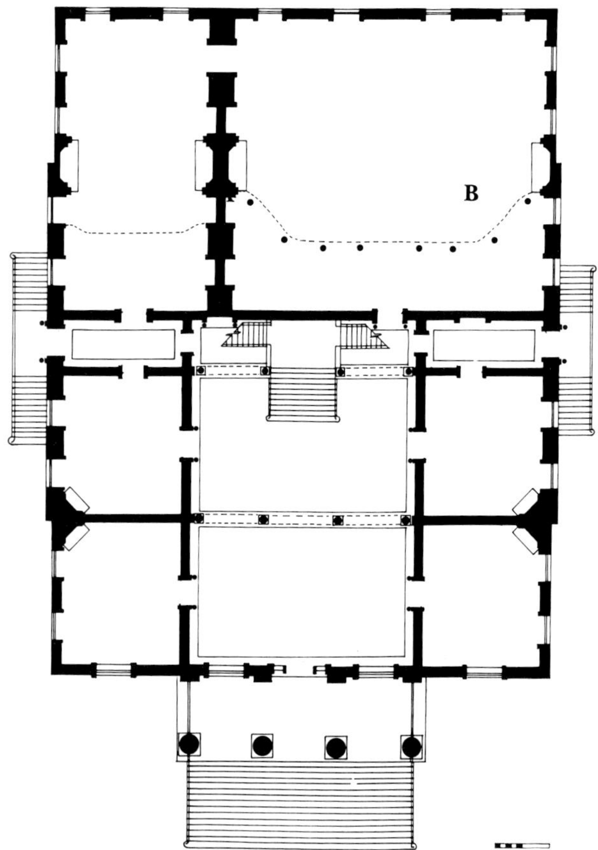

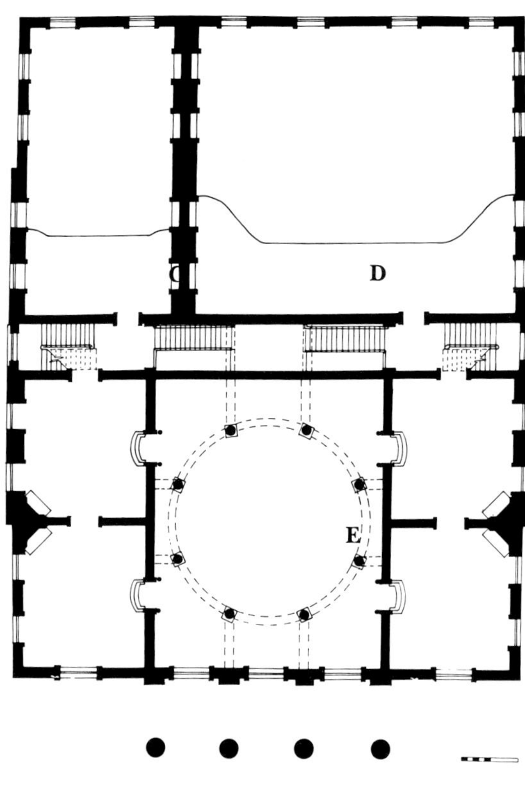

▲
Fig. 47. New York State Capitol, Albany (1806–9), first floor plan, including A. Senate Chamber and B. Assembly Chamber.

▶
Fig. 48. Second floor plan, after alterations of 1818, including C. Senate Chamber gallery, D. Assembly Chamber gallery, and E. Supreme Court Room. Reconstructed by W. R. Wheeler, 1991.

marble, from Berkshire county in Massachusetts. The north and south fronts have each a pediment of 65 feet base, and the doors are decorated with columns and angular pediments of free-stone. The ascent to the hall at the east or principal front, is by 15 stone steps, 48 feet in length.—This hall is 58 feet in length, 40 feet in width, and 16 in height, the ceiling of which is supported by a double row of reeded columns;—the doors are finished with pilasters and open pediments; the floor vaulted, and laid with squares of Italian marble, diagonally, chequered with white and grey. From this hall, the first door on the right hand opens to the Common Council Chamber of the Corporation of Albany; opposite this, on the left, is a room for the Council of Revision. On the right, at the W. end of the hall you enter the Assembly-Chamber, which is 56 feet long, 50 wide, and 28 feet in height. The Speaker's seat is in the centre of the longest side, and the seats and tables for the members are arranged in front of it, in a semi-circular form. It has a gallery opposite the Speaker's seat, supported by 8 antique fluted Ionic columns;—the frieze, cornice, and ceiling-piece, (18 feet diameter,) are richly ornamented in Stucco.—From this hall, on the left, you are conducted to the Senate-Chamber, 50 feet long, 28 wide, and 28 feet high, finished much in the same style as the Assembly-Chamber. In the furniture of these rooms, with that of the Council of Revision, there is a liberal display of public munificence, and the American Eagle assumes an Imperial splendor. There are 2 other rooms on this floor adjoining those first mentioned, which are occupied as lobbies to accommodate the members of the Legislature.*

▲
Fig. 49. New York State Capitol, Albany (1806–9), the Assembly Chamber, as it appeared c. 1870. Courtesy New York State Library, Albany.

From the west end, in the centre of the hall, you ascend a staircase that turns to the right and left leading to the Galleries of the Senate and Assembly-Chambers, and also to the Supreme Court room, which is immediately over the hall; its dimensions are 50 feet in length, 40 in breadth, and 22 in height. This room is handsomely ornamented in Stucco. An entresole or mezzanine story, on each side of the Court room, contains 4 rooms for Jurors and the uses of the Courts.

The attic story contains a Mayor's Court room, a room for the Society of Arts, and 2 other rooms yet unappropriated. This building is roofed with a double-hip, or pyramidal form, upon the centre of which is erected a circular cupola 20 feet diameter, covered with a domical roof, supported by 8 insulated columns of the Ionic order, and contains a small bell for the use of the courts.—The centre of the dome sustains a pedestal, on which is placed Themis, facing State-Street, a carved figure in wood of 11 feet in height, holding a sword in her right hand, and a balance in her left. The whole cost of the building, 115,000 dollars; and I regret to say that the roof is covered with pine instead of slate, with which the state abounds, and of an excellent quality .

**This violation of architectural proportions, is a deviation from the design of the Architect, Mr. Philip H. Hooker, of this city, whose abilities and correctness in the line of his profession are universally acknowledged.*[6]

Further information was provided in *Harper's Weekly* at the time the building was being razed.

In front the sombre walls of Nyack freestone are relieved by window trimmings and an Ionic portico . . . of grey marble from the Berkshire Hills. . . . the forty-foot columns are merely veneers of marble upon piers of brick, and . . . they have been reeded, instead of fluted, in order to make the deception more easy. The entablature of this portico of great pretensions is of wood, and the pediment . . . is of the same ignoble material. The "acroteria" which seem to promise so much have never held the statues for which they waited so long, while the apex of the pediment supports an urn, also wooden, and totally innocent of decoration. . . . within the round-topped doorway [under this portico] *was the imposing hall or vestibule which offered an open space of fifty-eight feet long and forty feet wide. . . .* [it featured a] *double row of Etruscan columns. . . . upon the broad landing of the stairway* [in this hall], *SEWARD took the gubernatorial oath.*[7]

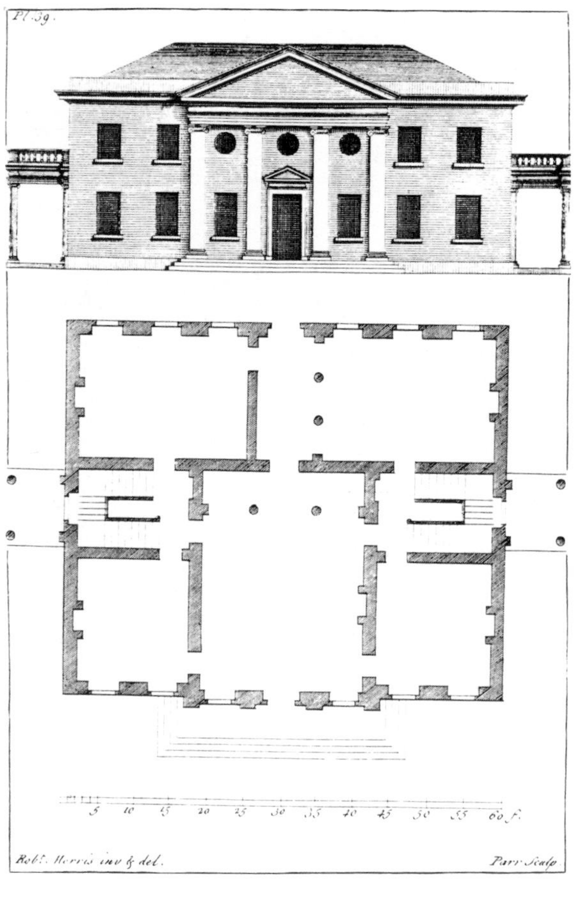

▶
Fig. 50. Robert Morris, *Select Architecture,* second edition (1757), Plate 39. Courtesy Cornell University, Ithaca, N.Y., Fine Arts Library.

The plans (figs. 47, 48), sections, and elevations of this first New York State Capitol have been reconstructed by the present author, using the above descriptions, the few surviving exterior photographs, a series of interior views dating from about 1870 (fig. 49), and the documentation published in legislative manuals from 1840 to 1870. In the T-shaped configuration of the three largest spaces, the plans resemble the arrangement illustrated in Plate 39 of Robert Morris's *Select Architecture* (fig. 50).[8] A variation of this scheme is found in the plan of the Samuel Hill house, attributed to Hooker (A7).

Much has been written about Hooker's treatment of the elevations, particularly the awkward juncture between the east front and the north and south elevations (figs. 12, 46). Hooker's intention appears to have been to address the public square to the east of the building with a facade whose scale was worthy of the space it fronted upon and which made an impression from a distance. The east elevation framed the view up State Street and was visible down to the banks of the Hudson River. The columned portico and large scaled windows were used to increase the appearance of the building's size. Unfortunately, the budget seems to have dictated a sense of economy in the treatment of the remaining elevations.

The capitol building underwent extensive improvements in 1818, likely to Hooker's designs (A20). An addition in the 1850s together with other modifications during that period changed much of the architect's interior design. The building was razed in 1883.[9] ✜

6. Horatio Gates Spafford, *A Gazetteer of the State of New-York* (Albany: H. C. Southwick, 1813), pp. 118–19.
7. Frederic G. Mather, "The Old Capitol in Albany," *Harper's Weekly,* XXVII, 1395 (15 September 1883), 587–88.
8. Robert Morris, *Select Architecture,* 2d ed. (1757; reprint ed., New York: Da Capo Press, 1973), pl. 39.
9. Root, p. 121.

16. TRINITY EPISCOPAL CHURCH

115th Street, Lansingburgh, N.Y.
Designed after 17 May 1804.
Built c. 1804–5; burned 23 December 1868.
Builder unknown.

▶
Fig. 51. Trinity Episcopal Church, Lansingburgh, N.Y. (c. 1804–5), the only known view, taken before 1869. Collection Frances D. Broderick.

On 3 May 1804 a committee was created by the vestry of the newly formed Trinity Episcopal Church *to procure a plan for* [a] *church and enquire of carpenters for estimates of sum.*[1] On the 14th of the same month William Bradley and John Rutherford were *appointed a committee to procure an estimate for the church at forty five by fifty-five feet.*[2] Although the wording of this minute suggests that a plan was in hand at this time, it is clear from another dated 17 May that this was not yet so.

> *Resolved that Joseph S. Mabbett, John Rutherford & David Smith be appointed a committee to purchase materials to enclose and complete the church, and employ workmen for building the same; and also to purchase materials and employ masons to complete the foundation.*
>
> *Resolved that William Bradley be authorised to procure a plan for the church of Mr. Hooker.*[3]

It appears that the church's wooden construction and its size, with seats for approximately 300,[4] were decided before Hooker was consulted.

Construction had begun by 12 June 1804[5] and was completed by 1806 at a cost of about $5,000. A steeple was added to the church in 1820, but the person responsible for its design is not known (fig. 51).[6] The building burned on 23 December 1868.[7] ✤

1. Protestant Episcopal Church Vestry Minutes, 3 May 1804, Archives, Trinity Episcopal Church, Lansingburgh, N.Y.
2. Ibid., 14 May 1804.
3. Ibid., 17 May 1804.
4. Nathaniel Bartlett Sylvester, *History of Rensselaer Co., New York* (Philadelphia: Everts & Peck, 1880), p. 315.
5. Protestant Episcopal Church Vestry Minutes, 12 June 1804.
6. Ibid., 2 October and 10 November 1820.
7. Miscellaneous note, Protestant Episcopal Church Vestry Minutes.

17. ST. PAUL'S EPISCOPAL CHURCH

Third and Congress streets, Troy, N.Y.
Designed before 2 July 1804.
Built 1804–5; altered 1819; steeple added 1839; razed.
Builder unknown.

The congregation of St. Paul's Church in Troy shared both its rector and its architect with Trinity Episcopal Church in Lansingburgh (cat. 16).[1] Information on the construction of St. Paul's Church is provided in an early twentieth-century newspaper article.

> *A church building was erected on the northwest corner of Congress and Third Streets, the architect being Philip Hooker of Albany. . . . The bricks were supplied by the Wilson Brothers, one of whom was Samuel Wilson, the original Uncle Sam. . . . The cornerstone was laid July 2, 1804 by Rev. Mr. Butler.*[2]

▶ Fig. 52. St. Paul's Episcopal Church, Troy, N.Y. (1804–5), view, 1819, evidently before enlargement. Courtesy W. R. Wheeler, Troy, N.Y.

The church was built of brick with five round-arched windows on each side, the first of which was *blind.* This device, frequently employed by Hooker, maintained a consistent rhythm on the facade while permitting flexibility in the placement of the stairs up to the gallery. An engaged entrance tower was capped by an octagonal belfry (fig. 52).

The building, lengthened by thirty-five feet in 1819, served St. Paul's parish until 1831, when it was sold to the recently formed St. John's Episcopal Church. Its members added a steeple in 1839 and used the building until 1853. It was then purchased for $9,000 by Gardner W. Rand, who agreed to the congregation's stipulation that the structure be razed.[3] ✤

1. Arthur James Weise, *Troy's One Hundred Years, 1789–1889* (Troy, N.Y.: William H. Young, 1891), pp. 61–62.
2. Acc. 72.96.4, Collection, Rensselaer County Historical Society, Troy, N.Y.
3. Weise, pp. 63, 125, 172.

18. SOUTH DUTCH REFORMED CHURCH

Beaver Street, Albany, N.Y.
Designed between 26 November and 4 December 1805.
Built 1805–11; burned September 1892.
Builders: Philip Hooker, Elisha Putnam, and John Boardman.
Stonemasons: Scrymser and McNab.

On 26 November 1805 the consistory of the Dutch Reformed Church resolved that *Messers Dox, Bleecker & Ten Eyck be a Committee to view the old burying ground, and report as to the eligibility of erecting a church thereon, together with* [presenting] *a draft of such church.*[1] Two days later they further resolved to reserve rights to the materials, chiefly stone, remaining from the razing of the congregation's 1715 church (fig. 2), the site of which was being sold to the city of Albany.[2]

Hooker had worked with this congregation on the construction of the first of its new *collegiate* churches, the North Dutch Reformed Church (cat. 1), and had drafted the original proposal for the South Dutch Reformed Church in 1799 (cat. 4). Therefore it comes as no surprise that he was again chosen architect by the building committee, as recorded in their 4 December 1805 report.

> [The building committee] *report*[s], *that in their opinion it appears the centre of the lot would be a proper spot to erect a church as the graves are chiefly placed there, besides the building would be much less exposed in case the adjoining houses and other buildings should take fire, than placing it near either the west east or south side. That before any part of the building is begun, a vault should be made and placed on the outside of the spot intended for the church, instead of the inside, as it is probable a vault constructed in the inside should interfere with the stone pillars to be erected for the support of the timbers of the first floor. That from the situation of the graves in different parts of the ground on the outside, the spot pointed out for the erection of the church, more of the remains of the dead are necessary to be removed. . . .*
>
> *That with respect to the north side along the range of Beaver Street the whole space ought in their opinion to be closed with a fence similar to the one in front of the North Church.*
>
> *That for further information respecting the situation of the ground etc they refer the board to the sketch and a plan of the said church drawn by Philip Hooker herewith handed.*[3]

This site plan indicates that the church had been designed by 4 December, the date of the report, because the portico and tower are clearly shown (fig. 53).

On 3 January 1806, the consistory appointed a committee *to get lime and brick started and a lime house and carpenters shop* [were ordered] *to be built.*[4] Five days later, Elisha Putnam was appointed superintendent; his duties were to include *procuring and purchasing the necessary materials and . . . projecting & altering the plans of said building.* He was also responsible for keeping *accounts of all expenditures.*[5] It is probable that Hooker was not available to superintend the building because of his work on the state capitol at this time (cat. 15).

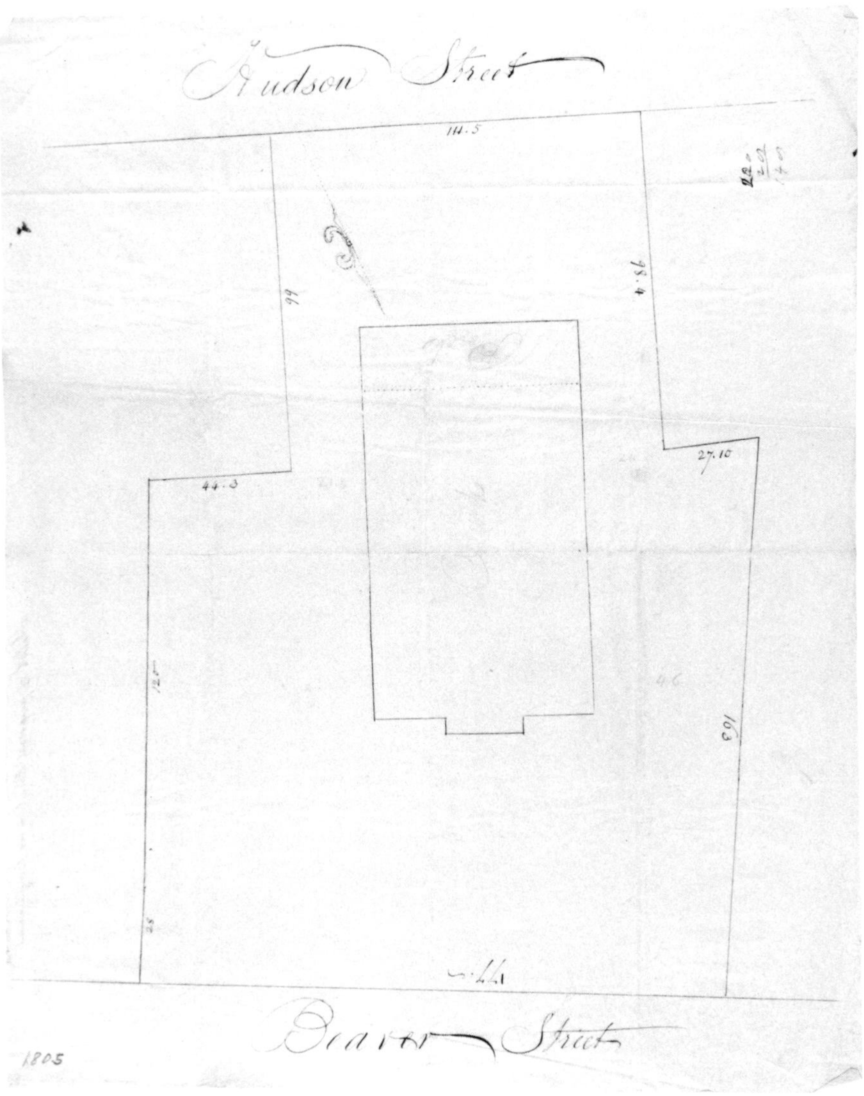

▶
Fig. 53. South Dutch Reformed Church, Albany, Hooker's site plan sketch for the proposed building, 1805.
Ink on paper. Archives, First Church in Albany.

On 29 January 1806 the consistory received a letter from Scrymser and McNab introducing themselves and asking to be selected as stonemasons for the project. James and Lucas Hooghkirk had been previously chosen, but there is no evidence to suggest why they were replaced.[6]

The consistory minutes noted on 27 February that it was *expedient to commence the operation of digging for the foundations of the . . . church in the next week.*[7] During March 1806 the old church at State and Market (now Broadway) was taken down, its stone to be used in building the new church.[8]

On 1 April 1806 Putnam submitted a report as part of his duties as superintendent requesting between $2,500 and $3,000 to pay for the construction during the next two months.[9] Money was appropriated and work continued. Putnam's 5 April communication to the consistory, which begins with a plan for the interment of the remains of the dead removed from the old church, continues with a proposal for what might have been the earliest central heating system installed in North America.

Since it has become necessary for the consistory to provide a vault or some suitable plan for the interment of the remains taken out of the old church and also for those which may become necessary to take up in order to obtain a foundation for the new intended church, it is suggested that the space within the tower walls will be amply sufficient for that purpose and that no additional expence will be incurred to make a compleat vault but the turning an arch; the walls of the tower answering for the abutments.

And as the south front of the church will, from the natural decent of the surface, be elevated about 6 feet, and the ground within the walls should be taken to the depth of about 2 feet below the surface in front and continued on a level to the rear will give the floor an ellivation of about 7 feet from the ground within, and it is more than probable that this ellivation will be attended with many benificial effects; it will afford a fine circulation of air, tend to preserve the timbers, keep the floors dry and prevent any noxious evaporation. All this may be done with little or no additional expense in or about the church.

Should this measure be adapted, the way will be prepared to make a very important & it is believed a successful experiment and that is to warm the church in winter from the heat of two horizontal pipes under the floors from stoves at the one end of the church & leading to funnels carried up in the walls at the other end. These pipes, by means of dampers, will contain collums of hot air extended in parrallel directions which may be admitted through the floors by small venturlaters in every seet if necessary and thereby distribute an equal degree of heat throughout the church.

Should this project of warming the church eventually fail, the stoves may be brought up and placed as usual; as they are at present in the N[orth] *Church. The funnels will be carried up in the same manner within* [i.e., whether] *the stoves are below or above the floor.*

If this plan an [i.e., as] *a fair experiment should be successful, that unequal degree of heat in some parts of the church experienced at present will be converted into a uniform and equal temperature throughout. The noise & disturbense ocationed in tending the fires avoided & probably much less wood will be required and the use of foot stoves entirely superceeded because the floors will be both dry & warm from the continued ascent of the rarrafied air.*[10]

In accordance with this proposal the consistory directed Putnam to provide a vault, but the minutes are silent regarding the heating system.[11] Putnam subsequently suggested further alterations.

The superintendent for building the new church presented to the board an elevation of the new church showing the improvement of long and a single row of windows for the said building. Resolved that the alterations and plan be accepted.[12]

Members of the church also recommended changes in the design: *It was suggested by some Brethren . . . that the new church should be rusticated with free stone, and it being represented by the superintendent that the added expense would be inconsiderable, as well as more durable and ornamental, resolved that the said measure be adopted.*[13] This decision to articulate the corners, doorways, and most of the windows with brownstone quoins and voussoirs necessitated the purchase of additional materials, and was eventually the source of many problems.

The cornerstone was laid on 30 April 1806, an event reported in the next day's *Albany Gazette.*

1. Dutch Reformed Church (hereafter DRC) Consistory Minutes, 26 November 1805, A FCA.
2. Ibid., 28 November 1805.
3. Ibid., 4 December 1805.
4. Ibid., 3 January 1806.
5. Ibid., 8 January 1806.
6. Ibid., 29 January 1806.
7. Ibid., 27 February 1806.
8. Ibid., February and March 1806, 28 November 1805. The cemetery under and around the church was left chiefly undisturbed and remains under the intersection of State and Broadway.
9. Ibid., 1 April 1806.
10. Doc. 101-16 (in Putnam's hand), DRC Collection, A FCA.
11. DRC Consistory Minutes, 5 April 1806.
12. Ibid., 21 April 1806.
13. Ibid.

▶
Fig. 54. South Dutch Reformed Church, Albany (1805–11, portico 1816), Hudson Street facade, before 1881.
New York State Library, Albany.

"Yesterday the Corner stone of the Second Dutch Church in this city was laid by the Rev. Mr. Bradford. This church, in its plan and style, is much the same as that of St. Paul's church in New York, and when finished will probably be the most elegant of any in this part of the state. It is situated upon the old cemetery, between Beaver and Hudson streets. . . . Its dimensions are 102 feet in length including the steeple and portico, by 66 in breadth. . . . This church and the new State House now erecting, together with the removal of the old Gothic structure, which lately incommoded our streets, will in some degree show the extent and rapidity of our improvements. We trust the time is at hand, when we shall rival our sister cities in the elegance and neatness of our public buildings, and show that the advantage of our situation is not lost upon us, but improved to a proper degree in point of interest and ornament."[14]

▶
Fig. 55. South Dutch Reformed Church, Albany (1805–11, first section of steeple 1818–20), Beaver Street facade, before 1881. New York State Library, Albany.

The stonecutters appear to have had trouble acquiring enough cut stone for the work to progress smoothly. The fact that brownstone was being used for the quoins as well as the trim required that it be constantly available as the walls were carried up. On 1 July 1806 the escalation of the problem prompted the consistory to propose the suspension of work due to the delay caused *by the want of freestone for Rustics &c.*[15]

On 13 August 1806 the consistory resolved that *it appears expedient & necessary that the work carried on at the new church should be suspended untill next spring* [and that] *the superintendent* [and] *all carpenters, joiners, masons & labourers* [should] *be discharged.*[16]

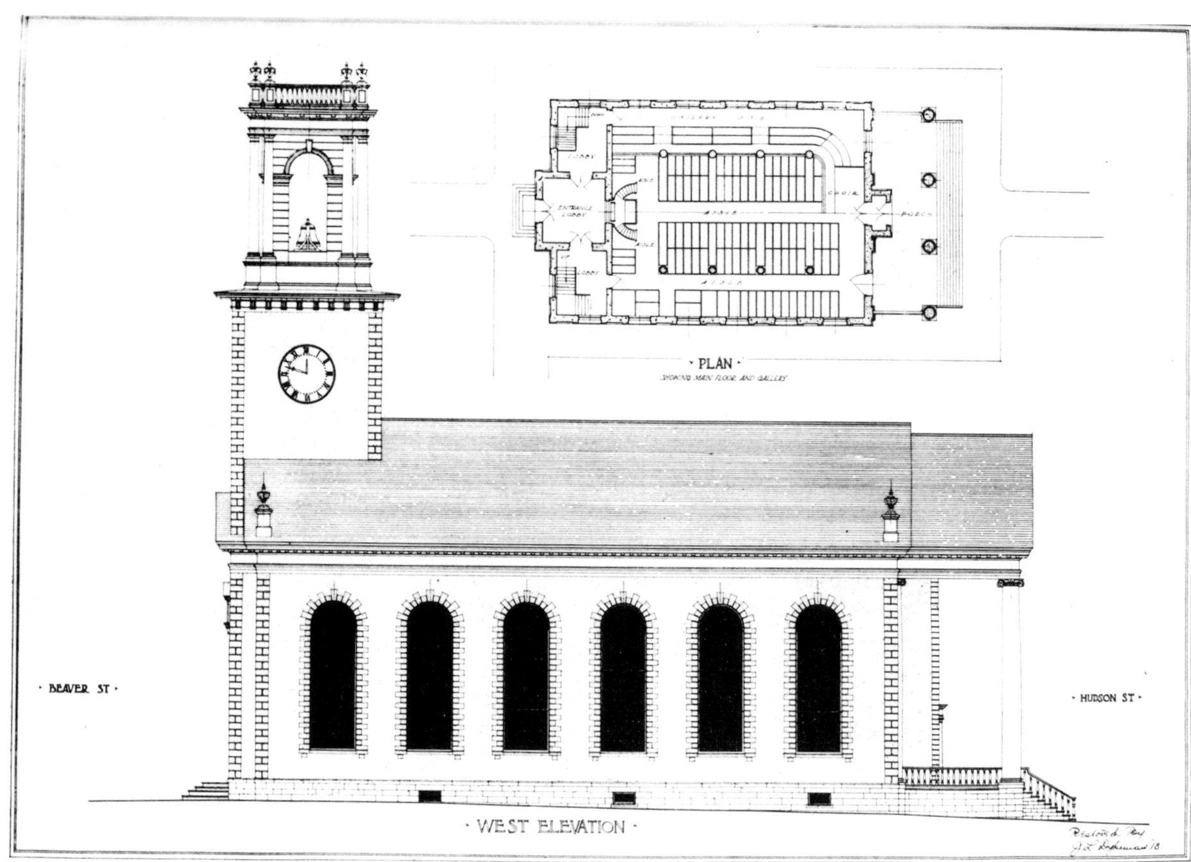

▲
Fig. 56. South Dutch Reformed Church, Albany (1805–11, portico 1816, first section of steeple 1818–20), plan and west elevation, restored by J. L. Dykeman, 1918. Courtesy New York State Library, Albany.

Putnam submitted a report to the consistory on 31 December 1806.

For all free stone together w[ith] *brick, lime, rough stone, water etc.*

amounts to	*7,860.50*
All the carpenters & joiners work	*1,421.39 1/2*
All the masons & labourers work including sand, scaffolding, poles, cordage, etc.	*4,161.07*
All the timber, boards & plank	*2,765.75 1/2*
Iron & smith work	*138.18*
Nails, sheet lead etc	*177.22*
Painting, putty and glazing etc.	*190.00*
The above statement comprises all the free stone	*16,714.85*

ash[l]*ar, water table, window sills, arches, consoles, plinths and bases together with about 1/4 part of pillasters and about 1/2 of all the rustick blocks, both for corners, doors & windows.*

The stonecutters have since the 18th of October been preparing the free stone, which is the only account I believe that is not settled to that date. There is on hand brick, lime, sand and rough stone nearly sufficient to bring the church to the side wall height; also all the timber for the roof & flooring sawed and prepared for framing. There is also a considerable quantity of boards and plank on hand and nearly all the outside cornishing prepared fit to put up. I have, in the course of the season, sold materials of the old church & others nearly to the amount of 100—which I shall credit on my account for superintendance, which should leave at present a small balance in my favour, but as I have not as yet collected all the money have deferred it on that account.

All which is respectfully submitted by your obedient servant

Elisha Putnam Super[intenden]*t*[17]

The stoneworkers were given permission to continue work in order to provide the large amounts of material needed for the coming season. On 10 January 1807 Scrymser and McNab requested *the advance of $300.00 on account of the freestone prepared for the new church and . . .* [stated] *that they have prepared stone to double the amount of the advance now required thereupon.* On the same day a committee was appointed *to report a system . . . to prosecute the building of the new church the ensuing season.*[18]

This committee presented its proposal on 31 January 1807. It included paying the superintendent a salary, to save *embarrassment, cost overruns and delays.*[19] On 12 May the consistory suspended building operations for the next year, due to lack of funds.[20] Efforts were made to raise money,[21] but it seems that work did not resume until the spring of 1809. At that time Hooker replaced Putnam as superintendent, and John Boardman took over the role of master carpenter from Lucas F. Hooghkirk.[22]

The church was opened for worship on 17 February 1811 (fig. 55),[23] and on 10 March, Boardman presented a proposal for finishing the steeple, presumably to the original design.

> *A proposal for building by contract a steeple on the tower of the new Dutch Church agreeable to the design adopted.*
>
> *Said steeple to be 130 ft in addition to the said tower; the whole height to be 200 ft.*
>
> *The principal posts of the frame (8 in number) to extend down the tower about 20 ft & framed into timbers plain*[e]*d for that purpose.*
>
> *The whole frame to be of good substantial timber framed & braced in the best possible manner & secured with strong iron bands & bolts.*
>
> *The first section to be finishing according to the Dorrick order on the rectangular plan with eight pillasters, pedestals & entablatures & four bold pedements & four circular headed windows with green blinds.*
>
> *The 2d section to be built after the Ionic order on the rectangular plan with eight collumns, pedestals & entablatures & four circular headed windows with green blinds. The spaces between the collumns to be formed into panels with a bold recess.*
>
> *The 3d section to be finished after the corinthian order (which is the master piece of architecture) also on the octangular* plan with eight* collumns, pedestals, & entabletures & four circular headed windows with green blinds. The spaces between the collumns to be formed into panels, as the other sections described.*
>
> *The attic section to be finished with a bold bass* [i.e., base] *& cornice with eight panels & in each panel an oval window with sashes & glass. A floor to be laid for each section & one at the footing of* [the] *frame making five in number. The floor on which the bell will be placed to be elevated in the center & so constructed as to carry off the water.*
>
> *Convenient stairs to be built, commencing at the stairs now built & ascending to the attic section, which is something over one hundred feet.*
>
> *The spire to commence at the top of the attic section with a verry bold bass* [i.e., base] *which spire is to be 48 ft to the fane** [i.e., weather vane]. *The first half of the spire to be formed into eight pannels of a bold recess & girded with a bold astragal molding.*
>
> *The upper part of the spire to be covered with the best of double white tin & finished with a large astragal & elevated above this, a gilt ball of at least 2 ft diameter. The fane* [i.e., weather vane] *to represent a blazing star elevated above the ball & fane; to be iron suitably strong & proportionable extended above the fane, the tip of which to be swelled & gilt.*

14. Root, p. 104, from *Albany Gazette,* 1 May 1806.
15. DRC Consistory Minutes, 1 July 1806.
16. Ibid., 13 August 1806.
17. Ibid., 31 December 1806.
18. Ibid., 10 January 1807.
19. Ibid., 31 January 1807.
20. Ibid., 12 May 1807.
21. Ibid., 24 March 1808.
22. George W. Featherstonhaugh Papers, 1771–1856, MK AIHA; Doc. 109-7, A FCA. Hooker mentions his work on this church in a letter to Featherstonhaugh (cat. 19).
23. Root, p. 102.

The whole of the proportions to be secured from leakage by white tin & painted. The whole of the wood work in the outside to be painted with three coats of good paint. The whole to be done in a masterly, elegant & substantial manner on or before the first day of October next, for the sum of five thousand eleven hundred & fifty dollars.

John Boardman

Albany, March 10th 1811[24]

*Root's published text differs.

On the following day Boardman submitted an account of unpaid bills, including that of cabinetmaker John Meads for *mahogany & venitian* window.[25] Again for financial reasons Boardman's proposal for the steeple was not acted upon.

Work resumed in August 1814 when a contract was signed with Samuel Dodd to provide the cut stone necessary to complete the portico. However, the terms of this agreement had not been met by 4 April 1816, when the consistory reviewed the scope of the contract.

◀ Fig. 57. South Dutch Reformed Church, Albany (1805–11), stereo view of the interior from the gallery, before 1881.

◀ Fig. 58. Stereo view of the interior, looking back to the organ, before 1881. Archives, First Church in Albany.

[In] *the contract* [of] *1 August 1814 . . . Samuel Dodd agreed to deliver, . . . on dock at Belleville, N. J. the quantities of freestone of the dimensions following to wit.*

4 Cap[ital]*s 4 ft 6" sq each 2 ft thick at 50—*	*200.*
2 Round bases for columns 4'6" in dia[meter] *each + 15" thick @ 32.50*	*65.*
4 Plinths 4'6" square each & 8" thick @ 16—	*64.*
56 Round blocks for shafts of column 4 of which to be 3'3" in d[iameter] *and the residue to be 3' in d*[iameter] *2' thick each @ 25—*	*1400.*
936' running measure for steps 12 pcs of which to be 4' in length each and the residue to be not less than 6' in l[ength] *each, the whole to be 19" wide and 7" thick @ 62 1/2 ¢ for each running ft*	*585.*
1 Platform 10' long 5' wide 7" thick	*55.*
	2369.
Brought forward	
1200 ft flagging 2' wide & not less than 2' in l[ength] *18 1/2 ¢ for each sq. ft*	*225.*
	2594.[26]

On 6 April 1816, apparently in light of Dodd's failure to deliver, the consistory contracted with John Boardman to complete the portico and north stoop using wood (fig. 54).

▲
Fig. 59. South Dutch Reformed Church, Albany (1805–11), stereo view of the pulpit, before 1881. Archives, First Church in Albany.

The church still lacked the planned steeple, but a subsequent building campaign provided the first stage of a tower (cat. 40). A contemporary account includes additional information:

> [N]*early 5 years were consumed in its erection and it was dedicated to the worship of God on 17 February 1811. Its cost exclusive of the land, was nearly 100,000 and yet it was left incomplete. The southern portico and the steeple, at the north end, of 5 sections in heighth, all to be built of stone, according to the original design, were not erected. . . . Some years . . .* [later] *. . . a sort of wooden portico was put up. . . .* [27]

Although the South Dutch Church has been said to have been inspired by St. Paul's Chapel in New York, aside from the general form and disposition of its tower and portico (fig. 56), the resemblance is slight. The arrangement of the elliptical arches and their juncture with the flat ceiling is most unusual but not unique in Hooker's work (figs. 57, 58). A similar treatment was utilized in the design of the Lutheran Ebenezer Church (cat. 37). The *architectural treatment of the wall* behind the pulpit (fig. 59) is apparently original,[28] and recalls earlier works by Hooker. The pulpit, however, is evidently a replacement dating before 1840. Root's source, Dr. Bartlett, described the original as having been cylindrically shaped, ornately carved, and surmounted with a sounding board featuring a dove on top.[29] It may have been similar in appearance to the one designed for the North Dutch Reformed Church (fig. 26).

The church was last used for its original purpose in 1881, and was then converted to a market and destroyed by fire in 1892.[30] The tooled brownstone foundations were briefly exposed during the construction of the parking garage that now occupies the site. ✣

24. Doc. 110-115, A FCA.
25. Doc. 110-112, A FCA.
26. DRC Consistory Minutes, 4 April 1816.
27. Phelps Family Papers, 1781–1919, DZ 10760, MSC NYSL.
28. Root, p. 106.
29. Ibid., pp. 105–6.
30. Ibid., p. 106.

19. COUNTRY SEAT FOR GEORGE W. FEATHERSTONHAUGH

Mariaville, Schenectady County, N.Y.
Designed between 20 September and 27 October 1808.
Built c. 1809; burned 1828.
Builder unknown.

George William Featherstonhaugh came to the United States from England in 1806. By the time of his return in 1839 he would distinguish himself as a linguist, geologist, railroad developer, diplomat, and author whose works included a translation of Cicero's *Republic* and a play, *The Death of Ugolino, A Tragedy*. Featherstonhaugh also founded the monthly *American Journal of Geology and Natural Science*. From 1844 until his death he served as British Consul at Le Havre, France.[1]

Featherstonhaugh's visit to America to study the people became a long term residency when he met Sarah Duane, to whom he was married on 6 November 1808. Even before their wedding, Featherstonhaugh had been in contact with Philip Hooker concerning the building of a house on land willed to Sarah by her father, James Duane.[2]

Significant information pertaining to this project as well as to Hooker's other activities during this period is preserved in three letters from the architect to Featherstonhaugh. On 17 October 1808 Hooker wrote:

> *Dear Sir/*
>
> *I find that it will be extremely inconvenient for me to meet you at Schenectady tomorrow according to appointment, as we have this morning commenced with the Collonade in front of the State House* [New York State Capitol, cat. 15] *which requires my particular attention, and I also find, that, from my pecuniary circumstances, I shall not be able to undertake to erect your building, agreeable to your proposition & independent of that circumstance, I clearly percieve that it would interfere too much with my business in Albany. As soon as I can be dispensed with at the State house, my attention is required in superintending a church of considerable magnitude, for the Dutch congregation in this city* [South Dutch Reformed Church, cat. 18] *I shall, however, be happy to assist you in arranging your plans, making estimates or procuring workmen to undertake your work, or any other services which may be in my power. I sincerely wish it was in my power to undertake my self, but it is not, without injury to my self.*[3]

The second letter is dated 6 February 1809.

> *Dear Sir/*
>
> *Your favor of the 30th Jan*[uar]*y, I duly received; Mr. C. Allen, was in Albany, about ten days since, who informed me that he had got 100 loads of stone upon the grounds* [and] *that he had procured a considerable part of the plank & boards, timber all hewn, & logs but for the scantling, which he should have conveyed to the mills on his return, had made a contract for the lime, & was about purchasing 10,000 bricks for the partition walls in the cellar. He appears to be anxious to have, aggreeable to your expectations, every*

thing in readiness; he rec[eive]*d from Mr Ka*[illegible] *$150 & some two months since, he rec*[eive]*d $100, in all $250 to enable him to get the materials upon the ground by sledding. He informed me that Mr. Bradshaw was recovering; from what he cou*[ldn't] *learn. He, Bradshaw, was perfectly agreed to make an exchange of lands with you, but that nothing further had been done in the business.*
With respect to your queries—
a stone building, wou[ld] *cost double the sum that your building will cost, upon the plan contemplated. It undoubtedly wou*[l]*d require more time in the erection, unless an extra number of workmen were employed.*
The walls of a stone house are always cold, consequently damp. When the air is in a rarified state, coming in contact with the surface of a cold wall, it is condensed, [*& runs down* (stricken by Hooker)] *into water. The only expedient to obviate this inconvenience is to fur the walls with battins of board or plank, & lath and plaister on those battins, which will leave a vacuity between the wall & plaistering. The first information I receive relative to your business, which will be interesting to you, I shall advise you* [of] *without delay.*[4]

The third letter is dated 8 November 1809.

Dr Sir/
You had the goodness to offer me payment (for the business which I had done for you) when last at Featherstone. I at that time declined receiving it, as I did not stand in need. But having been disappointed in some money which I ought to have received ere now, your profer will be very acceptable, at this time, I have charged you as follows:
1808

Sept[embe]*r 20th*	*To a journey to Princetown*	*$5.*	
	Expenses of horse & chair toll &c	*3.*	*$8."*
Oct[obe]*r 27*	*To a design for a villa ———*		*25."*
1809 Sept[embe]*r*	*To business at sundry times with Mr. Allen*		*12.'*
Oct[obe]*r*	*To a journey to Featherstone & expenses*		*15."*
			$60.~

If you consider the above charges too high, you will give me what you think is right. Any further services which is in my power to render you will be done with cheerfulness.
Your sash weights are ready at Mr. Townsend's. I promised Mr. Allen to endeavor to procure a Mr. Fuller to carry up your stair case, but he has finally declined; having a large family, he cannot do it without considerable inconvenience.[5]

Construction of the house began in the spring of 1809. It was a large building, sixty feet in depth and stretching one hundred and forty feet along Featherstonhaugh Lake.[6] Since the structure was destroyed by fire in 1828, only nineteen years after its completion, our knowledge of it is fragmentary. We do know that the building was constructed *in the style of architecture to be found on gentlemen's estates in England,* and that the interior had a hall with a *great fireplace.*[7] A painting by Thomas Cole, executed for Featherstonhaugh, depicts the house in its park-like setting.[8] ✜

1. George W. Featherstonhaugh Papers, 1771–1856, MK AIHA.
2. George S. Roberts, *Old Schenectady* (Schenectady: Robson & Adee, [1904]), pp. 188–89.
3. George W. Featherstonhaugh Papers, 1771–1856.
4. Ibid.
5. Ibid.
6. Roberts, pp. 188–89.
7. Ibid., pp. 189–92.
8. [George R.] Howell and [John H.] Munsell, eds., *History of the County of Schenectady, N.Y., from 1662 to 1886* (New York: W. W. Munsell & Co., 1886), p. 163.

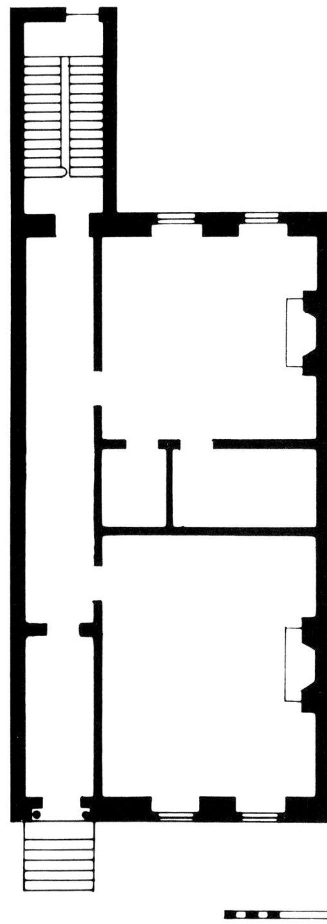

▲
Fig. 67. Consistory House, with dwelling, for North Dutch Reformed Church, Albany (1814–15), original plan of first floor, reconstructed by W. R. Wheeler, 1991.

set up, & compleately finish, an edifice of the form & dimentions as follows.

Twenty seven feet in front, twenty seven feet eleven inches in the rear, & fifty feet in depth from front to rear, & two stories in height. The first fifteen in the clear including an arched ceiling. The second twelve feet in the clear. To have a cellar under the whole eight feet high in the clear. The foundations whereof are to be substantially built with stone & mortar. The partitions in the cellar are to be of hard brick, eight inches in thickness, erected on stone foundation, 18 by 8 inches, laid without mortar. The foundation wall in front, above the surface of the street, is to be faced with free stone, crowned with an eight inch water table (to be on a line with the water table of Mr. John Bleecker's house aforesaid) rubbed smooth.

The walls of the superstructure are to be of good merchantable bricks laid in good lime & sand mortar & well grouted. None but the best hard bricks are to be exposed to the weather. The front & rear walls are to be two, and the flank walls, one brick or 8 inches in thickness. The front & chimney tops are to be neatly painted and penciled. The beams of the first floor are to be 12 by 4 inches, & those of the second floor 12 by 4 inches; the whole two feet from centre to centre. The beams of the garret floor, 11 by 4 inches, three feet from centre to centre. The roof is to be supported, with a substantial frame of trussed work. The rafters are are [sic] *to be 8 by 4 inches at bottom 6 by 4 inches at top & placed two feet seven inches from centre to centre, the whole to be of good, sound timber, free from blue sap & rotten knots. The roof is to be covered with sound plank and the best kind of American slates, laid not exceeding one third of their length to the weather. The back of the chimney tops are to be secured against leakage, with sheet lead; the sides of the chimnies, ridge of the roof & scuttle, with patent ribbing. The scuttle is to be well made, hung with hinges of wrought iron, lined on the outside with tin, & secured with a hook; to have suitable steps to the same. There is to be a neat cornice gutter & handsome balustrade in front, a plain gutter & strong railing in the rear, well secured with iron work. Two tin conductors of 2 1/2 inches in diameter in front & one of 3 inches diameter in the rear. There are to be five windows in front, 12 panes each of the best crown glass, of 20 by 13 inches. Those in the first story are to be finished in the best manner with inside shutters, cut in the middle, properly hung, and to be furnished with proper latch fastenings, pendent rings &c— & the sashes with the best kind of sash fastenings. The three windows in the second story in front are to be finished with framed jambs, backs, elbows, soffits & double faced architraves; and outside standing blinds, hung with wrought iron hinges, to have suitable fastenings, weather hooks &c, and painted a handsome green colour, to have three coats. Four windows in the rear to have 12 panes each of 18 by 12 inch glass; to have outside shutters with hinges, fastenings, & weather hooks. Two cellar kitchen windows of 12 panes* [margin note: *Made 16 panes*] *of 11 by 9 inch glass, to have shutters as above. All the sashes are to be hung with weights to have proper pullies, cords &c. Also, two windows in front, in the cellar story of proportionable size, to be properly finished. There is to be a well finished flight of stone steps & iron railing to the front door similar to Mr. Bleecker's aforesaid. The front door is to be 1 3/4 inches* [margin note: *2 inches*] *in thickness, framed in nine panels* [and] *to have frame, jambs & soffits to be neatly cased inside, hung with three 5 inch butts* [margin note: *2 inch lock*] *and furnished with a seven inch mortice lock, and painted* [in imitation of] *mahogany, sattin wood, or such other colour as shall be directed by the said parties of the first part. The back doors in the first & second stories are to be framed in six panels, 1 1/4 inches in thickness, neatly cased & hung with 4 1/2 inch butts & to have seven inch knob locks. Two inside doors in the second story* [are to be] *finished in the same manner. The doors in the cellar story are to be framed in four panels, 1 1/4 inches thick* [margin note: *Doors 1 1/2 inches thick*], *flush on both sides, neatly cased & hung with 3 1/2 inch butts & to have the strongest kind of thumb latches.*

The floors of the first & second stories are to be neatly planed, tongued & grooved, gauged thicknessed, joints broken & well nailed. The first story with yellow pine not exceeding nine inches in width, & second story with white pine not more than six inches in breadth. The garret floor is to be [of] *tongued & grooved planks of common width, but not planed. The cellar floor is to be laid with sound plank, on good sleepers of green timber. The kitchen and passage* [floor] *to be yellow pine; the bed room, pantry & root cellar* [of] *white pine. The floors of the kitchen & two bed room*[s], *pantry & passage are to be planed, tongued & grooved, & the floor of the root cellar square edged and not planed. The cellar kitchen is to have a proper fire place with a crane & a flue cover* [margin note: *crane not in the original & not to be included*]. *A large hearth to the kitchen fire place. The pantry is to be neatly shelved. The kitchen, bed room, pantry & passage are to have a neat plane wash board & finished with two good coats of mortar suitable for white washing. The walls of the root cellar are to be neatly pointed.*

The first & second stories are to have a handsome moulded base[board] *all round the rooms & cornices with stocco & finished with three coats of good mortar; the walls with a hard finish & the ceilings with putty and the casings of the doors & windows are to be in a neat modern style. The ceiling of the first story is to be arched.*

The second story is to be divided into two rooms & a passage. In which passage, a closed stairs is to be carried up to the garret [margin note: *Furnished with 2 doors*], *to have a framed door at the bottom neatly cased & hung with 3 1/2 inch butts— and to have a knob latch. Four stone tubes is to be placed in the south wall & flues carried up for stove pipes to be topped a sufficient height above the roof and capped with free stone. The kneelers are also to be capped with free stone.*

The stair case is to be carried up in the rear of said building, encompassed by an eight inch wall of hard brick, and covered with a shed roof well slated. [It is] *to have a plain cornice gutter & two inch tin conductor. The stair case is to be lighted with one window* [margin note: *Now two wind*[ow]*s*] *containing 12 panes of 14 by 10 inch glass neatly finished & sashes hung. The stairs are to be neatly made* [and are] *to have mahogany handrail & banisters & iron banisters when necessary. A plain framed stairs* [is] *to descend to the cellar underneath the principal stairs, to be also lighted with one window of 12 panes of 11 by 9 inch glass.* [A] *door from the bottom of the cellar stairs to lead to the yard* [is to be] *similar to those before described in the cellar* [and] *to have an eight inch knob lock. The stair case is to be plaistered with three coats; the cellar part with two for white washing. All the joiners work is to be painted with two coats of good paint of suitable colours. The first story in front is to have 4 projecting piers crowned with moulded imposts of freestone conected by three semi circular architraves, similar to the second story of Richard Lush's house in Market Street.* [It is to have] *moulded window sills in the second story, to continue through the whole length of the front. All the arches in the first & second stories, to the door & windows, are also to have mouldings, the whole of freestone rubbed smooth. A brick drain is to be laid from the rear of said building, through the yard & gangway, to the main drain in Steuben Street, and an apperture left in the front cellar wall for the reception of the waterworks. The whole to be compleated in every respect, according to the true intent & meaning of the parties, notwithstanding any ambiguities, or omissions in their presents, on or before the first day of May next* [This passage struck: *and that the said building shall be under roof on or before the fifteenth day of October next. And further, that there shall be blinds in the manner before mentioned to all the front windows of the said house and also window shutters on the inside of all the said windows. And further that the plank on which the roof as aforesaid shall be laid, shall be feather edged, and shall lap one* [and] *an half inch.*]. *And the said parties of the first part for themselves & their successors do*

1. Doc. 124-1, Dutch Reformed Church (hereafter DRC) Collection, A FCA.
2. Doc. 124-3, DRC Collection.
3. Doc. 124-2, DRC Collection. The miscellaneous notes at the end appear in the original.
4. Doc. 124-3, DRC Collection.

hereby covenant, promise & agree with the said party of the second part and his legal representatives to pay to him for the purpose of aforesaid and in consideration of the said promises on or before the first day of November next, the sum of one thousand dollars; on or before the first day of December next, the further sum of two thousand dollars; on or before the first day of March next, the further sum of one thousand five hundred dollars and when the said building shall be completely finished according to the terms of the contract, the further sum of one thousand dollars. In witness thereof, the parties of the first part have caused their seal to be hereunto offered and their president to subscribe the same and the said party of the second part hath hereunto put his hand & seal the day & year first above written.
Sealed and delivered
in presence of

The blinds to all the front windows. Inside shutters to all the front windows. The plank for the roof to be feather-edged; to lap 1 1/2 inch[es].[3]

Hooker was paid for his services on 4 July 1815 after the completion of the building.[4]

The structure was used for its original purpose until the provision of new facilities for the consistory (cat. 73) permitted its alteration for occupancy as a parsonage (cat. 70).[5]

Hooker's design for the street facade of the Consistory House and dwelling closely resembles that of the Wool house in Troy (A9, fig. 174). A similar elevation appears in Asher Benjamin's *The American Builder's Companion.*[6] Hooker indicates that the second story of the Richard Lush house on Market Street (now Broadway) in Albany also featured an arcaded treatment. His direct reference to the Lush house and his known design of a stable for Richard Lush (cat. 12) point to his possible involvement in the design of that house as well.[7] ✥

5. E. P. Rogers, *A Historical Discourse on the Reformed Prot. Dutch Church of Albany* (New York: Board of Publication of the Reformed Protestant Dutch Church, 1858), p. 48; "1814 Consistory House Erected," A FCA.
6. Asher Benjamin, *The American Builder's Companion,* 6th ed. (1827; reprint ed., New York: Dover Publications, Inc., 1969), pl. 51.
7. Hooker also mentions the Bleecker house on North Pearl Street. The intended similarities in water table height and in the front steps and railing may have been because Mayor Bleecker's residence was immediately adjacent to the Consistory House.

32. LANCASTER SCHOOL

Eagle Street at Jay and Tyger (now Lancaster) streets, Albany, N.Y.
Designed between 28 February and 10 July 1815.
Built 1815–16; altered c. 1838; razed 1927; fragments survive.
Master carpenter: Lewis Farnham.
Master mason: John Turner.
Stonecutters: Hamilton and Wilson.

▲ Fig. 68. Lancaster School, Albany (1815–16), sectional elevation, from a drawing by Hooker, published in 1820. Engraving. Albany Institute of History & Art, McKinney Library, Photograph Collection.

Joseph Lancaster (1778–1838) founded the first Lancaster school in England in 1801, basing its organization on the theories of Andrew Bell. Because professors taught only the most advanced students, who in turn acted as monitors, the system decreased the need for professional staff. Consequently it was seized upon by the Albany Common Council as a means to cheaply educate the poor of the city. Lancaster schools were also established later in other New York communities.[1]

The site for the proposed schoolhouse had been selected and purchased by late May 1814. On 28 February 1815 the common council appointed a special committee to procure "*a suitable plan or plans*" for the building. Excavations for the foundations were ordered to be begun on 3 April 1815, although the plans may not have been finalized until 10 July, when a committee was appointed "*to superintend the building*" and "*to proceed*

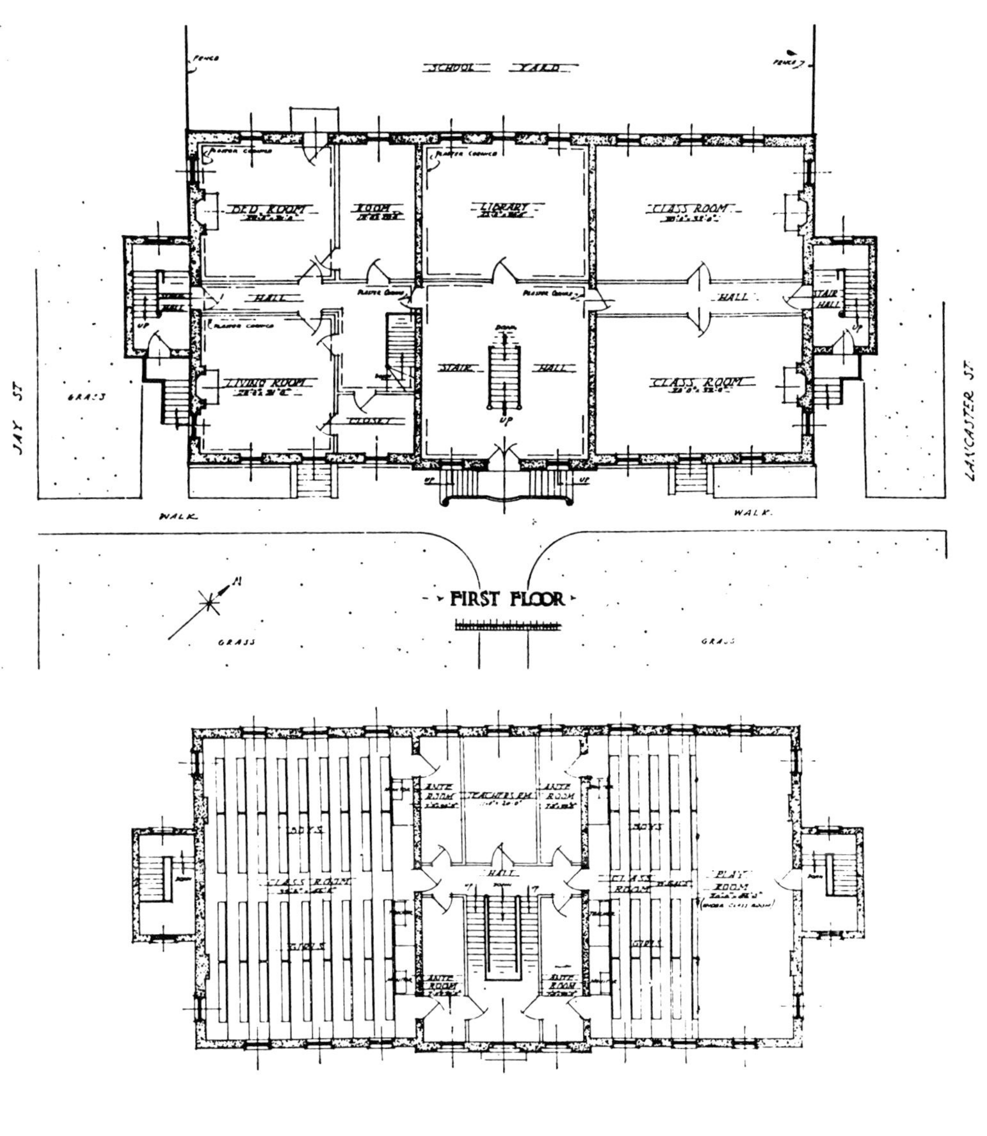

▶ Fig. 69. Lancaster School, Albany (1815–16), first and second floor plans, measured and restored by J. L. Dykeman, 1917. Courtesy New York State Library, Albany.

in Erecting the same without unnecessary delay, agreeable to a plan herewith submitted."[2]

Hooker appears to have acted as superintendent as well as architect. He billed $50.00 for his work up to 13 November 1815 drawing *plans, estimate & sundry services rendered, in leveling, laying out & directing masons, stone cutters, &c &c.*[3] The building was completed in the following year, its date stone naming the building committee, master carpenter, master mason, stonecutter, and "*P. H. HOOKER Architect.*"[4]

An engraving of the school was adapted from a drawing by Hooker and published in 1820 (fig. 68). This is the second known use by Hooker of a sectional-elevation technique to simultaneously depict the exterior and

▶
Fig. 70. Lancaster School, Albany (1815–16), exterior, before 1920. New York State Library, Albany.

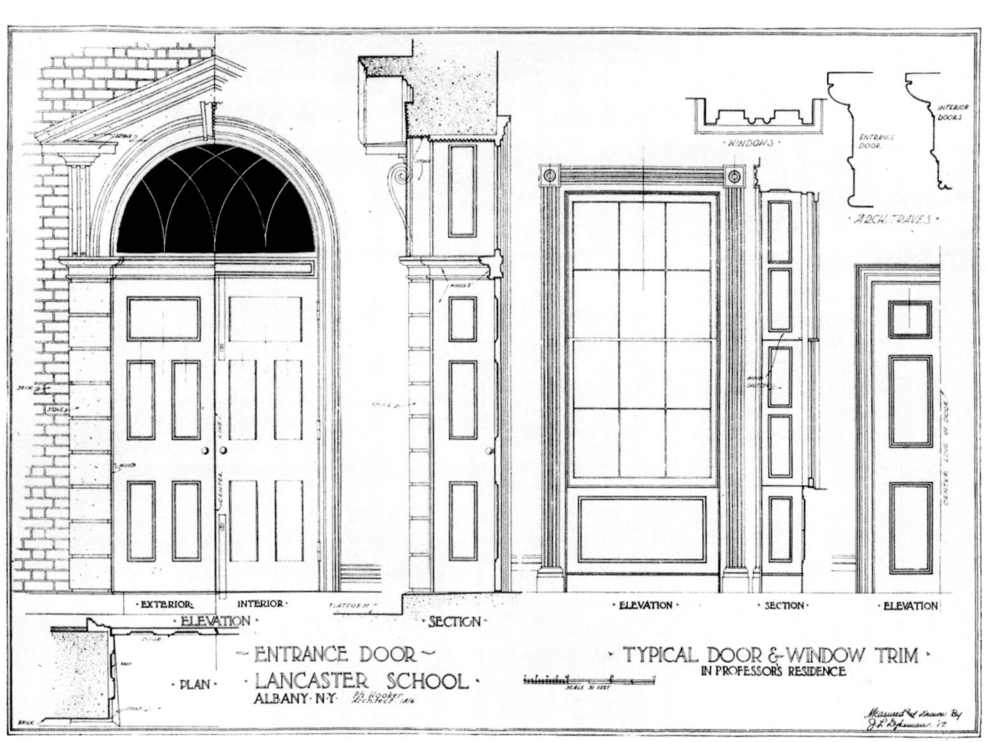

▶
Fig. 71. Lancaster School, Albany (1815–16), entrance door and interior trim, measured by J. L. Dykeman, 1917. Courtesy New York State Library, Albany.

▶ Fig. 72. View of 1843 showing the former Lancaster School, Albany (1815–16), in use as the Medical College. Modern print from original lithograph. Albany Institute of History & Art, McKinney Library.

interior of a building, the first having been in the facade drawing for the North Dutch Reformed Church (fig. 25). The engraving of the Lancaster School shows a hipped roof, but a simple gabled roof was apparently substituted in construction. A lithograph of the building dating from 1843 depicts the north elevation, whose oval and circular gable windows and blind arch are typical of Hooker's work (fig. 72).

Restored plans of the school (fig. 69) show the main stairhall, library, and administrative spaces centrally located behind the pedimented entrance pavilion. On the first floor were the principal's quarters and classrooms, while on the second story, double-height classrooms facilitated the implementation of the Lancaster system.[5] An enclosed stairway served each end of the main block.

The building remained a school until 1832. Before it was razed in 1927, it served as a hospital, then as the Albany Medical College (fig. 70).[6] Its entrance doorway (fig. 71) and at least two mantelpieces were incorporated in the college's new building, occupied in 1928.[7] ✥

1. William H. Harris and Judith S. Levey, eds., *New Columbia Encyclopedia,* 4th ed. (New York and London: Columbia University Press, 1975), p. 1523.
2. Root, p. 143, from Albany Common Council, Manuscript Minutes, 28 February and 10 July 1815.
3. MSC NYSL.
4. Root, p. 144.
5. J. L. Dykeman, "The Lancaster School, Albany, N.Y., Philip Hooker, Architect," *Architecture,* XXXVI, 6 (December 1917), 245–46.
6. Root, p. 146.
7. Richard T. Beebe, *Albany Medical College and Albany Hospital. A History: 1839–1982* ([Albany], 1983), pp. 210–11.

33. ALBANY ACADEMY

Public Square (now Academy Park), Albany, N.Y.
Designed by Thomas C. Taylor before 9 March 1815.
Hooker redraft of Taylor design between 5 April and 6 June 1815.
Built 1815–16; altered 1935 by Marcus T. Reynolds; extant.
Builder: Seth Geer.
Master mason: William Murray.
Stonemason: Peter McNab.
Woodcarver: Henry Farnham.

▲
Fig. 73. Albany Academy (1815–16), view from Academy Park (part of the former Public Square), before 1920.
Albany Institute of History & Art, McKinney Library, Photograph Collection.

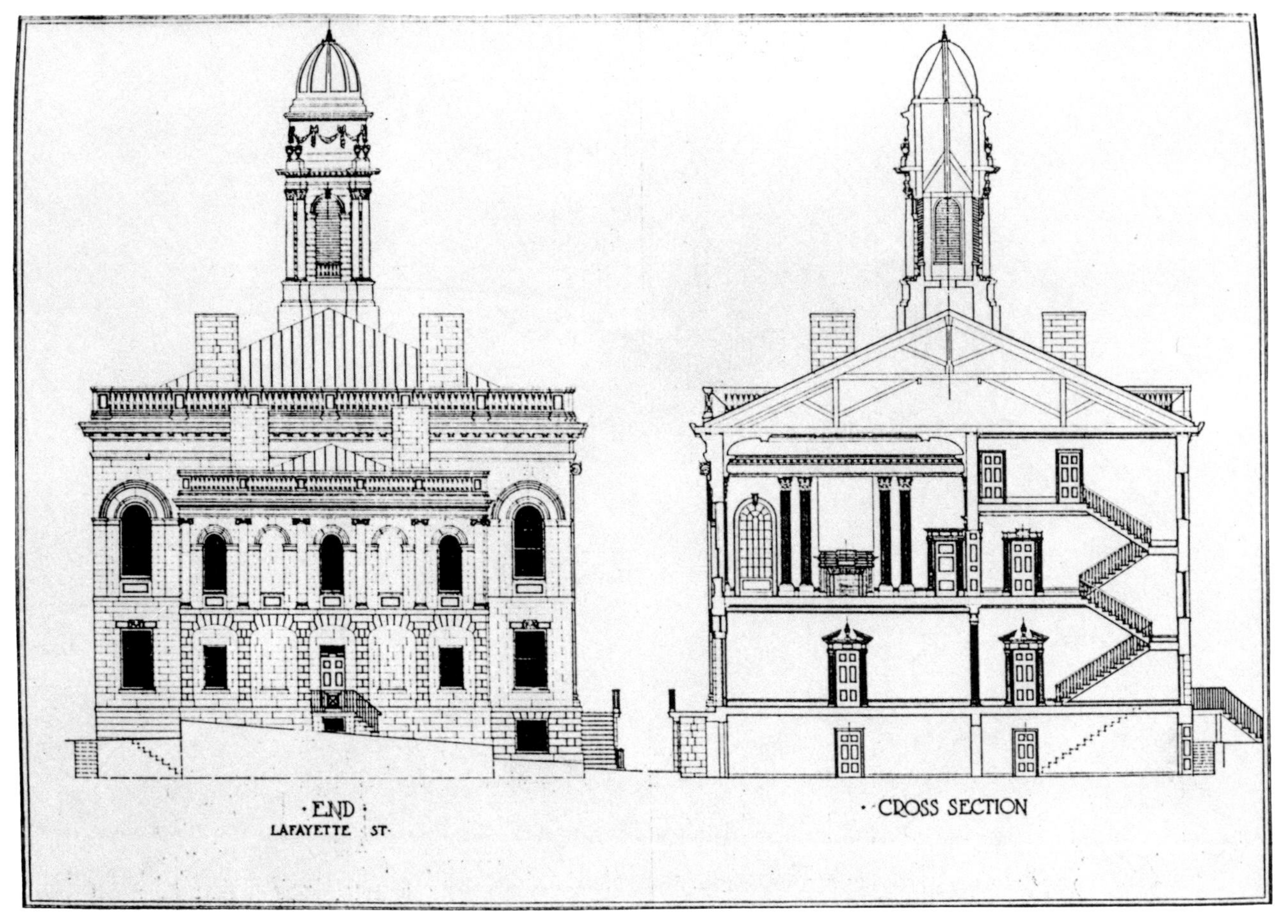

▲
Fig. 74. Albany Academy (1815–16), end elevation and cross section, published in 1916.
Courtesy Cornell University, Ithaca, N.Y., Fine Arts Library.

By 1813, the Albany Common Council's various attempts to encourage the establishment of a private academy had faltered. As a result the council finally opted in formal proceedings to partially subsidize the operation of such a school and took action towards the construction of a building to house it. In its first few years of existence, the Albany Academy operated in a house on State Street. Hooker's original plan for a new building, presented to the academy's trustees in 1814 (cat. 30), was abandoned after 13 February 1815, when the city assumed financial responsibility for the project.

Parallel committees were set up by the academy trustees, on 14 February, and the Albany Common Council, on 28 February 1815, to consider building proposals. They met together on 9 March and resolved to *adopt a plan of the building drawn by Thomas C. Taylor, as the most eligible of any of those exhibited* and indicated the acceptability of altering Taylor's design, noting that *in case the Corporation should be desirous of omitting the wings, they are requested to erect the central building only.*[1] On 29 March, the building committee that had been appointed by the common council accepted the proposal of builders Geer & Riley and chose Seth Geer to superintend the construction of the new academy.[2]

It seems that Hooker had not been invited to submit a second plan, but on 5 April he addressed the building committee with a proposal recorded by them.

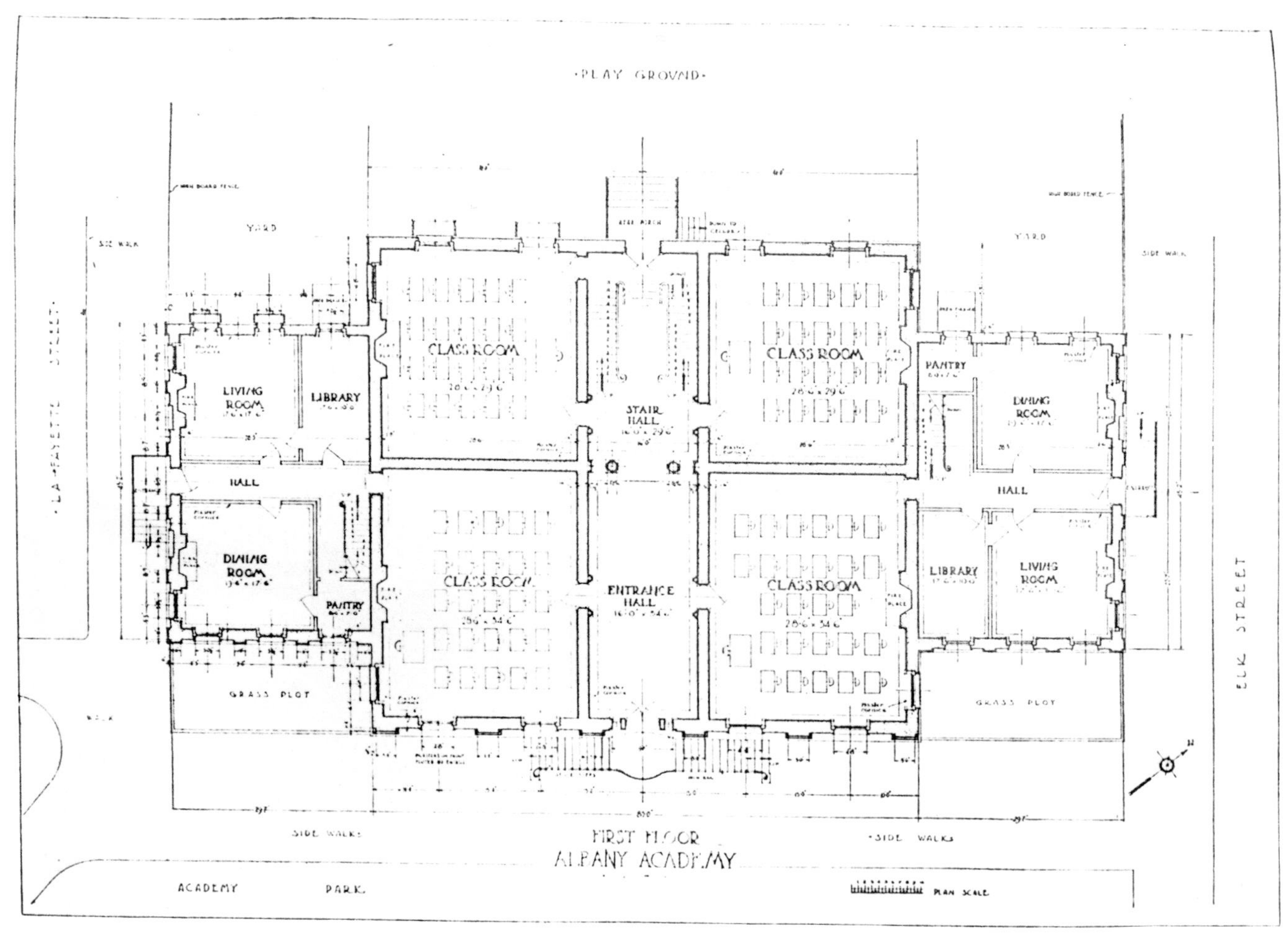

▲
Fig. 75. Albany Academy (1815–16), first floor plan, published in 1916. Courtesy Cornell University, Ithaca, N.Y., Fine Arts Library.

" . . . *as Mr. Philip Hooker is of opinion that he can improve on the Plan already* [*adopted* is crossed out] *agreed to, that he be disired to make a New Plan with such improvements as soon as possable and submit it to the Committee.*"[3]

Hooker's later handwritten bill indicates their acceptance of his proposal.

"1815		*Albany Academy* *To P. Hooker—*	
Feby 11th	*Estimate*	*p*[e]*r order of A. Hand*	*$5 . . —*
Mar: 14th	*Bill of timber*	*p*[er order of] *G. Stewart*	*5 . . —*
June 6th	*Arranging & drawing a full set of plans for the Building by order of the Committee*	}	*50 . . —*
	Laying out & drawing the basement for stone Cutter		*10 . . —*
	Making out a bill of All the freestone for the quarry		*5 . . —*
	Stationary & binding for the plans		*3 . . —*
			$78 . . —"[4]

On 20 June Hooker offered further services to the committee.

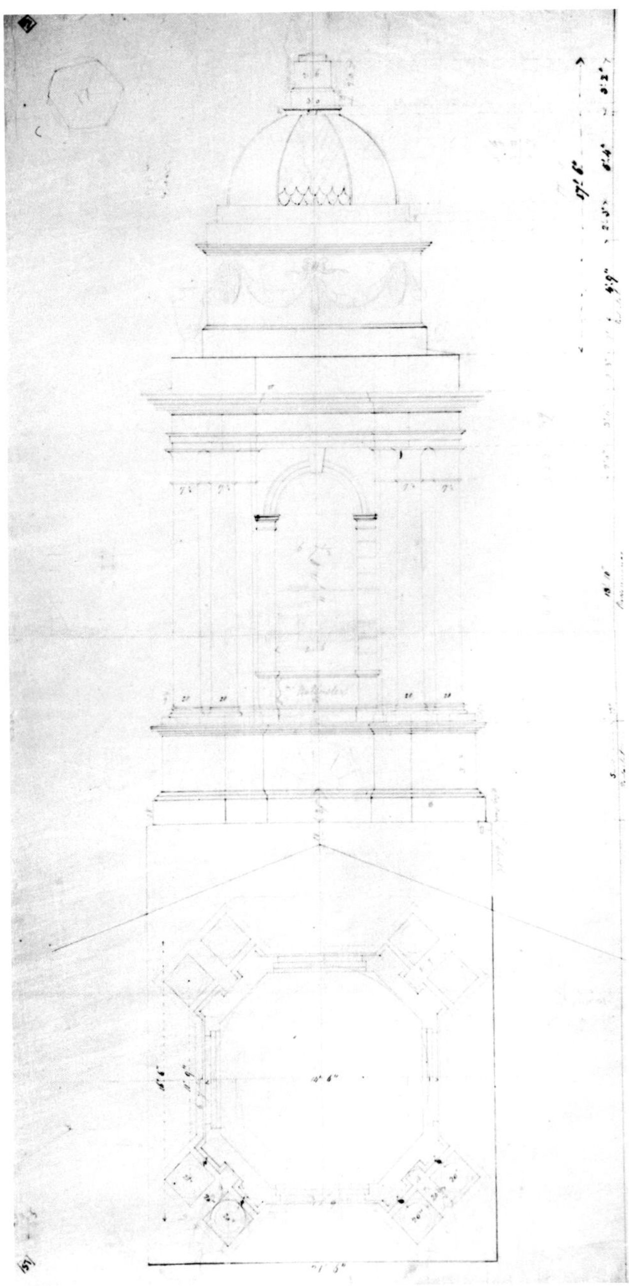

▲
Fig. 76. New York City Hall (1802–11), original cupola, drawn by John McComb, Jr. Ink on paper. The New-York Historical Society, New York, N.Y.

> *"Gentlemen*
>
> *"I avail myself of an opportunity, of offering to you, my services as Architect, to the Academy, the duties of which, I will undertake to perform, for the sum of One hundred dollars, which sum (I conceive) will be completely saved—by the relief it will give Mr Geer—in the time that would necessarily be taken up in drawing plans & directions, for stone cutters—smiths Carpenters Joiners &c &c—which could be applied to procuring materials, looking after, workmen and inspecting the work—*
>
> *"By this application I would not wish to be understood—that I doubt the abilities of Mr Geer—of whose integrity and Judgement as a builder I have a very high opinion—and I think the Committee were Judicious in selecting him as their superintendent*
>
> *"But I hope I shall not be considered vain when I suppose that I can be of some assistance to him—after an experience of twenty-five years in building and a close application in the research of antient and modern architecture. be that as it may, it is an old maxim that 'two heads is better than one'*
>
> *I am with respect Gentl*[me]*n*
> *Y*[ou]*rs Ph: Hooker"* [5]

On 21 August 1815, the committee resolved to accept Hooker's proposal *aggreeable to his . . . letter of 20 June last.*[6] Surviving records indicate that between this date and 20 December 1817 Hooker was paid $150 for his work on the project.

Bills relating to the construction of the Albany Academy have recently been discovered. That of stonemason Peter McNab contains a wealth of information about the costs of various services he provided, while a bill from Henry Farnham solves a long-standing mystery about the artist responsible for the remarkable woodwork in the building (fig. 77).[7]

Confusion over the authorship of the academy's design derives not only from the above references but also from the record of a copper plate placed at the time the cornerstone was laid, naming Seth Geer as the architect.[8] The respective contributions of Hooker's architectural skills and Geer's superintendence may be understood in light of Hooker's letter of 20 June 1815 and a date stone formerly on the rear wall of the building, since installed in the main hall. In addition to naming members of the building committee, the master mason, and stonecutter, the inscription identifies *"Ph. Hooker"* as the *"Architect"* and *"Seth Geer"* as the *"Master Builder."*[9]

▶
Fig. 77. Albany Academy (1815–16), first floor hall and stairs, c. 1925. Collection Morris Gerber, Albany.

1. Albany Academy Building Committee Minutes, Vol. 110-50, SARA, ACHR.
2. Root, p. 132. Geer was first listed in the Albany city directories in 1815, and before he moved to New York City in 1819, worked with fellow carpenter Asher Riley on at least one other building for which Hooker was the architect, the Lutheran Ebenezer Church (cat. 37). In New York Geer worked as a contractor and builder and as a speculator-developer. Information provided by Regina Kellerman.
3. Root, pp. 132–33, from Albany Academy Building Committee Minutes, 5 April 1815.
4. Root, p. 133, from the document, found in the State Education Building vault.
5. Ibid., p. 134, from the document, found in the State Education Building vault.
6. Albany Academy Papers, ACHR.
7. Ibid., Box 110-6, SARA, ACHR.
8. Root, p. 130.
9. Root, p. 130, from the date stone.
10. Root, pp. 136–38.
11. Ibid., p. 133.
12. Albany Academy Building Committee Minutes, 21 March and 27 March 1815, Vol. 110-50, SARA, ACHR.

Hooker's role in the design of the academy building vis-a-vis that of Thomas C. Taylor is less clear. Taylor seems not to have been an Albanian, and city records provide no further information about him with respect to this project.[10] At the same 5 April 1815 meeting that the building committee heard Hooker's offer of a new plan, they also approved an advertisement for 780,000 bricks.[11] This indication that the committee planned no radical changes, whatever Hooker would propose, coupled with the knowledge that Taylor's plan comprised a central block and wings, suggests some basic similarities between the original scheme and the executed one. Yet certain features discussed in the March 1815 building committee meetings—the height and ground level of the building's first floor and the facing of the front of the basement story— do not correspond to the structure as erected.[12]

Root has pointed out the distinction of the Albany Academy with respect to Hooker's prior public buildings in that it incorporates no pediment (fig. 73), yet he places its interior planning and ornamental detail fully within Hooker's works. The exterior is characterized by the two-story-high pilasters and large, arched windows of the central block. These and the detailing of the cupola reflect the influence of the rather recently completed New York City Hall (fig. 76), by Joseph Mangin and John McComb, Jr.[13]

The grand scale of the central block on its park facade corresponds to the location of the primary room, the second-story chapel (fig. 78), on this side of the building. The continuation of the large windows on the north and south elevations immediately adjacent to the wings maintains that

▶ Fig. 78. Albany Academy (1815–16), the chapel on the second floor, c. 1925. Collection Morris Gerber, Albany.

scale, although the rear or west elevation reflects the three-story division of that side of the building (fig. 74). A similar juxtaposition, but between the front and sides of the building, occurred in Hooker's design of the New York State Capitol (fig. 46), which also faced the Public Square. In this later structure, however, the problem is handled with greater skill. The plan of the academy building is merely an enlargement of the typical five-bay house plan, with the addition of two flanking wings which served as faculty residences (fig. 75). The facades of these north and south wings are treated as separate town houses, compatibly scaled to the nearby residences. In sum, the quality of its workmanship, proportions, and detailing all contribute to make the Albany Academy a masterpiece of Federal architecture.

In 1935, the building was renovated according to plans by Marcus T. Reynolds.[14] The original wooden staircase (fig. 77) was replaced by one of marble and its configuration was altered. Generally inferior plaster and woodwork were added to the building at that time. The wooden cupola, which was originally painted white and later in imitation of brownstone, was duplicated in copper and many of its details were simplified.[15] In addition, the fenestration of the rear or west facade was altered to accommodate the insertion of a Palladian window. The chapel, however, was not affected by Reynolds's renovations. Recently it and the main hall were returned to their original color scheme: terra cotta for the walls of the chapel and light grey for those of the hall, with cream trim in both.[16]

Still used for educational purposes, the building currently houses offices for the Albany City School District. ✤

13. Root, pp. 140–42.
14. Marcus T. Reynolds Papers, Collection, Kenneth G. Reynolds.
15. Fragments of the original cupola (swags, urns, column capitals, and modillions) are extant in the attic of the academy building.
16. A paint analysis was undertaken by Douglas G. Bucher in November 1989 to determine the original and subsequent color schemes in the former chapel. The original color, a terra cotta (Munsell number 7.5 YR 7/6), was similar to the stone found on the exterior. The woodwork has always been painted in shades of cream/ivory. The plaster ceiling was originally unpainted white plaster. Information provided by Douglas G. Bucher.

34. PROPOSAL FOR A TOWN HOUSE FOR THE GANSEVOORT FAMILY

Unknown location, Albany, N.Y.
Designed c. 1815.
Building history unknown.

▶ Fig. 79. Hooker's elevation of an unidentified house for the Gansevoort family, Albany, probably c. 1815. Ink and wash on paper. New York Public Library, New York, N.Y., Gansevoort-Lansing Collection, Manuscripts and Archives Section.

Features shared with Hooker's designs for the Consistory House of the North Dutch Reformed Church (cat. 31) and the Albany house for George Clarke (cat. 36) suggest a date of about 1815 for the drawing which documents this proposal (fig. 79). Typical of Hooker's graphic style, this drawing features finely drafted lines, but the hand-drawn elements such as the balusters and the cellar doors are tentative and suggest a discomfort with freehand work.

Hooker's drawing indicates an ornately patterned semicircular fanlight over the door. Returns at the corners coupled with the blind arches on the first story give the illusion of a masonry plane passing behind the arcade.

35. ONTARIO BRANCH BANK

West side of Genesee Street, Utica, N.Y.
Designed before 19 June 1815.
Built 1815; altered c. 1861; razed c. 1900.
Builder unknown.

▶
Fig. 80. Ontario Branch Bank, Utica (1815), exterior, 1874. Utica Public Library.

The cornerstone of the Ontario Branch Bank was laid on 19 June 1815, an event noted in that day's edition of the *Utica Patrol*: "... *this building will not be inferior to any building for the same purpose in the state. It reflects the highest honor on the architect, Philip Hooker, Esq., of Albany.*"[1]

The building was ready for occupancy by December 1815 and served until the bank's failure in 1857. It was remodeled around 1861, when the level of the first floor was lowered, the exterior stairs removed, and the interior adapted for a store.[2] The structure seems to have been razed sometime about the turn of the century.[3]

The design of the facade of the Ontario Branch Bank was a virtual copy of Hooker's New York State Bank in Albany (fig. 38), modified to fit a narrower site. Photographs indicate, however, that the detailing of the Utica example (fig. 80) was more coarse than that of its predecessor. Both structures owe much to the work of the Adam brothers, particularly the building for the Society for the Encouragement of Arts, Manufactures & Commerce in London (fig. 37). ✥

1. Root, pp. 125–26.
2. John J. Walsh, "Vignettes of Old Utica, Persons, Places and Events," unpublished manuscript, 1975, p. 52. Typescript on file at the Oneida County Historical Society, Utica, N.Y.
3. This conclusion has been drawn from a review of photographs in the collections of the Utica Public Library and the Oneida County Historical Society, both Utica, N.Y.

36. PROPOSAL FOR A DWELLING HOUSE FOR GEORGE CLARKE

Unknown location, Albany, N.Y.
Designed before 20 June 1816.
Unbuilt.

George Clarke (1768–1835), great-grandson of the George Clarke who had been Secretary and then Lieutenant Governor of provincial New York, inherited his forbear's properties in the state, totaling about 120,000 acres. Clarke came to Albany from Oxfordshire, England, in 1806 and rented a house on the southeast corner of State and Eagle streets on the Public Square. In 1815, Clarke bought three acres *on which to build a house*, and it was probably sometime thereafter that he contacted Hooker, initiating a professional relationship that would continue for more than a decade.[1]

A bound volume, measuring 10 5/16 inches by 8 inches, contains the drawings (figs. 81–89), brief text, and bill for timber which document this project.[2] The title page states that the house was *designed by George Clark* [sic] *Esq*[r]*, delineated by Philip Hooker, Albany, June 20th, 1816.* The similarity of the elevations to other projects by Hooker indicates that he was responsible for more than its delineation. However, it is likely that Clarke made suggestions about room sizes and arrangement, and thus to some degree determined the plan. Hooker's task would then have been to incorporate his client's ideas into an architectural design, for which he executed the drawings. The alteration of Hooker's two original elevations by the addition of flaps to present alternate cornice and roofscape designs (figs. 85–88) may reflect the architect's responses to Clarke's critique of the initial proposal. Only the alternate scheme is depicted in the simple line drawing of the third elevation (fig. 89). Pencilled emendations to the basement plan concerning room use are in Clarke's handwriting (fig. 81). Hooker's bill for his work was $30.00.[3]

The drawings and the design are explained by Hooker's accompanying estimate of materials, keys to the plans, brief descriptions, and bill for timber. Although the intended site for the house is not clear, its elevations and plans suggest a location with a view to be enjoyed from the piazza and with a garden to be reached from the dining room.

Materials—[4]

Bricks	*500 m*
Stone	*720 loads*
Lime unslacked	*6000 bush*[els]
Slates	*60 squares*
Copper gutter	*300 feet*
Ashler freestone	*700 feet supr*
Water Table	*140* [feet] *run*
Window frames & sills	*244* [feet run]
Yellow pine 1 1/4 inch plank	*1000* }
White [pine] *1 1/4* [inch plank]	*1400* }
[White pine] *2 inch* [plank]	*250* }
[White pine] *1 inch board*	*1500* }
60 m Split Laths	

1. George Hyde Clarke Papers, Coll. 2800, Department of Manuscripts and University Archives, Olin Library, Cornell University, Ithaca, N.Y. The property was purchased from Philip Livingston for $5,000. Clarke owned considerable real estate in and around Albany, and it is not clear where this particular parcel was located.
2. Collection, Friends of Hyde Hall, Inc., Springfield, N.Y.; photographic copy in the George Hyde Clarke Papers.
3. Ibid.
4. Pencilled notes on prices and dimensions, in Clarke's handwriting, accompany some of the listings. Also noted is the statement that all the wood was *to be clear free from knots not comformable to Albany custom which is held to be clear if there are 2 knots not large.*

▶
Figs. 81–84. Dwelling House for George Clarke, Albany, plans, 1816.
Ink and wash on paper, bound. Photographs courtesy Friends of Hyde Hall, Inc.

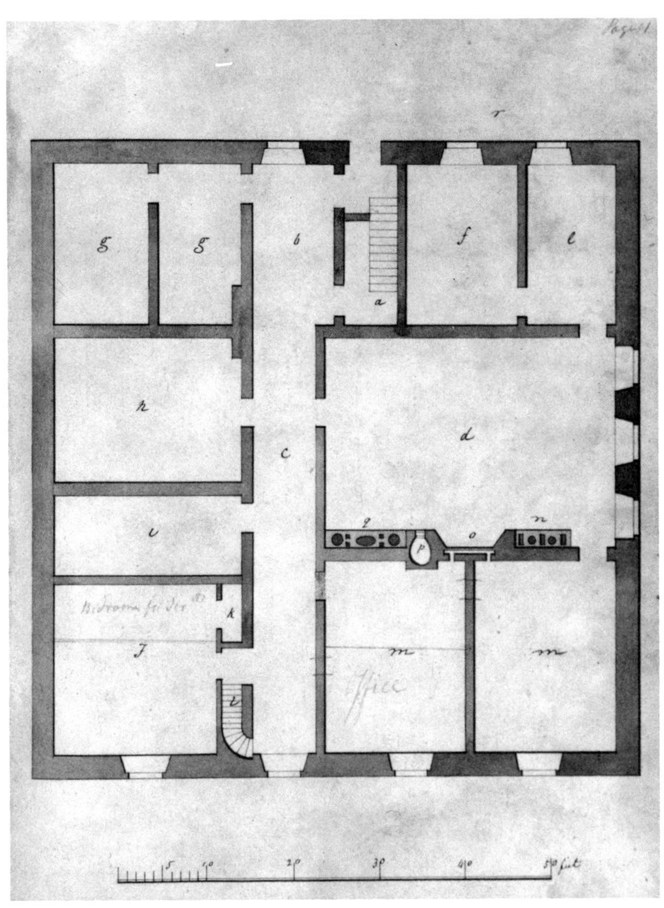

Plan of the Basement [fig. 81]
To be 8 feet in the clear from floor to ceiling

		Feet		*Feet*
a	*cellar stairs*			
b	*place for cleaning knives &c.*	*17 1/2*	*by*	*9 1/2*
c	*passage*	*47 1/2*	—	*7*
d	*Kitchen*	*34*	—	*23 1/2*
e	*Scullery*	*17 1/2*	—	*10 1/2*
f	*Larder*	*17 1/2*	—	*13*
g g	*Wine Cellars*	*17 1/2*	—	*10*
h	*Root Cellar*	*21 1/4*	—	*16*
i	*Beer Cellar*	*21 1/4*	—	*9*
j	*Servants Hall*	*18 1/2*	—	*18 1/2*
k	*Closet*	*5*	—	*2 1/3*
l	*private stairs to Hall door*			*2 1/3*
m m	*Bed rooms*	*21 1/4*	—	*16 1/3*
n	*range of stew holes*			
o	*Fire place*			
p	*Oven*			
q	*range of boilers*			
r	*Area*			

Base of the stone walls 4 feet—Stone walls above Cellar floor two feet Six inches in thickness. Principal partitions two bricks length—small partitions one brick length—NB the piers and appertures in the Back front are to be altered to correspond with those in the chamber story—(see plan 3d)

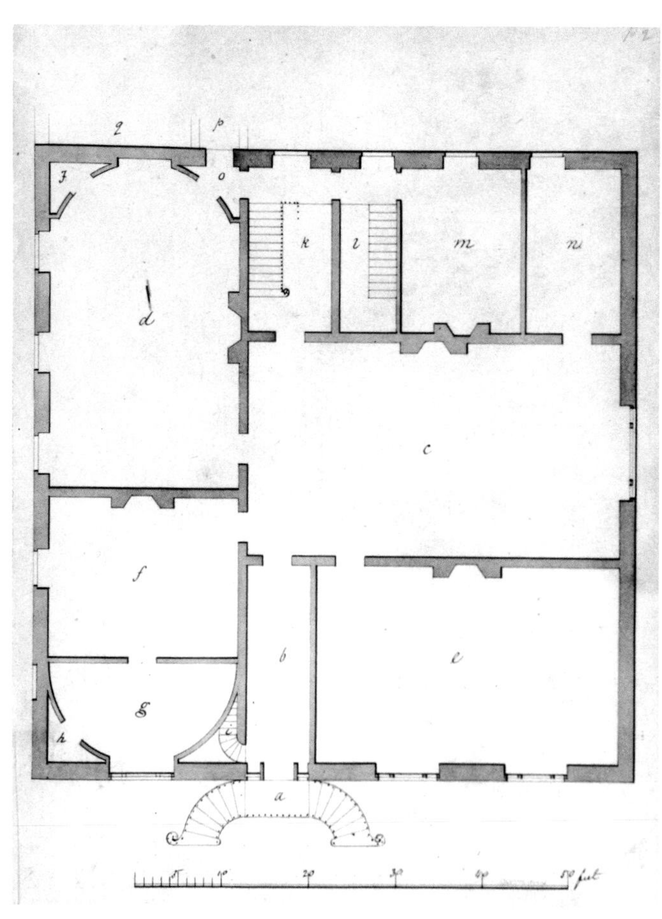

Plan of the Principal Story [fig. 82]
To be fourteen feet in the clear

		[Feet]		[Feet]
a	*Stone Steps to Entrance*			
b	*Entrance or Vestibule*	*22*	*by*	*7 1/3*
c	*Hall*	*43*	—	*24*
d	*Dining room*	*36*	—	*22*
e	*Drawing* [room]	*35*	—	*22*
f	*Library*	*22*	—	*18*
g	*Dressing room*	*22*	—	*11*
h	*Closet*			
i	*Porters stairs*			*2 1/3*
j	*Glass closet*			
k	*Grand stairs*	*18*	—	*10*
l	*Back* [stairs]	*18*	—	*6 1/2*
m	*Butlers Pantry*	*18*	—	*14*
n	*Conservatory*	*18*	—	*10 1/2*
o	*Lobby*			
p	*passage to garden*			
q	*Green House*			

Exterior walls, 3 bricks length—
Principal partitions 2 bricks length—

NB—the piers & appertures in the back front are to be altered to correspond with those of the chamber story.

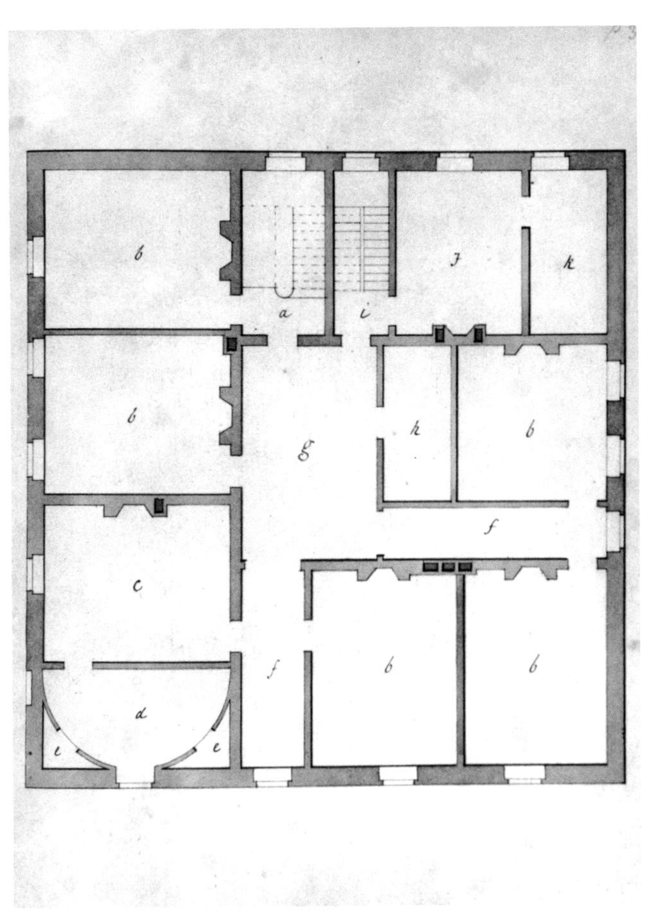

Plan of the Chamber Story [fig. 83]
To be twelve feet in the clear

			[Feet]		[Feet]
a	*Landing of Best Stair Case*				
bbbbb	*Bed Chambers*	*22 by 17 one of which is*	*17*	*by*	*17*
c	*Mrs. Clarks room*		*22*	—	*18*
d	[Mrs. Clarke's] *dressing room*		*22*	—	*11*
ee	*Closets*				
ff	*Passages*	*one of 22 by 7 1/3 feet the other*	*26*	—	*5 1/2*
g	*anti chamber*		*24*	—	*16*
h	*Linen closet*		*17*	—	*8*
i	*Back Stairs*		*18*	—	*15*
j	*Nursery*		*18*	—	*6 1/2*
k	*bedroom*		*18*	—	*9*
	External walls 2 1/2 bricks—				
	Principal partitions 2 Bricks				
	minor [partitions] *studs 6 by 4 inches*				

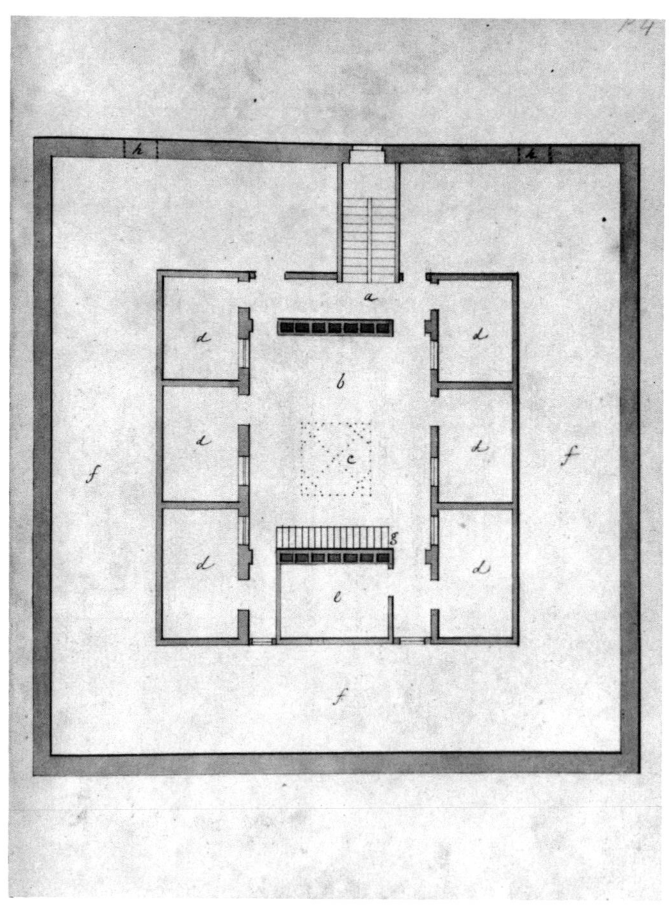

Plan of the Garret [fig. 84]

a	*Landing of back Stairs*
b	*Open area under Skylight*
c	*Skylight above*
dd&c	*bed rooms for servants*
e	*Smoak Room*
fff	*open garrett*
g	*Steps to the lead flat* [roof]

Smoak room floor to be laid with courses of bricks flatwise—Joints broke, fine salt to be mixed with the mortar—Stone sill & iron frame to the door which is also to be iron, or lined with plate iron, the sides & ceiling to be lathed & plaistered in the best possible manner— to prevent any cracks— an aperture is to be made in the flue of the kitchen chimney Just above the brick floor, and another aperture near the ceiling in to some other flue of the chimney farthest distant from the former.

Two dormer windows are to be made in the roof, to give light & air to the garret (see dotted lines hh [in west wall]*)*

Elevation of the East front [figs. 85, 86]

The rusticated walls of the Basements, the steps, door & window frames, 2nd story window sills, & the chimney tops—to be of approved freestone. The walls of the superstructure, are to be faced with the best moulded hard bricks—laid with a thin joint of best mortar. Struck off & pointed flush—to be painted a light, or portland stone colour.

The windows in the principal story are to have Stone sills pilasters & lintals—The centre to contain 12 panes of 20 by 13 inches in two casements of Mahogany Sashes—The side lights 4 panes Each Same size & finish—The Centre Sashes only, to be hung. The Sash frames are to be calculated for four fold of shutters on a side—which are to close the whole opening—which will require a base of about 5 inches deep on Each Side to receive the shutters. Mahogany pully pieces to sash frames—

Elevation of the South [or Garden] *front* [figs. 87, 88]

To be finished as before described—

The ground, taken from the excavation of the cellar, is to be thrown on the south side to form a gentle Slope from the Piazza to the garden—

The long windows in the principal story are to contain 18 panes of 20 by 13 inches—in two casements—12 in the lower & 6 in the upper—the sash frame so constructed, that the lower sash can rise to give a clear head way of 7 feet, and calculated for two folds of shutters, a side.

The windows of the chamber story throughout, to contain 12 panes of 18 by 13 Inches. Seven windows in the Basement 8 panes 14 by 10 in two casements 4 panes wide & one high—

Three [windows in the Basement] *12 panes 14 by 10—two casements to face the area, in the back front—*[5]

Hall window north front—Venetian, [fig. 89]
Centre, 24 panes 18 by 12—two casements
sides—12 panes 18 by 12 two [casements]
to have 5 fold of shutters on a side, or perhaps
as the window is very wide, it will be better
to finish with four pilasters, with boxes behind
Each—with two shutters for Each Side light &
four for the Centre—

Bill of Timber

166	*Beams 24 feet*		*14 by 4*	*1st & 2nd floors*
66	[Beams] *26* [feet]		*14 by 4*	
66	[Beams] *20* [feet]		*12 by 4*	
56	[Beams] *24* [feet]		*12 by 4*	*garret floor*
22	[Beams] *26* [feet]		*12 by 4*	
22	[Beams] *20* [feet]		*12 by 4*	
12	*pieces wall plate 25* [feet]		*12 by 4*	*Roof*
4	*rafters*	*40* [feet]	*12 by 4*	
40	[rafters]	*29* [feet]	*8 by 4*	
8	[rafters]	*26* [feet]	*8 by 4*	
8	[rafters]	*23* [feet]	*8 by 4*	
8	[rafters]	*20* [feet]	*8 by 4*	
8	[rafters]	*17* [feet]	*8 by 4*	
8	[rafters]	*14* [feet]	*6 by 4*	
8	[rafters]	*11* [feet]	*6 by 4*	
8	[rafters]	*8* [feet]	*6 by 4*	
8	[rafters]	*14* [feet]	*6 by 4*	
4	*Sills*	*42* [feet]	*7 by 5*	

▶
Fig. 85. Dwelling House for George Clarke, Albany, Hooker's elevation of the east front, first version, 1816.

▶
Fig. 86. Hooker's elevation of the east front, second version, 1816. Ink and watercolor on paper, bound. Photographs courtesy Friends of Hyde Hall, Inc.

▶
Fig. 87. Dwelling House for George Clarke, Albany, Hooker's elevation of the garden, or south, front, first version, 1816.

▶
Fig. 88. Hooker's elevation of the garden, or south, front, second version, 1816.
Ink and watercolor on paper, bound. Photographs courtesy Friends of Hyde Hall, Inc.

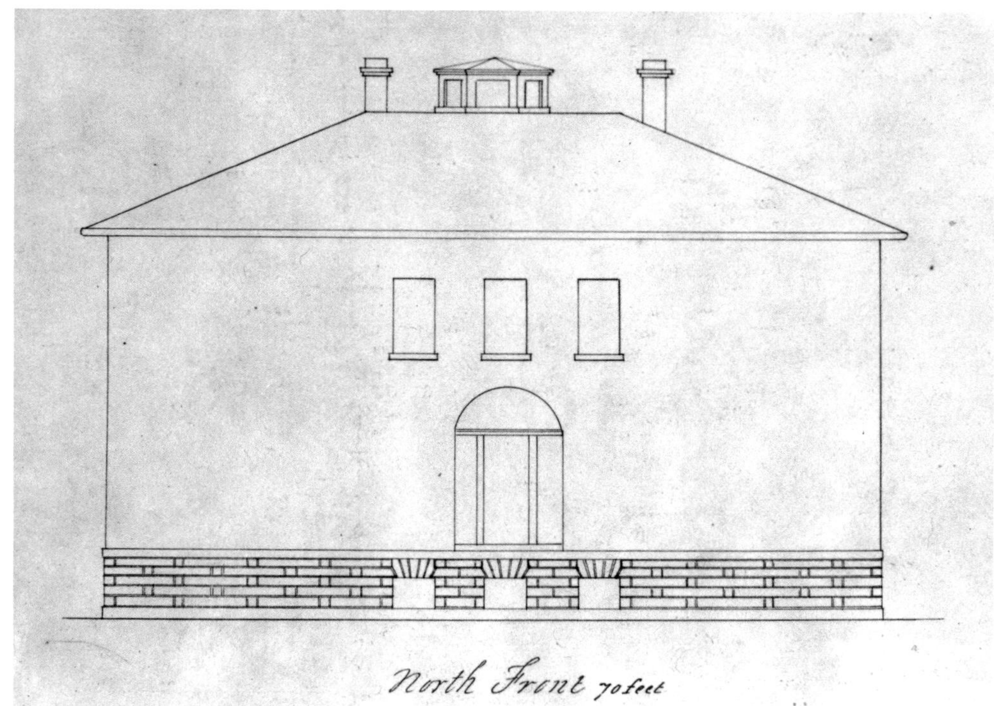

Fig. 89. Dwelling House for George Clarke, Albany, Hooker's elevation of the north front, 1816.
Ink on paper, bound.
Photograph courtesy Friends of Hyde Hall, Inc.

4	*plates*	*42* [feet]	*11 by 5*
16	*posts*	*7* [feet]	*12 by 5*
36	*Braces*	*14* [feet]	*6 by 4*
10	*deck beams*	*24* [feet]	*16 by 4*
10	[deck beams]	*9* [feet]	*15 by 4*
	Truss frame in Roof, north side of flat.		
2	*pieces*	*26 feet*	*12 by 5*
4	[pieces]	*14 feet*	*12 by 5*
2	[pieces]	*12 feet*	*7 by 5*
950	*feet run*[nin]*g of various lengths from 20 to 30 feet of wall plates - 8 by 4 1/2 inches —*		
34	*lintals*	*5 1/2 feet*	*12 by 4 1/2*
4	[lintals]	*9 1/2 feet*	*12 by 7 1/2*
1	[lintal]	*11 feet*	*12 by 9 1/2*
200	*pieces scantling*	*14 feet*	*6 by 4*
150	[pieces scantling]	*14* [feet]	*4 by 3*[6]

Despite the elaboration of this proposal, there is no evidence that Clarke's house was constructed. It would have been one of the most sophisticated buildings of its day. The blind arches in the east elevation are a continuing design theme in Hooker's work, only here with wider windows than those in the facades of the earlier Gansevoort (fig. 79) and Alexander (fig. 44) houses. The simplicity of the elevations, especially evident in the untinted drawing of the north front, is reminiscent of the work of Ledoux. The organization of the flues into two great chimneys, as shown in the plans and the first version of the elevations, would have proved an unusual decorative device, offering a particularly memorable image on a cold winter morning. ✥

5. The statements regarding the basement windows were written in black rather than in brown ink.
6. Collection, Friends of Hyde Hall; photographic copy in the George Hyde Clarke Papers.

37. LUTHERAN EBENEZER CHURCH

Northwest corner of Pine and Lodge streets, Albany, N.Y.
Designed before 21 September 1816.
Built 1816–18; razed October 1868.
Builders: Seth Geer and Asher Riley.

▶ Fig. 90. Lutheran Ebenezer Church, Albany (1816–18), view, c. 1840. Courtesy W. R. Wheeler, Troy, N.Y.

The first reference in the Lutheran Ebenezer Church (now First Lutheran Church) Council Minutes regarding the construction of a new building occurs on 14 February 1816.[1] The church was designed between that date and the laying of the cornerstone on 21 September 1816.[2]

The church council engaged Hooker to prepare a foundation for the building before contractors were invited to bid on the project, a common practice at the time. On 21 October 1816 they *resolved that one hundred plank be purchased to cover the Foundation of the new Church* and that Hooker be *authorised to purchase from two to four hundred loads of stone for the new Church.* It was not unusual for clients to procure as much of the building materials as possible before commencing a project in order to assure even quality and continued work. Hooker acted as representative of the church in the selection and acquisition of these materials. The minutes quoted above also authorized him to *give directions to the Master Builders in this city to estimate to build the new Church by Contract and receive the Corporation lands as cash the estimates to be delivered to Mr Hooker.*[3] By 6 November 1816 Hooker had been paid $50.00 *on account of services done and to be performed as architect of the new church,* as well as an additional $30.00 *on account of drawing plans &c. for the Lutheran Church.*[4]

One example of the estimates submitted to Hooker survives.

> *Albany November 26 1816*
> *Dear Sir*
> *I have estimated the Church according to the plans & description given except the cut stone, according to the conversation* [we] *had when I last saw you; & the painting of the plastering outside I do not see mentioned therefore have ommitted it*
> *The aggregate of my estimate is $14,250.*
> *I have, to be sure, made the estimate in rather too much haste, being that I am going from home & having had a short time since the plans have been left me*
> *If a decision can consistantly be omited until my return (two weeks), I should prefer revising it.*
> *Very Respectfully Yours*
> *Mr P. Hooker*
> *John Boardman*[5]

Hooker submitted Boardman's estimate to the church council on 28 November 1816, along with the others he had gathered. The minutes of that day record the results.

> *That whereas the estimates have been delivered to P. Hooker & by him been delivered to the trustees for building the new church, that on examination it appears Messers Geer & Riley are the Lowest on the same.*
> *Therefore Resolved that the said Geer & Riley are intitled to the said Job or contract provided the said Geer & Riley Give Sufficient Security to the trustees For the true performance of the Same—according to the plan made by P. Hooker upon which the estimates are made by order*
> *Chris.r Monk Secty*[6]

The following contract for the project was prepared by Hooker and signed on 4 December 1816:

> *. . . Geer & Riley . . . will . . . erect, build, & completely finish a stone church, or edifice for public worship. On the foundation now laid, by the said trustees, at the junction of Lodge & Pine Streets, in the city* [of Albany], *of the form & dimentions as follows and according to plans made thereof by Philip Hooker: sixty feet in length, forty two feet 4 inches in width, & twenty eight feet 9 inches in height from the water table, to the top of the cornice of the side walls; with a tower of sixteen feet square, and a circular projection in the rear, according to the plan; an average of four feet as yet to be raised on the foundation walls, laid in good mortar & of the following thicknesses: tower walls three feet 10 inches; sides and ends two feet 7 inches; circular wall two feet; & the partitions two feet. These walls are to be crowned with an eight inch water table all round the building; to have a three inch wash; the walls above the water table as follows: the walls of the tower two feet 4 inches to*

the square, from thence two feet; the side & end walls two feet. Gables one foot six inches; the circular & partition walls two bricks length in thickness. The whole throughout to be laid in good mortar & well grouted. The external angles of the building are to be carried up with quoins of freestone. Header & stretcher alternately, to be one foot eight inches long, 11 1/2 inches wide & 10 1/2 inches in thickness, with the corner chamfered off and sand rubbed, & the face neatly tooled. One rusticated entrance in the front wall of the tower, similar to the doors of Mr. Chesters Church in Chappel Street [Second Presbyterian Church, A12]*; to be seven feet wide in the clear of the jambs, & nine feet high to the top of the impost. There are to be fourteen freestone window frames with plain jambs of 7 by 6 inches; sills 12 by 6 inches; & arches similar to those of M. Gregory's on the west side of the public square* [Congress Hall]. *These frames are to be seven feet 4 inches high, & four feet 1 inch wide in the clear. Sixteen frames with circular head to have imposts, locks & keys, opened in the face; to be seven feet 5 inches by four feet 1 inch in the square. Three sides of the tower walls are to be crowned with freestone: one foot 6 inches wide, & 8 inches in thickness, to project 4 inches; the upper part to be rabbited to correspond with the base of the pedestal of the first section of the steeple. A drip or channel is to be cut underneath & the whole will be cramped together with iron & lead. The entrance doors in front are to be framed in three thicknesses; the outer part composed of stiles, rails & muntins 1 1/4 inch thick, of proportionable width. The second the same, except the margins are to be wider & one inch thick. The inner door with pannels flush on both sides, 1 1/8 inch thick; the whole secured together and mouldings planted into each recess, which will form double sunk pannels. The jambs & soffit to correspond with the doors, to have a proper impost & fan sash over the same; finished plain inside. The doors are to be hung with substantial wrought iron hinges; hooks to have plates &* [be] *well secured with screws & rivets; two large flat sliding bolts suitable for such doors. A ten inch dead lock & the largest size brass thumb latch. Ten windows in the first range are to contain 24 panes of 18 by 10 inch glass, in two casements. Those in the upper range, 24 panes of 14 by 10 inches in the square, also in two casements. The circular head will compose a part of the upper casement. There is to be thirteen windows of this kind. The whole are to have boxed frames, 1 5/8th inch sashes; glazed with good clear glass, and properly hung with cords, pullies & weights. A 3/4th inch quirk oge is to be planted onto the face of the sash frames. The inside will have no finish but plaistering except a seat to each window. There is to be two circular windows in the south gable, two feet 4 inches diameter; to have stone frames 5 by 4 inches; to have green blinds hung with hinges & fastened with buttons. One semi-circular window in the north gable, to have a stone frame of the same size as the head of the gallery windows; to have a sash glaized with glass & so contrived that it may be taken out occasionally, & to be fastened with bolts or buttons. The building is to be surrounded with a neat plain dentel cornice, 11 inches high & 18 inches projection; balance* [of] *which is to be a frieze of 9 inches & an astragal & fillet of 3 inches. The cornice is to be carried up the gable and a pediment formed in the front of the tower. It is also to be continued round the circular wall in the rear. This circular projection is to be roofed with timber planks & stout sheet lead in the most approved manner, and surrounded with a handsome balustrade. The main roof will consist of six pair of principal rafters, with tie beams suspended from the principals, by iron bolts. The two center tie beams will be cut off by an arch in the ceiling, which are to be well secured against spreading by tieing them to the whole beams, by diagonal stays or ties. These two pair of principals are to have collar beams & posts from the inner ends of the tie beams. Intermediate pieces of timber are to be framed into or between the ends of the tie beams to sustain the lower ends of the small rafters, of which there is to be twelve pair, exclusive of those which will extend along each side of the tower. The principals are to be well connected by purlins & braces: principals 10* *by 5; tie beams 11 by 5; purlins 7 by 6; braces in principals 6 by 5; d*[itt]*o in purlins 4 by 3; small rafters 6 by 9 inches; the whole of good sound timber. The roof is to be covered with sound hemlock boards & the best kind of 19 inch white pine shingles, well jointed & nailed; the ridge to be well secured. The exterior walls above the water table are to have a coat of the best plaistering mortar, composed of clean sharp sand, lime, & hair, to be put on as thin as possible & cover the most prominent parts of stone work. After this is sufficiently dried, a finishing coat is to be laid on as thin as may be, composed of clean sand & lime; floated off to an even surface & jointed in to blocks; corresponding with the quoins at the angles. It is hereby expressly understood that* [Geer & Riley] *are to have the first coat of mortar above specified well worked into every crevice of the wall, with the points of the trowels used for that purpose, & that all dry dust and the like shall be washed off clean previous to spreading & working in the mortar as aforesaid. There is to be a door in the center of the circular wall in the rear, 7 feet high, 4 feet 1 inch wide in the clear of the jambs; to have a plain stone frame & sill. The doors in two parts: three pannels in each door to be 1 3/4 inches thick; flush on one side & sunk on the other; to be hung to a plain stile rabbited with a 3/4th bead between the door & stone frame; hung with 5 inch butts; to have suitable bolts & strong thumb latch. Steps and railing to the yard between 4 & five feet high. Above this door is to be placed in the wall a freestone tablet, 4 feet long, 2 feet 8 inches wide, with an inscription engraven thereon, as shall hereafter be directed by the said parties of the first part. The first section of the steeple* [is to be] *rectangular, encompassed by eight Doric Columns of one foot 8 inches in diameter, so disposed as to admit of five trigliphs in each front. The entablature & pedestal are to continue strait over each pair of columns and return into the body of the steeple, which is to be nine feet 8 inches square; in which is to be four circular headed windows, nine feet 6 inches high & five feet wide in the square; to have moulded imposts, architraves, & opened keys, and soffits one foot wide. The piers & jambs are to be rusticated in a bold style. This section will be about twenty one feet in heighth. The second section is to be also rectangular of the Ionic Order; to have eight columns one foot 3 inches diameter; 11 modillions on each front & 3 on each return. The entablature will break over each pair of columns, as in the order below, but each column will have its separate pedestal. The body of this section is to be seven feet 1 inch square; with a window in each front, 7 feet 10 inches high & 3 feet 6 inches in the square with circular heads finished as described in the first section, except that the jambs and soffits will be ten inches wide & plain. This section is to be 17 feet high. The third section is to be octangular; to have double trusses on four sides, & deep double sunk pannels on the other four faces, over the windows below. The body of this section is to be 4 feet 8 inches diameter & about twelve feet in heighth; the top to be* [surrounded] *with a plain bold cornice, and a well shaped Vase placed over each pair of trusses. The fourth section to be about Seven or eight feet high, four feet 8 inches at* [the] *bottom & one foot 4 inches at* [the] *top; to have a double plinth at bottom & an astragal at top; & cased off with a faint cove. In this section is to be a post to receive the spindle, to be banded with iron under the astragal. The spindle is to be 11 feet long to the vane to enter the post one foot; to have a collar wielded on at the head of the post. A ball of double tin gilt is to be placed on the spindle 30 inches above the head of the post, and the spine to be cased off from the astragal to the ball with a faint cove. The spindle is to be two inches square to the ball, and to taper from thence to one inch; to have light scroll work between the ball & vane, which represents a Comet, surmounted by a tulip; both of which are to be gilt, as also the points in the Scroll work; the rest painted black. The top of each section is to have a good slope; to be covered with tin soldered. All the wood work of the finishing of this steeple is to be well seasoned, & put together with white lead in the joints, and painted with two coats of good white lead ground in oil, free from any mixture of chalk, whiting, or the like; to have a mixture of any other colour which shall be directed by the* [Trustees of the Church] *and well sanded with clean, course sand as the last coat of paint is laid on; the windows excepted which are to have green blinds. The two first sections are to be floored similar to those in M[r] Chesters Church aforesaid. Step ladders are to communicate to the third section of the steeple. A moveable shutter is to be made in on*[e] *of the pannels of this section. The frame composing the body of this steeple is to consist of four posts . . . 56 feet long 10 inches square at bottom & 7 inches at top; to be united by six tier of interties, well braced. This frame will form a square of 11 feet at bottom & 5 feet at the top; the bottom of the posts to rest on diagonal piers of sound yellow pine across the angles of the tower walls; locked onto pieces of* [bond?] *timber six inches square; laid in the center of the wall & locked, or halved together at the angles. Triangular pieces of masonry is to be projected in the angles of the tower wall to support the diagonal pieces aforesaid; the upper sections to be secured to the top of the aforesaid principal frame. The ground floor of the church is to be well timbered, that is to say, timber of suitable proportions according to the bearings; Sound, free from blue or decayed sap & rotten knots. The floor of the aisles are to be laid with narrow planks; those of the tower & stair cases of common width, plained, tongued & grooved & well nailed. The floors of the pews are to be laid with white pine of common width planed, tongued and grooved & those before mentioned of yellow pine. The floors of the pews are to be raised four inches above the floor of the aisles. The flooring in the gallery is to be the same as the pews below. The gallery joists are to be 6 by 4 inches, two feet from centre to Centre with a firring between, with brackets raised thereon to elevate the seats one foot above another. The gallery beams are to be 10 by 7 inches into which the joists are to be framed at one end & the other is to be framed with dovetailed tenons into plates built in the walls for that purpose. The gallery beams are to be supported by two small columns & four posts of one foot square, which are to extend to the roof and assist in supporting the same. These posts are to be sustained by stone piers well sunk in the ground to be at least five feet square at their base, & diminished upwards. A sufficient number of small piers are also to be erected to support the ground floor of said church. Around the four posts above described, four Corinthian columns are to be formed, nineteen feet 6 inches in heighth including the base & capital, raised on sub plinths equal in height to the capping of the piers. The shafts are to be fluted, the bases well wrought, & the capitals executed in a masterly style, the whole of well seasoned & suitable timber. From the top of these four columns, four elliptical arches are to be raised, with rough firrings four feet 9 inches high, and the angles formed by these four arches are to be firred out in spandrils drawn from a common Centre so that, at the summit of the arches, a perfect circle will be formed. From this it is to be firred upright to the height of two feet with brackets in the upper part to form a Cornice. Above this is to be formed a concave ceiling to rise about five feet, in the centre of which is to be formed a handsome centre piece with stems & foliage in stocco, with a fixture for suspending a chandelier. In the spandrils aforesaid are to be sunk triangular pannels in a bold style, double without mouldings over against those four elliptical arches, already described. Four other arches equal & similar are to be formed on the opposite walls to project 4 inches in the soffit, to be supported by four rich wrought trusses of proportionate size. Eight other arches are to be formed at right angles with those before mentioned from the said columns to the walls, and the angles formed by these and the other arches are to be firred out in spandrils generating into elipsis' at the ceiling, which is to be horizontal. The four arches in the angles of the ceiling are to be groin*[e]*d & supported by four quarter trusses. A neat stocco cornice is to be run round at the base of the upper concave ceiling already specified. Two Corinthian pilasters are to be formed corresponding with the columns aforesaid, on the angles formed by the circular recess in the rear, the abacus of which is to be run round the circle in stocco as a small cornice or foot moulding, to an eliptical arched ceiling, coinciding with the arch in the rear wall. The circular heads of the windows will break into this ceiling, over which proper groins are to be formed, and the moulding returned against the wall. There are to be two other trusses on the south wall making in all for the support of the ceiling four column capitals, two pilasters* [capitals] *six full & four quarter trusses. All the plaistering is to be done in the best plain manner; the ceilings white & the walls hard finish, including the first story of the tower & the stair cases to the galleries. The soffits of the arches are to be sunk 1 1/4 inches without mouldings, having a margin of about 5 inches on each side. Their width will be equal to the neck of the columns. The gallery stairs are to be close work handrail height, & capped. Steps of pitch or yellow pine. There is to be four inside Six panneled doors, Seven feet high 3 1/2 feet wide 1 3/4 inches thick— to have framed jambs— and double faced architraves to two & single faced to the other two— to be hung with suitable hinges & furnished with Large Knob latches. The pulpit is to be placed in a concave surface against the tower wall, to be encompassed by an arch of 12 feet cord, Supported by pilasters, 15 feet high, including base & capital, which are to be ornamented with leaves— the shafts one foot 6 inches wide, to be opened or fluted. The arch will consist of a well-moulded architrave and key. The pulpit to have a commode front with pilasters in the angles; the front and ends panneled, to have a handsome base & cornice* [illegible passage struck by Hooker]. *The body of the pulpit is to be supported by two antique Ionic Columns in front, one under each angle & two pilasters in the rear— the reading desk is to have a swelled front with pilasters on the angles and a neat base and cap. A neat circular winding Stair case is to be carried up to the pulpit, with mahogany handrails & Balusters. The outside rail is to be continued round to enclose an oval space of 15 by 10 feet— which is to be raised 6 inches above the floor of the aisle— and a wicket is to be made in said railing at the bottom to the pulpit stairs on the most approved plan. There is to be thirty pews Seven feet 2 inches long & twenty eight pews 8 feet 8 inches long & 2 feet 4 inches wide— & four oblong Square pews about 6 feet on the ground floor. The whole to be finished in a similar style to those in Mr Chesters Church aforesaid. Except that, the Capping is to be cherry wood instead of mahogany. The gallery will have twelve pews of 10 feet, & six of 6 1/2 feet, & four circular seats— and a seat or bench to be extended all along the walls in the aisle of the gallery, Supported by brackets nailed to the walls. The gallery front is to be panneled in a neat bold style & instead of a cornice on the lower part— to have a run of neat fret work to be finished with a handsome capping. The gallery beams between the columns is to be supported* [by lining the] *gallery front herring bone with stout plank and strapping the beams to the lining in the middle & to be well secured. All the inside wood work is to be painted in a style Equal and Similar to Mr Chester's Church before mentioned. The outside Cornice & balustrade is to be painted & sanded like the Steeple.* [Illegible passage struck by Hooker.] *All the joiners work is to be done with well Seasoned wood and the whole of the Building is to be finished in all its parts in a Substantial & workmanlike manner. The Stone walls are to be regularly carried up, so that they shall settle as Equally as possible— and the Building is to be enclosed on or before the first day of December in the year One thousand eight hundred and Seventeen, & to be completed in all its parts, on or before the first day of July in the year, one thousand eight hundred & eighteen. The Steps to the front entrance excepted, which are not included in this Contract. . . . that the work & materials shall be subject to the inspection of Philip Hooker of Said City (who is to furnish the said parties with a regular set of plans to work by) or such other person as shall be appointed for that purpose by the* [Trustees of the Church]. . . . *The* [Trustees of the Church] *do hereby, for themselves & their successors in office— promise & agree to pay* . . . [Geer & Riley] . . . *Fourteen thousand nine hundred & ninety dollars. . . .*[7]

1. First Lutheran Church (hereafter FLC) Council Minutes, 14 February 1816, Archives, First Lutheran Church, Albany, N.Y. (hereafter A FLC).
2. Root, p. 148.
3. FLC Council Minutes, 21 October 1816.
4. Building Costs Account Book, A FLC.
5. Box A2, Folder 2, Collection, A FLC.
6. FLC Council Minutes, 28 November 1816.
7. Box A2, Folder 2, Collection, A FLC.

A photograph taken before the church was demolished in 1868 documents the exterior appearance and verifies that the contract was followed fairly closely.[8] Supporting information about the form of the building is provided by an early woodcut (fig. 90). As depicted, the top stage of the steeple follows Hooker's design for the cupola of the Lancaster School (fig. 68), with its attenuated scroll trusses, urns, and octagonal paneled core.

The sanctuary, for which no visual documentation has survived, is vividly described in the contract. From this we learn that the columns and the ceiling of the church received similar treatment to the sanctuary of Hooker's South Dutch Reformed Church (cat. 18) in which the roof and galleries were supported by a colossal order of Corinthian columns engaged to the face of the galleries. Here also elliptical arches intersected a flat plane to create a space which was at once divided into cells and unified as a whole. The major difference between these two examples is that in its central bay the Lutheran Ebenezer Church featured a domical ceiling punctuated by a large chandelier. This focus could only have been partially successful, however, since the placement of the apse and pulpit and the location of the galleries along the side walls would have created a strong linear spatial emphasis.

Geer and Riley apparently had trouble getting paid for their work, and in April 1818 they petitioned the city to require the church council to fulfill their part of the contract.[9] By 14 August 1818, when the church appears to have been completed, the builders received final payment on their contract.[10]

Structural problems plagued the building in later years, and the tower of the church leaned considerably. These problems were probably caused by the lowering of the surrounding grade, which exposed the building's foundation. St. Peter's (cat. 6), located two blocks to the south, was subjected to the same regrading and suffered a similar fate.[11] ✣

8. For a photograph, see Henry H. Heins, *Swan of Albany: A History of the Oldest Congregation of the Lutheran Church in America* (Albany: First Lutheran Church, 1976), p. 77.

9. Collection, Douglas G. Bucher.

10. Box A2, Folder 2, Collection, A FLC.

11. Root, p. 148.

38. *COTTAGE* FOR GEORGE CLARKE

Springfield, Otsego County, N.Y.
Designed before 30 July 1817.
Built 1817–22; extant as part of Hyde Hall.
Builders: Joseph Woodhouse, Enoch Sill, and Cyrenus Clark.
Mason: Isaac Smith.

While George Clarke had obtained plans for a house in Albany from Hooker in 1816 (cat. 36), he may have abandoned that project by the time he decided to build a country residence. On 3 May 1817, Clarke bought 340 acres in Springfield, Otsego County. Hooker's design for what he would later refer to as a *cottage* was likely prepared after that date but before 30 July, when Clarke contracted for the building of *a dwelling house according to a Plan or diagram drawn by Mr. Hooker, reference being thereunto had.*[1]

Construction of this project, which would be the first stage in a campaign that continued until 1835 and resulted in Hyde Hall, was well under way by 5 October 1817, when Hooker billed Clarke for *a plan of* [a] *Venetian window, bill of timber & sketch of framing & other plans,* for which he charged *$10.00.*[2] Before the *cottage* could be completed, however, the plans for this comparatively modest structure were altered to fit into a larger scheme for which Hooker would present drawings in January 1818 (cat. 39). Early indications of that amplified project are found in several undated drawings which may be the subjects of the October 1817 bill.

The *Plan & Elevation on the room side of a Venetian Window, for Mr. Clarkes Back room* (fig. 91) seems to predate the expanded plan, while the framing drawings that accompany the *bill of timber for Mr. Clarke's offices &c* and for a wood house (fig. 92) depict the added kitchen wing which would house various domestic offices.

A bill of timber for Mr. Clarke's offices &c—

4 sills–hemlock	*29 feet long*	*10 by 8* [inches]	*hewn*
2 [sills–hemlock]	*35 feet*	*10* [by] *8* [inches]	
6 Posts–oak	*16 feet*	*8* [by] *8* [inches]	
2 [Posts–oak]	*9 feet*	*8* [by] *8* [inches]	
2 Plates–ash	*38 feet*	*8* [by] *5* [inches]	
1 [Plate–ash]	*35* [feet]	*8* [by] *5* [inches]	
60 Beams hem[lock]	*18* [feet]	*10* [by] *4* [inches]	*mill*[ed]
6 interties–oak	*18* [feet]	*8* [by] *4* [inches]	
54 Rafters–hem[lock]	*20* [feet]	*6* [by] *4* [inches]	
20 Collar beams–[hemlock]	*25* [feet]	*8* [by] *4* [inches]	

150 pieces 14 feet, 4 by 3 hemlock studs & braces

Wood House

1 Sill hemlock	*30 feet*	*9 by 7* [inches]	*hewn*
2 [Sills hemlock]	*10* [feet]	*9* [by] *7* [inches]	
4 Posts–oak	*12 feet*	*6* [by] *6* [inches]	
4 [Posts–oak]	*8* [feet]	*6* [by] *6* [inches]	
2 Plates ash	*30 feet*	*7* [by] *4* [inches]	
4 tie beams	*10 feet*	*6* [by] *4* [inches]	
16 Studs	*8* [feet]	*4* [by] *3* [inches][3]	

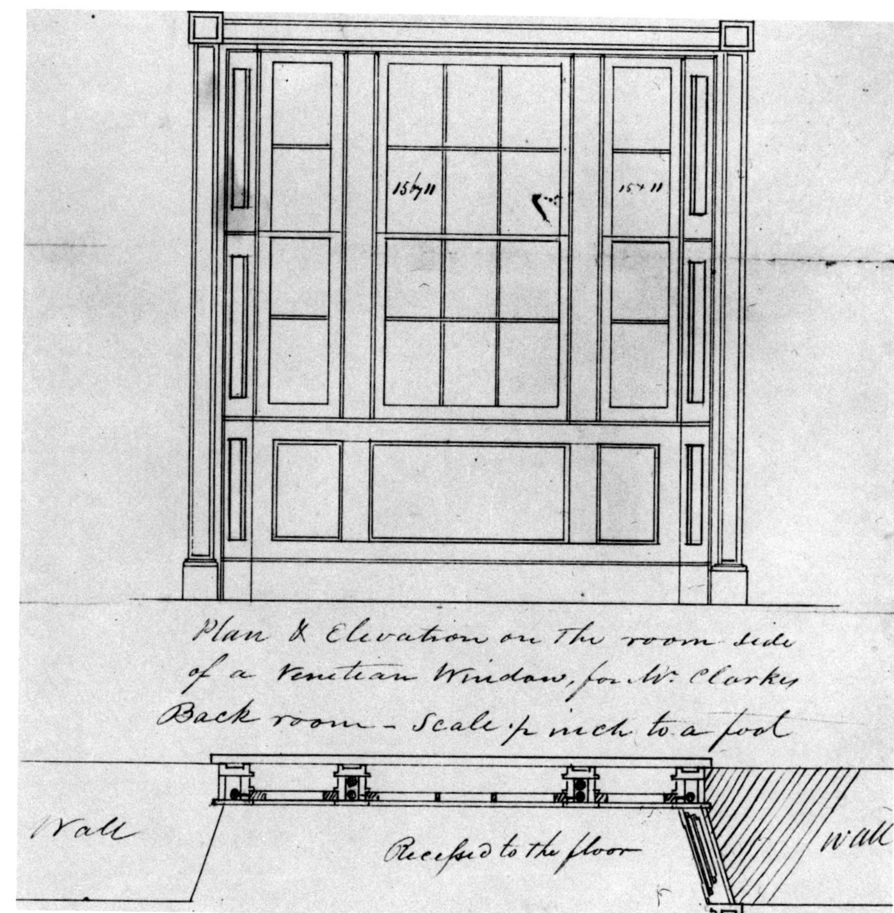

▶
Fig. 91. George Clarke *Cottage*, Hyde Hall, Springfield, N.Y., Hooker's plan and elevation of a *Venetian Window*, 1817. Ink on paper. Cornell University, Ithaca, N.Y., Olin Library, Department of Manuscripts and University Archives.

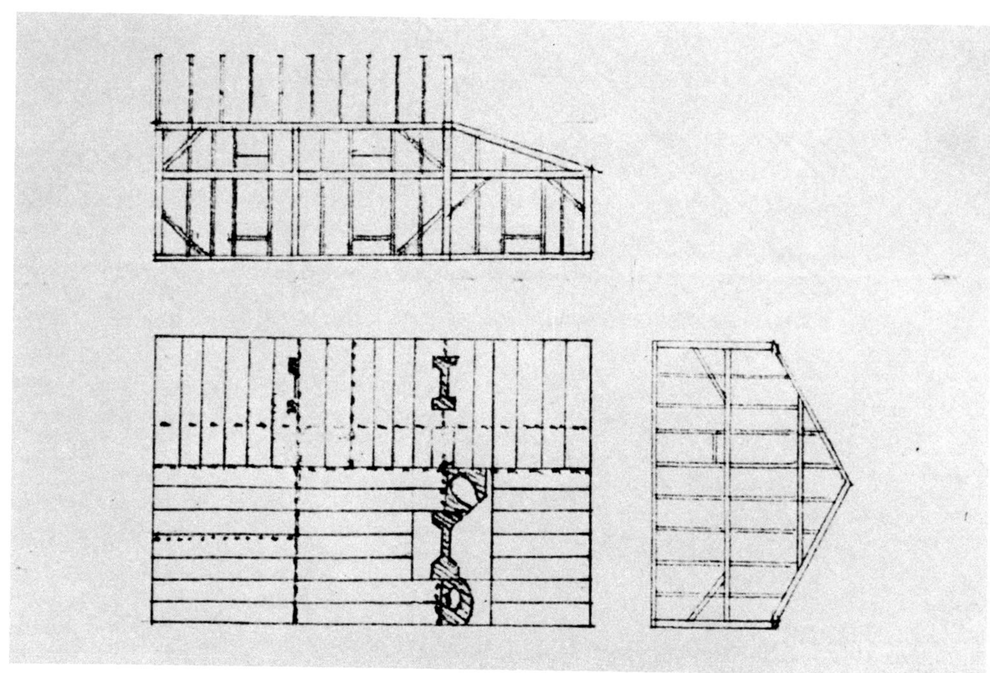

▶
Fig. 92. George Clarke *Cottage*, Hyde Hall, Springfield, N.Y., Hooker's drawing of timber framing for the kitchen wing, or domestic offices, 1817. Ink on paper. Friends of Hyde Hall, Inc. and Cornell University, Ithaca, N.Y., Olin Library, Department of Manuscripts and University Archives.

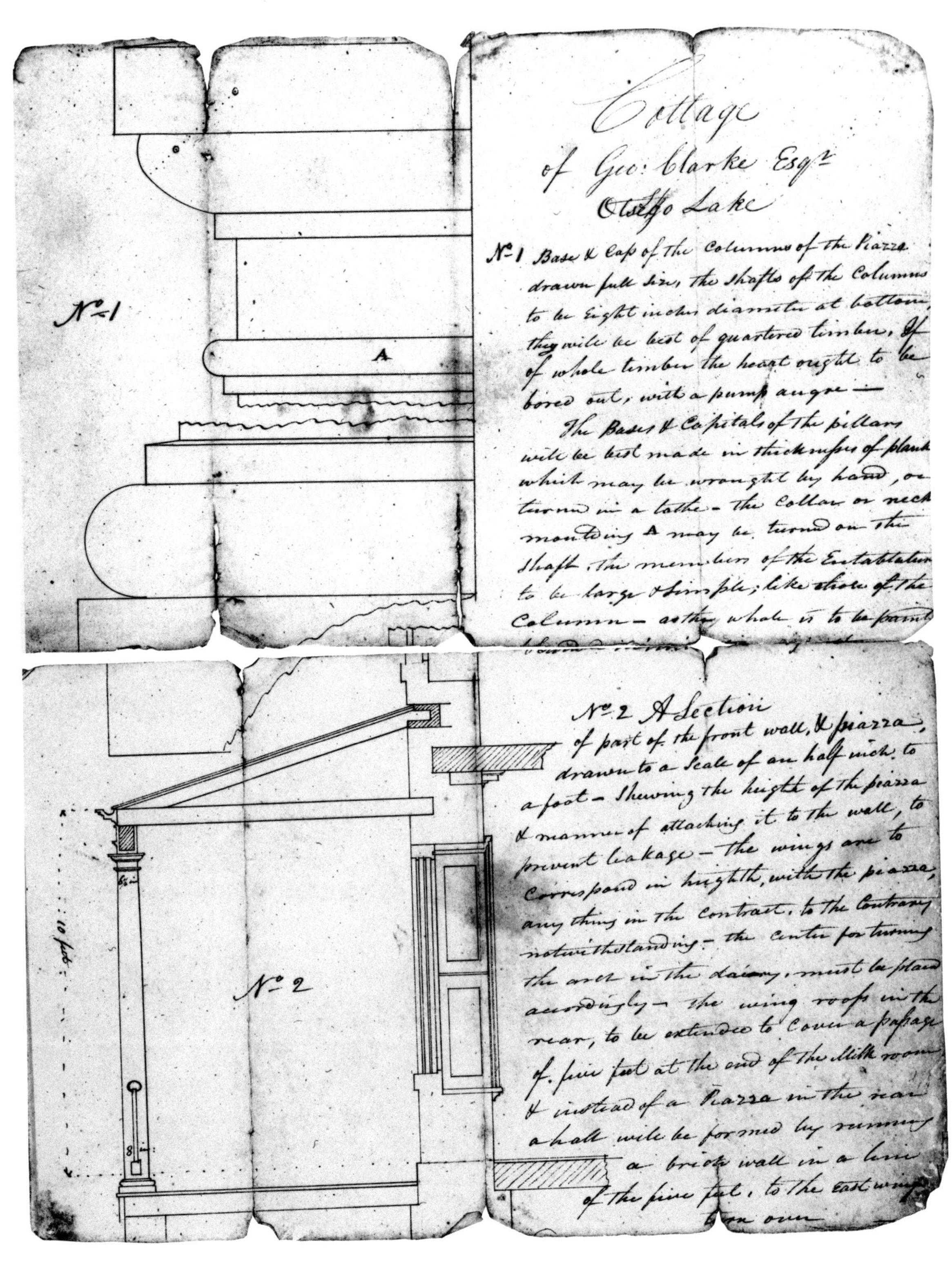

▲
Fig. 93. George Clarke *Cottage*, Hyde Hall, Springfield, N.Y., Hooker's drawing of the base and cap of the piazza columns, and his section through the front wall and piazza, 1817. Ink on paper. Photograph courtesy Friends of Hyde Hall, Inc.

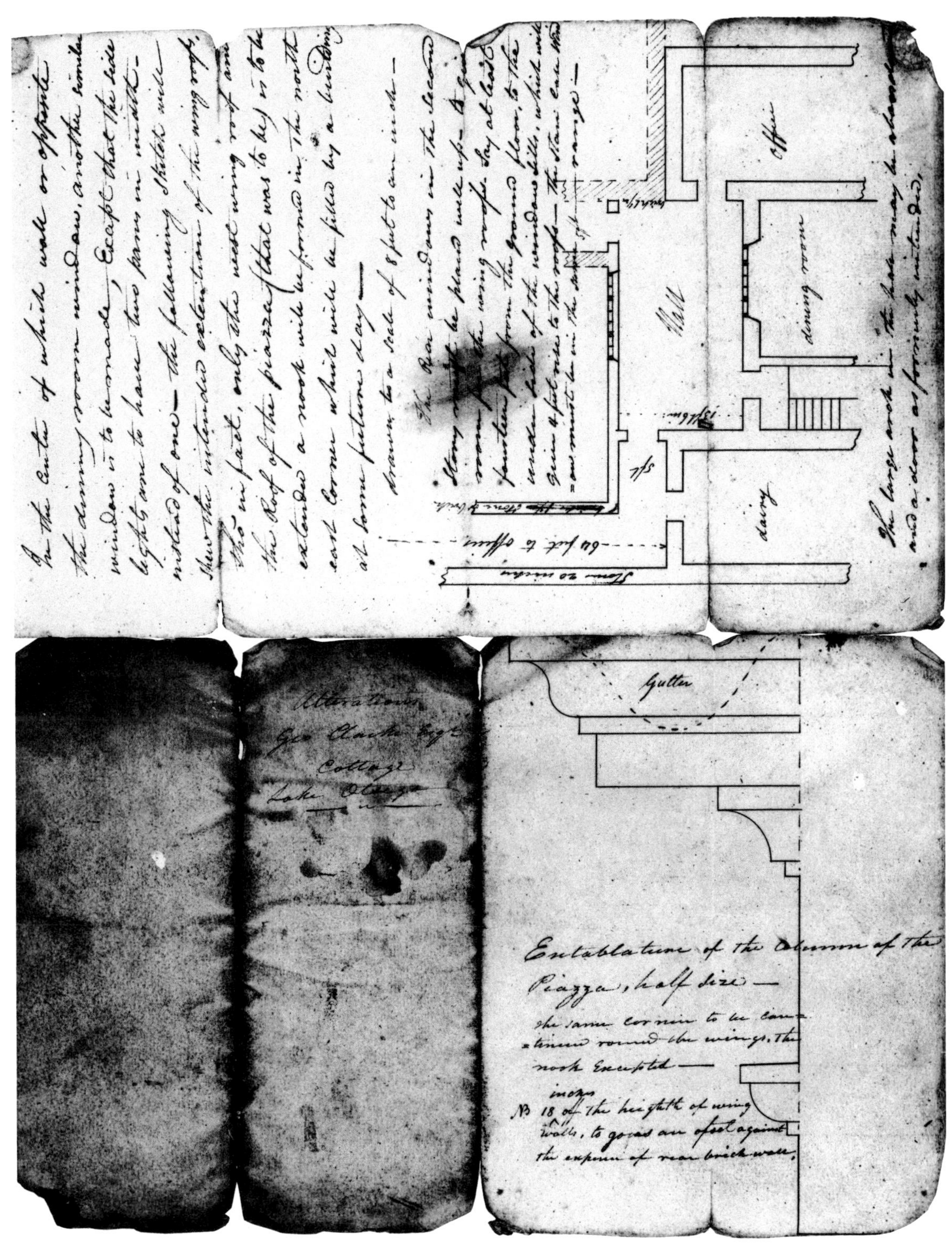

▲
Fig. 94. George Clarke *Cottage*, Hyde Hall, Springfield, N.Y., Hooker's drawings of a portion of the first floor plan, showing alterations and additions, and of the piazza entablature (the verso of fig. 93), 1817.
Ink on paper. Photograph courtesy Friends of Hyde Hall, Inc.

More informative about the character of the initial building and the nascent changes in the project were the drawings labeled *Cottage of Geo: Clarke Esqr Otsego Lake* (figs. 93, 94), which could be the *other plans* billed to Clarke in October 1817.

> *N° 1 Base & Cap of the columns of the Piazza drawn full size, the shafts of the columns to be Eight inches diameter at bottom. They will be best of quartered timber. If of whole timber, the heart ought to be bored out, with a pump augre—*
>
> *The Bases & Capitals of the pillars will be best made in thicknesses of plank which may be wrought by hand, or turned in a lathe. The Collar or neck mounting* **A** *may be turned on the shaft, the members of the entablature to be large & simple, like those of the column— as the whole is to be painted and sanded in imitation of stone.*
>
> *N° 2 A Section of part of the front wall, & piazza drawn to a scale of an half inch to a foot— showing the height of the piazza & manner of attaching it to the wall, to prevent leakage— the wings are to correspond in heighth, with the piazza, anything in the contract, to the contrary notwithstanding— the center for turning the arch in the dairy, must be placed accordingly— the wing roofs in the rear, to be extended to cover a passage of five feet at the end of the Milk room & instead of a Piazza in the rear a hall will be formed by running a brick wall in a line of the five feet, to the East wing In the Center of which wall or opposite the dining room windows, another similar window is to be made, Except that the side lights are to have two panes in width— instead of one— the following sketch will show the intended extention of the wing roofs, tho' in fact, only the west wing roof and the Roof of the piazza (that was to be) is to be extended. A nook will be formed in the north east corner which will be filled by a building at some future day—*
>
> *The Rear windows in the second story must be placed well up to give room for the wing roofs— Say at least fourteen feet from the ground floor to the under side of the window sills, which will give 4 feet rise to the roofs— the stair case window must be in the same range.*
>
> *The large arch in the hall may be abandoned and a door as formerly intended.*
>
> *Entablature of the Column of the Piazza, half size—*
>
> *the same cornice to be continued round the wings, the nook excepted—*
>
> *N.B. 18 inches off the heighth of wing walls, to go as an ofset against the expense of rear brick walls.*[4]

Although this plan (fig. 94) and the drawings of January 1818 (figs. 95-98) depict an expanded *cottage,* the latter identifying altered room uses, they do provide a sense of that building as it must have been initially conceived. Known to workmen as the *Stone House* for its ashlar limestone walls,[5] the *cottage's* simple hip-roofed, two-story central block had a broad front piazza that wrapped around the sides to meet one-story wings. Small oval windows, typical of Hooker's work of the period, were placed over the wings. A rear porch was intended between the wings, just outside the *Venetian Window* detailed by Hooker. In the expanded scheme, this porch would be enclosed to form a hall, an indoor link between the original *cottage* and passages to the domestic offices and to the projected main house or east wing. The intended dairy would become a dressing room, the laundry would be turned into an office, and the central rooms on the first story into libraries, all part of a more gracious country residence.[6] ✤

1. George Hyde Clarke Papers, Coll. 2800, Department of Manuscripts and University Archives, Olin Library, Cornell University, Ithaca, N.Y. Clarke would continue to rent a house in Albany until spring 1819, when he moved to his new Otsego County residence.
2. Ibid. It is not known when the billed drawings had been provided.
3. Ibid. This wing would be altered in the January 1818 plans.
4. Ibid.
5. Ibid.
6. Douglas R. Kent, "Hyde Hall: America's Greatest Country House," *Newsletter: Preservation League of New York State,* XII, 4 (Fall 1986), 4. The laundry has already been identified as an office in the drawing illustrated in fig. 94.

39. COUNTRY SEAT FOR GEORGE CLARKE (HYDE HALL)

Springfield, Otsego County, N.Y.
Initial design from before 5 October 1817 to 25 January 1818.
Built 1818–35; extant.
Carpenter: Cyrenus Clark.
Masons: Isaac Smith and Lorenzo Bates.

The *cottage* (cat. 38) that George Clarke had begun in 1817 from Hooker's plans was enlarged and otherwise altered during construction to facilitate its incorporation into a more extensive project for a country residence. The later scheme, which guided a prolonged building campaign, is represented by a bound set of drawings, lists of materials, and specifications (figs. 95–105), and bears the following inscription:

Plans Designed by George Clarke Esquire.
for his Country residence,
North end of Lake Otsego.
Drawn by P, Hooker, Albany 25th Jan[uar]*y 1818.*[1]

The roles of client and architect here were probably similar to those assumed in the earlier planning of the Albany house (cat. 36), with Clarke making suggestions and directing Hooker to favored design sources. Hooker would then have assimilated this information to produce the final design.

▶
Fig. 95. Hyde Hall, Springfield, N.Y., Hooker's elevation of the front to the lake, or the south front (the *cottage* side), 1818. Ink and wash on paper, bound. Photograph courtesy Friends of Hyde Hall, Inc.

▲
Fig. 96. Hyde Hall, Springfield, N.Y., Hooker's elevation of the east front (the *Great House* side), 1818. Ink and wash on paper, bound. Photograph courtesy Friends of Hyde Hall, Inc.

The drawings provided by Hooker are accompanied by the following text:

> *This front* [fig. 95] *commands a full view of the lake, and the handsome village of* [*Utica*—Hooker's strike] *Cooperstown, situate on its southern extremity, a distance of about eight miles. The eastern shore of the lake is some what indented, forming here & there a bold bluff, with intervening inclinations in the most picturesque style; while the western shore rises in more gentle acclivities, which are under a good state of Cultivation, with the exception of here & there a promontory to diversify the scene. This forms a pleasing Contrast to the wild Luxuriance of the opposite Shore. It seems as tho' nature had formed this for an agreeable place of retirement.*

> *This front* [fig. 96] *commands a view of the north east end of the lake and a rich vale extending several miles, through which, Mill Creek takes a devious course, beyond which are hanging farms backed by a Picturesque ridge clothed with forest trees. The cultivated part of Mr. Clarke's grounds lies in this direction. This front extends ninety seven feet and tho' plain will have a good appearance at a distance, from which it will generally be viewed. The offices, which appear on either side in the drawing, are to be screened by planting, elevated ground, clothed with a thick hanging wood, will form the background, and a screen from the north west winds.*

Plans follow the elevations, with references:

References [Plan of the Principal floor, fig. 97]

a	*Hall*	*24*	*by*	*18 feet*
b	*Dining room*	*36*	[by]	*24 feet*
c	*With drawing room*	*36*	[by]	*24 feet*

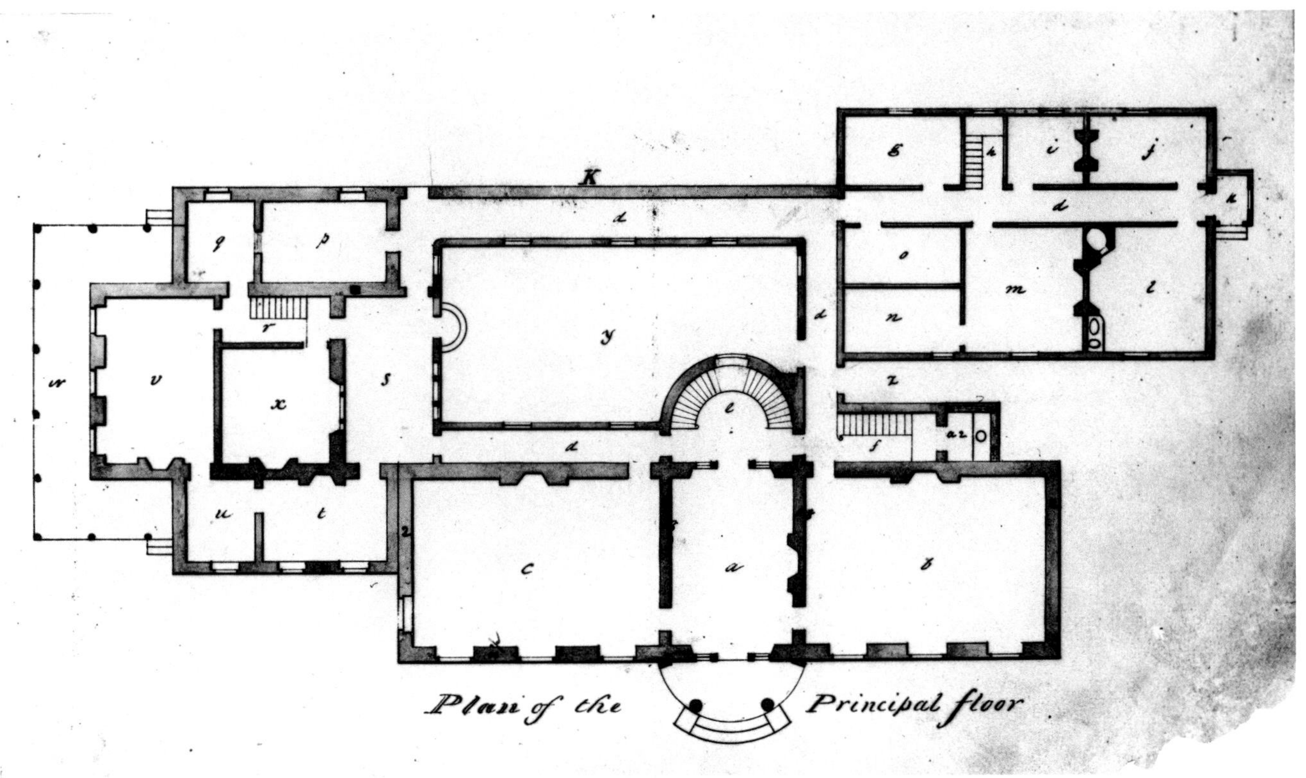

▲
Fig. 97. Hyde Hall, Springfield, N.Y., Hooker's plan of the principal, or first, floor, 1818. Ink and wash on paper, bound. Photograph courtesy Friends of Hyde Hall, Inc.

d	*Corridors, or passages*		*5 feet*
e	*Grand stair case*		~~ [by] ~~
f	*back Stairs*		~~ [by] ~~
g	*house keepers room*	<u>*stove*</u>	*17* [by] *12* [feet]
h	*Stair case*		*12 1/2* [by] *6 1/2* [feet]
i	*Butlers pantry*		*12* [by] *11 1/2* [feet]
[j]	*Laundry*		*18* [by] *12* [feet]
[k]	*Portall*		*7* [by] *5* [feet]
[l]	*bake & brew house*		*18* [by] *18* [feet]
[y]	*Court*		*53* [by] *25* [feet]
m	*Kitchen*		*18 by 18 feet*
n	*pantry*		*17* [by] *9 1/2* [feet]
o	*Larder*		*17* [by] *7* [feet]
p	*Milk room*		*18* [by] *12* [feet]
q	*Vault*		*12* [by] *10* [feet]
r	*Stairs*		*17* [by] *6 1/2* [feet]
s	*Anti Chamber*		*24* [by] *13 1/2* [feet]
t	*Office*		*18* [by] *12* [feet]
u	*bed room*		*12* [by] *10* [feet]
v	*library*		*24* [by] *16* [feet]
w	*piazza*		*8 1/2 feet*
x	*breakfast room*		*17* [by] *17* [feet]
z.	*back Entrance*		~~ ~~
	a2— water closet		

[Wall K to] *be the heighth of the walls of the milk room, & the passage "d", to be covered with* [a roof slop]*ing into the court, the windows semi circular, placed near the ceiling.*

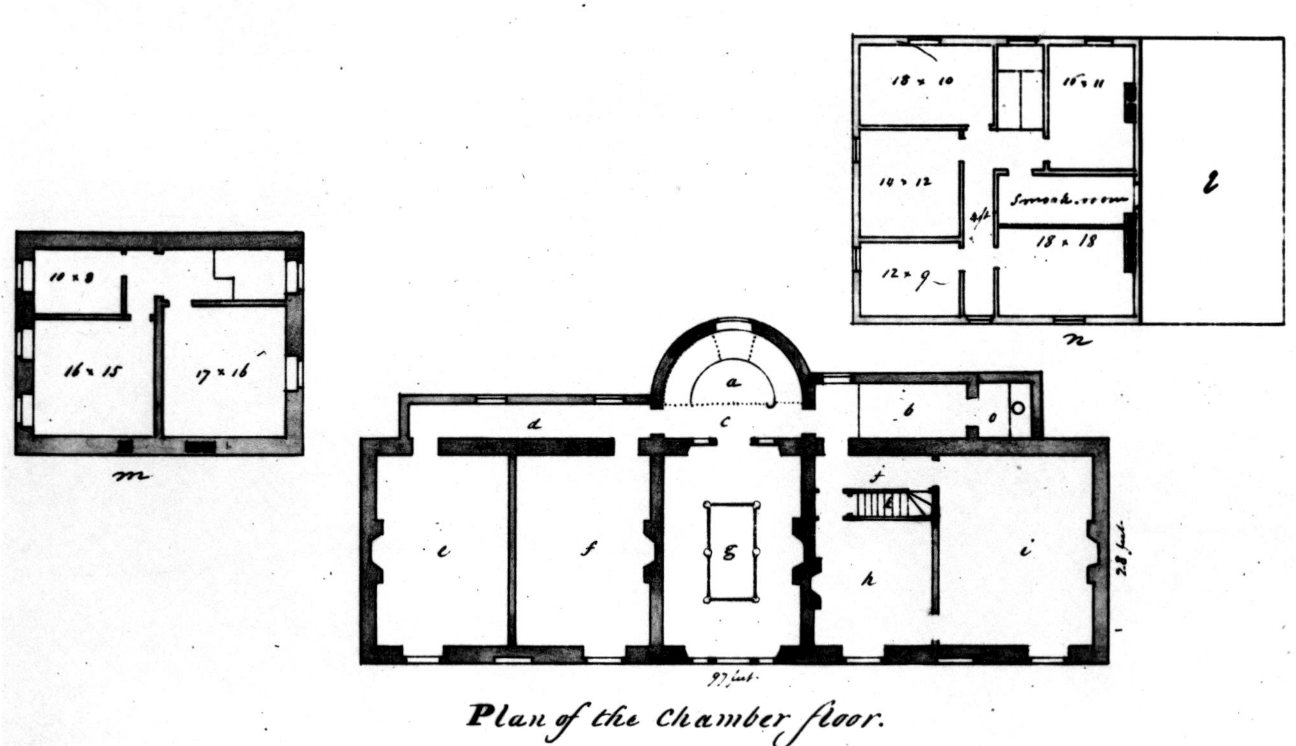

▲
Fig. 98. Hyde Hall, Springfield, N.Y., Hooker's plan of the chamber, or second, floor, 1818. Ink and wash on paper, bound. Photograph courtesy Friends of Hyde Hall, Inc.

References [Plan of the Chamber floor, fig. 98]

a	*Grand stairs*	
b	*back* [stairs]	
c	*Landing*	*5 feet*
d	*passage*	*5* [feet]
e	*bed chamber*	*24* [by] *17 3/4* [feet]
f	[bed chamber]	*24* [by] *17 3/4* [feet]
g	*Billiard room*	*24* [by] *18* [feet]
h	*dressing room*	*16* [by] *15* [feet]
i	*Bed Chamber*	*24* [by] *20* [feet]
j	*passage*	*4 feet*
k	*Garret stairs*	*3* [feet]
l	*Roof of brew house and laundry*	
m	*Bed chambers over library &c*	
n	[Bed chambers] *over offices*	
o	*Water closet.*	

A plan of the cellars is also provided (fig. 99). The documents conclude with detail drawings (figs. 101–5), a section (fig. 100), and a materials list. The text accompanying the section is as follows:

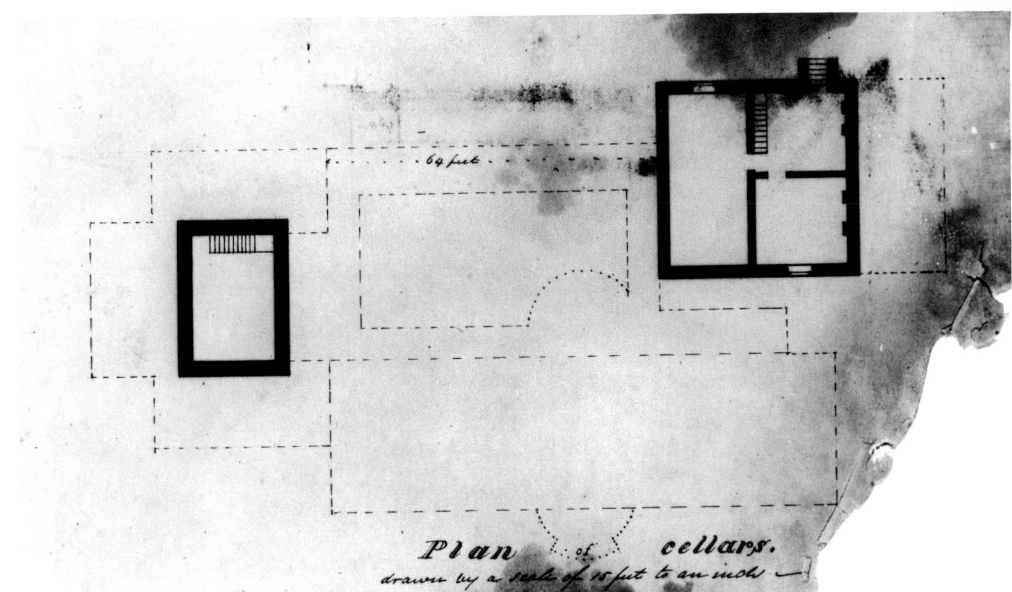

Fig. 99. Hyde Hall, Springfield, N.Y., Hooker's plan of the cellars, 1818. Ink and wash on paper, bound.

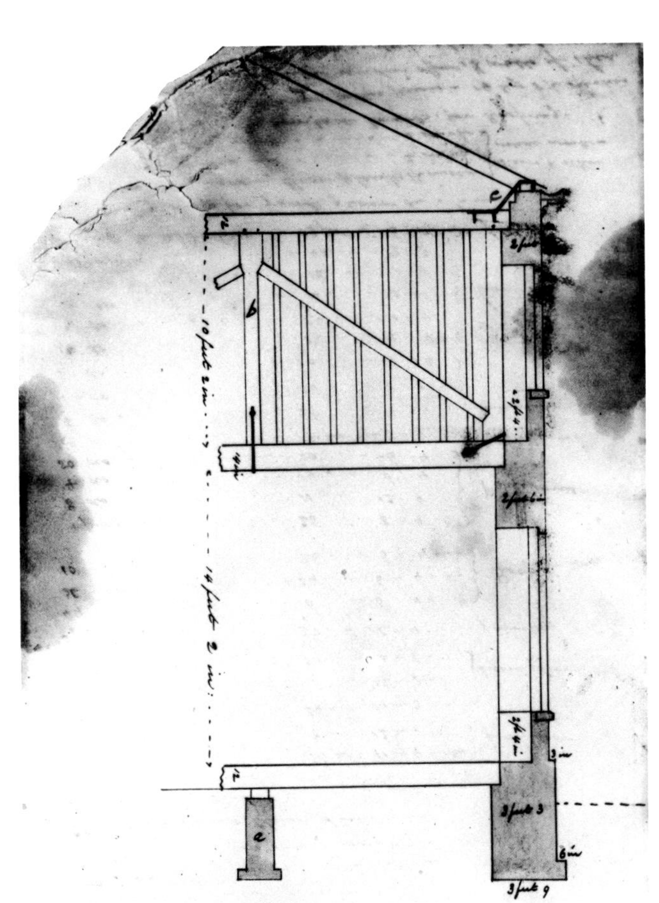

Fig. 100. Hooker's section, taken through the east wing, 1818. Ink on paper, bound. Photographs courtesy Friends of Hyde Hall, Inc.

Section of the Building 1/4th inch to a foot [fig. 100]

Front & rear walls of 1st Story	*2 feet 6 in*
[Front & rear walls] *in 2nd story, & end walls*	2 [feet] *0—*
First floor to be supported by a wall	*a.*
Truss partition 2nd story	*b.*
Anchors to wall plate 12 feet apart	*c.*
Hall Partitions 18 inches thick	

And the materials list:

Materials for the large building

1833 loads of stone
2962 bush[els] *slacked lime*
55,000 bricks for chimnies & partitions
12 tierces Rhode Island lime
25 bushels boiled plaister
16,000 split laths
30 Bushels of good dry hair
320 loads sharp, clean sand
37 squares of slates

50	*floor joist*	*24 feet, 11 by 4 inches*	*first floor*
24	[floor joists]	*18* [feet], *12 by 4* [inches]	
72	[floor joists]	*25* [feet], *14 by 3* [inches]	*second floor*
28	[floor joists]	*19* [feet], *12* [by] *3* [inches]	
1	[floor joist]	*20* [feet], *12* [by] *8* [inches]	
37	[floor joists]	*27* [feet], *12* [by] *4* [inches]	*garret*
44	*Rafters*	*16* [feet], *6* [by] *4* [inches]	*roof*
38	[Rafters]	*24* [feet], *6* [by] *4* [inches]	
10	[Rafters]	*26* [feet], *6* [by] *4* [inches]	
4	*pieces*	*25* [feet], *8* [by] *4* [inches]	*partitions*
8	[pieces]	*11* [feet], *12* [by] *4* [inches]	
4	[pieces]	*14* [feet], *6* [by] *4* [inches]	
50	[pieces]	*10* [feet], *6* [by] *4* [inches]	
20	[pieces]	*12 two lengths 7* [by] *4* [inches]	*passage floors*
8	[pieces]	*25* [feet], *8* [by] *4* [inches]	*wall plates*
1	[piece]	*34* [feet], *8* [by] *4* [inches]	
1	[piece]	*30* [feet], *8* [by] *4* [inches]	
14	[pieces]	*5 1/2* [feet], *12* [by] *4* [inches]	*lintals*
14	[pieces]	*5 1/2* [feet], *10* [by] *4* [inches]	
4	[pieces]	*14* [feet], *12* [by] *6* [inches]	
4	[pieces]	*12* [feet], *10* [by] *6* [inches]	
14	[pieces]	*4 1/2* [feet], *12* [by] *3* [inches]	

[missing passage] [pieces] *clean battins* *13 feet, 6* [by] *1 1/2 in*[ch] *floor*
[missing passage] . . . *: planks for garrett floor &c*
[missing passage] *board measure. clear planks* *1 1/2 inch* — *stairs, & other inside work*
[missing passage] . . . [measure. clear planks] *2 inch*
[missing passage] . . . [measure. clear planks] *1 inch*
[missing passage] . . . *: 1 1/8th inch hemlock boards, for roofing*
[missing passage] . . . *white pine gutter pieces—14 by 5 1/2 inches*
[missing passage] *for cellar under offices, & walls of the*
[missing passage] *to the same— will be about 350 loads—*

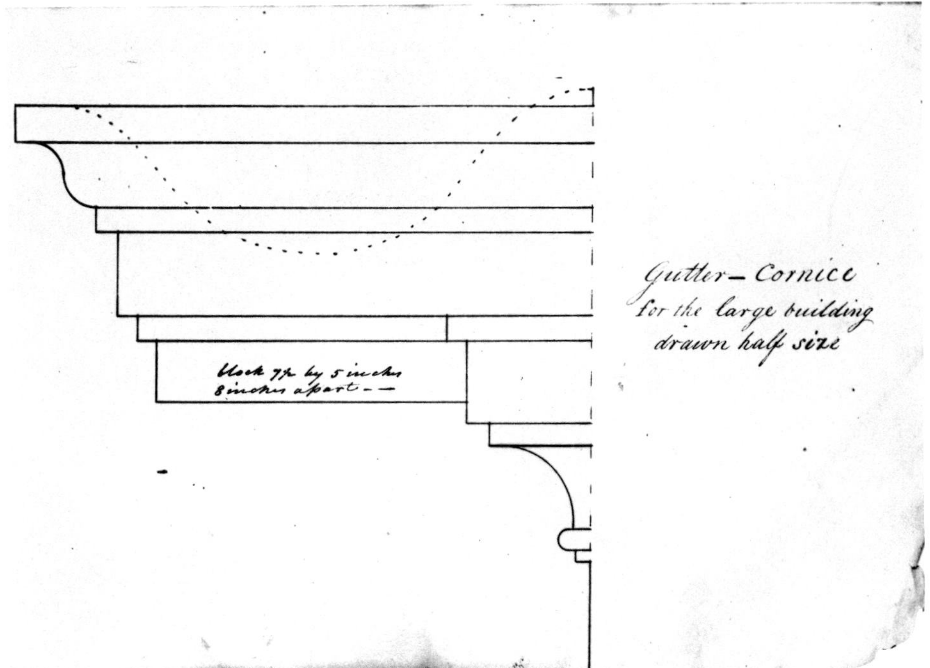

▶
Fig. 101. Hyde Hall, Springfield, N.Y., Hooker's drawing of the gutter-cornice for the east wing, 1818.

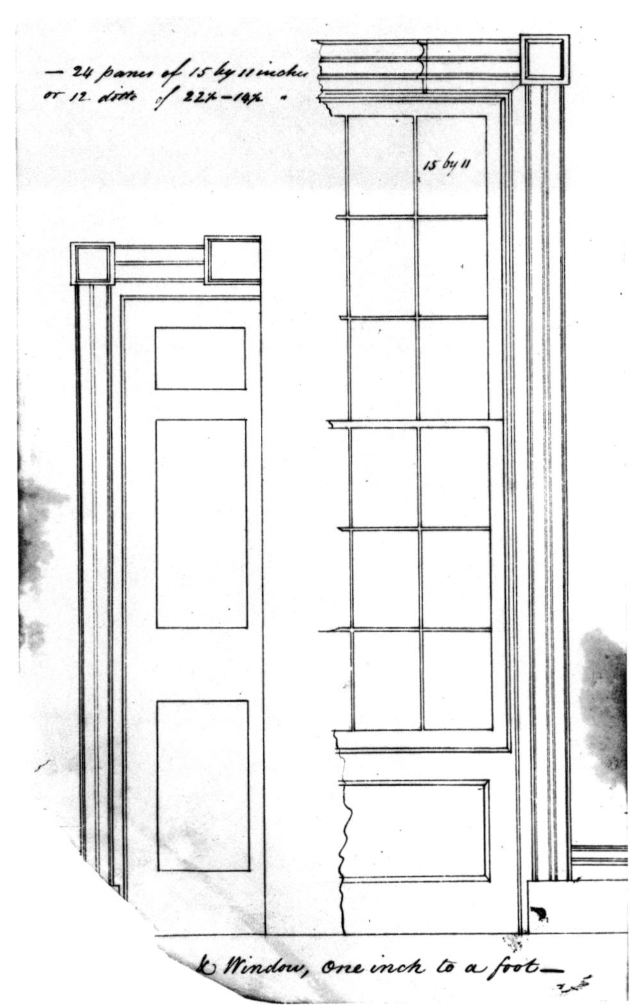

▶
Fig. 102. Hooker's elevations of a door and window, 1818. Ink on paper, bound. Photographs courtesy Friends of Hyde Hall, Inc.

Fig. 103. Hyde Hall, Springfield, N.Y., Hooker's drawing of the drawing room cornice, 1818.

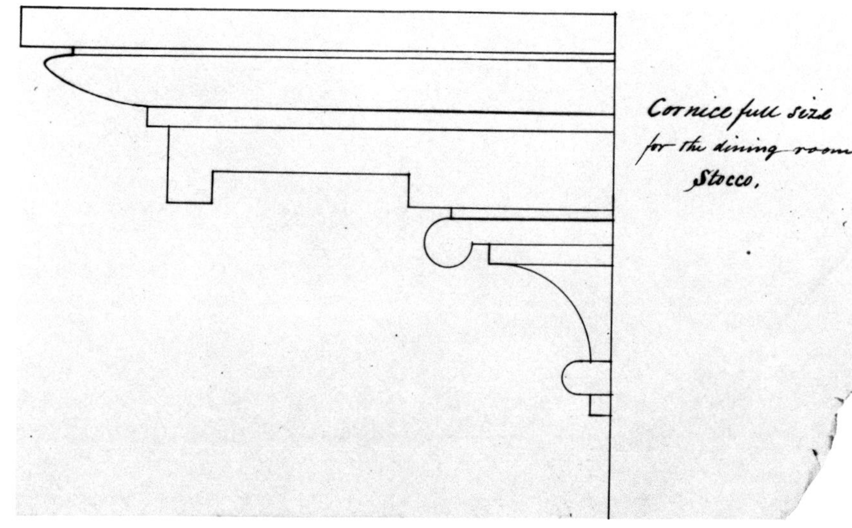

Fig. 104. Hooker's drawing of the dining room cornice, 1818.

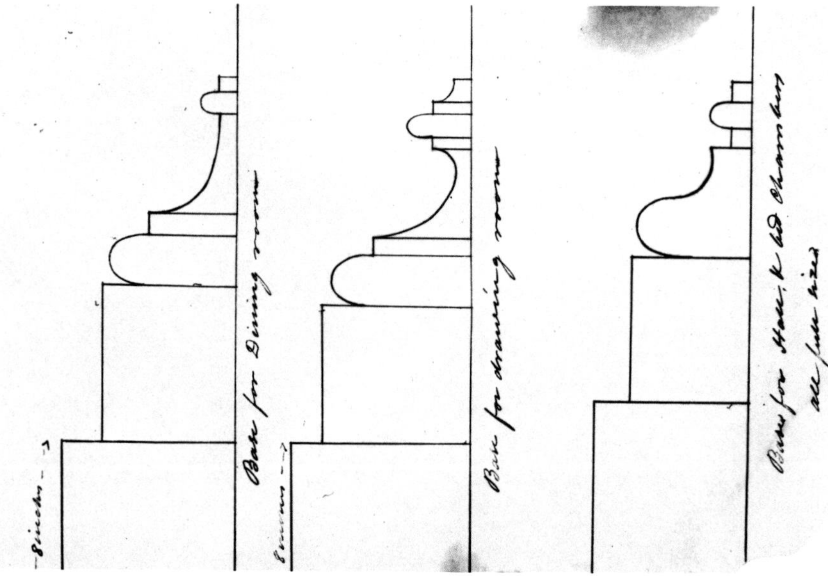

Fig. 105. Hooker's drawing of baseboards, 1818.
Ink on paper, bound.
Photographs courtesy Friends of Hyde Hall, Inc.

Hooker, who received $50.00 for his initial work,[2] visited Springfield in October 1818.[3] Construction activity increased soon afterward, and would continue until 1835. The northwest wing containing the domestic offices, or the kitchen wing, was built during 1820–23.[4] As completed, it differs from previous proposals (figs. 92, 97, 98) and also from a drawing in Hooker's hand which possibly dates to his October 1818 visit (fig. 106).[5] The text accompanying that drawing follows:

> *Plan of offices 20 ft to an inch. walls, stone, 16 ft high 20 inches thick. Partitions, bricks— 9 inches* [thick] *Basem*[en]*t walls 4 1/2 ft high, 26 in*[ches] *thick under the Laundry & bakery— a cellar under the remain*[der] *of the building—walls 7 feet high—partitions bricks— Bakery & Laundry* [are to be] *one story of 9 feet in the clear.*
> *Stone for walls & foundations &c 725 loads*
> *Bricks for partitions & chimnies* 72 *thousand*
> *Slates for covering roofs* 26 *Squares* } *or 20 thousand good 18 inch shingles*

120 floor Joist	*19 feet long*	*10 by 4 inches*
46 Rafters	*23 feet* [long]	*7 by 4* [inches]
16 Collar beams	*30 feet* [long]	*8 by 4* [inches]
16 King posts	*8* [feet long]	*12* [by] *4* [inches]
52 braces	*9* [feet long]	*6* [by] *4* [inches]
2 plates or 4 pieces 21 feet spliced	*40* [feet long]	*8 by 4* [inches]

> *500 feet running measure of wall plates & bond timbers of convenient lengths 8 by 2* [inches]
> *900 Bushels stone lime.*

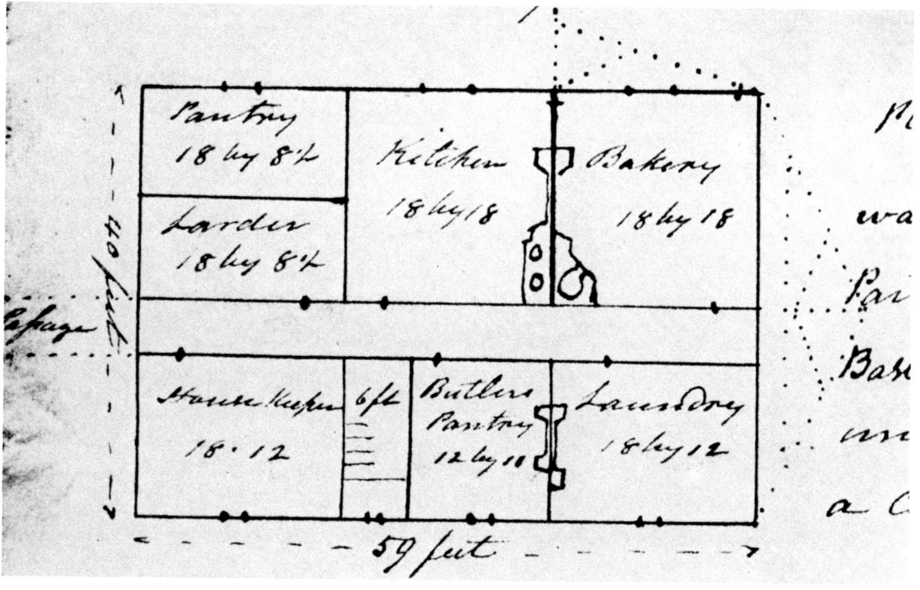

▶ Fig. 106. Hyde Hall, Springfield, N.Y., Hooker's drawing for the masonry version of the kitchen wing, possibly October 1818. Ink on paper. Friends of Hyde Hall, Inc. and Cornell University, Ithaca, N.Y., Olin Library, Department of Manuscripts and University Archives.

A series of rooms erected off the passage that connects the *cottage* and the kitchen wing indicates another, in this case undocumented, diversion from the original plans.[6] By 1827, when the last phase of construction was initiated,

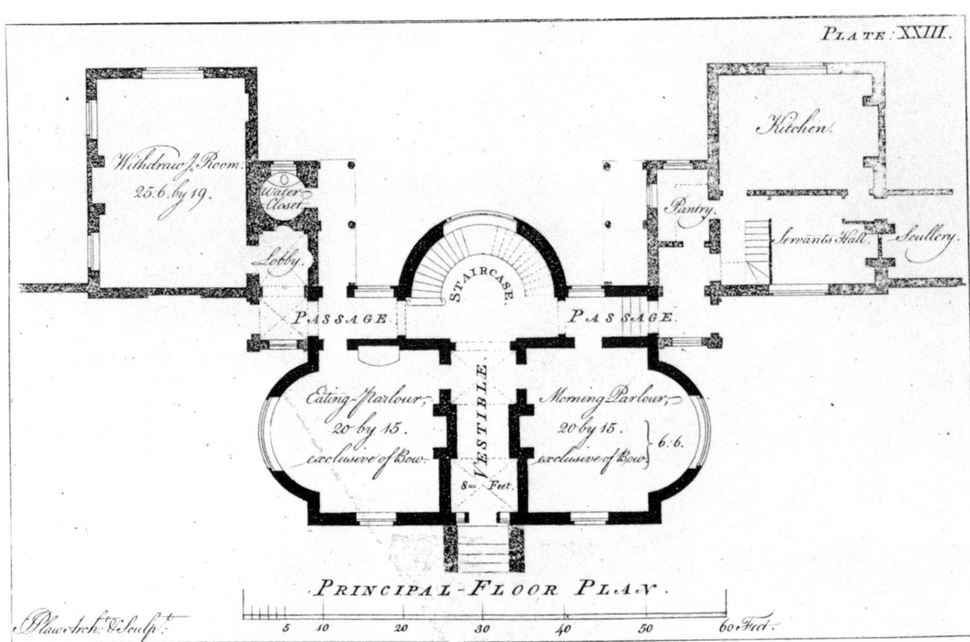

▶ Fig. 107. Plan of a Villa, from John Plaw's *Rural Architecture*, 1785. Courtesy Friends of Hyde Hall, Inc.

the *Great House* had been entirely redesigned (cat. 67), although features of its first floor plan were retained.

Hooker's design for Clarke's country residence thus accommodated the slightly earlier *cottage* scheme, making it part of an assemblage of separate structures. In the disposition of the units as well as in the floor plan of what would be the *Great House* (fig. 97), the architect seems to have been guided by such published sources as John Plaw's *Rural Architecture* of 1785 (fig. 107). George Clarke is known to have owned a copy of one of Plaw's later publications,[7] and he may well have envisioned his new residence as an English country house, whether appearing entirely new or as one that had been added to over time. While the juxtaposition of the *cottage* and the *Great House* is awkward, some contrast between these and the kitchen and service wings is gained by the treatment of the latter in rough stone. Hooker's suggestions for plantings to screen the wings on either side of the main block may have been intended to address the situation.

The open court around which the individual units are grouped is, in many ways, the most important element of the design. In plan it serves as a great ordering device for the distinctly different pavilions, and in space it provides a reference point for persons inside the house. The play of the seasons in the courtyard gives the house a dynamic presence.

The decorative program of the interior did not wholly follow Hooker's original intentions. Some of the door and window trim matches his specifications, but other trim and the plaster work were superseded by his later proposal for the *Great House* (cat. 67). Hooker's relationship to the project in the 1830s, when the plaster work of the drawing and dining rooms was executed, is unclear.

Hyde Hall is currently undergoing an extensive restoration sponsored by Friends of Hyde Hall, Inc. ✤

1. Photographic copies of this material are held in the Collection, Friends of Hyde Hall, Inc., Springfield, N.Y.; and the George Hyde Clarke Papers, Coll. 2800, Department of Manuscripts and University Archives, Olin Library, Cornell University, Ithaca, N.Y.
2. George Hyde Clarke Papers.
3. Ibid.
4. Ibid.
5. Ibid.
6. For a drawing of the existing first floor plan showing these rooms, see Douglas R. Kent, "History in houses: Hyde Hall, Otsego County, New York," *Antiques*, XCII, 2 (August 1967), 191.
7. Information provided by Douglas R. Kent, Curator, Friends of Hyde Hall, Inc., Springfield, N.Y.

40. STEEPLE FOR SOUTH DUTCH REFORMED CHURCH

Beaver Street, Albany, N.Y.
Designed between 11 March and 1 April 1818.
Built 1818–20; burned September 1892.
Builders: Lewis Farnham and John Goodrich.

The consecration of the South Dutch Reformed Church (cat. 18) on 17 February 1811 marked the end of the original building campaign,[1] although the edifice was still without its portico and steeple. Both were intended to be constructed of stone.[2] The portico was finally erected of wood, however, and on 11 March 1818 *Messrs Dewitt and La Grange* were appointed to *obtain a plan and estimate of the woodwork of the steeple so far as will be necessary to hang the bell.*[3]

Hooker submitted his design for a wooden tower by 1 April 1818.[4] Lewis Farnham was awarded the contract,[5] and the first stage, intended to house the bell, was constructed by 14 October 1818 at a cost of $1,615.78.[6] This section may not have been realized according to Hooker's proposal, however, for on 4 May 1819 the consistory resolved *to obtain from Mr. Goodrich the lowest terms on which he will engage to finish the first section of the steeple—according to Mr. Hooker's plan.*[7] Goodrich's estimate was approved on 22 July 1819.[8]

The language of the minutes suggests that Hooker's redesigned tower was to have had more than one stage, although only the first was completed (fig. 55). Its design shares features with the steeples of Hooker's Lutheran Ebenezer Church (fig. 90), St. Peter's Episcopal Church in Albany (fig. 35), and Hamilton College Chapel (fig. 127). ✣

1. Phelps Family Papers, 1781–1919, DZ 10760, MSC NYSL.
2. Ibid.; Root, p. 102.
3. Dutch Reformed Church Consistory Notes, A FCA.
4. Ibid.
5. Ibid.
6. Ibid.
7. Ibid.
8. Ibid.

41. PROPOSAL FOR A TOWN HOUSE AND STORE FOR JOSEPHUS BRADNER STUART

Probably Albany, N.Y.
Designed before 22 May 1818.
Probably unbuilt.

▶
Fig. 108. Town House and Store for Josephus Bradner Stuart, Hooker's elevation of the west front, 1818. Ink and watercolor on paper, bound. William L. Clements Library, University of Michigan, Ann Arbor.

Josephus Bradner Stuart (1787–1828), a prominent businessman, was active in ventures in New York and Ohio and served as Chancellor to the United States Consulate in London in 1815–16. His most noteworthy enterprise after his return to the United States was the construction and operation during 1818–19 of the *Walk-in-the-Water*, the first steamboat to operate on lakes Erie, Huron, and Michigan. Stuart's engagement to Ann Leonard was probably the inspiration for commissioning this design. Business losses during 1819, however, forced the newly-wed couple to settle at Stuart's family farm in Jamesville, New York, and it is unlikely that Hooker's design was executed.[1]

Hooker was paid $10.00 for a bound set of plans, a brief description, and an estimate of material expenses for the building. Stuart received the plans on 22 May 1818.[2] The drawings (figs. 108–12) depict a structure which utilizes detailing common to buildings of the previous century. The text of the book provides valuable construction details for a typical modest building of the period.

The annexed plans are designed for a dwelling house & Store, to be constructed of frame work— 45 feet 8 inches front & Rear, & 50 feet in depth, 23 1/2 feet posts— to be divided into two stories of 11 & 9 feet in the clear. The frame to be substantial, of good sound timber framed with posts & interties— 4 posts in front. The same in the rear, & one in each End— which are to be connected by ties through the building in the partitions of Each story. The rafters are to be supported in the middle by an oblong Square frame so constructed and braced— as to throw the weight, on each end & on the Middle or Hall partitions— the timbers to be proportionate, to the size of the building— Say— sills 10 by 8, Corner posts 10 by 10— intermediate posts–10 by 5— interties 8 by 5—plates–10 by 7—Rafters 7 by 4— Braces, studs 5 by 4 or 3—floor Joists 11 by 4— 2 feet from Center to Center— with One firring between, if split laths are used— these Joists may be spliced on the partitions— breaking Joints alternately— the frame in the garret will consist of 2 sills 45 feet 8 inches long–8 by 4 2 plates or bearing beams of the same length 9 by 5— 8 posts–10 by 4— 8 tie beams 22 feet, 8 by 4— 8 braces 10 feet, 6 by 4 inches, besides other small beams— the whole to be put together in a workmanlike manner— the frame to be enclosed with narrow clapboards— neatly planed & thicknessed— the roof well boarded & Shingled—. Cornice Gutters front & Rear, to have proper pipes & leaders— Windows [the following is crossed out on the original: *of first story 12 panes of 18 by 12 inches, second story 12 panes 16 by 12 inches*] [written above crossed out words: *of both storys 24 panes 8 x 10 inches*]*— hall door to be finished with Columns, Pediment, & fan light. Store doors plain— with a row of square lights over— to raise them in a line with the windows— a tier of oval windows in the center of the South or garden End— The inside to be finished throughout in a neat plain style—Except the store, & loft over the same— the Cellar walls of Stone one foot 8 inches in thickness— partitions of hard-bricks— the length of a brick in thickness. The whole laid in good mortar—Piazza in the rear 22 by 7 feet, with steps to the yard— The Hall, & two rooms in the first story to have narrow blind nailed floors— the others of Common width, principal stairs to have a continued rail of hard wood—*

Prices for labour only—

Stone walls p[er] *perch,*	*16 1/2 cubic feet*	*$1 .—*
plaistering 2 coats		*.15*
[plaistering] *3* [coats]		*.21*
Stocco Cornice plain p[er] *foot run*		*.15*
Bricks p[er] *thousand*		*4..—*

— ~ —

framing timber p[er] *100 feet board meas*[ure]*:*	*1..—*
Clapboarding p[er] *100 sq. feet*	*2..50*
Boarding & Shing[les]*:* [per 100 sq. feet]	*2..25*
plain moulded Cornice Gutter p[er] *ft run*	[?]
Block & Lintil [per ft run]	[?]
Parapet railing p[er] *foot*	*1..50*
Sash frames boxed for weights— each	*2..75*
Astragal & hollow sashes p[er] *light 18 by 12 in.*	*..16*
front door, frontispiece & fan light	*30..—*
Shop doors—Each finished	*9..—*
Inside [doors] *6 pan*[els]*: 1 1/4 inch thick cased with architraves*	*7..50*
Inside 2 inch doors cased with pilasters & tablet caps	*$10. —*
windows, framed backs & pilasters	*6. —*
[windows] *plain* [backs] *& d*[ou]*bl*[e]*: architraves*	*4. 50*
[windows] *without backs & single* [architraves]	*2..75*

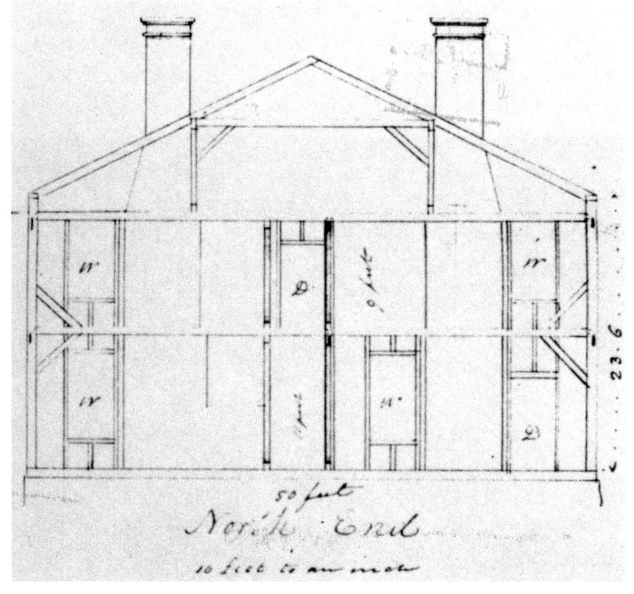
50 feet
North End
10 feet to an inch
23.6
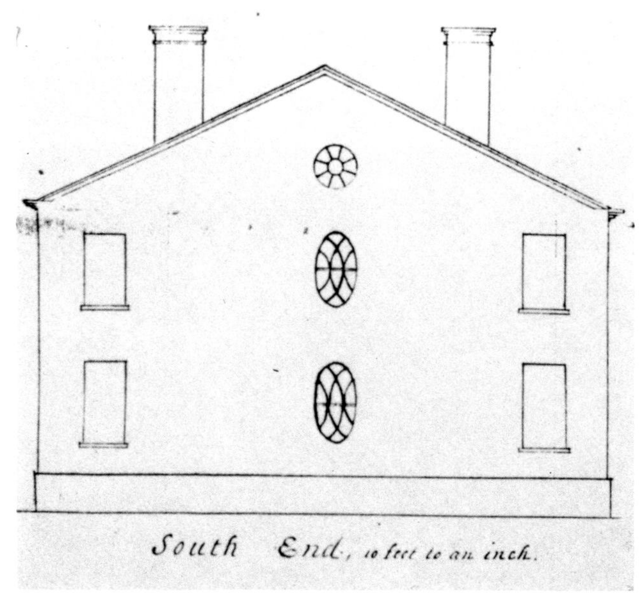
South End, 10 feet to an inch.
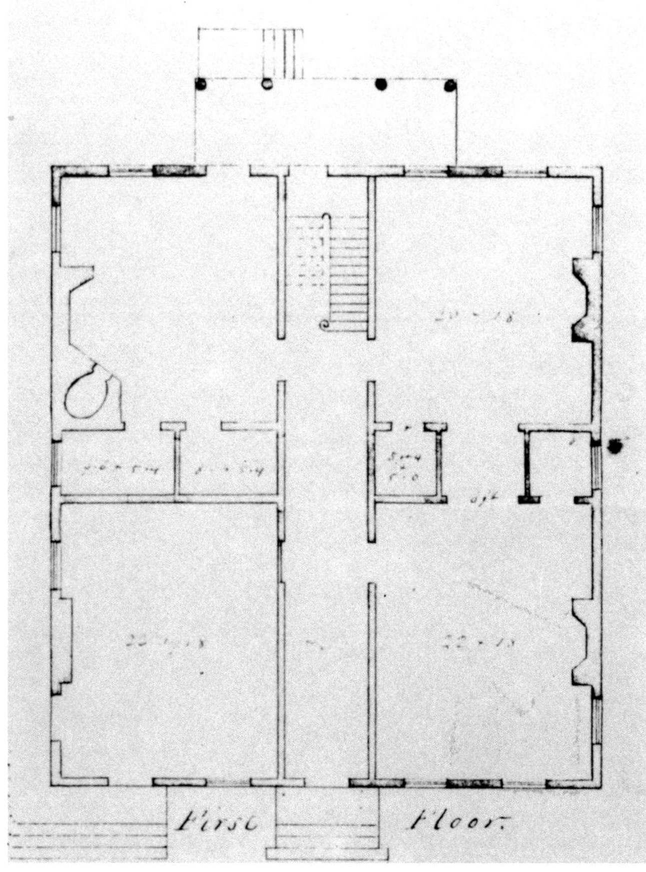
First Floor.
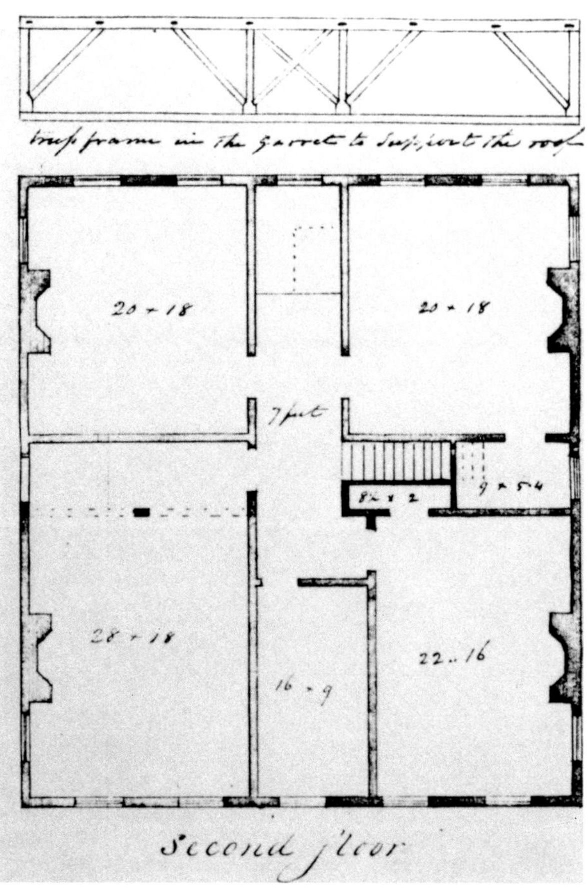
truss frame in the garret to support the roof
20 × 18
20 × 18
7 feet
9 × 5.4
28 × 18
22 × 16
16 × 9
Second floor

◀
Figs. 109–12. Town House and Store for Josephus Bradner Stuart.
Fig. 109. Hooker's framing drawing of the north end, 1818. Ink and watercolor on paper, bound.
Fig. 110. Hooker's elevation of the south end, 1818. Ink on paper, bound.
Fig. 111. Hooker's plan of the first floor, 1818. Ink and wash on paper, bound.
Fig. 112. Hooker's plan of the second floor and truss elevation, 1818. Ink and wash on paper, bound. William L. Clements Library, University of Michigan, Ann Arbor.

Stair case, with continued hardwood rail Scrol[l] *at bottom p*[er] *step*	*2..50*
Garret Stairs & Cellar [stairs] [per step]	*..75*
wash board & base moulding p[er] *foot run*	*..12 1/2*
handsome Mantle piece with Columns	*10..00*
[handsome mantle piece] *with pilasters*	*6..*
Narrow floors p[er] *100 feet*	*3. 25*
wide [floors] *planed tong*[ued]*: & grooved*	*2..25*
[wide floors] *not planed, but grooved*	*1..50*
Window shutters p[er] *pair, framed & hung*	*3..50*
[window] *blinds— Standing* [i.e., fixed slats]	*4..*
[window blinds] *moveable* [slats]	*5..50*

Estimate for Carpenters, Joiners & Masons work, to Mr. Stewarts house—

144 perches stone walls	*@ $1*		*$144..*
37 M bricks, in Cellar part[itions]*: & Chimnies*			*148..*
1666 yds plaistering	*15@*		*250..*
Stocco Cornice in two rooms & hall			*50..*
			592..
framing 15M feet timber 1 @		*$150..*	
Board'g & Shing[les]*: 26 sq*[uare feet]		*58.*	
Clapboard'g 4[?] *sq*[uare feet]		*108.*	
Cornice Gutter 90 feet		*36.*	
Railing	*115*	*22.*	
28 Sash frames		*75.*	
288 lights dowelled sashes		*46.*	
28 [lights] *Circular*		*7.*	
48 [lights] *plain ovals*		*4.*	
Hall doors Complete, & steps		*45.*	
Two shop [doors Complete]*— & steps*		*30.*	
Back doors		*12.*	
16— 6 pan[el]*: 1 1/2 inch doors neatly cased— d*[ou]*bl*[e]*: architraves in first story & Single* [architraves in] *Second Story*		*120.*	
21 windows finished in like manner		*84.*	
20 steps to principal stairs		*50.*	
Cellar & Garret [stairs]		*20.*	
600 feet wash board		*50.*	
2 Mantle pieces, [with] *pilasters*		*12.*	
3 [Mantle pieces] *plain*		*9.*	
12 sq[uare]*: narrow floor*		*39.*	
32 [square] *Com: width* [floor]		*72.*	
22 [square] *Garret, rough* [floor]		*33.*	
26 p[ai]*r Wn* [i. e., window] *Shutters & blinds*		*104.*	
Back Piazza		*40.*	
Outside Cellar door & steps		*12.*	
			1238..
			$1830..

No finish is Calculated in the Cellars— Shelving Store, & pantries to be added [3]

✜

1. Biographical information provided by Catherine Barnes to Curator of Special Collections, Hamilton College, Clinton, N.Y., 14 September 1990.
2. Josephus Bradner Stuart Papers, William L. Clements Library, University of Michigan, Ann Arbor, Mich.
3. Ibid.

42. GARDEN HOUSE, COUNTRY SEAT FOR GEORGE CLARKE (HYDE HALL)

Springfield, Otsego County, N.Y.
Designed before 20 June 1818.
Built 1818.
Builder unknown.

Along with the plans for the main house then under construction, Hooker was responsible for the *designing & drawings for a garden house* at Hyde Hall. He completed this small task by 20 June 1818 and was paid $3.00.[1] There is no visual record of this structure, which was built during the summer of 1818. According to the bill for materials, it was rectangular and constructed of wood with doors and windows.[2] ✤

1. George Hyde Clarke Papers, Coll. 2800, Department of Manuscripts and University Archives, Olin Library, Cornell University, Ithaca, N.Y.
2. Ibid.

43. ST. PETER'S EPISCOPAL CHURCH

Originally at Hamilton Avenue, Sherrill, N.Y.;
moved to Seneca Avenue, Vernon, N.Y.
Designed before 8 July 1818.
Built 1818–19; moved and altered 1840; razed c. 1955.
Builders: John Culver, Abraham Van Santvoord, and James Platt.

Hooker's bound set of drawings (figs. 113–18) and specifications for this project, intended as a church for the Oneidas, was evidently posted to the client, the missionary Eleazar Williams, who in the nineteenth century was rumored to be *the lost Dauphin*. The extent of Hooker's work on this project was probably the preparation of the plans, as it is unlikely that he traveled to Sherrill.

Hooker's specifications read:

> *Designed for a church for our Red Brethren at Oneida. To be of frame work, 50 by 40 feet in the clear, 24 feet posts. To have a stone foundation sunk sufficiently below the depth of frosts. The walls, above the surface of the ground, are to be laid in good mortar and neatly pointed, and to be one foot eight inches in thickness. Sixteen stone piers will be required for supporting the ground floor. The frame work of the superstructure is to be composed of good, sound timber, framed and braced in a substantial & workmanlike manner. (see plans Nos. 5 & 6). Sills 10 by 8* [inches], *corner posts 10 by 10* [inches], *intermediate posts 10 by 6* [inches] *interties 8 by 6* [inches] *plates 10 by 7* [inches], *principal rafters 10 by 5* [inches], *tie beams 11 by 5* [inches], *purlins 8 by 5* [inches], *small rafters, studs, braces &c. 6 by 4 inches. The posts of the spire* [are to be] *8 inches square at bottom & 5 inches at the top; girts, or interties, studs & braces in proportion.*
>
> *It is proposed to cover the front with flush work; narrow planks tongued & grooved similar to flooring. The tongues must invariably be placed upwards, and the joints are to be put together with white lead ground in oil. The tower, above the*

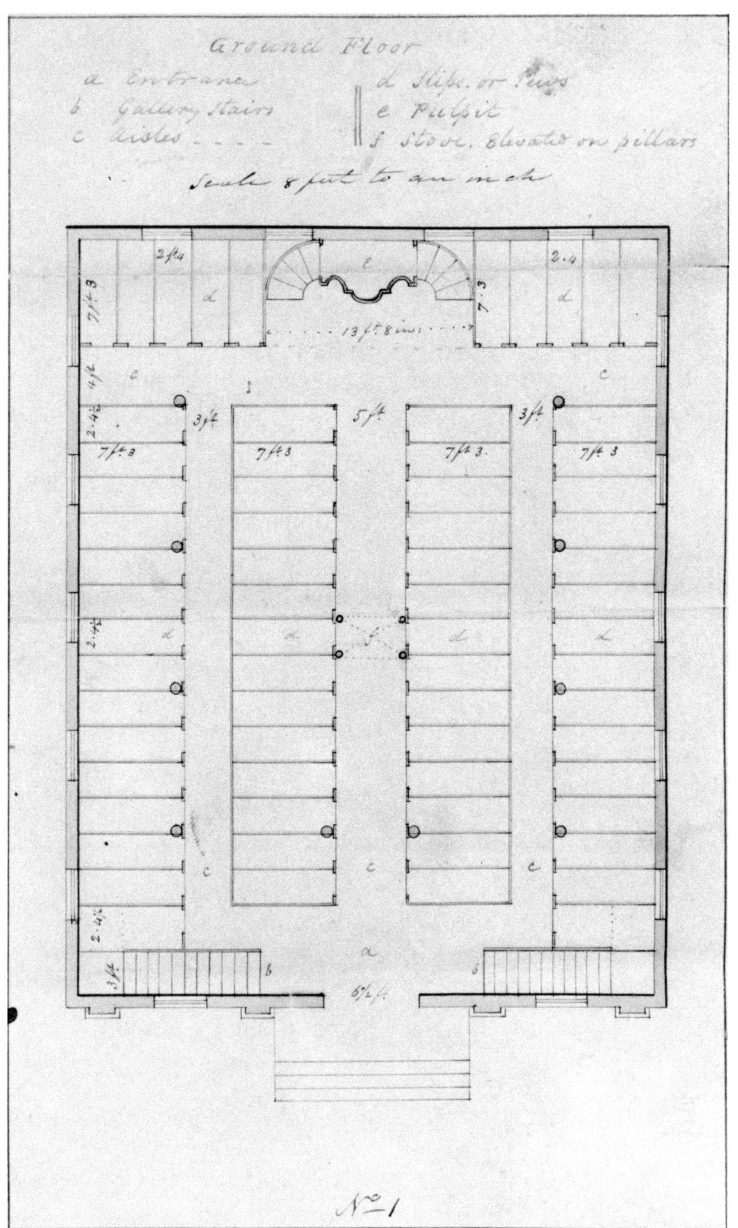

▶
Fig. 113. St. Peter's Episcopal Church, Sherrill, N.Y., Hooker's ground floor plan, 1818. Ink and wash on paper. The New-York Historical Society, New York, N.Y.

roof, is to be done in like manner. The sides & rear [of the building] *are to be covered with clapboards, neatly planed, thicknessed, capped and well nailed. The roof is to be well boarded & shingled. The side cornices are to have gutters. The water may be brought down, by conductors, or leaders placed on the angles* [i.e., corners] *in the rear. These ought to be of tin 3 1/2 or 4 inches in diameter, and the gutter pipes of lead, of nearly the same size. The windows are to contain 24 panes each, of 11 by 9 inches, to have proper sash frames, boxed— 4 1 1/2 inch ovolo sashes. The outside doors are to be made in two thicknesses of 1 1/4 inches framed and screwed together. The recess of the pannels to be equal to the outer thickness.* [The doors are] *to be hung with substantial hinges, well secured with screws & rivits* [and are] *to have a strong spring both at top and bottom and a good winch knob lock. The floor of the church is to be well timbered and laid with good sound planks, tongued and grooved. Those of the aisles are to be planed;* [the] *gallery floors in like manner. The pews are to be neatly made. The doors are to be framed in two pannels 1 1/4 inches thick. The stiles between the doors* [are to

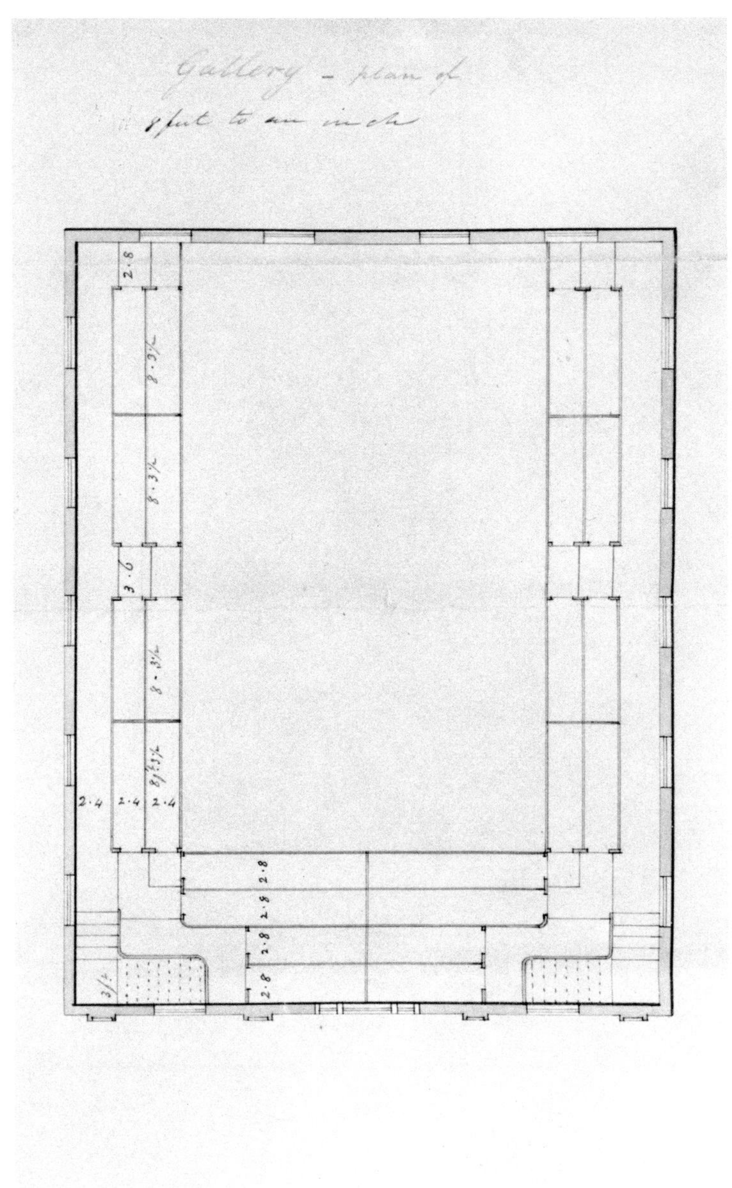

▶
Fig. 114. St. Peter's Episcopal Church, Sherrill, N.Y., Hooker's gallery plan, 1818. Ink and wash on paper. The New-York Historical Society, New York, N.Y.

be] *plain, of the same thickness. The fronts facing the aisles are also to be of framed work, as also* [are] *the backs of the pews; to be framed in one long pannel, the back to extend no lower than the underside of the seat. The partition below* [is] *to be placed under the middle of the seat thus: which gives more room for the feet. The lining* [i.e., wainscot] *of the sides of the church, (to be* [the] *heighth of the pews), may be of wide boards planed, tongued & grooved. The floor of the pews ought to be elevated at least the thickness of a plank above the floors of the aisles. The doors are to be hung with bolt hinges sufficiently wide to swing the doors clear of the capping of the pews, and each door to have a brass button. Neat plain stairs to the galleries, which are to be seated according to plan No. 2 and to be supported by ten turned pillars 6 inches in diameter, having a suitable plain moulded entablature along the gallery front, which is to be pannelled above* [and decorated] *with an open pilaster over each column. The whole* [gallery front] *to have a neat cornice capping. The pulpit is to be neatly made, with circular winding steps at each end. (See plans No. 1 & 6.)*

▶
Fig. 115. St. Peter's Episcopal Church, Sherrill, N.Y., Hooker's front elevation, 1818. Ink and watercolor on paper. The New-York Historical Society, New York, N.Y.

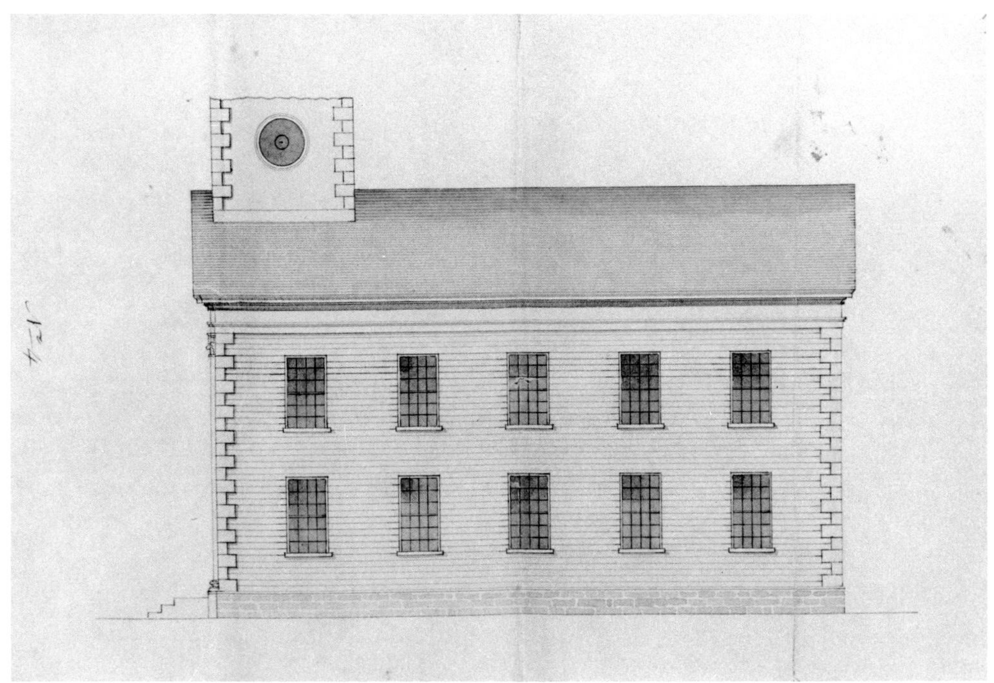

▶
Fig. 116. St. Peter's Episcopal Church, Sherrill, N.Y., Hooker's side elevation, 1818. Ink and watercolor on paper. The New-York Historical Society, New York, N.Y.

The ceiling & sides of the church above the pews is to be neatly lathed & plaistered with three coats of suitable mortar, the last to be like the churches in Utica. A small stocco moulding is to be run round at the foot of the arch [i.e., the arched ceiling] *and another at its termination on the ceiling. The steeple is to be enclosed with well seasoned stuff, & put together in the best possible manner, to prevent leakage. The deck of the belfry should be laid with two inch seasoned planks caulked & p*[ai]*n*[te]*d or which is better, two thicknesses of planks, breaking joints, with tarred sheathing paper between. The whole to be done in a neat, plain and workmanlike manner, and according to the plans or draughts hereto annexed. All the joiners work is to have two coats of paints of suitable colours.*

Several pages were left blank by Hooker for the inclusion of a contract, which was written by John Culver and features changes to Hooker's design.

We, John Culver, Abraham Van Santvoord & James Platt do hereby covenant and agree with Morris J. Miller and Nathaniel Williams, agents appointed to erect a church at Oneida, to erect a church on the site fixed upon by said agents according to the plan of directions contained in these sheets from page 1 to 17; the following alterations and additions excepted. The pulpit may be made with one stair case. The caps of the front pillars may be plain instead of carved. The side galleries and cornice gutters may be omitted. The windows are to be gothic, four on each side, of suitable dimensions, like those of the Episcopal Church in Utica [Trinity Church, cat. 11]. *The front of the church to be finished in a stile suitable to the Gothic plan. There is to be a suitable lightening rod from the top of the steple, a handsome railing in front of the pulpit for a Chancel with a proper kneeling board in front, and a suitable sheathing is to cover the building under the clapboards. The whole work to be completed according to said plan, with the above additions and alterations, on or before the first day of July next. The building is to be finished and painted on the outside before winter sets in, and the floors laid so that church may be held in it during the winter.*

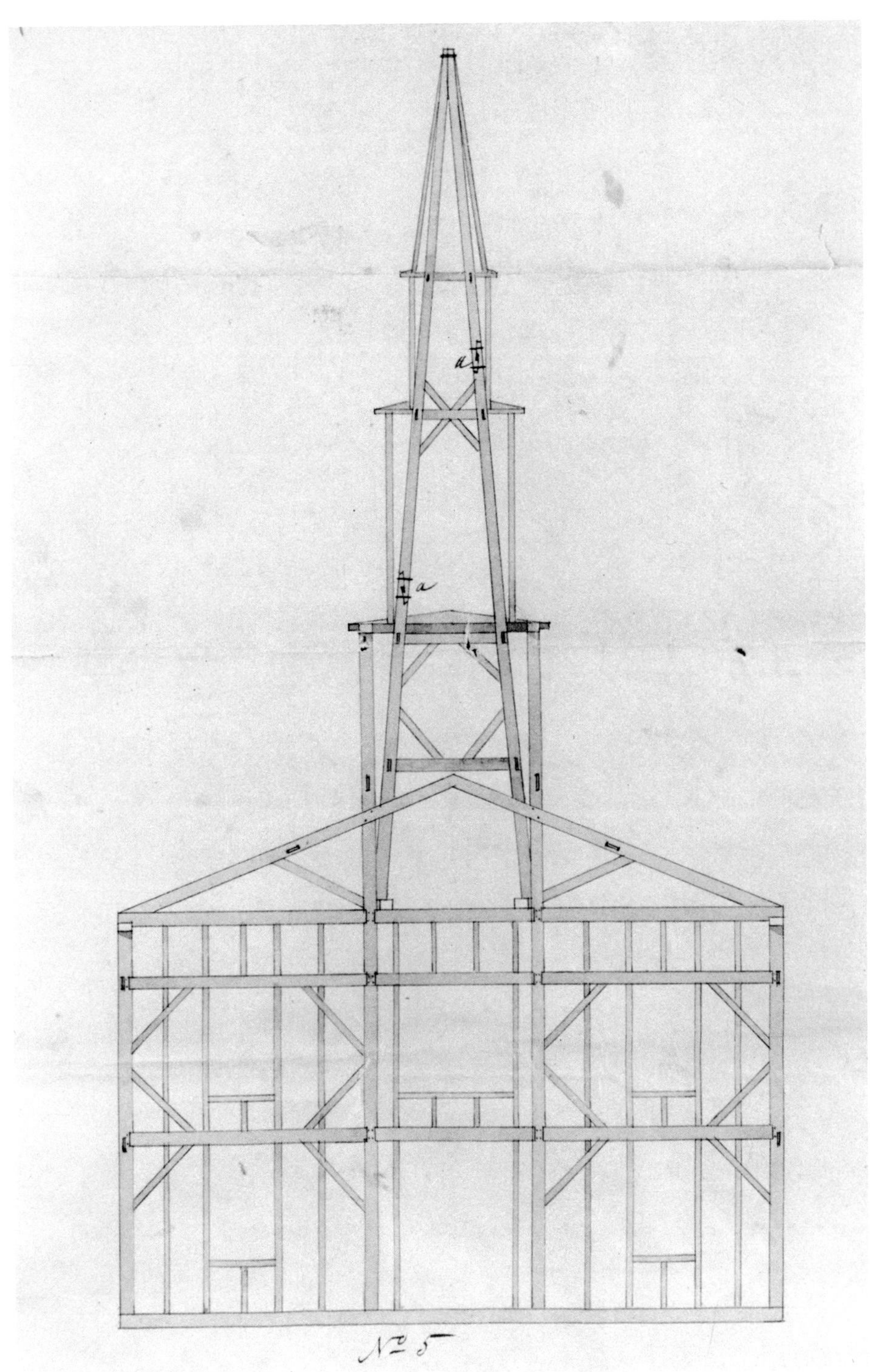

▶ Fig. 117. St. Peter's Episcopal Church, Sherrill, N.Y., Hooker's framing elevation of the front, 1818. Ink and wash on paper. The New-York Historical Society, New York, N.Y.

▶
Fig. 118. St. Peter's Episcopal Church, Sherrill, N.Y., Hooker's transverse section and structural details, 1818. Ink and wash on paper. The New-York Historical Society, New York, N.Y.

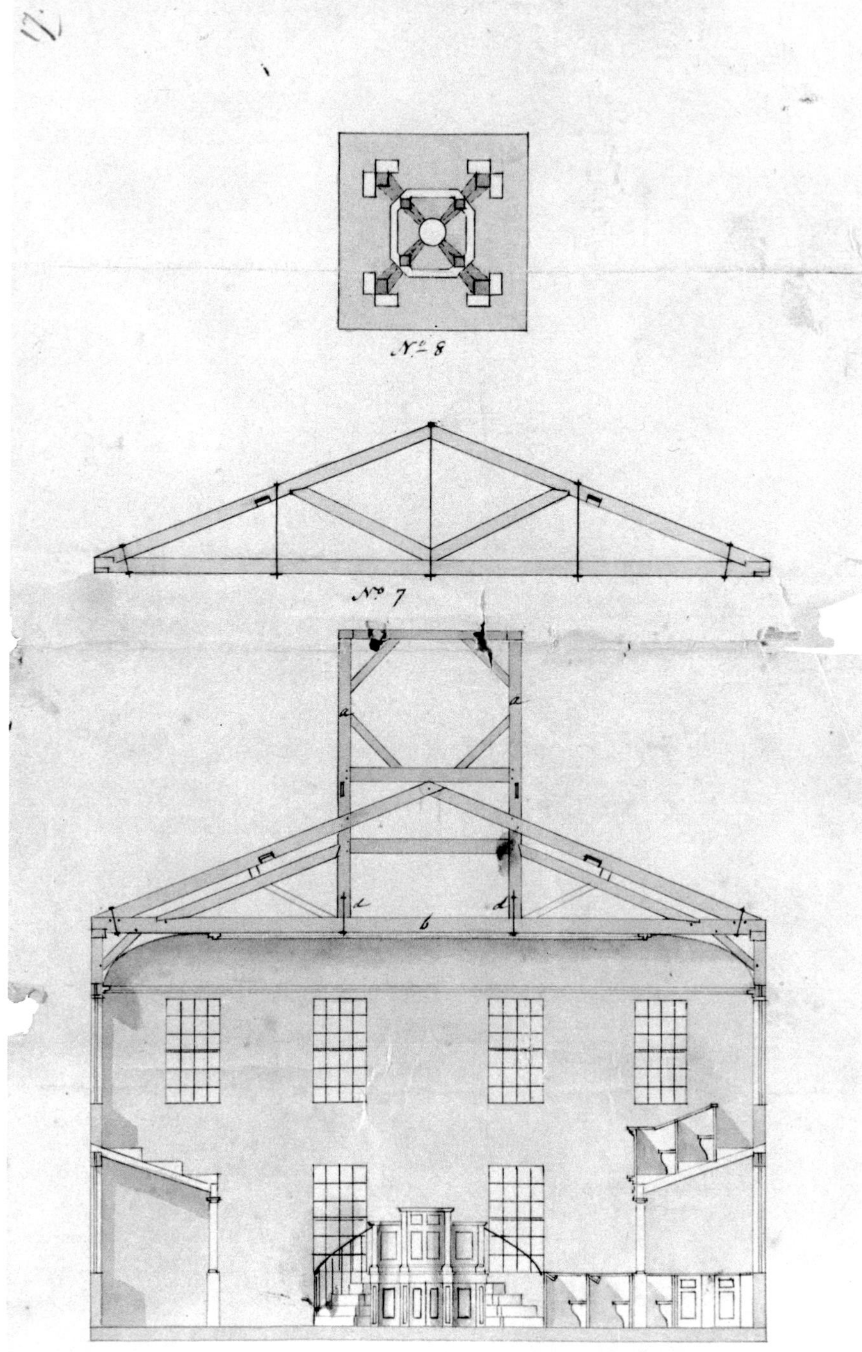

1. Utica, Misc., Manuscripts Division, NYHS.
2. John Henry Hobart, "Address," in *Journal of the Proceedings of the Annual Convention of the Protestant Episcopal Church in the State of New-York . . . 1819* (New York: Printed by T. and J. Swords, 1819), p. 17.
3. Ferne Kitson Patterson, *Pioneers of Vernon, Oneida County, New York, and the Root Family* (Interlaken, N.Y.: Ferne K. Patterson, 1985), p. 66.

▲
Fig. 119. St. Peter's Episcopal Church, after its removal from Sherrill to Vernon, N.Y., and enlargement with a portico and a rear addition. Vernon Historical Society.

Said agents are to pay for the work as follows viz— five hundred dollars down, one thousand dollars when the building is raised, one thousand dollars when the outside is finished and painted, five hundred dollars when the floors are laid, seven hundred and fifty dollars when the plastering is finished, and seven hundred and fifty dollars when the building is completed. . . .
In testimony whereof the parties have hereunto interchangeably set their hands and seals the 8th day of July 1818.
[written in the hand of John Culver]

Hooker's notes on the backs of several of the drawings provided further details on the construction techniques to be used.

No. 5 Skeleton, or naked frame, drawn to a scale of 8 feet to an inch [fig. 117]. *The corner posts being 10 inches and the intermediate posts only 6 inches thick, it will be necessary to cut away the internal angles 4 inches in order to make flush work, which will give the end of the post this shape:* 4 6 10 *where the posts to the spire are spliced at "aa" they are to be secured with screw bolts.*

Three pair of trussed rafters as represented at No 7 will be required exclusive of those connected with the tower— and the gable end rafters in the rear.

Number 6. Tra[ns]*verse section, shewing the manner of trussing the rafters to support that part of the tower which extends into the roof* [fig. 118]. *The posts "aa," are secured to the tie beam "b" by screw bolts "dd." The nuts are morticed into the posts in the same manner as those in a bedstead.*

No. 7 Plan of the other principal rafters beyond the tower [fig. 118]. *This method of framing principals is far preferable to that of king posts, and less expensive, as 2/3rds of the labour is saved in framing, having neither tenon or mortice, except where the braces are framed into the rafters. A groove is made in the upper end of each rafter, equal to half the size of the bolt. The same is done with the (feet) of the braces, which when put together forms a mortice and the bolt the tenon, which when screwed tight keeps the timber in their proper place. One inch square iron is sufficiently large & 3/4th inch* [square iron] *for the bolts at the feet of the rafters. The screws & nuts ought to have a good thread.*[1]

St. Peter's Church was constructed with the above modifications and was consecrated on 21 September 1819.[2] The building served its original purpose until the Oneidas left the area. In 1840, the building was dismantled, reassembled, and rededicated as the Unitarian Church in Vernon, New York. At that time a pediment and columned porch were added (fig. 119). After 1922 the structure served as the Vernon Town Hall until it was demolished around 1955.[3] ✤

44. ALTERATIONS AND ADDITIONS TO THE VAN RENSSELAER MANOR HOUSE

Head of Market Street (now Broadway), Albany, N.Y.
Designed c. 1818.
Built 1819; altered early 1840s; razed 1893;
fragments believed to have survived.
Builder unknown.

▲
Fig. 120. Van Rensselaer Manor House, Albany, drawing by Thomas Cole, 1839–40, showing one of the wings and the piazza added by Hooker in 1819.
Pencil on paper. The Detroit Institute of Arts, Founders Society Purchase, William H. Murphy Fund.

During 1818–19, Hooker was retained to design and superintend the construction of extensive modifications to the Van Rensselaer Manor House, built in 1765. Hooker worked on new sashes for the windows, a porch or piazza on the garden side of the house,[1] and the addition of two one-story wings, which included space for formal dining and service, a library, and a drawing room.[2] The house as enlarged by Hooker appears in a drawing by Thomas Cole (fig. 120). Its subsequent remodeling by Richard Upjohn in the early 1840s obscured much of Hooker's work.[3] The wings were destroyed when the house was dismantled and partially reconstructed in Williamstown, Massachusetts, in 1893.[4] Some of the interior woodwork is believed to have been incorporated into a row of town houses facing Washington Park in Albany, designed for the Van Rensselaers in 1897 by architect Marcus T. Reynolds. ✤

1. Philip Hooker, Bills, Receipts, etc., Hooker, Marvin, etc., Van Rensselaer Manor House, 1766–1836, MSC NYSL.
2. Van Rensselaer Manor Papers, SC 7079, MSC NYSL.
3. Everard M. Upjohn, *Richard Upjohn: Architect and Churchman* (New York: Columbia University Press, 1939), p. 207. According to Marcus T. Reynolds, "The Colonial Buildings of Rensselaerswyck," *Architectural Record*, IV, 4 (April–June 1895), 425, the wings designed by Hooker were torn down in the Upjohn remodeling and the *great wings* added. Based on stylistic evidence, this author believes that the Hooker-designed wings, with some of their detailing, were retained but enlarged and remodeled. For the window surrounds in the library, attributed to Hooker, see Architects' Emergency Committee, *Great Georgian Houses of America*, Vol. I (1933; reprint ed., New York: Dover Publications, Inc., 1970), p. 205.
4. Marcus T. Reynolds Papers, Collection, Kenneth G. Reynolds; Reynolds, "The Colonial Buildings of Rensselaerswyck," p. 433.

45. FENCES FOR LUTHERAN EBENEZER CHURCH

Pine and Lodge streets, Albany, N.Y.
Designed before 1 July 1819.
Built 1819.
Builders: Timothy Fassett and Lawrence Hallenbake.

Hooker had designed the church for this congregation in 1816 (cat. 37). His handwritten contract for the fences to enclose the churchyard provides a clear description of their design and construction.

> *Memorandum of an agreement entered into this first day of July in the year one thousand eight hundred & nineteen, between the Trustees of the Lutheran Ebenezer Church in the city of Albany of the first part & Fassett & Hallenbake builders, of said city of the second part as follows:*
>
> *The said parties of the second part do hereby (for the considerations herein after specified) engage to erect fences and palisades around three sides of the lot on which the said Lutheran Church is situated, according to the plans hereto annexed. That is to say, the palisade on Pine Street is to be erected on a stone wall 50 feet in length 2 1/2 feet thick at the bottom, & twenty inches at the top, 3 ft 6 inches high at the east end & 6 ft 6 inches high at the west end, to be well laid in good mortar. Holes of 5 inches square are to be made in said wall, to receive the fence posts which are to be of red cedar. This wall is to be capped with timber two feet wide, 6 inches thick in the middle & 4 inches at the edges, neatly dressed & planed, except that part which will be under the gates; it is to be capped with stone. Three plain, freestone steps equal to the opening of the gates will conduct you from the street to the area in front of the church. The style of the fence is to be similar to that in front of Mr. Gregory's* [Congress Hall, on the Public Square] *but somewhat larger in dimentions as shall be directed by the said party of the first part. The gates are to be well made & hung with wrought iron hinges. The hooks to have plates attached to the posts with strong woodscrews, to have fastenings similar to those in front of the 2nd Presbeterian, or Mr. Chester's, Church* [A12]. *From the east end of said fence, or palisade, is to extend along Lodge Street, as far as the south east angle of the Church (about 6 feet), a similar fence, (with a pair of gates in the center)* [built] *except* [without] *the stone foundation, but there will be anchors to the feet of the posts. From the north end of the last described fence, is to be extended a pale fence 76 feet along Lodge Street, at the end of which is to be a single gate of 3 feet. This fence is to be composed of chestnut posts, squared & planed above the ground, connected by two rails of proportionate dimentions; a plank at the bottom, above which it is to be faced with flat pales about 2 1/2 inches wide & the same distance apart, to be fashioned at the top in the shape of an urn.* [The fence is] *to have a beaded batten nailed on the outside against the upper rail. A close boarded fence, 6 feet high, is to be made from the last mentioned single gate to Steuben Street, a distance of about 52 or 53 feet. The boards are to be sound, free from loose knots, neatly planed on the Street side, well lapped & well nailed. A similar fence is to be made along Steuben Street, with a pair of strong battened braced gates, 7 feet wide, to have a crossbar & hooks to fasten them. The bottom of the gate posts ought also to be anchored. The whole of the above described work is to be done in a good substantial manner, and with good materials, and to be completed on or before the first day of October, next ensuing the date hereof. In consideration of the true and faithful performance of which, the said parties of the first part agree to pay or cause to be paid to the said parties of the second part, or their lawfull attorney, the just & full sum of four hundred & fifteen dollars,*

money of account of the United States, as follows, to witt: On signing this memorandum of their agreements, the sum of two hundred dollars & when the whole shall be completed and approved, the residue two hundred & fifteen dollars. It is hereby further agreed between the parties that the said parties of the second part are to paint the palisades & paleing with two coats of good white lead ground in oil & the close fences & plinth of the paleing with two coats of yellow ocre ground in oil, & further that the said parties of the first part shall be at liberty to appoint a suitable person to inspect said work, as it progresses. And if any dispute shall arise relative to said work, or materials, or any part there of, the same shall be left to disinterested persons, to be chosen by each of the said parties, as is usual in such cases & whose determination shall be final and conclusive. And for the true & faithfull performance of all & singular, the aforesaid covenant & agreements to be kept, done and performed on the part & behalf of the respective parties to these presents, the said parties of the first part do hereby bind themselves & their successors in office & the said parties of the second part do also bind themselves, their heirs, executors, administrators and assigns in the penal sum of eight hundred and thirty dollars money as aforesaid, to be recovered with costs of suit. In testimony whereof the said party of the first part have caused this Secretary to subscribe his name & affix their common seal hereto, and the said parties of the second part have also subscribed their names & affixed their seals the day & year first above written—

In presence of — *John C. Feltmen*
Edward Burt — *Timothy Fassett*
Lawrence Hallenbake

A note by Hooker appears on the verso of the last page.

I have examined the church fence and am of opinion that Messrs. Fassett & Hallenbake have complied with the contract, except in the lock to the front gate which is different from Mr. Chester's but may answer as well, tho' rather low—

P. Hooker[1]

Hooker was paid $5.00 on 30 November 1819.[2] Since the fences would have been constructed by then, the fee probably included Hooker's payment for superintending the work.

An early painting of the church depicts the fences essentially as described in the contract.[3] ✣

1. Treasurers Book, Archives, First Lutheran Church, Albany, N.Y. (hereafter A FLC).
2. Ibid.
3. A FLC.

46. ADDITION TO THE EAGLE TAVERN

South Market Street (now Broadway), Albany, N.Y.
Designed before October 1819.
Built 1819; burned 1848.
Builder unknown.

Although Stephen Van Rensselaer III's relationship to this project is not completely understood, it was he who commissioned Hooker to design and supervise *sundry repairs and alterations, together with* [the design and supervision of] *an addition to the Eagle Tavern.* Hooker's bill, dated 29 October 1819, charges the patroon $666.66 for the above and for architectural services related to other Van Rensselaer property.[1] Additional bills of 1819 and 1820 document some of Hooker's other work at the Eagle, which included the repair of drains[2] and the installation of plumbing.[3]

Hooker had previously made a perspective drawing of the hostelry (fig. 169), and it is possible that he had designed the building itself (A2). ✥

1. Van Rensselaer Manor Papers, SC 7079, MSC NYSL.
2. Ibid.
3. Ibid.

47. PROPOSAL FOR A CHURCH

Unknown location, St. Lawrence County, N.Y.
Designed before 10 February 1820.
Building history unknown.

Among Stephen Van Rensselaer III's bills and receipts for the year 1820 is a bill from Hooker dated 10 February charging $5.00 *to designing and drawing a sketch for a church to be erected in the county of St. Lawrence* and $7.00 for *drawing plans.*[1] Since the Van Rensselaer papers contain no clues about the patroon's plans to fund the building's construction, he might have intended merely to donate the plans. The denomination of the congregation is not specified, and no further identification of the project has been made.[2] ✥

1. Van Rensselaer Manor Papers, SC 7079, MSC NYSL.
2. For the Van Rensselaers in St. Lawrence County, see Gates Curtis, ed., *Our County and Its People: A Memorial Record of St. Lawrence County, New York* (Syracuse: D. Mason & Company, 1894), pp. 325, 351.

48. PROPOSAL FOR A PULPIT FOR NORTH DUTCH REFORMED CHURCH

North Pearl Street at Clinton Square, Albany, N.Y.
Designed before 22 June 1820.
Unbuilt.

A bill, dated 22 June 1820,[1] indicates that Stephen Van Rensselaer III paid Hooker $10.00 for producing *plans with drawings* [illegible word] *member & embellishments, for a pulpit for the N*[orth] *Dutch Church, rejected by committee.* It was common for wealthy persons to propose improvements to their places of worship at their own expense, and a pulpit would have provided a conspicuous gift to the congregation.

It is likely that the proposed pulpit took the form of a platform raised on columns, with two staircases and no sounding board. This type appears in Hooker's drawings after 1815 (figs. 118, 149) and contrasts with the pulpit drawn by Putnam in 1797 (fig. 26), whose form was characteristic of seventeenth and eighteenth century examples. ✣

1. Van Rensselaer Manor Papers, SC 7079, MSC NYSL.

49. PULPIT FOR NORTH DUTCH REFORMED CHURCH

North Pearl Street at Clinton Square, Albany, N.Y.
Designed before 12 July 1820.
Built 1820; removed.
Builder: William W. Williams.

After the rejection of Hooker's initial design (cat. 48), he submitted a pulpit plan to the church consistory, billing $10.00 on 12 July 1820 for *drawing a design for a pulpit with embellishments at large for the workmen.*[1]

Two bills document William W. Williams's work on the pulpit, assumedly to Hooker's design. On 26 August Williams received $40.00 *on account of the pulpit,*[2] and on 6 November he billed the consistory:

To building pulpit	*275.00*
To extra	*7.00*
To 1/2 days work	*2.25*
To 2 letters	*.40*
	284.65[3]

This pulpit was removed and is presumed to have been destroyed during the renovations of 1857–59. Later, in 1913, the congregation installed the pulpit that had been obtained from the Netherlands in 1656 for its initial church at State Street and Broadway.[4] ✣

1. Doc. 132-27, Dutch Reformed Church (hereafter DRC) Collection, A FCA.
2. Doc. 132-26, DRC Collection.
3. Ibid.
4. Robert S. Alexander, *Albany's First Church and its Role in the Growth of the City, 1642–1942* (Albany: First Church in Albany, 1988), pp. 268–69. For a photograph of that pulpit, see Cuyler Reynolds, comp., *Albany Chronicles* (Albany: J. B. Lyon Company, Printers, 1906), opp. p. 52.

50. SUNDIAL STAND, VAN RENSSELAER MANOR

Head of Market Street (now Broadway), Albany, N.Y.
Designed before 17 August 1820.
Built 1820.
Builder unknown.

During the summer of 1820 Hooker was engaged by Stephen Van Rensselaer III to design and supervise the construction of a sundial stand for the manor house garden. Hooker billed Van Rensselaer $6.25 on 17 August 1820 for *timber, dressing, turning, carting, setting* [and] *painting a ballister for & setting a sun dial.*[1] Although the language of the bill suggests that Hooker did all the work himself, it is more likely that he merely supervised. ✤

1. Van Rensselaer Manor Papers, SC 7079, MSC NYSL.

51. STEEPLE FOR ST. PETER'S EPISCOPAL CHURCH

State and Lodge streets, Albany, N.Y.
Designed c. 1822.
Built 1822; razed 1859.
Builder unknown.

The steeple of this church (cat. 6) was originally designed by Hooker around 1802, but for financial reasons it was not constructed until 1822. A committee consisting of "*Mr. Van Rensselaer, Mr. Duer and Mr. Davis*" was appointed by the vestry "*to procure plans and estimates from the architect of the Church, Mr. Philip Hooker.*" He submitted at least two designs, and "*it was resolved 'that* [design] *No. 2 terminating in a spire be adopted.*' " The construction estimate was $2,170, but as built it cost $2,420.[1]

An undated estimate in Hooker's handwriting may refer to his design *No. 1*, of which no visual record exists, or to a design prepared at the time of the initial building campaign.

Estimate for finishing the steeple of St. Peters Church

Stone cutters bill for hewn stone		*$360.*
Carting & setting		*30.*
155 perches rough stone	*32/*	*620.*
124 yds of rough casting		*212.*
Cornice & circular ornament		
1st section compleat		*$1222.*
Timber work to spire, ironwork scaffolding & raising		*360.*
2nd section Ionic order compleat		*450.*
3rd [section] *Corinthian* [order]		*425.*
4th [section with a] *truss, ball & vane*		*225*

[To] *Painting*	*150.*
[To] *Compleating Gallery*	*372*
	3204.
Superintendence 8 p[er] *c*[en]*t*	*256.*
	$3460.

The above work, to be done in the best & most substantial manner, According to the design.[2]

The estimate closely matches the steeple as executed, with the exception of the fourth section. *Truss* probably refers to open-work scrolls similar to those which Hooker had used in the cupolas of the Union College building (fig. 10) and the Lancaster School (fig. 68). The phrase *Compleating* [the] *Gallery* might refer to work necessitated by the construction of the steeple, such as the building of steps and other details.

The steeple of St. Peter's Church (fig. 35) shares features with others designed by Hooker between 1815 and 1825. However, while the use of the architectural orders on all four elevations and the relationship of one stage to the next are typical of his designs, the rusticated first stage of this steeple is unique. ✥

1. Root, p. 79, from Joseph Hooper, *A History of Saint Peter's Church in the City of Albany* (Albany: Fort Orange Press, 1900).
2. Archives, St. Peter's Church, Albany, N.Y.

52. COUNTRY SEAT FOR JUDGE MORRIS S. MILLER

Rutger Park, Utica, N.Y.
Designed c. 1823.
Built c. 1823–30; altered c. 1870 and c. 1910; extant.
Builder unknown.

Landscaping in Rutger place, as it was subsequently known, was begun in 1820 by Judge Morris S. Miller.[1] The house was designed sometime before 1824 as the foundations were in place when Judge Miller died in that year.[2] The original plans were carried out by Mrs. Miller and her eldest son, Rutger B. Miller.[3] A contemporary memorandum, recorded by Root, indicates Hooker's connection with the project.

> "*The plan of the Miller house was drawn by a Mr. Hooker of Poughkeepsie* [sic] *considered the best architect of that day—in justice to him it must be said the plan was not strictly followed. At Mrs. Miller's suggestion the hall was made much wider—a great improvement to interior but not to exterior, the house not being proportioned in height.*"[4]

The house was occupied in the late spring of 1830.[5] Its walls were constructed of rubble stone, covered with stucco and scored to resemble cut stone (fig. 121). Blandina Dudley Miller, who grew up in the house, recollected in 1901 the original uses of the rooms.

1. Blandina Dudley Miller, *A Sketch of Old Utica*, ed. Helen Lincklaen Miller (N.p., 1909), p. 21.
2. Ibid., p. 22.
3. John J. Walsh, "Vignettes of Old Utica, Persons, Places and Events," unpublished manuscript, 1975, p. 85. Typescript on file at the Oneida County Historical Society, Utica, N.Y.
4. Root, p. 191, from a Miller family memorandum.
5. Walsh, p. 85.

▶
Fig. 121. Miller House, Utica (c. 1823–30), exterior, c. 1850. Utica Public Library.

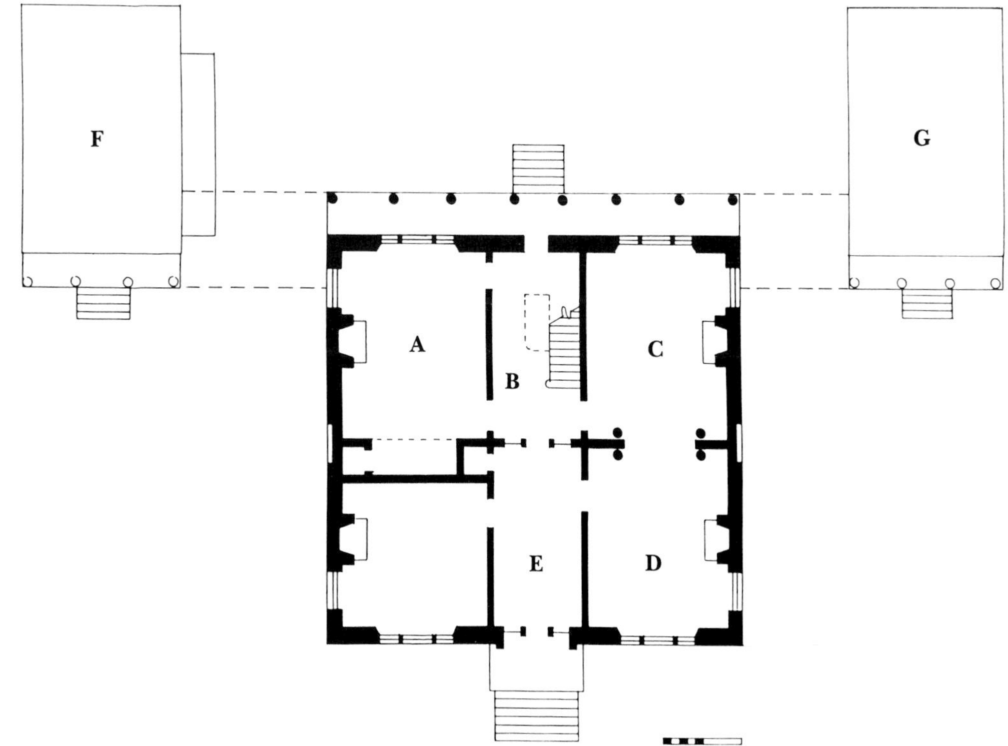

▶
Fig. 122. Miller House, Utica (c. 1823–30), first floor plan, with outbuildings:
A. Dining room,
B. Back hall,
C. Back parlor,
D. Front parlor,
E. Front hall,
F. House for coachman and gardener, and
G. Office;
reconstructed by W. R. Wheeler, 1991.

▶
Fig. 123. Miller House, Utica (c. 1823–30), interior view, showing glazed partition between entrance and stair halls. Collection Thomas S. Kernan.

> *The basement story contained the kitchen, with huge fireplaces, cellars for fruits and vegetables, servants' rooms and pantries. The first story had the wide hall* [divided into *front* and *back* halls by a glazed partition; fig. 123] *with two large rooms on either side* [used as parlors and a dining room]. *The staircase led from the back hall up to the sleeping and dressing rooms, through the upper hall, which opened through a small library room out on to the square upper porch. The back rooms of both first and second floors opened out* [onto] *wide piazzas which extended the entire width of the house. . . . On either side of the stone house was built a story and a half house of wood, for the coachman and gardener* [on the east side of the house] *and for an office* [to the west]. *The upper piazza ran across to the roofs of these buildings, forming a connected group* [fig. 122].[6]

It appears, based on materials and stylistic character, that alterations were made to the house about 1870 and 1910. The wooden dependencies have been destroyed—the office around 1850 and the gardener's house around 1950.[7] The main house, which measures 53 feet 4 inches wide by 51 feet deep, is extant but currently unoccupied. ✜

6. Ibid.
7. A photograph depicting the gardener's house shortly before its destruction is at the Oneida County Historical Society. In noting the general composition of the main house and dependencies, the author wonders whether Hooker might have had a role in the design of Ezra Prentice's *Mount Hope*, erected south of Albany about 1832.

53. CIRCULAR GARDEN PAVILION, VAN RENSSELAER MANOR

Head of Market Street (now Broadway), Albany, N.Y.
Designed before 22 May 1824.
Building history unknown.

54. OCTAGONAL GARDEN PAVILION, VAN RENSSELAER MANOR

Head of Market Street (now Broadway), Albany, N.Y.
Designed before 9 July 1824.
Probably built 1824; razed.
Builders: Timothy Fassett and Lawrence Hallenbake.

During the summer of 1824 Stephen Van Rensselaer III commissioned Hooker to design two garden pavilions. The first, designed by 22 May, was *a circular pavillion,* the design for which Hooker charged $10.00. Hooker charged $8.00 on 9 July for the design of the second pavilion, to be *octagonal.* It is not known whether this scheme was intended to supersede or to accompany the previous one. Finally, on 24 August Hooker billed Van Rensselaer $7.00 for *inspecting the erection* of the pavilion or pavilions and *directing the work of carpenters stone cutter &c.*[1] From other bills held in the same collection it appears that Fassett and Hallenbake were the builders.[2] ✣

1. Van Rensselaer Manor Papers, SC 7079, MSC NYSL. It is not known how these pavilion designs were related to Hooker's earlier schemes for a similar structure (cat. 24).
2. Ibid.

55. PEARL STREET THEATRE

South Pearl Street, Albany, N.Y.
Designed c. July 1824.
Built August 1824-May 1825; altered 1840;
burned January 1868; rebuilt; razed c. 1963.
Stonecutters: Brainard & Bruce.
Carpenter: Lewis Farnham.
Mason: John Turner.

Concerned citizens had struggled to maintain a theatre in Albany since before 1800. In 1812, the first structure in the city designed for that purpose was constructed by Lewis Farnham on Green Street. The enterprise failed, however, and the building was converted to a church in 1818.[1]

Encouraged by Albany's fast-growing population, another theatrical venture was attempted with the establishment of the Pearl Street Theatre. On 15 July 1824, the buildings on the intended site were sold at auction and were *to be pulled down immediately.*[2] Construction likely began soon thereafter.

▶
Fig. 124. Pearl Street Theatre, Albany (1824–25), exterior, c. 1925. Collection W. R. Wheeler, Troy, N.Y.

A contemporary description of the building, quoted in a later publication, provides information regarding its exterior appearance, plan, and decorative scheme.

> *"The new theatre is situated on the west side of Pearl Street, extending to William; sixty-two feet front, one hundred and sixteen feet deep; height in front forty feet; divided into a basement, principal and attic story. The entrance to the boxes is by three lofty arched openings; the piers and arches are of free stone, beautifully rusticated; they occupy three-fifths of the front; the entrances to the pit and gallery are on each side, in plain brick work. Above the rusticated basement, the center is embellished with six stone pilasters, supporting an entablature and angular pediment; the pilasters are coupled at the angles, and the order is the antique Ionic; the cornice only is continued the whole length of the front, which is crowned with a bold balustrade, surmounted with appropriate acroteria. The outer lobby is entered by two steps, from which you are conducted by easy flights of winding stairs to a spacious corridor surrounding the first tier of boxes. Over the*

1. H. P. Phelps, *Players of the Century* (Albany: Joseph McDonough, 1880), pp. 40–41.
2. Ibid., p. 63. The land the building was to occupy was reportedly subscribed by Hugh (or Isaac) Dennison [sic].
3. Ibid., pp. 63–64.
4. Cuyler Reynolds, comp., *Albany Chronicles* (Albany: J. B. Lyon Company, Printers, 1906), p. 453.
5. Ibid., pp. 453–54.
6. This was first issued as Pl. II in No. III, evidently in 1778, before the entire Vol. II was published in the following year; Robert Adam, *The Works in Architecture of Robert and James Adam,* ed. Robert Oresko (London: Academy Editions, and New York: St. Martin's Press, 1975), pp. 7, 60, 125.
7. *Albany Argus,* 10 February 1907; newspaper clipping in the Scrapbooks of St. Paul's Church, Albany, N.Y.
8. Root, pp. 150–51.
9. Collection, Don Carpentier.

outer lobby in the second story, is an elegant saloon or coffee room, with an adjoining chamber, and over these in the third story, are similar rooms for refreshments. The auditory is divided into a pit and three tiers of boxes, the gallery being in the front of the third tier; the boxes advance one seat in front of the columns which support them; the second and third tiers are brought forward on arches springing from the capitals of the pillars. The ceiling is in the form of a dome, painted in stone-colored panels, with rosettes. The glass chandelier is to be lighted from above and lowered through the fret-worked circlet in the centre of the dome. The proscenium and the panels of the boxes are to be splendidly ornamented. The stage is fifty-eight by fifty-two feet, above which are painting rooms, carpenters' galleries, etc. An adjoining brick tenement contains a green-room and very comfortable dressing rooms. The whole is furnished in handsome style, and is somewhat larger than the Baltimore theatre. Mr. P. Hooker is architect, and Mr. Grain the scene painter. The probable cost, including lot, is about $25,000."[3]

▲
Fig. 125. Pearl Street Theatre, Albany (1824–25), as depicted in a transfer print on a Staffordshire pitcher, 1825.
Albany Institute of History & Art.

The language indicates that the structure was not yet complete. Its technical nature further suggests that Hooker was the author.

On 26 March 1825 the nearly completed building was opened for public inspection,[4] and the first production was staged on 18 May.[5] An image of the Pearl Street Theatre has been preserved as a transfer print on a Staffordshire pitcher (fig. 125). Hooker's elevation recalls that of Robert Adam's Shelburne House in Berkeley Square, London, published in the second volume of *The Works in Architecture* in 1779.[6]

In 1839 the Pearl Street Theatre was purchased by the congregation of St. Paul's Church and, like the city's first theatre, converted into a church the following year.[7] The building returned to its original use in 1863, but was gutted by fire in 1868.[8] After being rebuilt, apparently incorporating portions of the Hooker-designed street facade (fig. 124), the theatre proved successful until around 1963, when it was razed.

Excavation for the Knickerbocker Arena in 1986 uncovered what appears to be a fragment of the cornerstone of the building with the following inscription:

[Phili]*p Hooker Esq*$^{\text{r.}}$ *Arch*^{t}
[Brai]*nard & Bruce.* ~
[Sto]*ne Cutters.* ~
[Lewi]*s Farnam Carpt*$^{\text{r.}}$
[Joh]*n Turner Mason*
~ ~ *1824*[9]

56. LOWVILLE ACADEMY

Lowville, N.Y.
Designed c. November 1824.
Built 1825–26; razed 1836.
Builders: Russell Hills, Oliver Bingham, and Luke Wilder.

The Lowville Academy was chartered in 1808. On 24 March 1824, Principal Stephen W. Taylor submitted a proposal for the organization of an ideal school as a condition under which he would accept a new contract.

> " . . . *the academy* [is to] *be large enough for 100 students, and . . . be built on a new plan, which is supposed to retain every important modification of the best plans hitherto in use . . . though secluded from each other* [the students] *are placed under the immediate inspection of the instructor.*"[1]

After the academy trustees agreed to Taylor's proposal, plans for the school building were drawn by Hooker *under the eye of the principal, and* [were] *approved late in 1824.*[2] They were patented by Taylor and John W. Martin on 16 April 1825.[3]

Franklin B. Hough provides descriptions of the building in his histories of the academy and of Lewis County.

> *This "patent-right academy" was a twelve-sided brick edifice . . . two stories high, above a high stone basement, and was surmounted by an attic story of wood and* [a] *tin-covered dome, from the center of which arose a cupola for the bell. There was a window on each side, in each story, except at the front doorway. Around the attic was a promenade, whose deck floor formed the roof of the outer portion of the main building. An immense twelve-sided column of timber in the center* [not indicated in the plans] *supported the attic and roof. The building was 70 feet in diameter between its parallel walls, and cost $8,200.*[4] *(Joiners', carpenters', painters', and glaziers' work and materials, five thousand and fifty dollars; mason work and materials, three thousand one hundred and fifty dollars.)*[5] *The building contract was awarded December 13, 1824 to Russell Hills, Oliver Bingham, and Luke Wilder. The basement* [used as a dormitory] *was 8 feet high, and the main story 10 feet under the galleries, and 13 feet above them. The attic was 10 feet high, and was used as the ladies department.*[6] *The* [original] *design proposed to have the pillars supporting the gallery twelve-sided; the teachers platform twelve-sided; and in short the duodecimal number was adopted throughout. The attic was designed under the contract of Dec. 13, 1824, to include twenty-four bed rooms besides entries and halls, but by a subsequent agreement (April 5, 1825), an alteration was made, and thirty-two boxes like those in the first and second stories, were to be built. This change was occasioned by the erection of the wings that were chiefly devoted to small rooms for one student each.*[7] *It was dedicated January 12, 1826.*[8]

Although the original drawings and contract have since been lost, they were extant when Hough prepared his history of the academy in 1859.[9] Hough's woodcut illustrations of the building (fig. 126) were taken from Hooker's plans and, when published in 1883, were accompanied by the following reference key:

1. Franklin B. Hough, *History of Lewis County, New York, 1805–1883* (Syracuse: D. Mason & Co., 1883), pp. 334–35.
2. Ibid., p. 336.
3. Ibid.
4. Ibid.
5. Franklin B. Hough, *Lowville Academy Semi-Centennial Anniversary* (Lowville, N.Y.: The Home Committee, 1859), p. 70n.
6. Hough, *History of Lewis County*, p. 336.
7. Hough, *Lowville Academy*, p. 70n.
8. Hough, *History of Lewis County*, p. 336.
9. Hough, *Lowville Academy*, p. 67.

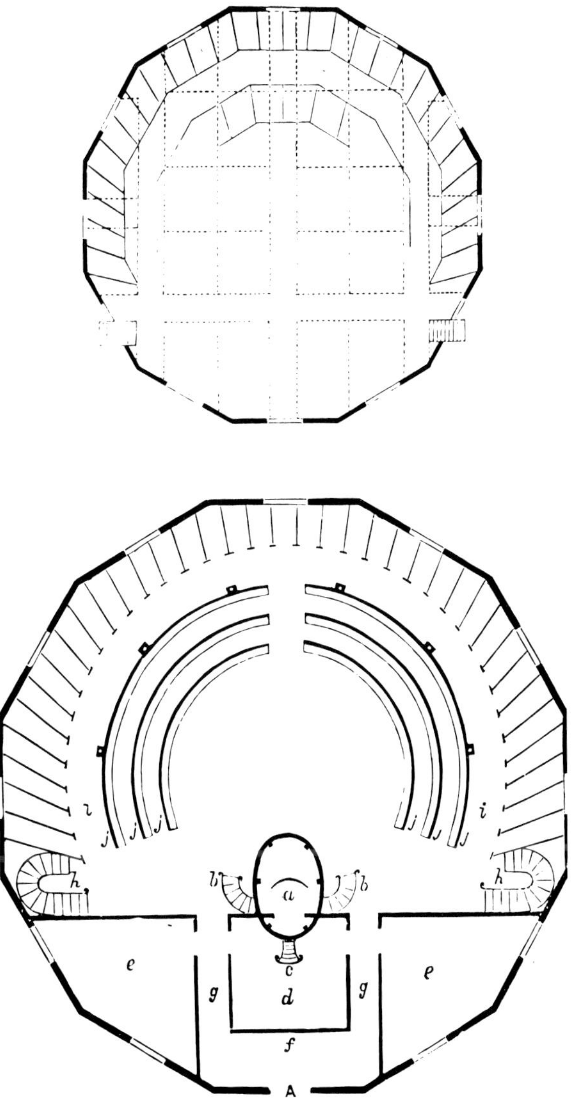

▶
Fig. 126. Lowville Academy, Lowville, N.Y. (1825–26), plans of the principal and attic stories, after drawings by Hooker. Courtesy New York State Library, Albany.

A. *the principal entrance on the west side, fronting upon the main street of the village.*

a. *The Instructor's stand and desk, commanding a view of every seat in the room. It was also used as a rostrum for exercises in declamation.*

bb. *Stairs to this stand and stage.*

c. *Stairs from the stand to the recitation room.*

d. *Recitation room sixteen feet square, with an entrance from each hall.*

ee. *Rooms opening into the halls. That on the right was used as a library, and the one on the left as the recitation room of an assistant teacher.*

f.g.g. *Halls.*

h.h. *Stairs to the gallery.*

i.i. *Depressed aisles, in front of the student's boxes. Around the margin of this aisle were six twelve-sided pillars supporting the gallery, which extended thus far into the room.*

j.j.j. *Circular seats for recitation of large classes. Each cell was furnished with a desk and chair.*

The smaller figure is upon the same scale as the larger, and shows the size of the attic story as compared with the main [floor of] *the building. The dotted lines represent the arrangement as first planned, for bedrooms, but this intention was changed before completion. It* [the attic] *was constructed upon the solitary-cell principle, however, like the main building below, it being apparently thought that the young ladies needed watching while at their studies, as much as the young men.*[10]

In his discussion of the Lowville Academy, Hough notes that *it has been said that the plan resembled that of some convict prison in Europe.*[11] Indeed, the spatial arrangement of the school building appears to have followed Jeremy Bentham's notion of the panopticon, developed for use in prison design.[12] Whether proposed here by Principal Taylor or by Hooker, whose second scheme for the Albany Jail (cat. 23) had reflected Bentham's ideas, the plan's effectiveness in establishing hierarchical relationships seemed to make it suitable for the academy's educational program. As constructed and put into use, however,

> *the new academic building proved a failure from the beginning. It was found that every noise in the main room was repeated in unpleasant echoes from the walls. The lower cells were in winter too cold, and those in the galleries were too warm. The furnaces in the basement were ill constructed, and insufficient. But most of all it was soon found that students of advanced age would not subject themselves to the espionage to which they were exposed—and finally the foundations of the building proved defective and the walls soon required support by the bracing of strong timbers from without. It became unsafe, and in 1836, it became necessary to take it down.*[13]

10. Hough, *History of Lewis County,* p. 337. Hough, pp. 337–38, reports that two small buildings, 22 by 32 feet, were constructed at the same time, intended as dormitories. They do not appear on the plans, and there is no indication whether or not Hooker designed them.
11. Ibid., p. 336.
12. Jeremy Bentham, *Complete Works,* Vol. IV, ed. John Bowring (Edinburgh, 1843).
13. Hough, *History of Lewis County,* p. 336.

57. SPECULATIVE TOWN HOUSE FOR LUTHERAN EBENEZER CHURCH

Pine Street, Albany, N.Y.
Designed after 29 November 1824.
Built 1825; razed.
Builders: Timothy Fassett and Lawrence Hallenbake.

On 29 November 1824 the Trustees of the Lutheran Ebenezer Church appointed Hermanus Henderer to *see our Philip Hoocker to make a draft for a two storey brick house twenty-one feet fronting Pine Street next to Mr.* [Frederick van] *Wormer's thirty feet deep.* On the first floor, there were to be *two rooms and a pantarey* and on the second *also two rooms.* There was to be a *celler under the whole and celler Kitchens* and *a good and suficient stone wall under the whole.*[1]

No further action on the project was recorded for the next eight months until the church trustees hired Fassett and Hallenbake to construct the building for a fee of $1,495.00.[2] The builders received the final payment on their contract on 25 November 1825.[3] Hooker was paid $30.00 for his services, indicating that he probably supervised the construction.[4] ✥

1. First Lutheran Church Council Minutes, 29 November 1824, Archives, First Lutheran Church, Albany, N.Y. (hereafter A FLC).
2. Ibid., 19 July 1825.
3. Treasurers Book, A FLC.
4. Ibid.

58. FRONT ELEVATION AND STEEPLE FOR THE CHAPEL, HAMILTON COLLEGE

Clinton, N.Y.
Designed after 23 November 1825.
Built 1825–27; extant.
Stonemason: Reuben Wilcox.
Carpenter: Isaac Williams.

▶
Fig. 127. Hamilton College Chapel, Clinton, N.Y. (1825–27), exterior, c. 1869. Archives, Hamilton College.

▶
Fig. 128. Hamilton College Chapel, Clinton, N.Y. (1825–27), front elevation measured by Bagg & Newkirk, Architects, 1927–28. Archives, Hamilton College.

No significant new information on Hooker's design for the Hamilton College Chapel (fig. 127) has come to light since the publication in 1929 of Edward W. Root's pioneering work, *Philip Hooker: A Contribution to the Study of the Renaissance in America.* Because of Root's closeness to his subject and in an effort to pay tribute to his part in documenting an otherwise little-known architect, much of his Hamilton College Chapel entry is reprinted below. The text reveals the quality of his insights and the flavor of his prose.[1]

> *Oren Root, a graduate of Hamilton College in 1833, and later its Professor of Mathematics, has left the following entry inside the cover of the book in which he kept his weather records: "Ham Coll Chapel designed by Hooker of Albany 1827." This memorandum taken in connection with a letter from Hooker in the College archives and the appearance of the building itself seems to establish the identity of the architect with some degree of certainty.*
>
> *At a meeting of the Board of Trustees of the College at the College Hall on the*

▶
Fig. 129. Stone Presbyterian Church, Clinton, N.Y. (1834), exterior, c. 1875. The Clinton Historical Society.

23d of August, 1825, it was resolved, "That the Treasurer proceed to build a chapel and cause the same to be completed as soon as practicable, consistent with due economy; and that Mess[rs] *Platt, Lothrop, & Hubbard be a committee to advise & direct the Treasurer as to the form & size & mode of finishing; and that the chapel be located south of Kirkland Hall. . . ."*

The Treasurer of the College at the time was Erastus Clark. The Lothrop mentioned was John H. Lothrop, one of the trustees and for many years a prominent citizen of Utica.

On the 6th of November, 1825, Clark died and Lothrop assumed his correspondence—in so far at least as it concerned the projected building. On the 23d of November Hooker writes to Lothrop:

"Dear Sir

"I have received your favour of the 19th instant I received a communication from the late M[r]*. E Clark dated the 8*[th] *of last month, giving me a particular description of the Scite & Buildings of Hamilton College—requesting me to forward a plan or Elevation of a front of a chappel, to have a Tower & Steeple Standing intirely without the Building which was to be 75 by 50 feet front—He informed me that the Building would be, 'Erected for other purposes, beside, Religious & Classical exercises' that it would have 'three tier of windows' and that it would be '33 feet in height above the watertable'*

"On the receipt of his letter I wrote to him to inform me of the distribution of the interior the better to enable me to design a front to answer the internal arrangement, and whether a Steeple with a proportionate Spire would be prefered—or whether Something of the Style of a cupola with two Sections finished with a dome would not be more proper for a chappel than a lofty Spire—the tower I presume ought to Contain a clock—and a College bell as a matter of course. If I understand the thing Correctly the Steeple, is to be placed in front, or at the East End—is the Stairs to be carried up in the tower or Elsewhere.

"If you will favour me with a few hints on the Subject, I Shall forward a drawing—for the same forthwith

Respectfully yours
P. Hooker

J. H. Lothorp [sic] *Esq*[r]*"* — *23*[rd] *Nov*[r] *1825*

▶ Fig. 130. First Presbyterian Church of Whitesboro, Whitesboro, N.Y. (1834), exterior, c. 1960. Oneida County Historical Society, Utica.

This letter is addressed on the outside "J. H. Lothrop, Utica," is postmarked, "Albany, Nov 24," and is indorsed in Lothrop's handwriting, "Philip Hooker's Letter, Nov 1825."

Professor Edward North's chronology of events in the history of Hamilton College states that "plans for the building were drawn by John H. Lothrop" and that two years passed before it was ready for occupancy. This fixes the date of its completion at the end of 1827. From the letter just quoted it appears that Dr. North's statement regarding the plans must refer to the design of the main body of the structure. This last, while pleasing, is devoid of the architectural treatment which has been given the facade, tower and steeple.[2]

Root went on to state that *the exterior of the building has suffered comparatively little from alteration.*[3] He noted the disappearance of the parapets above the eaves on the side elevations, an absence which continues to the present. Among the few other changes cited by Root, the one that disturbed him most was the later nineteenth century replacement of the small-paned, clear-glazed sash with stained glass windows. This alteration was reversed in 1949 as a result of the decision *to restore the Chapel to the spirit and style intended by its architects,* a project executed as a World War II memorial.[4] Root's comments about the original windows may enhance our appreciation of the building today.

> *Few people realize how much the good appearance of the Colonial and post-Colonial type of building depended upon the presence of the delicate sash bars or muntins that held the panes of glass in place. These muntins, when painted white, as in the case of the Chapel, transformed the window openings into dainty checker boards which greatly relieved the plainness of the walls.*[5]

In discussing the various changes to the interior of the building, Root noted that

> *originally the Chapel proper occupied the easterly two thirds of the two lower stories. In the westerly portion were recitation rooms for Greek and Physics on the first and second floors respectively. In 1897 these rooms were removed, the apse was built and the Chapel auditorium extended to the main wall on the west.*[6]

Still other changes made at that time were superseded by the 1949 work.[7]

Finally, Root commented on Hooker's design and paid tribute to the character of the building.

> *Apart from its commanding site and the beauty of its steeple the Chapel is remarkable as perhaps the only one of our earlier churches built in three stories. . . . The introduction of the third story, besides improving the main proportions of the building, has given Hooker another opportunity to solve the problem of providing three rather low stories with a dignified front. On either side of the tower entrance he has placed, as the pictures show, a single, large, semicircular-headed window running up through the two lower floors, and above each of these windows, on the wall of the third story, he has completed the design with a rectangular panel of painted wood* [fig. 128].
>
> *Not the least attractive feature of the Chapel is the color of its stone. Originally a neutral gray, but rich in iron, it has turned with the years a subdued, soft orange which contrasts ever so faintly with the slightly bluish, rusticated quoins. Altogether its exterior is one of the best proportioned and most charming of its kind in America and deserves more attention than it has hitherto received.*[8]

Although the chapel at Hamilton College has not received the critical attention that Root believed it was due, the design of its tower was apparently influential in the region. The steeples of the Stone Presbyterian Church of Clinton, 1834 (fig. 129), and the First Presbyterian Church of Whitesboro, 1834 (fig. 130), are identical to it in all but their uppermost stages. It is possible that the drawing for the chapel was preserved and used repeatedly by the same builder.

The steeple of the Hamilton College Chapel incorporates many design elements typical of Hooker's work of this period. Today, as the unique unmodified survivor among Hooker's ecclesiastical designs, it continues to demonstrate his skill as a master of detail and proportion. ✥

1. Root's substantive notes and citation notes have not been included here.
2. Root, pp. 151–53. The names of the stonemason, Reuben Wilcox, and the interior carpenter, Isaac Williams, are given in Walter Pilkington, *Hamilton College 1812/1962* (Clinton, N.Y.: Hamilton College, 1962), p. 187.
3. Root, p. 153.
4. Pilkington, *Hamilton College*, p. 192.
5. Root, p. 154.
6. Ibid., p. 155.
7. Pilkington, *Hamilton College*, p. 192.
8. Root, p. 156.

59. WAREHOUSE FOR HENRY VAN SCHAICK

West side of Quay Street, Albany, N.Y.
Designed before 3 April 1826.
Built 1826; razed.
Builders: John Boardman and John Nelligan.

60. WAREHOUSE FOR JOHN HOLME

West side of Quay Street at the corner of Mark Lane, Albany, N.Y.
Designed before 3 April 1826.
Built 1826; razed.
Builders: John Boardman and John Nelligan.

A letter from Hooker written around March 1826 to Henry Van Schaick provides information about these two related projects. Hooker had been retained separately by Van Schaick and John Holme to design buildings on their contiguous lots. He wrote to propose cooperation between the two clients and to indicate his availability to supervise the work.

> *Dear Sir*
> *I have obtained two estimates for the building of your store; the lowest of which is not out of the way. I have recommend*[ed] *to Mr. Holme to join with you in the erection of his building. I consider that it will benifit you both, as you will thereby save room: let him allow you the privelege of a small privy for the use of your back wall* [i.e., to share the structural support provided by it]. *Then there will be no vacancy between the buildings. One tier of windows in the rear of your store in the upper stories will open into the small yard (in rear of Mr Holme's new building) to give light and air. When you shall have made up your mind with respect to the plan I have proposed, I will obtain one or two more estimates & transact such other business as you shall direct. If it shall be your wish, I will see that your building be done according to any contract you may enter into, for a reasonable compensation.*

In the margin of the letter is Hooker's estimate of the probable cost of the two buildings:

Suppose H. V. S. building to cost	*$3000*
and Mr. J. H. [building to cost]	*4500*
	$7500 [1]

The proposal was accepted and a contract, between John Holme and Henry Van Schaick of Lansingburgh and the builders John Boardman and John Nelligan, was written by Hooker and signed on 3 April 1826. The builders agreed to complete the two stores by 1 September for a payment of $2,400 from Van Schaick and $3,567 from Holme.[2]

The specifications were written by Hooker as a separate document, a practice uncommon in his work before this time. Their language suggests that Van Schaick's intended building was to be used for merchandising grain.

▲
Fig. 131. Typical storehouses on lower State Street, Albany, circa 1915. Albany Institute of History & Art, McKinney Library, Photograph Collection.

Specifications of a store house to be erected on the west side of Quay Street, for Henry Van Schaick, of the following dimentions: twenty feet front and rear, and forty one feet in depth from front to rear; four stories high, the first, 8 [feet high]*, the second, 7* [feet high] *the third and fourth, 6 feet 9 inches between the floors & beams with a breast wall above the garret floor of 2 1/2 feet. The foundation walls to be made of the best stone and mortar.* [The] *front walls 2 feet, and sides and rear, 20 inches thick, 5 1/2 feet high, to be sunk four feet below the surface of the street. The foundation to be prepared by driving good and sufficient piles, 2 feet from centre to centre, in a zig zag form under the said walls; to be levelled off fair and even, on the top of which is to be laid sound timber, 6 inches in thickness, the width of said walls. The walls of the superstructure are to be of good, merchantable bricks, laid in good lime and sand mortar. The front wall in the first story, 2 1/2* [bricks thick]*; second and third stories, 2 bricks* [thick]*; and the remainder, 2 bricks in thickness. The first story to be faced with handsome, tooled stone, with a sufficient number of headers to bind the work, and resting on an eight inch water table of like stone. The rear wall, two bricks* [in thickness]*; the flank walls, 2 bricks* [in thickness] *in the first, second, and third stories; 1 1/2* [bricks in thickness] *in the fourth story; and one brick* [thick] *in the gables. Two tier of piles are to be driven two feet from center to center, and capped with timber, 18 inches wide, under two intermediate walls to be erected 18 inches thick and two feet high, for the support of the first floor, and posts for the support of the upper floors. Said walls to be built with the best flat Schodack* [New York] *stone. The beams of the first* [floor] *8 inches square, two feet from centre to centre; those of the second* [floor] *10 by 5 inches, 15 inches apart; those of the third and fourth stories, 9 by 4 1/2 inches, 16 inches apart; and those of the garret floor, 9 by 4 inches, 20 inches apart. Each floor to be supported by two bearing beams of 10 by 8 inches under the second and third* [floors]*, and 9 by 7 inches under the fourth and fifth floors, with posts of the same size to have cap*[ital]*s and bases of two inches* [of] *seasoned, white oak plank; the roof to be supported by a truss frame; purlin plates, 10 by 5* [inches]*; straining beams, 10 by 4* [inches]*; 4 posts, 10 by 5* [inches]*; 4 braces, 6 by 4* [inches]*; rafters, 6 by 4* [inches]*, 28 inches apart. The purlin plates, all the bearing beams, and three beams in each of upper floors, are to be secured to the walls with good and sufficient anchors of iron.* [The] *roof plank*[e]*d and slated in the best possible manner,* [word illegible] *gutter in front and two 3 inch, tin conductors with proper heads and pipes; double iron tin gutter and one 3 inch tin conductor in the rear. The water to be conveyed into a drain, 10 by 6 inches; plank bottom, brick sides & flat stone cover to be laid under the first floor and conveyed into the river. In front there are to be a pair of doors, and two windows in each story. The doors are to be made of narrow, or slit, plank, beaded and lined, with 3/4th inch boards put on with wrought nails, clinched and hung with strong hinges; the hooks to be leaded into stone blocks, laid fair in the walls. The door of the first story is to have an eight inch knob lock of the best kind, and two strong sliding bolts. Those of the upper stories are to have wooden cross bars and half staples; a dormer door in the roof. Sides and roof to be* *slated and secured with sheet lead and patent ribbing in the best manner against leakage, over which is to be a projecting pediment and proper fixture, with a large shive or roller of the most approved construction for hoisting. Two windows in the first story to contain 16 panes, 14 by 9 inch glass, to have proper made outside shutters similar to the aforesaid doors; and the windows in the upper stories are to be 4 by 3 feet, to have like shutters, without frames or sashes, but to shut into a rebatement made in the brick work and hung to stone blocks. All the doors and windows to have stone sills and lintals, and finished in the most substantial manner; black birch or white oak rollers of 2 feet* [illegible passage] *at each end to have turned gudgeons, one inch diameter, to roll in suitable eyes leaded into the lintals of the doors of the second, third and fourth stories; and a frame of white oak timber of 8 by 6 inch scantling is to be placed on the front of the wall and secured with suitable holdfasts, wrought into and anchored to the wall, to the door of the first story. The front corners of the stiles and lintals are to be rounded off in a handsome and workmanlike manner. Cast Iron plates of 3 feet high and 16 inches wide, the front edge and top end rounded off and secured to the wall with suitable anchors rivetted into the plates to all the other doors. One back window in each story of 4 by 3 feet* [margin note: *Back window 2 x 8*] *made like those in front, with the addition of tin or sheet iron lining, and a back door in the first story. The door and window sills, lintals, water table and facing, and the front of the first story are to be of the best kind of Bethlehem* [New York] *stone. The lower corners of the door lintals are to be rounded off. The floors are to be laid with sound, seasoned, yellow pine plank, tongued and grooved and well nailed; strong step ladders to each story; scuttle and steps to roof balustrade in front* [on roof]*; strong railing in rear, hoist wheel band and runner of the best kind. Counting room partitioned off with seasoned plank, tongued and grooved, and planed on counting room side; ceiling with narrow boards, tongued and grooved, to have a proper door and sash window. In the partition a proper flue is to be carried up in the wall for a stove pipe; the timber to be of the best yellow pine, free from sap. The outside woodwork is to be painted with two coats of good paint; the front of said building to be painted and penciled. The floors are to be scribed so close to the walls that no kind of grain* [passage illegible] *any of said floors. The drain, above mentioned, is to extend eleven feet west of said rear wall to a privy, which is to be built by the owner of the adjoining lot in connection with the above described store house.* [It] *is to be erected on the north side and on the corner of Mark Lane* [later Exchange Street] *and Quay Street. A similar structure for Mr John Holme, with the exception that Mr Holme's store will be twenty six feet, two inches in front on Quay Street and forty one feet on Mark Lane. The first story on each street to be faced with the Bethlehem stone in regular courses, handsomely tooled, and to have one pair of doors and two windows on each street in each story as described for that of Mr Van Schaick. The windows in the first story are to have 16 panes of 14 by 10 inch* [glass]. . . .[3]

Although they have not survived in total, the extant specifications describe a type of structure commonly built in Albany after the opening of the Erie Canal, which had its eastern terminus in this part of the city. The area along Quay, lower State, and Water streets was once occupied by many similar buildings, as early views attest (fig. 131). No image of these two specific buildings has yet been found. ✜

1. Van Schaick Family Papers, DD 10442, MSC NYSL.
2. Ibid.
3. Ibid.

61. FIRST PRESBYTERIAN CHURCH

Northwest corner of Washington and Liberty streets, Utica, N.Y.
Designed spring 1826.
Built 1826–27; burned January 1851.
Builder: John Culver.

▲
Fig. 132. View of the City of Utica, 1850, including First Presbyterian Church (1826–27), right side center. Also depicted are the remodeled Trinity Episcopal Church (cat. 11), Miller house (cat. 52), Ontario Branch Bank (cat. 35), and Bank of Utica (A13). Lithograph, hand-colored. New York State Library, Albany.

The First Presbyterian Church was the largest of Hooker's church commissions, built at a cost of approximately $30,000.[1] Moses Bagg, historian of early Utica, provides additional details from records which are now lost.

> *. . . In the summer of 1826, a plan having been furnished by Philip Hooker of Albany, the architect of Trinity* [Episcopal Church, Utica], *the foundations of the new edifice were laid, twelve feet north from the old one. Messrs. Thomas Walker, John Bradish and Samuel Stocking were the building committee, and John Culver took the contract and superintended the work; on the 8th of November, 1827, the new building having been completed, it was formally dedicated. It was a substantial brick structure, surmounting a basement of stone. In dimensions it was seventy-two feet by one hundred and six, and had a steeple two hundred and eight feet in height. The basement contained a session room for evening meetings, and*

two large rooms for the male and female departments of the Sunday school. The auditorium was roomy, well-lighted and conveniently seated, and over the pulpit was an organ fifteen feet by ten in superficial dimension, and six feet deep, and having twelve stops. For many years this fine Ionic edifice surpassed in magnitude and convenience any church structure in Central and Western New York; it was the pride of the village, and, with its ambitious steeple, a landmark the most conspicuous of any in the vicinity.[2]

Further recognition of the building's amplitude appeared in a 14 January 1851 article in the *Utica Daily Gazette,* which noted that *the wide gallery which was on all sides* [of the church] *could . . .* [seat] *two thousand people.*[3] An understanding of the building's scale may be gained from an 1850 view of Utica, which depicts the church in relation to neighboring structures (fig. 132). The building was destroyed by fire on 13 January 1851.[4]

1. Root, p. 159.
2. M. M. Bagg, *The Pioneers of Utica* (Utica, N.Y.: Curtiss & Childs, 1877), p. 461. Pomroy Jones, *Annals and Recollections of Oneida County* (Rome, N.Y.: Pomroy Jones, 1851), p. 569, gives the height of the tower and spire as 215 feet.
3. *Utica Daily Gazette,* 14 January 1851.
4. Root, pp. 158–59.

62. COUNTRY SEAT FOR ELKANAH WATSON

Port Kent, N.Y.
Designed c. 1826.
Built 1826–28; altered c. 1870; extant.
Builders: Sheldon & Merritt.
Mason: John York.

Elkanah Watson (1758–1842) became prominent through successful business ventures, including banking, land speculation, and agriculture. The success of the New York State Bank and the construction of canals through his major land holdings made him wealthy. His efforts in promoting the Erie and Champlain canals, starting in 1791, had made him a familiar face in Albany.[1]

It was through the New York State Bank project of 1803 (cat. 10) that Watson had first become acquainted with Hooker. The 1820s saw the Albany entrepreneur considering retirement with his wife and son, Charles, in Port Kent on Lake Champlain, and at some time in the spring of 1826 he may have commissioned Hooker to design a *country seat.* Watson, a man of resolute ego, had earlier claimed credit for the bank design, and he would unabashedly state with regard to his house in Port Kent that it was *finished with elegance & on my own plan & admired by everybody, compleatly furnished in every way with elegance.*[2] The existence of house and site plan sketches attributed to Watson (figs. 133, 134) and the absence of manuscript material in Hooker's hand raise questions about the nature of the architect's involvement in the project. Nevertheless, references in Watson's correspondence during the construction of the house make it clear that he consulted Hooker on matters of design and that the Albany architect produced drawings for at least portions of the scheme.[3]

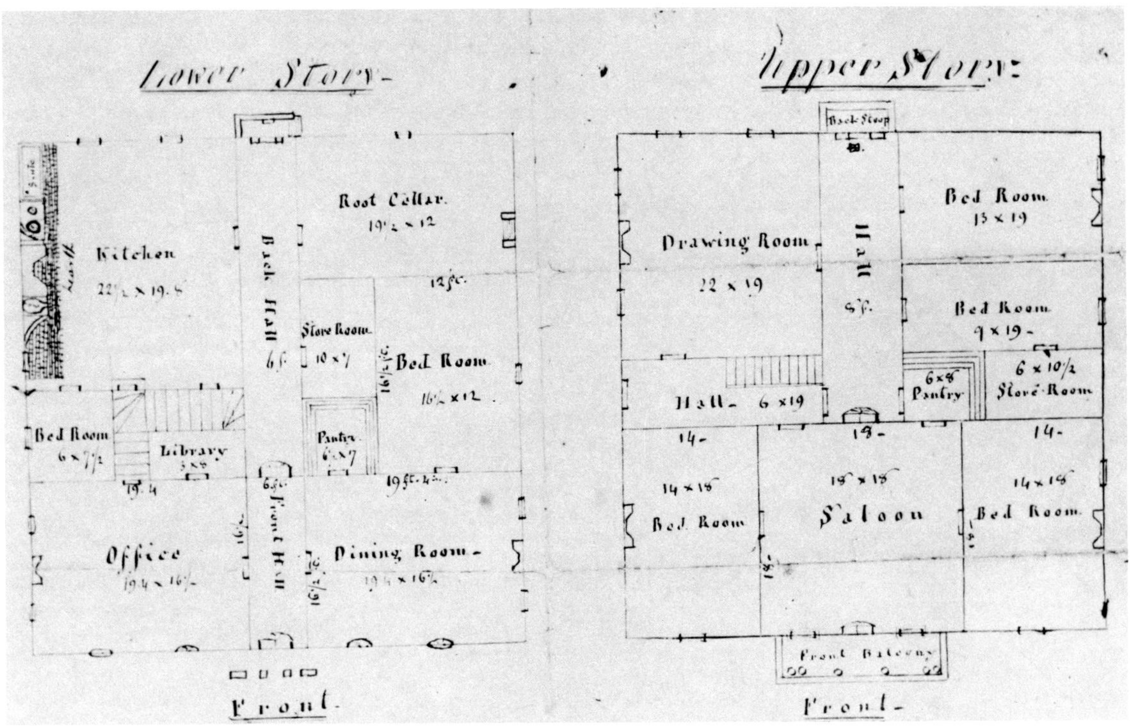

▲
Fig. 133. Elkanah Watson House, Port Kent, N.Y. (1826–28), plans of the upper and lower stories, attributed to Watson, c. 1827. Ink on paper. New York State Library, Albany.

A contract dated 1 July 1826 between John York of Peru, New York, and Watson indicates that work commenced on the foundation *50 feet square on the outside, ten feet in height, and two feet in thickness* by 15 August. York further contracted to *build the front wall as smooth & hansome as the stone furnish*[e]*d by said Watson will admit of* and to construct *four stacks of chimneys, ten feet in height, and to build in the one a comodious kitchen fire place & oven, and in the other three chimneys, a fire place in each.* York's compensation was $90.00 and a parcel of land in Port Kent.

Charles Watson, overseer for the construction of his father's house, contracted with builders Sheldon and Merritt to frame the building. Work progressed smoothly, and the roof was in place the next spring, as reported by Charles to his father in Albany.

> *Port Kent 27 June 1827*
> *. . . The roof was raised without any accident, and an eccellent peice of work it proves to be. It shal be covered and shingled (laying the shingles in cement) as soon as nails arrive. The stone has been laid at the base of the front pillars, and one week will complete the chimneys and balustrade agreeable to Hooker's plan. I have . . .* [illegible] *. . . off York, and sufficient remaining after paying Mayo and Follets bill, beams bill, &c &c., to pay the masons for finishing the cornish and balustrade out of the check of the bal*[an]*ce remaining in the Burlington Bank. . . .*

Charles wrote three days later from Burlington, Vermont.

> *My dear father,*
> *As soon as the nails arrive I shal have the whole exterior of your house compleated immediately.*

Enclosed, I send you the receipt of the Auburn Bank or the Mechanics Bank to enable me to close the contract with Sheldon for the entire completion of your building, agreeable to your instructions. The lower story by the 15 Oct and the upper story by the 1st April next . . . Sheldon & Merritt have offer[e]*d to compleat the building in the best style for $500. . . .*

On 9 October 1827, Elkanah Watson signed a second contract with John York to complete the interior finishes of the house.

. . . First, said York agrees & covenants to & with said Watson that he will make his plaster, and plaster in a good, workmanlike manner, all the basement, or lower story, of said Watson's house, now building in said village of Port Kent, on or before the first day of May next; that he will put on two coats of plaster & float & square the two front rooms.
Second, For the faithfull performance of the above agreement, the said York doth deposit, as an eskrow or security, a certain deed executed by said Watson to said York, dated the second day of June 1827, & conveying a "certain lot of land situate lying & being in Watsons Patent (so called) in the township of Peru & county of Clinton, being the south east corner lot number twenty three, to be in a square form & to contain fifty acres of land." The said security being for seventy dollars, which said York hereby acknowledges to have this day received for lathing & plastering said house. The said deed to be destroyed & the land revert to Watson, if the said York does not, on or before the first day of May next, lath & plaster the said basement story as aforesaid, or refund the said Watson seventy dollars in cash to said Watson on or before the first day of July next; or should said York lath & plaster the said basement story before the first [of] *May next as aforesaid or refund the said seventy dollars on or before the first day of July next, then, & in that case, the said Watson agrees to deliver over the said deed to said York.*
Third, the said York further agrees that if said Watson should have the whole or any part thereof lathed, then said York agrees to deposit, at the rate of three cents a square yard for such laths, & pay that amount thereof to said Watson. . . .

Charles wrote to his father, reporting the status of the work:

Port Kent 18 November 1827
. . . The house progresses very well. They finish their work faithfully. The first story is ready for the plaster. . . .

After this date, the existing correspondence appears to be incomplete. Watson wrote his son in a quick note on 27 December 1827: *How come the pillars?* referring to the columns for the portico of the house. Whether of wood or stone, these would have been one of the most expensive features of the house and, in Port Kent of the 1820s, difficult to obtain.

Upset over the lack of communication,Watson wrote to his son on 8 January 1828:

. . . I must be permitting to complain again while I have cause; not a word from you and Sheldon and Merritt; no map, no carpenters book, no long letter to fill in the gap of infamiliarity.

Elkanah wrote again on the following day.

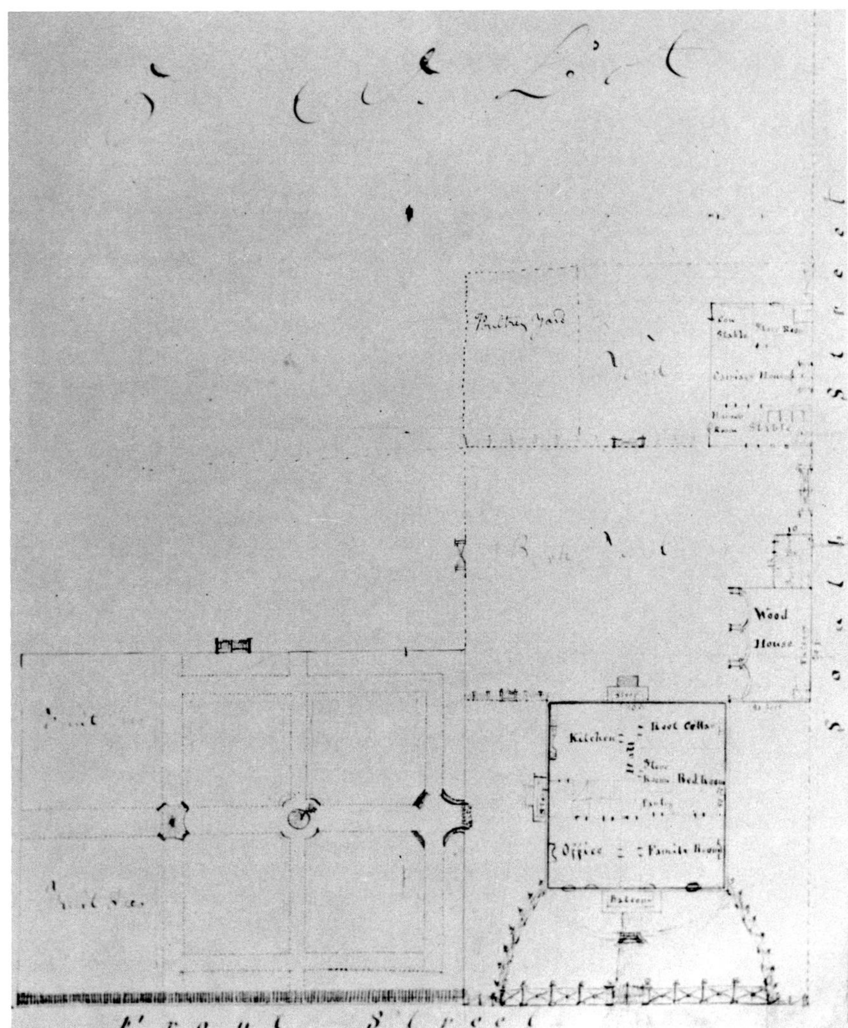

▶
Fig. 134. Elkanah Watson House and grounds, Port Kent, N.Y. (1826–28), sketch plan attributed to Watson, c. 1828. Ink on paper. New York State Library, Albany.

> *. . . I am really sorry you have not explained to me about the roof: what has been done; what is the true situation? I wrote to* S[heldon] *and* M[erritt to ask them] *to furnish that information. They too are silent. I know not why I should be kept in the dark; I ought not. . . . This information I seek at all counts as Hooker has furnished me with a method to attach the* [balustrade]*. . . . Hooker will have that expensive* n[orth] *wall. . . .*

The stone balustrade and the built-in gutters prepared for the building's roof had apparently taxed the builders' abilities. Shoddy construction aggravated the situation. Later correspondence suggests that the *carpenters book* had been lent by Albany carpenter John Boardman for use of the builders, and he requested its return. Again Elkanah wrote to Charles.

> *Albany 18 January 1828*
> *. . . Hooker has agreed to give me a plan on paper. As to the measures of fixing the roof, he says York's great mistake was to suppose himself in England, and that no experience of this entire city has* [illegible] *the impossiblility of making any quick gutters water tight. He mentions one instance where they expended $500.00 in copper all to no purpose. Even at this moment, I have noticed 2 scaffolds erected in the dead of winter to prostrate* [illegible] *walls. I* [illegible]

at the gutters [illegible] *under the eaves.* [Illegible] *that steep* [illegible] *York, to have involved me in so much unnessessary expen*[ses], *which I am ill able to* [afford]. . . .

. . . *Boardman, the carpenter, just called again; says with anger he must have the book; not another in the city. He can't make his contracts without it. Besides, I have fulfilled my promise by means of others. What a piece of work to get anything from the north. . . .*

On the same day Sheldon, of the builders Sheldon & Merritt, sent a letter to Watson.

Honored Sir

Yours of the 23 Dec did not come to hand till after Mr. Gross had been gone a number of days. Therefore I could not send the carpenter book as you requested, but [your] *son, Col. Charles, will forward it in a package which he informs me he is going to send you. As to the fifty dollars, your son has paid over according to contract and* [it] *is endorsed on the contract. Third, the roof is secured on the inside as agreed by Mr. Merritt. Fourth, as to the leaks of the roof, we did not secure it so permanently as we could, on account of the cement cleaving from the balustrade, which continues to fall more or less every week. We had a consultation respecting it and concluded to let it remain till spring when you should come to Port Kent and advise some measures about the balustrade, as it may injure the shingles in working over the balustrade. Fifth, the cold weather naped us up so close here that Mr. Merritt was not able to finish the stone work of his house. Consequently,* [he] *was not able to raise his house, but is a going on with it early in the spring.*

. . . *The second story of your house is going on well and the greatest precaution is taken as to fire. Your son or Mr. Barron, a very trusty hand, sleeps in the house every night. . . .* [4]

Previously, Elkanah had sent a disapproving letter, now lost, to the builders to which his son refers.

Port Kent 24 January 1828

My dear father,

In your pungent letter to Sheldon and Merritt, you express some alarm that one should have concluded to take down the wall of the north balustrade without consulting you. We had no such intention. I merely gave you our opinion; I believe the substance of any remarks was merely reccomendatory, for your consideration, if any way could be devised to secure your roof against leaking. . . . I should not under that consideration . . . consider it advisable to take down the wall. Some other substitute, however, will be necessary for the water cement. You can readily ascertain what composition would stand, as rough-cast work on the outside of buildings is common at the south, and York would put it on for nothing as he guaranteed the other. . . .

. . . *We shal want in the spring another keg of ground white lead, to paint the interior of the house, & sufficient black paint and varnish for the mantletree pieces which Mother wish*[e]*d to have painted black. . . .*

The *rough-cast* referred to here was a thin coat of cement placed over the exterior walls, smoothed and scored in imitation of cut stone. York apparently made an unsuccessful experiment with *water cement*; its name suggests it was a thinner mixture.

A letter Charles wrote to his father on 2 February 1828 seems to indicate that interior trim and windows were being installed. The same letter reports on *a conditional bargain* to provide builder Merritt with *a quarter acre lot in the village* in return for certain work on the project. Indeed, the letters and contracts indicate that most of the work in constructing the house and dependencies was bartered for and that Watson provided land and sometimes agreed to build small houses in exchange for services rendered. This arrangement was to Watson's benefit as it populated the town, Port Kent, which he was attempting to create and increased the value of the lands he retained.

Meanwhile, the roof remained a perpetual problem as Charles wrote:

> *Port Kent 12 February 1828*
>
> *. . . We have done nothing with the roof, waiting your final conclusion in regard to it. It will be important, however, to do whatever is done early in the spring as no plastering can be done untill the roof is fixt, as it leaks very much.*

Charles further reported:

> *Port Kent 13 February 1828*
>
> *. . . To save paying out cash for the hearths & facings in the fire places up stairs, I have partially agreed to sell Bingham & Page a village lot, & told them, if it met* [with] *your approbation,* [we] *would put them up a cheap building to the amount of a chimney piece in the drawing room. . . . We have the stuff on hand. . . .*

Elkanah's response followed five days later.

> *. . . I have never known till (your letter rec'd) this day that the roof "<u>leaks badly</u>"— nor do I yet know if the fense is made around the 5 acre lot. . . .*
>
> *You speak to me as to my final decision about the roof & yet wholly over look Hooker's letter, or rather draft with his directions to Sheldon and Merritt. . . . As to the manner of fixing the roof, their proposals for doing it, the manner they recommend by a plan on paper, no*[t] *a me*[a]*n sketch, but a regular draft of the roof, its assent* [illegible] *&c. . . .*

Sheldon, of Sheldon & Merritt, wrote to Elkanah on 19 February.

> *Sir, we read yours of the 23 Jan and also of 1st Feb requesting our views of the plan of fixing the roof; likewise Mr. Hooker's wishes of the plan of the gutters, balustrade &c. As to York, we shall* [have] *no further consultation respecting the roof or any part of it, as he has done the work entirely different from what Mr. Merritt and I got the idea when first conversing with him on the subject. Our views as* [to] *the finishing* [of] *the roof, is to take down the balustrade, carry out the roof, put on a wooden cornice and wooden balustrade, if the roof could be made tight as to leaks. As it is now the balustrade would have to be taken down and built up again for it is all coming to pieces already. We do not wish to have Mr. Hooker lay any stress upon our views of what way is most proper, but we would leave it with him as he is more experienced than what we are. We should be pleased to have Mr. Hooker give his plan in full, how it ought to be done, and we should like to have Mr. Hooker give a* [*plan* crossed out] *draught and explain every part of it fully.*
>
> *Yours respectfully Sheldon & Merritt*

Sheldon included a sketch, apparently of the existing treatment of the balustrade, gutter, and cornice (fig. 135).

A fragmented letter to Charles documents Elkanah's proposal to stop the leaky roof with pitch.

> *Albany 21 February 1828*
>
> . . . *I have enquired* . . . [illegible] . . . *of pitch of Follet, which* [illegible] *to put in our roof, for I am master ma*[n] *of that subject; even after* [those] *offensive walls are prostrated, & the roof brought over the eaves &* [cornice] . . . *for a leaky house is even worse than a leaky ship in a gale of wind.* . . .

Hooker corresponded with the builders and provided drawings and suggestions to them when difficulties arose, as noted in Elkanah's 29 February letter to his son.

> . . . *Hooker is preparing a plan to compleat that ill fated roof, as far as I can learn, & it* [conflicts] *with my opinion; no splicing the roof for new trouble & perpetual* [leaks] *but to knock* [down] *the n*[orth] *& e*[ast] *balustrades, & cornish & mark, smooth, & then continue the roof, so as to run over the eves; and a spout out side. He says the roof is sufficiently flatt.* [To] *splice on 6 feet upon that to make a joint & yet flatten that distance will be but half doing the work, & worse than 00. However, as I learn it to be guided by his own great experience, equal to any artist in America, I know not with certainty his exact* [illegible]. *His greatest difficulty appears to be here to combine the porticoed roof with the main roof, & as to taking up the present spouts to put out side, by keeping* [them] *cornice fashion & painting them white, combining the n*[orth] + *n*[orth] *1/2 of e*[ast] *at the n*[orth]*e*[ast] *corner of the house to carry off the water in that direction, & on the sueers* [i.e., sewers] *to bring the water to the s*[outh]*e*[ast] *corner to connect with the s*[outh] *1/2 of the n*[orth]*east spout, at that point leaving the n*[orth]*w*[est] *spout to carry the water into a great cistern. Such I collect to be his* [vision]. *He will send me a plan in a day or two, which I shall transmit to Sheldon & Merritt* . . . [with] *an injunction to follow the same implicity, or take the responsibility on their own shoulders, for I cannot take it on mine.* . . .

Charles wrote his father on the same date, indicating the status of the work.

> . . . *I have settled with J. R. Sheldon. The balance due you on his account is* [$] *64.00, which he wishes to apply on the balustrade. Sheldon & Merritt will make an offer as soon as they receive Mr. Hooker's plan of how much they will finish the roof, make new cornice & balustrade.* . . .
>
> . . . *The upper story of the house is in fine progress. They are doing some handsome work, more than could have been inforced by the contract. The capitols of the pillars they commence on next week; the pilars themselves can not be got out until we have Hooker's plan.* . . .

Interested in expediting a solution, Elkanah writes his son:

> *Albany 6 March 1828*
>
> . . . *On rec't of Hooker's plan, send me their proposals; to compleat the roof exactly upon that plan; to be annexed to the contract as part of it. Let them send*

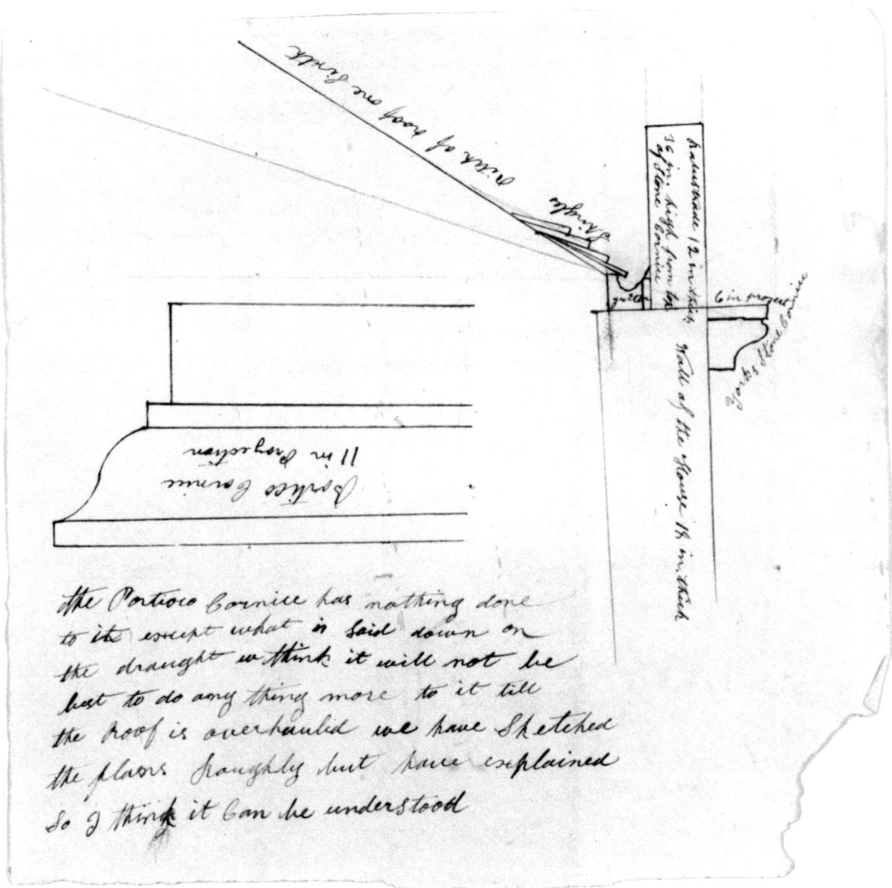

▶
Fig. 135. Elkanah Watson House, Port Kent, N.Y. (1826–28), sketch by contractor J. R. Sheldon of existing balustrade, gutter, and cornice, 1828.
Ink on paper. New York State Library, Albany.

me a intelligible, and plain, statement of what they will do it for compleat, . . . & I will answer you promptly by <u>*returning mail*</u> *after consulting Hooker, so as they can go as soon as the weather will justify it.*

And on 25 March 1828, Charles wrote to his father:

. . . Hooker's plan corresponds with Sheldon & Merritts views about the roof. They prefer, as I wrote you before, to do it by the day. . . . The hearths will be laid in the course of this week. . . .

Elkanah had earlier requested that Charles send him a map of the grounds about the house so that he and his wife could start to plan the landscaping. On 15 March he noted that

. . . as to the plan of the garden, your mother and myself having confidence in your good taste, will leave it to you. At the [illegible] *time the sketch enclosed* [coincides] *with our ideas, but* [the] *subject in toto to yours. . . .*

Charles reported on the site work in a letter dated 30 March.

. . . I will clear the garden of stone; make the land as mellow as possible; lay out the garden as near to your plan [fig. 134] *as its shape will admit off; plant out the fruit trees where you have directed; & deliver it over to you resigning all*

jurisdiction even of opinion after your arrival. . . . Quere. Shal I gravel the walks?
. . . I have sold two of the cooking stoves: one to Burges, which he pays by building [a] *stone-wall on the Hooker farm as you wish'd, between us & the Colvins. Colvin has agreed to build his half of the line in stone-wall, & I have agreed to build the other. . . .*

The owner of the *Hooker farm* remains a mystery. It is quite possible that it was Philip Hooker himself having accepted an exchange of land for architectural services.

Charles wrote again:

Port Kent 2 April 1828
*. . . Sheldon & Merritt have sent you their proposals as you requested them. I do not know what they have proposed, but to finish the three sides in the Ionic order, which is plainest from their debt I should think, was not worth over $100,* [$] *60. of which you know Sheldon now owes you. The roof cannot be fix't before the fore part of June, on account of spring raines, by which time I presume you will be here. I am apprehensive our house, from this delay, will not be fit to occupy before the middle of September.*

Elkanah replied:

Albany 8 April 1828
. . . I am aware, however, you cannot plaster till the roof is tight + compleat, & yet to be working up a large batch of mortar, and lay a while according to your [illegible] *plan is certainly an important prepatory step. . . . I shall hold myself in readiness to start the moment I hear the roof is compleat.*

Charles wrote to his father later that month, indicating that work was almost complete.

Port Kent 18 April 1828
. . . Sheldon & Merritt [have] *finish*[e]*d all the joiners' work under their contract that can be done before plastering.*

Elkanah Watson left Albany to begin residence in Port Kent by mid-May of 1828.

The roof problems were solved with the removal of the stone balustrade and its replacement with one of wood. This arrangement allowed water to pass under the balustrade, which could now be supported on posts. The stone balustrade had been a solid extension of the walls and prevented release of the water or snow which built up behind it.

Whether the sketch plans attributed to Watson (fig. 133) were drawn to guide the design of the house or to record its completion, they appear to be close to the layout as executed.[5] The building is cut into the side of a hill and its second floor is accessible from the carriage yard in the rear of the house. The lake front facade is a full two stories tall, and was built with a central pedimented pavilion containing a porch on each story. On the second story, the formal entertaining room overlooked Lake Champlain, while on the first story circular and semicircular windows framed the views.[6] ✤

1. Elkanah Watson Papers, GB 12579/GB 13294, MSC NYSL.
2. Ibid.; "Mixed Medley," Memoirs, 1821, MSC NYSL.
3. Elkanah Watson Papers. All the excerpts from documents and correspondence which follow are from this source.
4. The precaution against fire was well founded, for early notice by the resident watch saved the house from destruction about two months later; letter from Charles Watson to Elkanah Watson, 9 March 1828, Elkanah Watson Papers.
5. For a study of the building, see Susan Horst, "The Watson Manor: A Preliminary Historic Structure Report" (Master's thesis, Columbia University, 1980).
6. The first-story porch has since been extended, and the first-story windows altered.

63. SPECULATIVE DOUBLE TOWN HOUSE FOR HENRY VAN SCHAICK

Fox Street (now Sheridan Avenue), Albany, N.Y.
Designed before 15 January 1827.
Built 1827; razed.
Builders: Robert McElroy and John Sipple.

Bound with the specifications for the warehouses designed for Henry Van Schaick and John Holme (cats. 59, 60) is Hooker's handwritten contract dated 15 January 1827 and specifications for a *double dwelling house* to be built for Van Schaick by Robert McElroy and John Sipple.[1] No visual record of this project exists, but the specifications give valuable information regarding its construction and design.

> *The annexed plans* [now lost] *are designed for a double dwelling house to be built for Henry Van Schaick, on the north side of Fox Street in the city of Albany. Said double dwelling house is to be 39 feet, 10 inches, front and rear, and 24 feet deep, and 20 feet fronts divided into two stories; the first, 8 1/2 feet, and the second, 8 feet in the clear; to be constructed of sound timber; sills, 9 by 8* [inches]*; posts, 4 by 8* [inches]*; joists, 4 by 8* [inches]*; two feet, four inches from centre to centre in the first and second floors, and 9 by 4 inches & 2 1/2 feet apart on the garret floor; plates, 4 by 6* [inches]*; rafters, 4 by 6* [inches] *with coller beams 2 1/2 feet apart; studs & braces, 3 by 4 inches. The roof* [is] *to be well boarded & shingled; the ends & rear rough boarded with common sound tally boards; the whole well lapped and nailed. Neat cornice gutter in front, and plain gutter in the rear; one two-inch tin conductor in the rear and two in front. There is to be a cellar under said building, sunk three feet below the surface of the side walk. The walls of* [the cellar are to be] *stone, seven feet high & 18 inches thick, composed with good stone and morter; to have an 8 inch hard brick party wall, & fire places in the same, and subdivided by stud partitions, lathed and plastered, on stone foundations, according to plan № 5; finished neat and plain, with battened doors and plain casings; four windows in front of 6 pains of 14 by 10 inches; two windows in rear of 4 pains of 10 by 8 inches, hung with hinges; the front windows to have neat batten shutters. Stone steps, front & rear, walled round with stone. Cellar floors, laid on good sized chestnut sleepers, two & an half feet apart and well nailed. Front steps and railing on the platform, and back steps to the yard. The hall doors in six pannels to have 7 inch knob locks; the back and inside doors in four pannels, properly hung, to have the best thumb latches. The back doors to have bolts. Ten front windows of 12 pains of 10 by 8 inches; the lower windows to have outside shutters, hinges, and fastenings. The floors are to be laid with common, sound plank, plained, tongued and grooved, with the exception of the garret floor, the plank of which are not to be plained nor tongued and grooved. The upper tie beam to be cut at the chimney and secured with a flat bar of iron. There is to be a sky light scuttle in each tenement, with steps to the same. Neat plain casings to the doors and windows; wash boards* [i.e., baseboards] *scribed close to the floors. One double stack of chimnies on a stone foundation with four fireplaces, neat plain mantle pieces, brick hearth, and hard finished facings, & side closets to each room. Neat framed stairs with pine posts, and rails and balusters, and neat made step ladders to the garrets. All the rooms and halls and landings are to be lathed and plastered with two coats of good morter, fair and even, for white washing; the wood work to have two coats of good paint, including gutters. Hard wood buttons are to be secured to the frames to keep up the lower*

sashes [a passage struck from the contract follows: *the front of the said building is to be of hard brick, 8 inches thick, in flemish bond, neatly painted and penciled; to have brick arches to the doors and windows, 1 1/2 brick* [in thickness]*; the windows and door sills to be of freestone, and a freestone water table*]*; and four pains of glass, 8 by 10 inches, over each front door. Scrapers* [i.e., boot scrapers] *to the steps, and every other matter and their necessary, to* [be] *completed* [for] *said building in a neat style. To be completed on or before the first day of May next. Jan*[uar]*y 1827.*
*Note 1st * Insted of a brick front, the said building is to be faced with narrow clapboards, neatly planed. Said front is to be painted with two coats of good, white paint. The window shutter*[s] *are to be painted green.*[2]

The timber-framed dwellings described in the specifications were typical of middle-class residences built at that time. Following a tradition begun in Albany by Dutch settlers, the use of a brick veneer on the street front would have given the building an image of greater permanence and value without the cost of masonry construction. Henry Van Schaick, however, with legendary Albany-Dutch frugality, decided to do without brick entirely. ✤

1. Van Schaick Family Papers, DD 10442, MSC NYSL.
2. Ibid.

64. FENCE FOR NORTH DUTCH REFORMED CHURCH

North Pearl Street, Albany, N.Y.
Designed before 6 February 1827.
Built 1830.
Builder: Martin Van Alstyne.

▲
Fig. 136. North Dutch Reformed Church, Albany, Hooker's elevation of iron fence, 1827.
Ink on paper. Archives, First Church in Albany.

Hooker had been retained to design a new fence for the North Dutch Reformed Church on North Pearl Street by 6 February 1827, and on that date he billed the consistory $10.00 *to plans & estimate for* [an] *iron railing.* One of the drawings Hooker submitted to the church survives (fig. 136). The architect also charged an additional $1.50 for work completed by 10 February, which included *plans of stone plinth,* presumably the foundation for the fence, and *dimensions of iron, etc.*[1]

It was not until the spring of 1830 that the consistory contracted with Martin Van Alstyne to erect a fence according to the plans and dimensions provided by the church, the same design submitted by Hooker three years earlier.[2] It was agreed at the time of the contract signing that Hooker supervise the work. Hooker declined, however, indicating that he *was not a competent judge* of the techniques used in ironwork construction.[3] The fence was nearly complete on 17 May 1830,[4] but there were questions regarding the workmanship and the church withheld payment until a decision could be arbitrated.[5] On 30 December 1831 Van Alstyne was awarded $2,793.10 for the work, including interest.[6] ✤

1. Doc. 139-8, Dutch Reformed Church (hereafter DRC) Collection, A FCA.
2. Doc. 143-0, DRC Collection.
3. Doc. 143-17, DRC Collection.
4. Doc. 143-3, DRC Collection.
5. Diana S. Waite, *Ornamental Ironwork: Two Centuries of Craftsmanship in Albany and Troy, New York* (Albany: Mount Ida Press, 1990), pp. 38–41.
6. Docs. 143-21 and 143-22, DRC Collection.

65. DOUBLE TOWN HOUSE FOR CASPARUS F. PRUYN AND ANDREW D. LANSING

North Market Street (now Broadway), Albany, N.Y.
Designed before 4 August 1827.
Built 1827–29.
Builder: John Sipple with John Turner (masonry and plaster work).

This double house shares many features with that designed for Henry Van Schaick about seven months earlier (cat. 63). The contract, dated 4 August 1827, stipulates that Sipple and Turner would be paid $3,300 for constructing two houses *on the west side of North Market Street next, south of Cornelius Van Schoonhoven, according to the . . . specification & plans made thereof by Philip Hooker.*[1] Although the specifications were damaged in the capitol fire of 1911, enough of their text is readable to provide an understanding of the building.

> *Specification of a double dwelling house to b*[e built] *in N*[orth] *Market Street for Mess*[rs] *Pruyn & Lans*[ing with] *dimensions as follows: forty* [two?] *feet,* [front] *& rear, & forty two feet in depth from front to rear.* [Two] *stories high; the first nine feet four inches, and* [the] *second, eight feet four inches in the clear; with two* [feet?] *6 inches* [of] *breast wall above the garret floor. To have a* [cellar] *under the whole, seven feet in the clear. The walls of* [the cellar] *are to be 8 feet high, front & rear, walls 2 feet below* [the] *surface of the ground, and 18 inches thick above flan*[k walls]; *18 inches in thicknesses. The whole to be built with good* [blue?] *stone, coarse sand & lime mortar. The front, above* [the] *surfaces, is to be faced with blue stone blocks laid* [in] *regular courses and crowned with an 8 inch water* [table], *the top of which will be 3 feet 4 inches above the* [surface] *of the ground. One party wall, one brick thick and* [8 feet?] *high in the cellar. The basement story is to be* [built] *according to plan No. 1, with partitions of hard b*[rick] [? inches] *in thickness, to be laid in good lime & sand mortar.* [The] *superstructure will be a frame of timber, well j*[oined] *& braced, 4 posts in front & the same in rear, 9 by* [3?], *to be connected by tie beams in each floor of 10 by* [4?], *and by interties front & rear, 8 by 4 inches. The joists* [of] *the first & second floors, 10 by 4 inches, two feet from c*[enter to] *center; those of the garret floor, 9 by 3 inches, same* [spacing; the] *eave plates & rafters, 6 by 4 inches. The rafters to be su*[pported] *by a counter frame properly constructed. There* [?] *pair of rafters, studs & braces, 4 by 3 inches; the* [?], *the ends & rear to be placed a suitable distance* [from] *weather boarding. The front faced with good hard* [bricks] *& mortar, laid in flemish bond, neatly painted* [and pencilled]; *the rear & sides with good tally boards lapp*[ed] [?], *the rear & south end to be planed, & the roof board* [?]. *Shingled in the best manner with a scuttle to* [?] *building, properly hung & fastened with suitable* [?] *the same. Neat block cornice, gutters, frieze & archi*[trave] *in front, & plain gutters in rear, with two 3 inch* [diameter] *conductors in rear, & heads & gutter pipes & one* [?] *conductor with ornamented head in front, & suit*[able] [?] *pipes. 4 windows in cellar, 9 panes of 10 by 12* [inches]; *2* [windows] *in rear, 6 panes* [of the] *same size; 4 windows in f*[irst story] *in front, 12 panes, 15 by 10 inches; & 4* [windows] *in rear, 12 p*[anes], *14 by 10 inches; 6 windows in 2nd story in front, 12 panes* [?] *inches; & 6 in the rear, same size. The windows in f*[irst] *& second storey to have boxed frames, 1 5/8th inch ovolo sas*[h] *hung with cords, pullies & weights; to have outside* [?] *moveable blinds in front with proper hinges & faste*[ners]. *The windows in the rear & cellar windows in front* [to have] *outside framed shutters, proper*[ly] *hung & fastened.* [The] *sashes are to be glazed with the best crown glas*[s] [and]

cased to correspond with the doors. The hall doo[rs] *in 6 pannels, sunk on the outside & bead & but on t*[he inside], *1 3/8th* [inches] *thick, to be cased with framed* [*plain* added in pencil] *jambs, pilaste*[rs], [?] *beaded grounds, blocks & imposts and ornamented obl*[ong] *square lights. 4 inch butts & best 8 inch knob locks* [?] *handsome front steps and railing of wood. The back* [doors] *in 4 pannels, cased neat & plain, to have 3 inch butt* [?] *thumb latches & bolts. The hall doors in the cel*[lar], *front & rear the same, & stone steps, walled round* [with] *stone according to plan No. 1, & an ash pit is to be* [built] *under each back stoop. The doors in the basement are to be made of narrow plank, batten*[e]*d, cased plain doors of the front rooms in the first storey, 1 3/4th inches in six pannels faced on both sides. Those in the be*[st] *rooms* [are to be] *1 3/8th* [inches] *thick, faced on both sides; those on the sec*[ond] *story in 4 pannels, 1 1/4th inches thick, sunk on o*[ne side]; *the other bead & but. The whole to have patent hinges of suitable size & the best 7 inch scotch* [spring] *knob locks, cased with double architraves in hall* [and the] *large rooms in first story. Those in the second story,* [and the small] *rooms in first story,* [are to be] *cased with single architraves. Floors are to be laid with sound, well seasoned p*[lank], *on common width, planed, tongued & grooved,* [gauged] *thicknessed. Joints broke & well nailed. Stairs f*[rom] *first to the second story with cherry wood com*[?] *hand rail & balusters; close stairs to the garrets* [?], *pantries underneath, & framed stairs to cellars.* [?] *place with crane eyes, mantle bar, & flue, oven in* [the] *cellar kitchen, and two fire places in each story above* [?] *each building, and proper sheet iron tubes or collars for* [flue] *papers in each story. The chimney to be carried 3 feet a*[bove the] *ridge of the roof & painted & pencilled. The water tab*[le] *of freestone; front doors & window sills & channel* [?] *of freestone. Neat, plain, column chimney pieces in* [large] *rooms in first story, & neat plain pilasters in* [the] *rooms & in the second story. All to have freestone* [hearths] *& facings. The first story to be plastered for paper h*[anging]; *the large rooms & halls in the first story to hav*[e] [?] *ceilings & light stucco cornices. The second story pla*[stered] *for white washing; the cellar walls & partitions to* [be] *pointed & whitewashed with thin grout; the pan*[try], *hard finished, to be properly shelved; to have a 13* [inch] *shelf & closets underneath. A back stoop is* [to be] *made in the rear of each building, enclosed w*[ith] [?] *boards, 3 feet high, planed, tongued & grooved. Shing*[les], *plain gutters & conductors; floor of plank, plan*[ed] *& grooved, gauged thicknessed; joints broke & well* [nailed]. [To] *have a stone foundation & to be finished neat* [?] *(see plans Nos. 1 & 2). All of the above specified timber is to be* [sound] *& durable. A sink is to be made in each kitchen. The woodwork is to be painted with two coats of unadulterated paint of suitable colours. The b*[linds] *green, three coats, and every other matter & the* [?] *be done to complete said buildings acco*[rding to] *said plans, including stoop scrapers* [i.e., boot scrapers], *clo*[sets], *shelving, &c, &c. The frame is to be filled in w*[ith] *burnt bricks all round to the roof. The midd*[le] [par]*tition also filled in & lathed & plastered to the gar*[ret]; *the filling to extend to the roof. One plain window to be made in the rear in each house, with* [glass] *8 by 10 inches, the cellars to be cieled.*[2]

Extant bills for this project cover the period from 8 September 1827 to 10 January 1829 and indicate that in April 1828 Pruyn and Lansing negotiated with the builders to add one-half brick thickness to the front wall for an additional $53.50. The builders used a cost of $9.50 per 1,000 bricks in their estimate of the charge. On 10 May 1828 an additional $265.02 was added to the contract, bringing the total cost to $3,618.52.[3]

The contract, a draft of which is preserved, stipulated that Hooker supervise the work and that it be *subject to his approval.* He was paid $15.00 for his services.[4] ✜

1. John V. A. Lansing Papers, SC 16832, MSC NYSL.
2. Van Rensselaer Manor Papers, SC 7079, MSC NYSL.
3. John V. A. Lansing Papers.
4. Ibid.

66. PROPOSALS FOR THE GANSEVOORT HOUSE STOOPS

Unknown location, Albany, N.Y.
Designed c. September 1827.
Building history unknown.

Hooker created *sundry designs for stone steps and iron railing*[s] for the house of General Peter Gansevoort in Albany, billing him $4.00 for his design services on 29 September 1827.[1] Three drawings in the Gansevoort-Lansing Collection of the New York Public Library, though unsigned, appear to be the subject of this bill.

The first is rather tentatively drawn in pencil (fig. 137) and carries a later inscription, which is probably an estimate.

> *$75*
> *1828 5 Sept*[embe]*r*
> *Mr* [Town?] *offers to make the stoop of free stone, $10 less than Hill in marble.*
> *Mr* [Town?] *includes all the mason work (including the Foundation and the freestone)*[2]

The second drawing, also in pencil, offers an alternative stoop design and an areaway rail design (fig. 138). It carries the inscription *$120. Iron.*[3] These two drawings, which feature square newels, appear to have been part of a single sheet of paper that was subsequently separated to facilitate the solicitation of individual estimates.

The third sheet, drawn with greater care and using ink and wash (fig. 139), offers two additional designs for iron railings, this time with round cage newels.

Three estimates of the construction costs of stoops for General Gansevoort are preserved. In addition to the one already cited as an inscription on the first drawing, there are proposals from Joseph B. Hill and Brainard & Bruce, each for two stoops. Hill's estimate reads:

Platform & steps (moulded)	*60 feet @ $1.25*	*$75.*	*Dwelling*
Wrought @ $1.25	*18* [feet @] *62 1/2*	*11.25*	
Ashler 62 1/2 cts	*two blocks $8 =*	*16.*	
Blocks eight doll[ar]*s each*	*setting*	*12.*	
Setting 12 d[ollar]*s*		*114.25*	
Plain steps & platform	*45 feet—*	*$45.*	*Office*
@ $1.00 per foot	*18 ft ashler*	*11.25*	
Ashler 62 1/2 cts	*setting*	*6.*	
Setting 6 d[ollars]		*62.25*	
		$176.50	

Jos. B. Hill
Green & Lydius Sts[4]

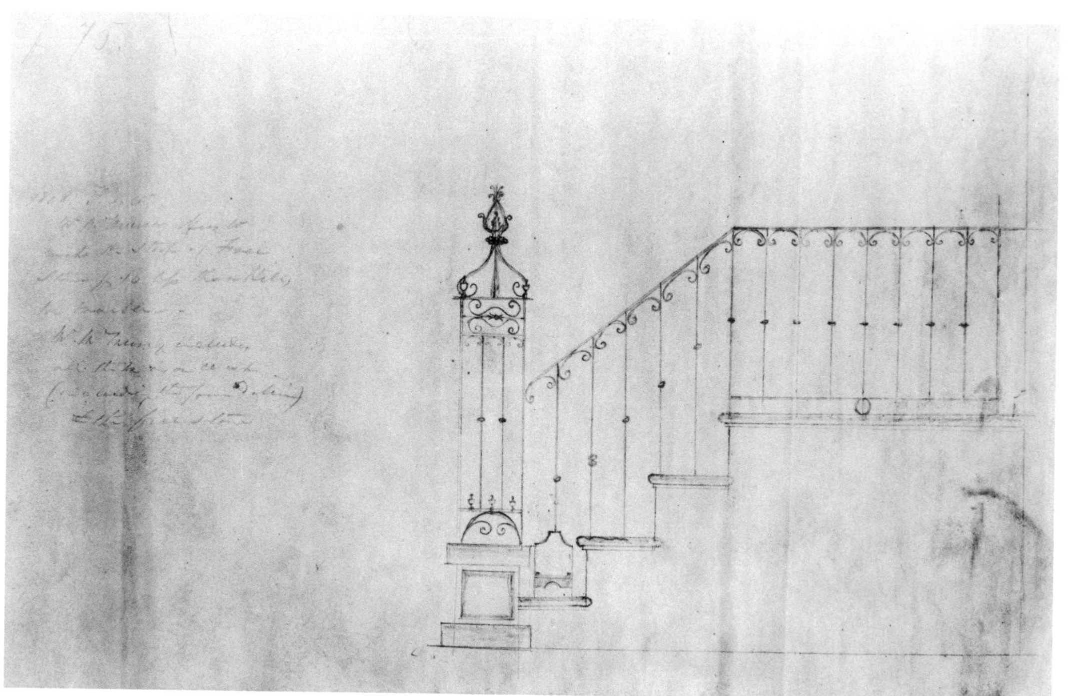

▶
Fig. 137.

▶
Fig. 138.

Figs. 137 and 138. Elevations, likely by Hooker, of designs for a stoop for the Gansevoort house, Albany, c. 1827. Pencil on paper. New York Public Library, New York, N.Y., Gansevoort-Lansing Collection, Manuscripts and Archives Section.

▲
Fig. 139. Elevations, likely by Hooker, of two designs for a stoop for the Gansevoort house, Albany, c. 1827. Ink on paper. New York Public Library, New York, N.Y., Gansevoort-Lansing Collection, Manuscripts and Archives Section.

The estimate furnished by Brainard & Bruce provides further information.

> *Agreeable to the plans shewn by P. Hooker Esqr for two stoops for Gen*[era]*l Peter Gansevoort. We give the following list of prices— viz—*

77 ft moulded steps & platform	*8/—*	*77.00*
52 [ft] *plain* [steps & platform]	*6/—*	*39.00*
39 ft stoop ashler for both	*4/—*	*19.50*
2 Pedestal blocks— at $6— ea		*12.00*
		$147.50

> *The above are prices for free stone— Marble will be 2/— per foot higher— which with the difference in pedestal blocks will amount to about $50. more than the above estimate.*
> *Albany Sept*[embe]*r 28th 1827 ~* *Brainard & Bruce*[5]

It is not known which, if any, of these designs were finally chosen, nor to whom a contract was awarded.

Hooker's designs have close counterparts in wrought iron railings that were erected elsewhere in New York State. The designs on the first sheet resemble the ironwork which formerly decorated the stoop of 71 Hudson Avenue in Albany. The details of the second drawing, with its Gothic Revival-inspired tracery, are similar to the ironwork on the steps of the Stocking house in Utica, a project which Root ascribed to Hooker.[6] The railings still in place at 25 Second Street, Troy, have details in common with the designs presented in the third drawing. ✥

1. Gansevoort-Lansing Collection, NYPL.
2. Ibid.
3. Ibid.
4. Ibid.
5. Ibid. It is likely that one of the two stoops was for General Gansevoort's residence and the other for his office.
6. Root, p. 207.

67. *GREAT HOUSE,* COUNTRY SEAT FOR GEORGE CLARKE (HYDE HALL)

Springfield, Otsego County, N.Y.
Designed by 1827.
Built 1827–35; extant.
Mason: Lorenzo Bates.

▲
Fig. 140. Hyde Hall, Springfield, N.Y. (1817–35), exterior, c. 1920.
New York Historical Association, Cooperstown, N.Y.

▲
Fig. 141. *Great House,* Hyde Hall, Springfield, N.Y., Hooker's elevation of the east front, the second design, by 1827.
Ink and wash on paper. Photograph courtesy Friends of Hyde Hall, Inc.

The final building campaign of Hyde Hall commenced in 1819, when foundations for the main, east wing were laid on the lines of the January 1818 scheme (fig. 97).[1] Erection of the walls, however, was delayed until 1827, by which time this *Great House* had been redesigned (fig. 141), exhibiting greater sophistication and formality.[2] Since bedrooms had been provided for in the rear wing, those originally intended for the second level of this portion of the house could be dispensed with, and the ceilings of the dining and drawing rooms could rise to a grand height of nineteen feet (figs. 142, 143).[3] The first floor plan remained the same, except for the substitution of a cast iron stove and flanking wood doors for what would have been a glazed door with two sidelights separating the front and rear halls. The original arrangement would have been virtually identical to the screened wall in the Miller house in Utica (cat. 52). The billiard room, initially planned for the second floor, occupied a central attic pavilion where it opened onto the balcony atop the portico. Construction continued until the death of George Clarke in 1835, when the work was permanently suspended.

▶
Fig. 142. *Great House,* Hyde Hall, Springfield, N.Y. (1827–35), the dining room, an early twentieth century view. Collection Friends of Hyde Hall, Inc.

▶
Fig. 143. *Great House,* Hyde Hall, Springfield, N.Y. (1827–35), the drawing room, c. 1845, view reconstructed by Douglas G. Bucher, 1989. Watercolor on paper. Collection Friends of Hyde Hall, Inc.

▶
Fig. 144. *Great House,* Hyde Hall, Springfield, N.Y. (1827–35), the main stair hall, an early twentieth century view. Collection Friends of Hyde Hall, Inc.

1. George Hyde Clarke Papers, Coll. 2800, Department of Manuscripts and University Archives, Olin Library, Cornell University, Ithaca, N.Y.
2. Ibid. Bills for work on this structure term it the *Great House.*
3. Measurements taken in the summer of 1991 recorded the ceiling height, which differs from the previously understood figure of seventeen-and-a-half feet; information provided by Douglas R. Kent, Curator, Friends of Hyde Hall, Inc., Springfield, N.Y.
4. Root, p. 197 and figs. 5, 6, cites Asher Benjamin, *The American Builder's Companion,* 2d ed. (1811) as the source for the frieze in the drawing room.

The sculptural character of the building, its fine proportions, and its bold detailing are all typical of Hooker's best work (fig. 140). These qualities are maintained on the interior, as evidenced in the handsome stair (fig. 144) and in the drawing and dining rooms. The plaster work of the latter rooms may be to Hooker's designs, but obviously draws on Asher Benjamin's *The American Builder's Companion.*[4] Renderings depicting the two rooms as they would have looked around 1845 have been made for Friends of Hyde Hall, Inc. (fig. 143), which is currently restoring the building. ✤

68. DUTCH REFORMED CHURCH OF NISKAYUNA

Troy Schenectady Road, Niskayuna, N.Y.
Designed before 25 March 1828.
Built 1828–29; razed 1852.
Builders: Charles T. Clark, James J. Staat, Hiram Pardee, Timothy Livingston, and John Fremyre (all of Amsterdam).

An undated minute of around December 1827 records the directives set forth by the consistory for the planning of its new church edifice.

> *Size of the church 45 feet by 55* [feet]
> *Length of Posts 16 1/2* [feet]
> *Windows one tier, width of seets 2 feet 4 inches*
> [The] *model of the church & shape of* [the] *cieling over head* [is to be] *after the model of the Church of Amity* [now Vischers Ferry] *or such other churches including the Churches of Washington* [south of Watervliet] *& the new Presbyterian Church at Waterford as they may deem proper.*[1]

On 25 March 1828 Hooker billed the congregation $15.00 for producing a set of drawings (figs. 145–49) and specifications.[2]

> *Specification of a church to be erected in the Troy & Schenectady turnpike road near Clutes tavern, in the town of Niskayuna of the form & dimentions as follow and according to plans made thereof by Philip Hooker, to wit. Said building is to be 65 feet in length, 50 feet in breadth* [and have] *23 1/2 feet* [high] *posts. A frame of good, sound, square-edged timber,—framed & braced in a workman-like & substantial manner. Sills 10 by 8* [inches], *posts 12 by 6* [inches], *except* [the] *two front tower posts, which are to be 12 by 10 inches. Tie beams 14 by 6* [inches] *at the ends & reduced to 10 by 6* [inches] *in the middle. Girts or interties 8 by 6* [inches],*— studs & braces 4 by 6* [inches], [the] *principal rafters 12 by 4* [inches], *small rafters 6 by 4* [inches], *purlins 9 by 7* [inches], *roof braces 6 by 6* [inches], *cieling joists 6 by 2 1/2* [inches], *floor joists 8 by 4 inches, supported by bearing beams of 10 by 8* [inches] *and proper posts or piers in the basement. Gallery beams 12 by 6* [inches], *joists 6 by 4* [inches], *having proper brackets of two inch yellow-pine plank to carry the floors of the gallery slips. The joists to be two feet from centre to centre, having one furring of plank edgewise between. Cieling joists 16 inches from centre to centre, floor joists 2 1/2 feet from centre to centre. The aisles and the slips should be floored length-wise. The floors of the slips on the ground floor should be raised about four inches above the floor of the aisles; the floor to have an elevation of from 16 to 18 inches in the length of the middle range of slips. The outside of said building is to be faced with narrow clapboards neatly planed & thicknessed and well nailed. The roof, boarded & shingled* [on the] *side & in front. A pair of entrance doors* [are to be] *framed in twelve pannels each, neatly cased & hung* [and are] *to have proper bolts & 10 inch tin scotch-spring knob-lock & a row of sash lights over the same. Said doors are to open at least 8 feet wide in the clear; and* [the] *two six panneled doors in the rear 7 feet high & 3 feet 2 inches wide cased neat & plain,* [are] *to have suitable hinges & strong wrought iron thumb latches & inside bolts. Ten windows as p*[e]*r plan* [are] *to have box frames & sashes hung with cords, pullies & weights and inside fastenings of hooks & eyes or bolts. All the floors are to be of sound well seasoned plank, planed, tongued, grooved, gauged, thicknessed, joints broke & well nailed.* [There are to be] *two inside doors on the ground floor & two gallery doors framed in six pannels, to be cased in a proper manner.*

[They are] *to have suitable hinges and handsome wrought thumb latches. Convenient stairs with cherry or birch wood handrails & balusters on each side of the church to the galleries. The slips are to be made in a neat & workmanlike manner; the doors framed in two pannels, the divisions planed, the backs plain, tongued & grooved and a little leaning back; to have suitable book boards, a suitable capping to the doors, plank seats 14 inches wide, a little elevated in front & partitions under the middle of the seats. The front of the front slips opposite the pulpit to be of frame work in a handsome style. The front of the gallery to be panneled, to have a neat moulded capping, to be supported by nine columns of six inches diameter, Doric caps & bases, over which is to extend, all round the front of the gallery, a neat plain moulded entablature. The galleries are to be seated in a proper manner. The form of the slips generally are to be similar to those in the church lately built in Waterford* [the First Presbyterian Church, finished in 1826, A26]. *The sides of the church are to be lined with boards, tongued & grooved and neatly planed as high as the bottom of the windows, and the remainder including the cieling, stair ways and entrance, is to be lathed & plastered with the best lime sand & hair mortar. The cieling* [is] *to be finished white with putty, gaged with boiled plaster. The sides, stairways &c hard finished. A small neatly formed moulding is to be run at the spring of the arch of the cieling. The pulpit is to be paneled in front, having suitable pilasters, doors, cap & base mouldings; to be supported by four fluted Doric columns with two circular flights of winding stairs & cherry wood hand rails & balusters and astragal brackets & handsome turned newels of like wood. Suitable steps to the entrance doors front and rear. The principal floor is to be five feet above the surface* [of the ground], *under which is to be a good stone wall twenty inches in thickness, laid in good mortar & sunk a sufficient depth below the frost. The side walls, for 34 feet on each side, and two cross walls, are to be 8 feet in height; and one partition wall of hard brick 8 inches thick, 30 feet in length to form two rooms under said church to be properly floored, cielings lathed and the whole plastered for white washing.* [The room is] *to have plain wash boards, two windows of 18 panes of 12 by 10 inches 6 panes wide & 3 panes high in two casements, 12 in the lower & 6 in the upper casement, jamb plastered, outside shutters & proper hinges & fastenings.* [Also] *two pair of sash doors, 6 panes of 12 by 9 inches in each half door, the doors made double, to have moveable shutters with suitable screw fastenings. The doors* [are] *to have suitable hinges & bolts and 8 inch best scotch-spring knob-locks. Two plain doors* [are] *to open under the outer lobby where wood &c may be kept. Suitable loop holes are to be made in the foundation walls for the admission of air; also holes for stove pipes in the basement story rooms. Two brick flues are to be carried up from the cieling of the church to rest on square stones, having holes in the same for stove pipes. Said stones are to be well secured by rabbeting the sides to rest on the timber of the cieling. Said flues are to be carried sufficiently above the roof & cap*[pe]*d with stone, into which sheet iron cylindric*[al] *tubes are to be fitted, and to which proper turn caps are to be adjusted. The shingling to be made tight around said flues, to have sheet lead on the upper side. A room is to be partitioned off from the stair ways & over the entrance, which will be come at by a narrow projecting gallery having a railing to be entered from the last slip of the gallery stairs* [and] *having a suitable door to the same. Said room to be properly floored & otherwise finished; from which room steps are to ascend through a scuttle in the cieling to have a trap door, & from thence by suitable steps to the top of the roof or tower. Instead of king posts, the tie beams are to be suspended from the heads of the principal rafters by screw bolts of tough 1 1/8th inch square iron, having a head under the beam & a washer or square plate & nut above, the points of the rafters being cut off for that purpose. The rafters mitred together & a groove in each to receive the bolts, the foot with a birds mouth on the plate & bolted to the beam 3/4 inc*[h] *iron.*

▶
Fig. 145. Dutch Reformed Church, Niskayuna, N.Y., Hooker's drawing of the front elevation, 1828.
Ink and wash on paper.
New York State Library, Albany.

The circular head of the window above the entrance will rise above the cieling of the room over the same which will be [backed?] *up behind & painted black. The whole to be painted inside & out with two coats of unadulterated paint of pure white lead, except the doors & fronts of the slips & cappings of the same and the front & other doors* [which are] *to be painted in imitation of mahogany, the roof excepted. The blinds in the tower & oval windows are to be painted green. The roof of the tower is to be made tight by a double plank covering, elevated in the centre forming a flat pyramid, the hips to be secured with strips of stout sheet lead laid in thick white lead. To have a scuttle in the same, well secured against leakage, and the tower is to be finished by a bold cornice & crowned with a handsome balustrade. The windows are to be glazed with the best quality of clear crown glass.*[3]

The contract to construct the church, at an estimated cost of $2,500, was signed on 19 April 1828.[4] An autumn 1828 note to the consistory from John Humphrey documents some of the subsequent changes to the specifications.

[The Ven]*itian window over the front door to consist of 16 lights in the* [?] *10 by 12* [inch] *glass. The other windows to consist of 60 lights 10 by 12* [inch] *glazing agreeably to the plan mentioned by Mr Witbeck. As to the width of the gallery, I have put it down, which is 13 ft and must be so unless there is a diference in length of the pews, or you can have the gallery only 9 ft wide and the pillows on the other side of the isle, which I think would be the best.*[5]

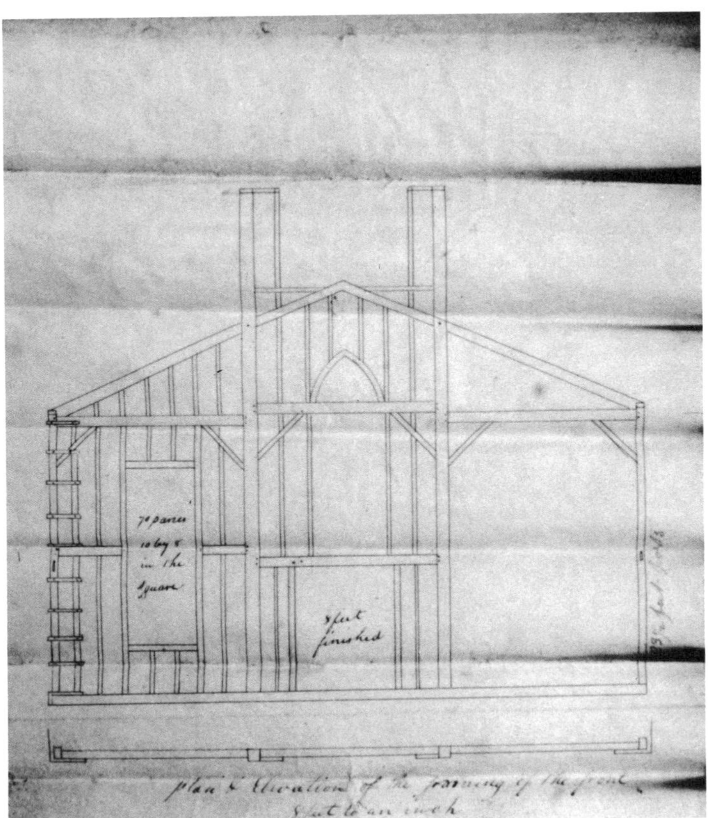

▶
Fig. 146. Dutch Reformed Church, Niskayuna, N.Y., Hooker's framing drawing of the front, with a partial plan, 1828.
Ink on paper. New York State Library, Albany.

Hooker's drawing of the front elevation, rendered in delicate washes (fig. 145), seems to correspond to the original specifications, with their mention of oval windows and a circular-headed window above the entrance. The other drawings offer a somewhat different, more fully detailed, and perhaps slightly later scheme. As depicted in the elevation of the front framing (fig. 146), the tower is broader and shorter, and the roof of the building has a slightly lower pitch. Furthermore, while the front elevation shows a projecting entrance tower and a Palladian window set into a recessed arch, the framing drawing depicts an unbroken facade, articulated by what appear to be four pilasters and featuring a central lancet-arched window. Pilasters are also indicated in the plan (fig. 149) and the side framing drawing (fig. 148), while the lateral section (fig. 147) shows another lancet-arched window in the rear wall of the church.

The note about the Palladian or [Ven]*itian* window in the amendments to the specifications and a later reference to *circular headed windows* indicate that these were part of the church as executed.[6] While it is possible that the entire building followed the design represented in the front elevation, it seems more likely that these features were borrowed from that proposal and incorporated in the scheme depicted more extensively in the other drawings.

Evidently some of the changes to the specifications were never discussed or were misrepresented by the builders, for on 28 February 1829 the consistory met to consider *defects in the new church.*[7] On 17 March the

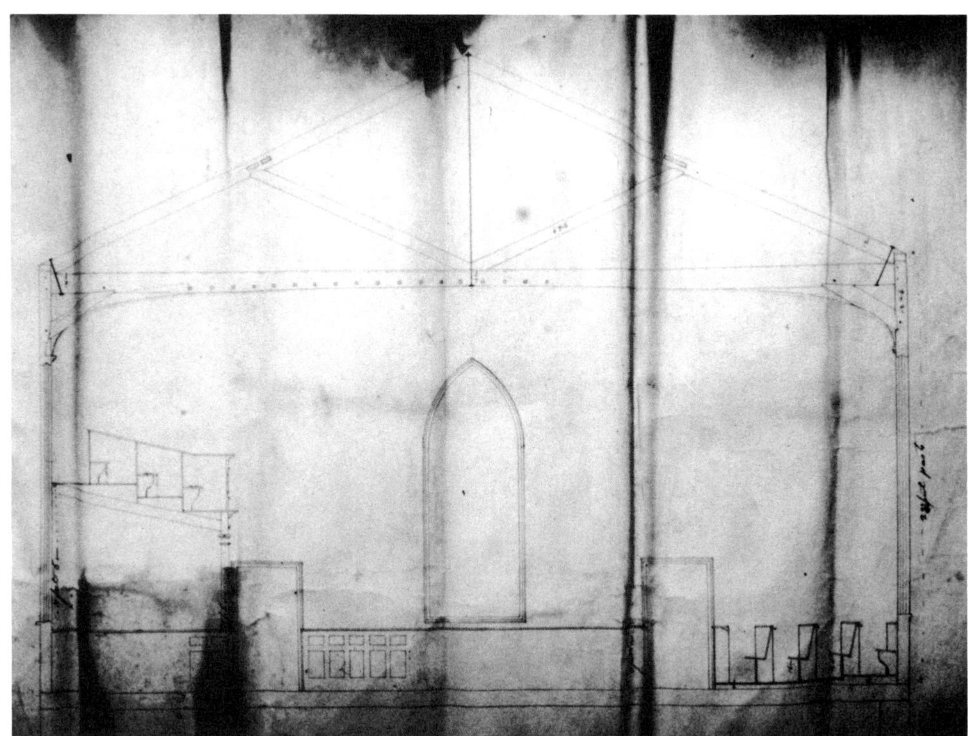

▶ Fig. 147. Dutch Reformed Church, Niskayuna, N.Y., Hooker's lateral, or transverse, section, showing lancet-arched window, 1828. Ink on paper.

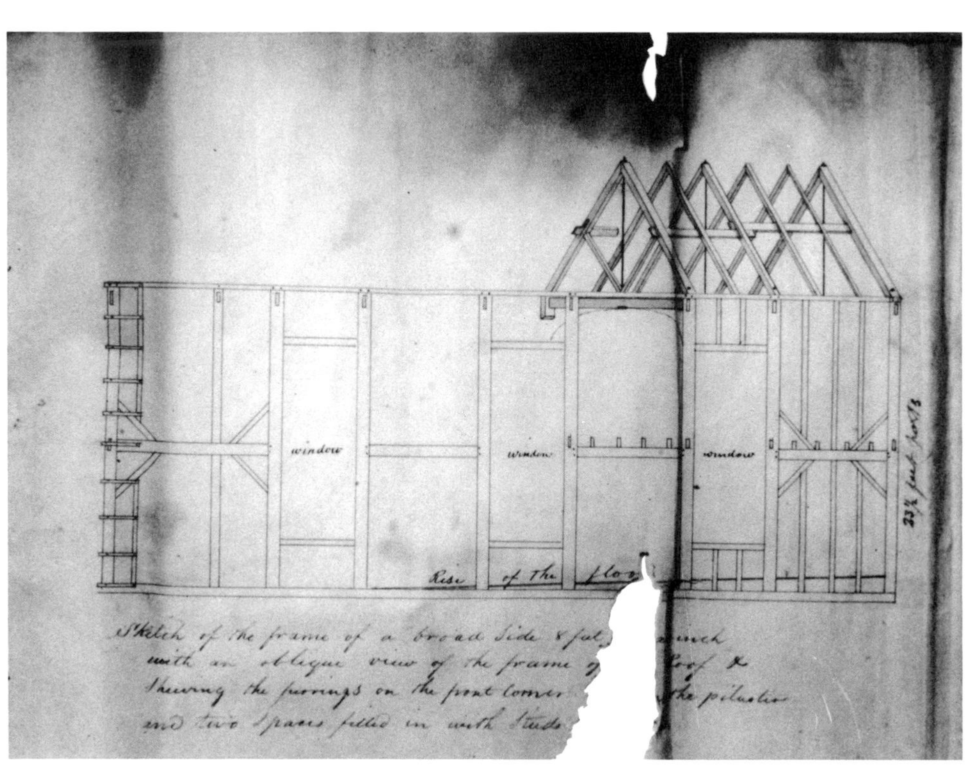

▶ Fig. 148. Hooker's framing drawing, showing the side elevation and the sanctuary roof construction, 1828. Ink and wash on paper. New York State Library, Albany.

consistory members met with the contractors. Charles T. Clark, speaking on behalf of the builders, claimed the church was finished *agreeably to contract* and proposed that *three regular taught mechanics take the contract and specifications and examine the church.* It was agreed that all parties would abide by their decision.[8]

Hooker and John Boardman were contacted and submitted this report:

> *Estimate of the deficiencies & defects on the contractors part in building a church on the Troy & Schenectady Turnpike road in the Town of Niskeuny for the Trustees of said church*
> *To wit: The foundation irregular*
> [To] *A bad roof*
> [To] *Circular headed windows deficient in size, badly made* }
> *Sashes not hung* [deficient in size, badly made] }
> *Depression in the he*[i]*ght of building*
> *The seating below & above badly done*
> *Clapboarding & nailing insufficient*
> *Bad floors in gallery*
> *Hand railing & balusters to gallery stairs*
> *Want of elevation to the gallerys*
> *Slight stoeps front & rear*
> *Stone chimn*[e]*ys not according to contract*
> *Want of stone foundation to some of the* }
> *collums supporting the gallery* }
> *Difficiency in cieling joist & other timbers of roof*
> *Plastering not done according to contract*
> *Hard finish & putty cieling*
> *Some of the doors badly trimed*
> *Whole amount of the above deficiencies*
> *estimated @ six hundred & two dollars* $602
> *Albany March 21 1829—*
> *John Boardman*
> *P. Hooker*[9]

The dispute had still not been resolved by mid-June of 1829 when Hooker and Boardman submitted a second report, this time in a standard legal format.

> *At the request of the Trustees of the new Church lately erected on the Troy Turnpike in the Town of Niskayuna, the undersigned have examined the same. It is, however, evident that the whole as to form and workmanship is at variance with the plans & specifications made thereof by P. Hooker. In the first place, the building wants one foot eight inches in height, in consequence of which the galleries are depressed, the windows shortened. The foot of the arch of the ceiling protrudes within the church and so low as to interfere with the head room. One window omitted on each side, and those put in 10 by 8 instead* [of] *12 by 10. The columns supporting the gallery stand in, and are an obstruction to, the aisles instead of being placed within the slips as they were to have been by plan & specification. The work generally slight in nowise conforming to said plans & specification and not executed in a workmanlike manner. Thin board seats instead of plank; weak hinges & screws to pew doors, weak railing to stairs. In short the work generally is badly done and in such* [a] *manner as to render it impossible to make it conform to the true letter of the specifications & plans. It is*

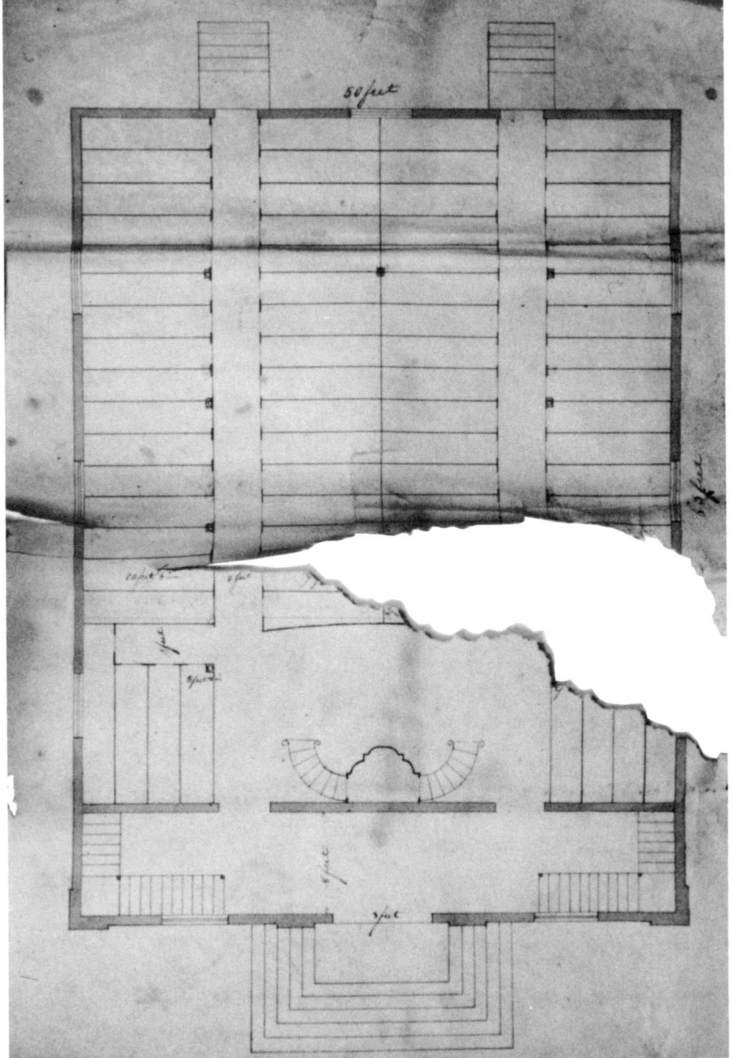

Fig. 149. Dutch Reformed Church, Niskayuna, N.Y., Hooker's plan, 1828. Ink and wash on paper. New York State Library, Albany.

difficult to determine what sum would compensate for the disappointment to the trustees and those who are interested. If we have a correct view of the contract, we are of opinion that the sum of five hundred dollars would be moderate—

P. Hooker
John Boardman

June 16th 1829[10]

By August 1829 the church had brought suit against the builders. In September the case was in the State Supreme Court, but the judge's decision is not known.[11]

Hooker's drawings for this project reflect his roughly contemporary use of several styles. In using a Palladian window in a recessed arch, he was relying on a motif that had been a part of his neoclassical architectural vocabulary for at least twenty-five years. At virtually the same time, he was experimenting with features common to the Greek and Gothic revival styles. In addition to proportions and pilasters which may suggest the Greek Revival, Hooker's indication of lancet-arched windows marks the first documented instance of his exploration of the Gothic mode.

1. Item 365, Archives, Niskayuna Reformed Church, Niskayuna, N.Y. (hereafter A NRC).
2. Van Rensselaer Manor Papers, SC 7079; and John V. A. Lansing Papers, SC 16832; MSC NYSL.
3. John V. A. Lansing Papers.
4. Item 340, A NRC.
5. Item 354, A NRC.
6. John V. A. Lansing Papers.
7. Consistory Minutes, 28 February 1829, A NRC.
8. Ibid., 17 March 1829, A NRC.
9. John V. A. Lansing Papers.
10. Ibid.
11. Elizabeth D. Shaver to the author, 29 May 1991.

69. ST. PAUL'S EPISCOPAL CHURCH

South Ferry Street, Albany, N.Y.
Designed before 14 May 1828.
Built between May 1828 and August 1829;
remodeled c. 1870 and c. 1910; extant.
Builder: Henry Peers.
Mason: J. Clement.

▲
Fig. 150. St. Paul's Episcopal Church, Albany (1828–29), view, before 1839. Engraving, hand-colored. Collection Douglas G. Bucher.

A mid-nineteenth century source identifies Hooker's involvement in this project.

> *Having become incorporated . . .* [sixteen days earlier]*; . . . on the 28th of November, 1827, the wardens and vestrymen appointed a committee to purchase as a site for a church edifice, two lots on the north west corner of Ferry and Dallius streets, for the sum of $2500; and on the 15th of June, 1828, they directed said committee to purchase an adjoining lot at the price of $500. Previous to the purchase of the last lot, a building committee was appointed, who on the 14th of May, 1828, accepted the proposal of Henry Peeres* [sic] *to build a church edifice on said lots for the sum of $12,550; and on the 11th day of June, 1828, the Rt. Rev. Bp. Hobart laid the corner stone of the proposed building, which was to be constructed agreeably to a plan drawn by Philip Hooker, of Albany, architect, of the Gothic order of architecture, and to be 56 by 85 feet, the walls to be built of rough blue stone, &c.*[1]

There is no reason to doubt the veracity of Hooker's connection to the design of the church. The language suggests that this account was transcribed in part from the original building contract, unfortunately now lost.

Contemporary reports of the completed St. Paul's Church provide further details regarding its design (fig. 150).

This ediface is situated at the corner of Ferry and Dallius Streets in this city. The building was commenced a year ago last May, by Mr. Henry Peers, the builder and contractor, and Mr. J. Clement, the mason, and is now [22 August 1829] *completed.*

The design is from an ancient Gothic temple. The width of the main body of the building is fifty six by eighty five [feet] *long; fronted with a semi-octagonal vestibule of thirty two feet diameter, with a corresponding roof rising into the front pediment of the main roof. The walls of the whole building are of unwrought stone 3 1/2 feet thick in the basement—the upper walls two feet. There are five windows on each side, and two in front, supported by center reeds, diverging at the head, so as to form three distinct gothic arches to the casements and frames of each window. The mullions are diagonally disposed, and contain glass of 5 1/4 inches square. The angles of the walls and the partition wall at the landing of the gallery stairs, are supported by buttresses of two feet square having in each three abutements cowped* [i.e., coped] *with cut* [free] *stone, and surmounted with quadrangular Gothic pinnacles. The eaves* [are] *finished with a deep Gothic frieze and cornice, and the parapet* [is] *carried up in the form of battlements.*

There are niches in the right and left angles of the entrance way, prepared for statuary. The front door is ten feet wide on each side of which are columns supporting the arch of a window above the impost of the door. The eaves of the vestibule roof are finished with a cornice and chainwork and the angles [are] *surmounted with pinnacles.*

The interior finish is also gothic, and painted (by Messrs. Russel and Davis of this city) in imitation of oak; there are 138 pews below, and 66 in the gallery—

The pulpit, screen and altar were designed and drawn by Mr. George Vernon, architect, and built by Mr. J. Biggelow. The screen is 24 feet wide, supported by four octagonal gothic columns, in panel work, and rising about 18 feet from the chancel floor. The columns are finished at the top with pinnacles, ornamented and encircled with carved leaves and vines; in the centre of the screen and immediately over the pulpit, there rises a pediment supported by clustered columns and an arch; the pediment [is] *also surmounted with a richly ornamented pinnacle extending to the ceiling and standing in relief, in a niche prepared to receive it. The top of the screen and bases of the pinnacles are finished with castellated battlements, and the panel work in quatre foils. . . . the building and interior finish has been done under the superintendance and direction of Mr. W. W. Dougherty.*[2]

In visiting this church . . . we noticed a peculiar softness in the light of the house, which has been effected by transparent paintings of the head lights of the side windows, and the whole of the front windows, and the tints so modified and arranged as to present a warm yellow atmosphere through the whole church. . . . [3]

An account published in 1837 reiterates portions of one of these descriptions and states in addition that *the original plan embraces the erection of a stone tower in the rear, of twenty two feet square, elevated two sections above the belfry; to be surmounted with turrets to correspond with those on the main building. . . .*[4]

The new St. Paul's Church, evidently without its proposed tower, was well received.

The whole building may be considered as an excellent specimen of Gothic architecture. . . . It is an ornament to the city, and will do credit to the age in which it was built.[5]

1. J. Munsell, comp., *Annals of Albany,* Vol. III (Albany: Joel Munsell, 1852), p. 245.
2. *Albany Gazette,* 25 August 1829.
3. Ibid.
4. *Letters about the Hudson River and its Vicinity* (New York: Freeman Hunt & Co., 1837), pp. 148–49.
5. *Albany Gazette,* 28 August 1829.
6. Ibid.
7. The first example, erected in 1826–28 by St. Paul's Episcopal Church in Troy, replaced that congregation's earlier building by Hooker.
8. A few additional facts and refinements to the above measurements are suggested by the parts of the original building that remain. As measured in August 1991, the overall dimensions of the main body are 56 feet 7 inches wide and 84 feet 9 inches deep. The vestibule, now razed, probably extended the front of the building another 15 feet 3 inches to meet the edge of the South Ferry Street property line. (*Albany Argus,* 12 June 1828.)

   The inner vestibule, with staircases on either side, occupied an area measuring 52 feet 7 inches by 13 feet 5 inches if the thickness of the walls is taken to be 2 feet. The wall between this room and the sanctuary was located in line with the rear buttresses of the towers. The sanctuary occupied the remainder of the building and was 52 feet 7 inches wide and 65 feet 1 inch deep.

▶
Fig. 151. St. Paul's Episcopal Church, Albany (1828–29), exterior, before c. 1910.
New York State Library, Albany.

8. (continued) The buttresses, originally six in number, project 2 feet from the walls and are, on the average, 1 foot 11 inches wide. The buttresses, which have brownstone copings, step back approximately 12 feet 8 inches above the watertable to a depth of 1 foot 5 inches. At approximately 25 feet 4 inches in elevation the buttresses step back again to only a 10-inch depth. The top portions of the buttresses have not been preserved.

The windows of the side elevations were 6 feet 2 1/2 inches wide on average and the tops of their brownstone sills were 3 feet 8 inches above the watertable. A bricked-in opening on the rear of the building, probably one of two that originally existed, is of the same width but its brownstone sill is only 2 feet above the watertable. The latter measurement is an estimate because the watertable extends only around the two street elevations.

> *In taking into consideration the external structure, together with the whole interior arrangements and construction of this ediface, it has never fallen to our lot to examine one more classically chaste in design, execution or finish.*[6]

To modern eyes, St. Paul's Episcopal Church may appear poorly proportioned and awkwardly composed. Even if the proposed rear tower had been built, the relatively broad form, squat front towers, and rough stone walls of the church would have countered the sense of verticality expected in Gothic Revival buildings. However, to those who viewed the church as only the second example of the style in the region,[7] it may well have seemed *an excellent specimen.* Further, by identifying its design as *from an ancient Gothic temple* and as *classically chaste,* contemporary writers suggest a different, more sympathetic vantage point.

After having lost its battlements in an earlier remodeling (fig. 151), most of the building's remaining details and its original fenestration were removed in an unsympathetic renovation around 1910.[8] ✤

70. ALTERATIONS TO THE NORTH DUTCH REFORMED CHURCH CONSISTORY HOUSE

North Pearl Street, Albany, N.Y.
Designed before 18 May 1828.
Possibly built c. 1828–30; altered; razed.
Builder unknown.

By May 1828 Hooker had completed *plans & specifications & estimates for altering* [the] *consistory house* of the North Dutch Reformed Church. He was paid $10.00 for this service, which involved the conversion of the consistory house (cat. 31) to a parsonage.[1] On 3 June Hooker billed an additional $2.00 for *altering* [the] *plans & specifications.*[2] This scheme seems to have been tied to the provision of new facilities for the consistory.[3] Since that project was deferred (cat. 73), the status of these particular plans is unclear, although it is known that the building was subsequently occupied as a parsonage.[4] ✜

1. Doc. 139-8, Dutch Reformed Church (hereafter DRC) Collection, A FCA.
2. Ibid.
3. E. P. Rogers, *A Historical Discourse on the Reformed Prot. Dutch Church of Albany* (New York: Board of Publication of the Reformed Protestant Dutch Church, 1858), p. 48.
4. Ibid.; "1814 Consistory House Erected," A FCA.

71. PROPOSAL FOR WASHINGTON, OR CENTRE, MARKET

South Pearl Street between Howard and William streets, Albany, N.Y.
Designed before 29 May 1828.
Unbuilt.

The Albany Common Council had considered the construction of an additional market in 1818 and 1819, but had taken no action on its committee's recommendations (A22). Finally, on 29 May 1828, the council approved proposals to erect two new markets, one of them on the previously suggested South Pearl Street site,[1] and to renovate an existing market. Special preparations were necessary to fund the anticipated construction.

> *Resolved that the lots fronting on Fly Market Square as laid down on a Map thereof made by Philip Hooker to be sold by public auction on the first Monday of September next; and that from the avails of the sale of said lots there be appropriated a sum, not exceeding three thousand five hundred dollars, for the erection of a new market & offices in South Pearl Street pursuant to the plan drawn by Mr. Hooker. . . .*[2]

Similar appropriations from the said *avails* were to be made for the other market projects (cats. 72, 81).

The map showing the property to be sold and the site of the proposed market on South Pearl Street, to be named the Washington Market, bore the following inscription:

▲
Fig. 152. Washington, or Centre, Market, Albany, Hooker's first design, elevation, 1828. Ink and wash on paper. Albany County Hall of Records, Albany.

> *"A Map of the Fly Market Ground laid out into Seven Building lots. The Market to be Erected along & fronting South Pearl Street. 79 feet in length, having 10 stalls. When Mr Scovils lease shall have expired 37 feet may be added, containing six stalls. Making in all sixteen stalls & scales to each over which May be 4 or 5 Rooms for offices.*
>
> *Surveyed 20th April 1827*
> *by P. Hooker City Surveyor*
> *by order"* [3]

Root notes that

> *this map shows the site of the Fly Market on the south west corner of Howard and William Streets laid out into building lots. It shows also that the area between South Pearl St., Howard St., William St., and Beaver St. contained a vegetable market along Howard Street, a hay market in the centre and two buildings (one presumably Mr. Scovil's) on the north-west corner of South Pearl and Beaver Streets.*[4]

No action was taken on the resolution, and this first project was superseded by one submitted on 9 February 1829 (cat. 82).

Hooker's elevation of the South Pearl Street facade is the sole surviving drawing depicting this first version (fig. 152). Stout Doric columns support the second story, which was treated in a stripped down manner and featured a triple window similar to those of the Miller house (fig. 121). The columns are reminiscent of those which appear in Hooker's elevation for the *Great House* at Hyde Hall (fig. 141). Recessed panels are featured in the otherwise blank entablature, in the solid balustrade, and in the base of the

1. For a description of the site, purchased in 1816, see Root, p. 169 n.
2. Albany Common Council Minutes, 29 May 1828, ACHR.
3. Root, pp. 168–69, from map cited as number 154 in the City Engineer's Office, Albany.
4. Root, p. 169 n.

cupola. A fanlight in the base of the cupola, with perhaps another on the opposite elevation, is an ingenious device which admitted light to the interior of the upper story.

Vestiges of Federal-era design are evident in the cupola. However, Hooker's choice of a shallow dome rather than the vertical elements that capped his earlier cupolas (figs. 28, 68) was an effective means of simplifying the building's outline. The proportions and detailing make this one of the finest designs of Hooker's late period. ✤

72. PROPOSAL FOR CLINTON, OR SOUTH, MARKET

South Market Street (now Broadway), Albany, N.Y.
Designed before 29 May 1828.
Building begun spring 1829; not completed.
Builders: Vanderlip and Huxley.

Within the resolution passed by the Albany Common Council on 29 May 1828 relative to the city's markets (cats. 71, 81) was its approval of the appropriation of *one thousand four hundred Dollars for the erection of a Market at the watering place in the fourth ward pursuant to the plans drawn by Mr. Hooker. . . .* [1] A drawing identified as the *Plan of Clinton Market* may represent this proposal (fig. 153).

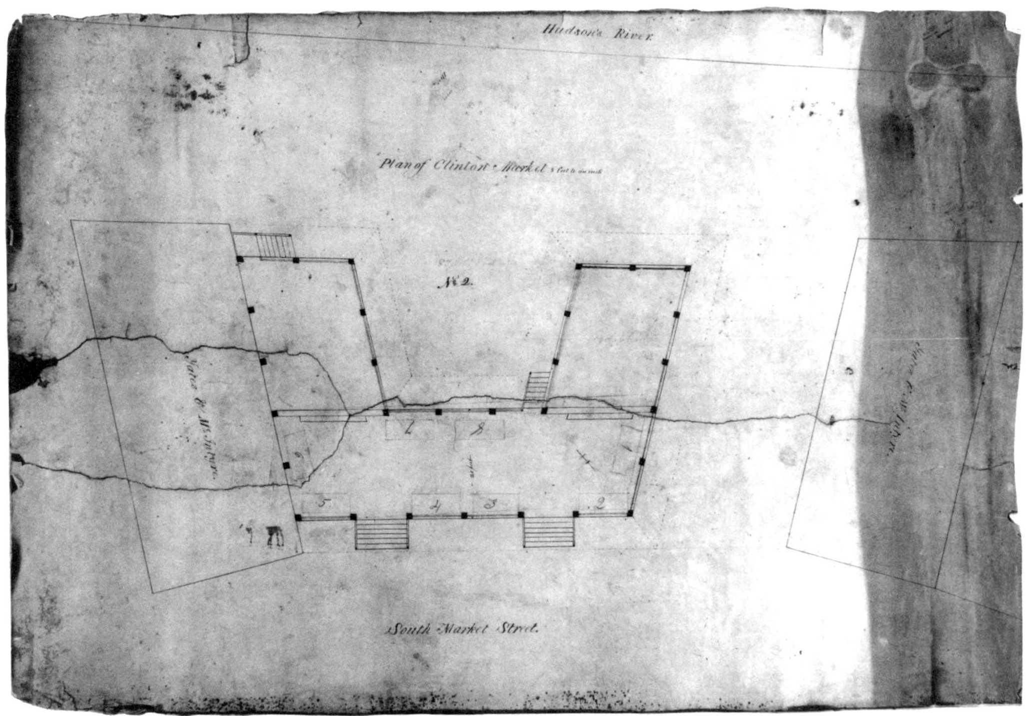

▶ Fig. 153. Clinton, or South, Market, Albany, Hooker's plan, c. 1828. Ink and wash on paper. Albany County Hall of Records, Albany.

No further action was taken until 29 December 1828, when the market committee was directed to *procure plans . . . with an estimate* for the market.[2] Hooker apparently presented his previously approved scheme, together with plans and an estimate for an addition to the North Market and a new market on South Pearl Street (cats. 81, 82; fig. 157). On 9 February 1829 the committee submitted Hooker's *plan of a market house . . . to be built with stone cellar underneath, divided into five rooms either for stores or the use of the butchers and vegetables; the dimensions 78 feet by 22 feet with a wing for a fish market. Estimated expence about two thousand dollars.* The plan was approved and a resolution was drafted the same day, indicating the market committee's preference for Hooker to act as superintendent of the project.[3]

A contract between the common council and Vanderlip and Huxley was agreed upon on 30 March 1829 "*for the erection of a new Market at the watering place agreeable to the plan & specifications drawn by Philip Hooker for the sum of one thousand four hundred and ninety three Dollars.*" [4]

The Clinton, or South, Market was presumably under construction when the contract for its erection was superseded by a second contract with the same builders. As approved on 22 June 1829, it provided for the construction of a second story (cat. 86).[5] ✤

1. Albany Common Council Minutes, 29 May 1828, ACHR.
2. Ibid., 29 December 1828.
3. Ibid., 9 February 1829.
4. Root, p. 171, from Albany Common Council Minutes, 16 March 1829.
5. Root, pp. 171–72.

73. CONSISTORY HOUSE, WITH DWELLING, FOR NORTH DUTCH REFORMED CHURCH (WITH ROBERT HIGHAM)

Chapel Street, between Orange and Van Schaick streets, Albany, N.Y.
Designed before 11 July 1828.
Built 1830–31; razed 1938.
Builders: John Boardman and Norman Francis.

On 11 July 1828 Hooker billed the consistory of the North Dutch Reformed Church $10.00 for *plans and specification of a lecture room,*[1] but work was not begun on the project until nearly two years later.

The 12 June 1830 contract between the church and *John Boardman and Norman Francis, builders of the city of Albany,* indicates that they agreed to construct this new building for $1,900.[2] In its provision of a large room with an arched ceiling, along with a basement apartment, this structure seems to have superseded the Hooker-designed consistory house on North Pearl Street (cat. 31).[3] Although the original specifications have been lost, a typescript of much of their contents yields valuable information.

The contract called for a building 50 feet long and 26 feet wide, height of side walls 16 feet.
The building to have a basement under it.
Walls to be 20 inches in thickness.
The front, on Van Schaick St., will be 8 feet above the surface of the sidewalk.
The walls to be 16 inches thick, having a stone plinth and reticated [i.e., rusticated] *piers.*
The basement was to be divided into a hall, 30 x 6 feet. One room with a fireplace, 18 x 16 feet. A bedroom, 10 x 7 feet.
A pantry or storeroom, 7 x 5 feet. A vegetable cellar, 15 x 8 feet.
A wood cellar, 18 x 14 feet, divided by 8 inch walls of hard brick.
The last two mention[ed], *vegetable and wood cellars, to be paved with small pebbles. The others are to be floored.*
The walls of the basement on 3 sides to be finished with a water table of free stone.
The inside walls to be plastered and whitewashed.
The fireplace to be a plain mantle and brick hearth with cran[e]*s' eyes to fireplace.*
The store room and pantry to be properly shelved.
A well made, 6 panel entrance door to the basement story, with a[n] *8* [inch] *knob lock.*
3 four paneled, inside doors, and 2 battened doors for the cellars.
The 2 windows in front to have 8 panes, 13 x 11 [inches], *with inside shutters.*
The 4 on the side to be 2 of 16 panes, 10 x 8 [inches]*; 2 of 8 panes, 10 x 8* [inches]*; to have outside shutters.*
The walls of the superstructure are to be of good merchantable brick and good mortar, 1 foot in thickness, having 4 projecting pilasters; at each end 6 [inch] *projection, to be finished at the top with square abacuses or caps* [i.e., capitals] *of hewn stone, above which the entablature is to be finished with clear, sound, white pine, painted and sanded in imitation of stone.*
The roof to be shingled and painted in imitation of slate.
8 windows, 18 panes of 14 x 11 [inches] *and one venetian window of 30 panes, same size, to have box frames; sashes hung with cord, pullies and weights.*
The large room to be floored with sound, well seasoned, white pine plank, planed, tongued, grooved, gauged to a width and thickness, joints broke and properly nailed. The plank not to exceed 9 [inches] *in width; the floor joists 10 x 4* [inches], *2 feet from center to center; to have a base and plinth around the room of suitable proportions.*
The windows cased with pilasters and blocks.
The ceiling to be furred to a segment of a circle, versed sine 3 1/2 ft., to be lathed and plastered with good puttly [i.e., putty] *well gauged with baked plaster.*
The side walls hard finished.
The entrance doors, Orange Street, are to be made in a bold style according to the plan, 6 ft. wide and 9 ft. high. Each door in 5 panels with heavy grecian mouldings. Doors to be 3 inches in thickness. To have proportionate hingles [i.e., hinges], *locks and bolts.*
A small vestibule of framed work is to be made on the inside with light inside doors, hung to open outward. The walls to be laid in flemish bond and penciled.
The steps in front, Orange St., to be substantially built with plank and timber; heavy stone blocks carried up at each end as per plan.
Collars and stoppers for 2 stovepipes above and i [probably *1* in the original] *in the basement.*
The stone sills to the doors, windows, and chimney tops to be caped with stone.
Cornice gutters, and friese [i.e., frieze] *on the east and west side with* [two] *3* [inch] *tin conductors to each, and a corresponding piedmont* [i.e., pediment] *at each end.*[4]

1. Doc. 139-8, Dutch Reformed Church (hereafter DRC) Collection, A FCA.
2. Typescript of Contract, DRC Collection.
3. The July 1828 bill describes the plans as being for a *lecture room.* E. P. Rogers, *A Historical Discourse on the Reformed Prot. Dutch Church of Albany* (New York: Board of Publication of the Reformed Protestant Dutch Church, 1858), p. 48, identifies the new construction at the rear of the church lot as a *Consistory Room.* A map published just prior to the 1857–59 construction of an addition to the church shows one building, situated along Chapel Street, on the lot behind the church; Hoffman, Pease & Tolley, *Map of the City of Albany* (N.p.: Sprague & Co., 1857). For the 1857–59 addition, see Joel Munsell, ed., *Annals of Albany,* Vol. X (Albany: Munsell & Rowland, Printers, 1859), pp. 422–23.
4. Typescript of Contract.

Work appears to have started immediately after the signing of the contract. The cut stone was to be quarried at Sing Sing state prison and shipped north by steamboat. A letter dated 6 July 1830 from prison superintendent Elam Lynds expresses his regret that the stone could not be worked on until September, due to previous commitments. On 15 September 1830 Hooker and cabinetmaker John Meads examined and approved the work done, including extras totaling $22.12, with the exception of *the hanging of the doors at the entrance so as to fold back to leave a free opening the whole width of the outer opening,* which they insisted should be done.[5]

The stone was still not ready to be shipped on 22 September 1830, when Elam Lynds wrote John Bogart of the building committee expressing his regret that *they* [the column capitals and bases] *are not all done yet . . . men will be put right at work on the caps so that they will be done with less delay.* On the verso of this letter is a reference to the stonework: *The top of the collums is 2 ft 5 inch*[es], *on which the cap*[i]*t*[al] *is to rest, from which you will be the best judge* [of what] *the size of the capps ought to be.*[6] A letter from Lynds dated 11 October assures the consistory that *we are this day loading a vessel for Albany and shall put on board the baises* [i.e., bases] *for columns for church,* but makes no mention of the capitals.[7]

On 18 October 1830 John Bogart sent Lynds a letter expressing his concerns.

> *Dear Sir*
> *The superintendent of the Hall* [the Albany City Hall, cat. 87, also utilizing Sing Sing marble] *Mr* [Jonathan] *Lyman informs me that the dimensions of the caps for the columns of the North Church* [consistory] *have been mislaid by Mr. Joy, of which we have much reason to regret, as the season is rappedly drawing to a close, & if they are not forwarded to us soon, all our work will have to lay over untill spring as the finishes can not go on before the caps are in their places. The dimentions of the cap ware* [i.e., where] *it will rest on the top of the colum must be two feet five inches. Mr. Joy will know what debth will be nessary. Mr. Hooker says he furnished you with his draughts.*[8]

The correspondence as preserved ends at this point.

The building, with its end facades dignified by pilasters and pedimented gables, appears to have been completed in 1831. On 11 March 1831 Hooker and Robert Higham, his recently appointed junior partner, billed the church $2.00 *to plans for a front door in altering consistory house.*[9] Measured drawings of the structure, submitted to but not approved by the Historic American Building Survey, indicate that modest changes may have been made to the contract specifications in the construction of Hooker's design.[10] The building was razed in 1938.[11] ✤

5. Doc. 142-5, DRC Collection.
6. Doc. 142-7, DRC Collection.
7. Doc. 144-7, DRC Collection.
8. Doc. 142-6, DRC Collection.
9. Doc. 144-4, DRC Collection. For further information on Higham, see pp. 44, 50 n. 76.
10. Drawings, "The First Dutch Church in Albany, N.Y.," 1939–41, Historic American Building Survey, Division of Prints and Photographs, Library of Congress, Washington, D.C. The exterior of the building was similar to that of the consistory house and dwelling erected for the South Dutch Church in 1828 (A28; visible in figs. 54, 55).
11. Robert S. Alexander, *Albany's First Church and its Role in the Growth of the City, 1642–1942* (Albany: First Church in Albany, 1988), pp. 294–95.

74. COACH HOUSE AND STABLES, VAN RENSSELAER MANOR

Head of Market Street (now Broadway), Albany, N.Y.
Designed before 16 October 1828.
Built 1828–29; razed before 1900.
Builder unknown.

▶ Fig. 154. Coach House and Stables, Van Rensselaer Manor, Albany (1828–29), exterior. Albany Institute of History & Art, McKinney Library, Photograph Collection.

On 16 October 1828 Hooker submitted his bill, totaling $6.00, to Stephen Van Rensselaer III for *plans, directions, and attendance to building* [a] *new coach house and stables.*[1] These service buildings were designed for the Van Rensselaer Manor and were recorded in a photograph (fig. 154), which shows them with later alterations.

1. Van Rensselaer Manor Papers, SC 7079, MSC NYSL.

75. BUILDING

South Market Street (now Broadway), Albany, N.Y.
Designed before 21 October 1828.
Building history unknown.

76. BUILDING

Church Street, Albany, N.Y.
Designed before 21 October 1828.
Building history unknown.

77. BUILDING

Westerlo Street, Albany, N.Y.
Designed before 21 October 1828.
Building history unknown.

According to a receipt in the papers of Stephen Van Rensselaer III, Hooker was paid $5.00 for *plans for buildings on S*[outh] *Market, Westerlo and Church Streets, procured by Chas. Conklin.* Hooker executed designs for these buildings, which were either speculative houses or commercial buildings or both, by 21 October 1828.[1] The amount of Hooker's fee suggests that they were simple in design, and it is possible that he prepared one set of drawings to serve all three sites. ✜

1. Van Rensselaer Manor Papers, SC 7079, MSC NYSL.

78. BUILDINGS FOR STEPHEN VAN RENSSELAER III

South Market Street (now Broadway), Albany, N.Y.
Designed before 30 October 1828.
Building history unknown.

Hooker was paid $15.00 for work done by 30 October 1828 for *an elegant* [plan and speci]*fication for buildings opposite the Eagle* Tavern.[1] We have no record of the appearance of these buildings, of their use, or even if they were built. It is likely that Hooker's scheme included first floor commercial space, for the street was well-established as a business center. ✜

1. Van Rensselaer Manor Papers, SC 7079, MSC NYSL.

79. PARSONAGE FOR NORTH DUTCH REFORMED CHURCH

Unknown location, Albany, N.Y.
Designed before 25 November 1828.
Building history unknown.

On 25 November 1828 Hooker provided the North Dutch Reformed Church with *plans, specifications &* [an] *estimate for* [a new] *parsonage house* and billed the consistory $12.50 for his services.[1] The appearance of this design is unknown, and its intended site and relationship to Hooker's earlier plans for remodeling the consistory house into a parsonage (cat. 70) remain unclear.[2] ✥

1. Doc. 139-8, Dutch Reformed Church Collection, A FCA.
2. "1814 Consistory House Erected," A FCA.

80. FOURTH PRESBYTERIAN CHURCH

North Market Street (now Broadway), Albany, N.Y.
Designed before 24 December 1828.
Built 1829–30; razed summer 1865.
Builders: Timothy Fassett and Lawrence Hallenbake.

On 1 December 1828 the newly formed congregation of the Fourth Presbyterian Church met and elected their first board of trustees, among them Philip Hooker. At a meeting on 24 December 1828, the trustees agreed upon a site and selected a design that had already been prepared.

> *"Resolved that the church be located on Moncius Lot on North Market Street.*
> *"Resolved that the model no*[.] *one be adopted—estimated to cost eleven thousand five hundred Dollars with the alteration of making the middle Aisle seven feet wide—"*[1]

The minutes of the trustees' 29 December meeting identify Hooker as the architect, for it was "*resolv^d^ to adopt plan no 1. as furnished by Mr. Hooker.*"[2]

Estimates from contractors were received by the trustees in the spring of 1829. Root records one that was dated 13 May.

> "*Gentlemen*
> *"We will build your Church agreeable to the plans & specification made and shown to us by Mr. P Hooker for eleven thousand two hundred and seventy five Dollars, if the foundation is piled we add two Hundred seventy five Dollars*
> *Fassett & Hallenbake*
> *N.B. if the jobb falls to us we will take one thousand Dollars worth of stock*
> *F & H*"[3]

The trustees responded quickly to this tempting offer and one week later a contract and specifications were signed with Fassett and Hallenbake. Root transcribed much of the text of the documents, which are now lost.

> *"Articles of agreement made & concluded this twentieth day of may, in the year of our Lord one thousand eight hundred and twenty-nine Between the Trustees of the fourth Presbyterian Church of the City of Albany of the first Part & Timothy Fassett & Lawrence Halenbake Builders of the said city of the second Part, Witnesseth: That the said parties of the second Part . . . do, hereby covenant promise and agree . . . that they . . . shall & will . . . erect, build and finish an Edifice for Public Worship in all respects, as set forth in the preceding specification . . . the whole to be done according to the plans now made & to be made theirof by Philip Hooker or such other person as shall be appointed for that purpose. . . . "*
>
> *The specification called for a building "86 feet in lenght, 60 feet in width, and 30 feet in height from the water table to the eaves, having a projection of 4 feet in front . . . containing three entrances to be erected on a basement story, the walls of which" were "to be built with good flat stone." Above the water-table the "west end and north and south sides" were "to be laid in flemish bond and painted with two coats of white lead"; the "east front" was "to be stuccoed in imitation of marble, with regular blocks, returned on the sides" and "the cupola" was "to be finished in the same manner." The "Dome" of the latter was to be covered with "Boards and tin plate" and "surmounted with an open lantern of eight Doric columns supporting an entablature and small dome." Above the last was to be "a spindle, gilt ball and vane." The west front was to have "a cornice continued up the rake of the roof forming an angular pediment, supported by Four brick pilasters." There were to be "twelve windows containing 72 panes," another window of 24 panes and, in the east front, a "Venetian window" of 12 panes. The latter was to have stone pilasters. The basement was to have ten windows with "stone sills and brick arches 1 1/2 brick high," and in the tympanum of the west pediment were to be three "loop holes with splay'd Jambs."*
>
> *Within, the galleries were "to be finished similar to those in the second presbyterian church in relation to seating front and support," except that the columns were to be "Grecian Doric fluted insted of ionic." The ceiling was to be "arched and panneled" and "divided into 126 bold recessed pannels" and the whole building was to be completed by May 1, 1830.*[4]

Even while it was under construction, the church building attracted attention. The following letter appeared in the *Albany Argus*:

> *Mr. Editor—I have been much gratified with the appearance of the new Presbyterian church now erecting in North Market street, (the Colonie) since the marbleizing of the front and base of the cupola. It is a handsome architectural ornament to that part of the city, as well as a valuable addition to our means of public worship.*
>
> *Allow me to suggest, through the Argus, the propriety of marbleizing the front and Lodge-street side of St. Peter's church* [cat. 6]. *The present plaster, or imitation, has become considerably defaced, and was never remarkable for the beauty of its appearance. Such an improvement, I am persuaded, would be as gratifying to the congregation, as it certainly would be to*
>
> *An Episcopal Layman*[5]

Marbleizing was the practice of coating the brick or rough stone walls of a building with a thin layer of cement, which was then scored in imitation of cut stone and painted to resemble marble. Less frequently, the finish coat

▶ Fig. 155. Fourth Presbyterian Church, Albany (1829–30), view, published in 1858. Courtesy New York State Library, Albany.

was mixed with powder of the actual stone, producing a more realistic effect but at greater expense. The same technique was used to imitate other stones, the most common being brownstone and granite.

Hooker's bill for services during the project was recorded by Root.

> *"The trustees of the 4th Presbyterian church in the city of Albany*
> *To Philip Hooker Dr.*
> *To plans, elevations, sections, specifications and other drawings.*
> *Journey & expenses to New York—superintending & directing the work of their New Church & its appendages.* *$150 . .—*
> *Albany 23rd June 1830 Recd payment*
> *P. Hooker"* [6]

A description of the completed building, taken from a contemporary newspaper, was published and illustrated in Munsell's *Annals of Albany* (fig. 155).

> *Among the improvements recently made in the city, is the Fourth Presbyterian church, just finished in the fifth ward. This building is situated in the centre of a handsome open area, extending from North Market to Orchard street, between*

▶ Fig. 156. Fourth Presbyterian Church, Albany (1829–30), interior view toward rear gallery, 1860. Albany Institute of History & Art, McKinney Library, Photograph Collection.

Patroon and Wilson streets. The grounds about the church are tastefully laid out in paved and graveled walks and parterres. The edifice is substantially built with stone and brick, marbleized, and designed in the most simple style of Grecian architecture; dimensions 90 by 60 feet, having a tower in which is a belfrey surmounted by a dome and small turret—a high basement, which contains a lecture room and two capacious school rooms—the body of the church is lighted by one tier of oblong windows; the ceiling a cylindric paneled arch, being a small segment of a large circle; a gallery on three sides; the nave divided by three aisles, the whole seated in a neat modern style. The chancel is enclosed with bold paneled work, screening the stairs to the pulpit, which rises in the centre in the form of an altar, in the same bold style, producing a pleasing and fine effect. The principal entrance is from North Market street, by a glacis and flight of stone steps thirty feet in length, terminated at each end by solid stone blocks or socles, supporting the lamp piers, which are of heavy ornamental iron work. What renders this building particularly interesting, is the novelty and simplicity of the design, which was founded on economy, and which has rendered it, and perhaps justly, the subject of criticism. The small windows over the entrances were not in the original design; blank recesses would have supplied their places with better effect. The original design was made by Philip Hooker.[7]

Hooker utilized many features typical of Greek Revival design in this building. His application differs, however, in that the Greek-derived details are reduced to pure forms. In the steeple, usually a showcase for the classical orders in Hooker's work, he utilized bold panels. A pediment is suggested by a continuous piece of boldly cut trim. The interior (fig. 156) appears to have followed suit in its severe coffered ceiling which spanned the sanctuary in a low arch. ✜

1. Root, p. 162, from the minutes, Fourth Presbyterian Church. It is likely that *model* as referred to here was synonymous with *design*.
2. Ibid., p. 163, from the minutes, Fourth Presbyterian Church.
3. Root, p. 163, from the document, Fourth Presbyterian Church.
4. Root, pp. 163–65, from the contract and specifications, Fourth Presbyterian Church.
5. *Albany Argus*, 24 September 1829.
6. Root, p. 166, from the receipted bill, Fourth Presbyterian Church.
7. Joel Munsell, *Annals of Albany*, Vol. IX (Albany: Munsell & Rowland, Printers, 1858), p. 210.

81. ADDITION TO NORTH, OR WASHINGTON (LATER LA FAYETTE), MARKET

North Market Street (now Broadway), Albany, N.Y.
Designed between 29 December 1828 and 9 February 1829.
Built 1829–30; razed.
Builder unknown.

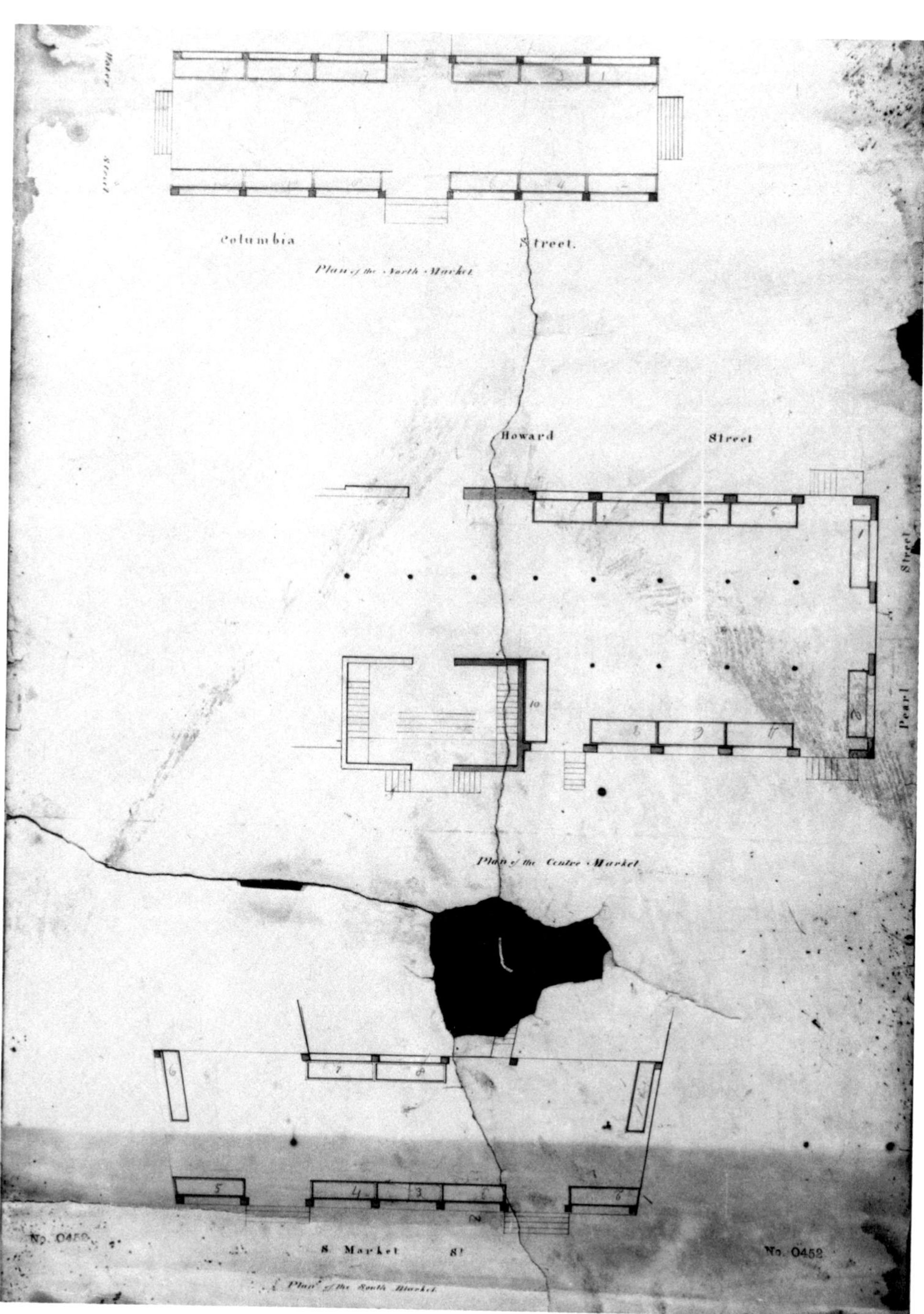

▶ Fig. 157. Plans of the North, Centre, and South markets, Albany, c. 1829.
Ink and wash on paper.
Albany County Hall of Records, Albany.

An addition to the North or Washington (later La Fayette) Market, initially constructed in 1807, was first contemplated by the Albany Common Council on 29 May 1828, when it was resolved to appropriate a sufficient sum of money *for the repairs and improvements of the Washington Market, and the appropriation for that purpose be not less than five hundred or more than one thousand dollars.*[1] By 29 December 1828 the resolution had not yet been acted upon, and the common council requested that plans and specifications be submitted.[2] The market committee report was submitted on 9 February 1829 and included plans and specifications for the addition as well as for the two new market buildings (cats. 72, 82). The project was described as . . . *an addition to the North Market erected on the east end of the present market for the purpose of retailing fish; to be built on a stone foundation without cellars, dimensions 22 by 22 feet, estimated cost five hundred dollars.* The plans, approved that same day, were drawn by Hooker.[3]

The committee advertised for sealed proposals for construction and indicated their preference for Hooker as superintendent of the project. The addition was completed by the spring of 1830.[4]

It is difficult to ascertain the relationship between the project description quoted above and the recently discovered *Plan of the North Market,* drawn on a sheet with the plans for the two new markets (fig. 157). The drawing depicts a market in which a wide aisle is flanked by stalls for twelve vendors, with entrances centered on the long sides. This scheme is similar to, though smaller than, that of the Centre Market, drawn below it on the sheet. ✤

1. Albany Common Council Minutes, 29 May 1828, ACHR.
2. Ibid., 29 December 1828.
3. Ibid., 9 February 1829.
4. Root, p. 172.

82. WASHINGTON, OR CENTRE, MARKET

South Pearl Street, between Howard and William streets, Albany, N.Y.
Built 1829; razed summer 1864.
Builder: Lewis Farnham.

Hooker had presented his original proposal for this market in May 1828 (cat. 71). Seven months later the Common Council requested that the plans be resubmitted. As there is no mention of dissatisfaction with Hooker's original proposal, it appears that he provided the second design on his own volition. The market committee submitted this new scheme with the plans for two other markets (cats. 72, 81; fig. 157) on 9 February 1829.[1]

Construction of the building was evidently under Hooker's supervision, and the new Washington Market was ready for occupancy on 1 October 1829 (fig. 158).[2] An early description of the market is recorded in an insurance survey conducted by John Boardman and dated 10 May 1830.

▶
Fig. 158. Washington, or Centre, Market, Albany (1829), exterior, c. 1855. Albany Institute of History & Art, McKinney Library, Photograph Collection.

Fronting on S[outh] *Pearl St 36 ft* *on William St 36 ft* *length 126* [ft]	*Two stories high, shingled roof* *Basement walls stone with* *a grocery east front meat*

cellars &c–b[ric]*k—superstructure brick*
First story constructed with peirs & arches open for
Meat & Sau[?]*e markets & so ocupied*

Second story 12 feet high, one public justice room
one city court room—one city surveyors office
one city superintendents office
two wood rooms—four councel & private conference rooms
stair way & entry
the garret in one—a scuttle in the roof—
with steps to the same a cupola in the center & ballustrades on each side
4th class value 9,000[3]

The *quiet and dignified classicism* of this building, described by Talbot Hamlin in his *Greek Revival Architecture in America*,[4] demonstrates Hooker's mastery of utilitarian forms and his deepening commitment to the language of the Greek Revival. ✤

1. Albany Common Council Minutes, 9 February 1829, ACHR.
2. Root, p. 172.
3. Box 16, Folder 109, SARA, ACHR.
4. Talbot Hamlin, *Greek Revival Architecture in America* (1944; reprint ed., New York: Dover Publications, Inc., 1964), p. 265.

83. ST. MARY'S ROMAN CATHOLIC CHURCH

Northwest corner of Pine and Chapel streets, Albany, N.Y.
Designed c. February 1829.
Built 1829–30; razed summer 1867; fragment survives.
Builder: Henry Peers.

▶
Fig. 159. St. Mary's Roman Catholic Church, Albany (1829–30), view, published in 1858. Courtesy New York State Library, Albany.

The documents relating to this project were transcribed and published by Root, but have since been lost. From the minutes of the church trustees come the following entries:

> *"Feb. 25, 1829. . . . Resolved that Mr. Morange be & is hereby appointed to call on M^r. Hooker, & request of him to loan any plans which he may have for the inspection of the trustees also to ascertain from him the difference of cost between a stone or a Brick Marbled Church.*
>
> *"May 19, 1829 . . . resolved that Mr. Morange, Mr. Duffan & Mr. Reynolds be a committee to inquire and obtain from Mr. Hooker a plan for building an addition to the church and the cost of the same."* [1]

By the time of the trustees' 15 August meeting, the decision had been made to construct a new building rather than an addition to the existing one.

> "*The proposals to errect S^t^. Mary's church having been opened it appeared that Henery Peers proposal was the lowest being for the sum of Ten thousand nine hundred and eighty dollars. Therefore resolved that Henry Peers proposal be and is hereby accepted, provided he completes the two upper sections of the steeple.*
>
> "*Resolved that Phillip Hooker Esqre be and is hereby appointed to superIntend the erection of S^t^. Mary's Church.*" [2]

The articles of agreement and specification for building the church are dated 15 September 1829.

> "*The body of the building shall be sixty-one by seventy-five feet, with a semi-circular Vestry of 23 feet projection according to the plans drawn by Mr. Philip Hooker, and a Portico and steps of 24 feet projection. To be 31 feet 4 inches high from the top of the water table to the top of the cornice and ten feet six inches from the ground on Chapel Street to the top of the watertable. . . . Four Grecian columns, of the Doric order, in front of bricks on a proper foundation of stone . . . 10 windows in the body of the building, . . . and nine windows in the vestry. . . . A neat pulpit, Altar, railing &c around the Chancel, the pulpit stairs to have a Mahogany rail & balusters and mahogany caps to the chancel rail. Suitable turned columns with caps and bases of the Doric order to support the galleries and four of the Grecian Ionic in front of the orchestra, the breastwork of the Gallery to be framed in pannels and capped with a suitable Cornice. . . . The whole of the exterior to be stuccoed with good sharp sand and lime mortar in imitation of Portland Stone, including the portico, columns, cieling of the same &c. . . . And the said Henry Peers doth hereby covenant, contract, promise and agree to and with the said Trustees, that he will faithfully honestly and skilfully obtain and procure all the said materials herein above mentioned and intended by the Specification and plans made by . . . Philip Hooker. . . . And it is further mutually agreed by and between the said parties, that the said Trustees may from time to time, make or direct to be made any alteration or improvement in the plans, specification or materials and if the said parties cannot agree upon the price or worth of such alteration or improvement, the subject matter shall be submitted to Philip Hooker Esqr. whose decision in the premises shall be final & conclusive. and his opinion, in case of disagreement between the said parties, relative to the goodness or quality of any of the materials or relative to the goodness or style of workmanship shall also be conclusive and said parties shall govern themselves accordingly.*" [3]

If we can judge from the small woodcut image of the church which comes down to us (fig. 159), Hooker provided St. Mary's Church with a design which was torn between the Federal and Greek Revival modes. The traditional steeple of the church sits awkwardly on what would otherwise have been a rather fashionable temple-form structure. Furthermore, Hooker renders this steeple in the Federal style, utilizing many of the elements common to his designs of the previous twenty years. The amalgamation of the tower and the temple was explored by other architects as well throughout the Greek Revival era, and was never satisfactorily resolved.

St. Mary's Roman Catholic Church was razed in 1867.[4] The tabernacle which graced its altar is now in the collection of the Albany Institute of History & Art.[5] ✜

1. Root, p. 174, from the minutes, St. Mary's Church.
2. Ibid.
3. Root, p. 175, from the articles of agreement and specification, St. Mary's Church.
4. Root, p. 176.
5. The tabernacle consists of columns supporting a stepped dome, which was formerly surmounted by a finial.

84. PROPOSAL FOR AN ADDITION TO THE NEW YORK STATE CAPITOL

State Street, Albany, N.Y.
Designed before 23 February 1829.
Unbuilt.

The burgeoning bureaucracies of the city, county, and state governments, all occupying the 1809 capitol (cat. 15), forced these bodies to look for additional space. The state expanded its office building (cat. 85), and Mayor John Townsend of Albany retained Hooker *to* [provide] *plans & estimate to enlarge the Capitol.*[1] For this service Hooker was paid $4.00.

Never carried out, this proposal was superseded by plans solicited by the city and county for construction of a separate city hall (cat. 87). ✣

1. Account by Philip Hooker of his work for the city, 23 February 1829 to 4 February 1830, typescript addressed to Mayor Erastus Corning II from John J. McEneny, 1972, in Philip Hooker, Historian's File, ACHR.

85. ADDITION TO THE STATE HALL

State and Lodge streets, Albany, N.Y.
Designed before 27 February 1829.
Built c. 1829; razed c. 1857.
Builder unknown.

The State Hall was erected in 1797 from the design of William Sanders, and was used as New York State's first office building (fig. 7).[1] It was still serving this function when Hooker was engaged to design and superintend the construction of an addition. The report of Simeon De Witt to the New York State Assembly dated 27 February 1829 provides further details.

> *In contracting for building the wing to the State Hall, it was agreed to allow Philip Hooker $50 for attending to the erections in their progress, and to see that every part of the work was done in a proper manner. He charges besides, for drawing plans and making estimates $10, with alterations and specifications of the buildings, $6, and for drawing contract $4 making in all $70. . . .* [2]

The addition was constructed to the south of the original building, but no record of its appearance exists. ✣

1. Cuyler Reynolds, comp., *Albany Chronicles* (Albany: J. B. Lyon Company, Printers, 1906), p. 355; A. O. Springer, *Albany's Bi-Centennial*, 2d ed. (Albany, 1886), n.p. For Sanders, see pp. 45, 50 n. 81.
2. *Journal of the Assembly of the State of New-York at their Fifty-second Session* (Albany: Printed by E. Croswell, 1829), p. 986.

86. CLINTON, OR SOUTH, MARKET

South Market Street (now Broadway), Albany, N.Y.
Designed before 27 May 1829.
Built 1829; razed c. 1845.
Builders: Vanderlip and Huxley.

As originally planned, the Clinton Market was to be one story in height with stalls for vendors; the cellar below was also intended to serve the market function (cat. 72). A second proposal, featuring plans and specifications by Hooker, included a second story with provisions for office space. This proposal was submitted to the Albany Common Council on 27 May 1829, and $2,404 was allocated for the project.[1] The revised contract with Vanderlip and Huxley was approved on 22 June 1829.[2]

That the building was required to be completed and ready for occupancy on 1 October 1829[3] indicates that construction had already begun when the original contract was cancelled. ✥

1. Albany Common Council Minutes, 27 May 1829, ACHR.
2. Ibid., 22 June 1829.
3. Ibid., 14 September 1829.

87. ALBANY CITY HALL

Eagle Street, Albany, N.Y.
First design between 26 June and 20 July 1829.
Built 1829–32; burned February 1880 and razed.
Builder: Jonathan Lyman.

On 12 June 1829, a building committee consisting of Mayor John Townsend, Recorder James McKown, and Messrs. Staats, Wasson, Hart, Maher, and Beck resolved *"to offer a premium of $100. for the best plan of a City Hall & to publish the following advertisement.*

> *"City Hall—$100 will be paid to the architect who may furnish a set of plans which shall be approved of by the Common Council for the City hall which is to be erected on the east side of the public square, between Maiden-lane and Pine-street.*
>
> *"The ground in front is nearly level. Pine-Street has a descent of 8 ft on 100 feet.*
>
> *"The building is to consist of a high basement & 2 stories of proportionate height. Plans of each floor will be required, elevations in front & profile, and at least one section.*
>
> *"The basement to be arranged for offices & convenient apartments for the keeper and his family, two rooms for the county clerk, one for the surrogate, & one for the sheriff. These offices should be fire proof. The first floor to contain rooms for the common council, chamberlain's office, mayor's office, mayor's court & jury room.*
>
> *"The second floor to contain a spacious room for the circuit court, jury rooms, a room for the supervisors & grand jury, vestibules, halls, stairs & other necessary appendages.*
>
> *"The general proportions will be determined by the taste & skill of the architect. The building is not to exceed 95 feet front, & from 80 to 85 feet in depth; or, if an exact square of 90 feet = 8100 feet area, will lay out to the best advantage, that dimension may be adopted. It is proposed to face the basement with sandstone of good quality, & the decorative parts of the superstructure with marble. Plans, with descriptions, will be received until the 15th day of July next.*
>
> *John Townsend, Mayor"* [1]

It was resolved to amend the notice on 26 June 1829.

> *"City Hall—Architecture—Notice is hereby given to Architects intending to exhibit plans for the City Hall, to be erected in the City of Albany that in consequence of the purchase of another lot of ground the dimensions of the front will not be confined to 'ninety five feet.' The late purchase opens a square, bounded by 3 streets, to wit: Eagle St. public squares on the N. W. extent of front 125 feet—Maiden Lane on the south, 133 feet—and Pine Street on the north, 111 feet. The principal front on Eagle Street may extend 100 feet, more or less; leaving room for iron palisades, steps, &c. on Pine Street & Maiden Lane. The depth from front to rear, may be from 70 to 80 feet, more or less, as may be required for the various apartments, described in former advertisements; the arrangement of which will be left to the designer. It may be proper to repeat, that the ground in front is nearly level; that Pine St. has a descent of 8 feet on 100 feet, & Maiden Lane something less.*
>
> *"The time for receiving plans, with descriptions, will be extended to the 20th of July next."* [2]

Responses arrived from across the northeast as well as from Albany and environs. The following letter to the mayor, dated 17 July 1829, came from Boston:

Sir:

Having noticed in one of the Albany papers that a premium has been offered for the best plan of a City Hall about to be erected in your City, I have taken the liberty to sketch a plan in haste, not having had sufficient time to finish one up properly since I saw the Advertizement but as they are I w[oul]*d wish to offer them for the examination of the committee. They are perfect in dimension altho' not highly finished in drawing. According to the lot of ground specified, I have constructed a set of plans 110 ft. in front & 80 ft. in depth which will have 7 1/2 ft. on each end in which I propose to build a level, & to descend by means of steps from the centre of each end into "Maiden Lane" & "Pine St" & at the lower end into the yard & to set the building back to allow sufficient room in front to build suitable steps with an arch under the same to ascend into the "recess*[ed] *portico", level with the principle floor. I have divided the basement into rooms suitable to be vaulted, which may answer for the several apartments required on the basement floor, with entry & suitable light & also a flight of stairs in the rear of the building to the principle 2d & 3d floor—I have divided the first floor into the apartments which may be required for "offices", "court rooms"; I have also divided the 2d floor in to "offices", "jury rooms" & "large halls" for "Circuit Court" & other purposes; furnished with gallery's and private stair ways to connect with the first floor.*

The occupation of the rooms for the purpose mentioned will be left (of course) with the committee; for that reason I have not marked any particular room as a "Circuit Court room," jury room &c. As there is a choice in the rooms, the committee will occupy them for that purpose which they may think the best adopted.

I w[oul]*d wish to have it understood that the exterior ornaments of this plan will be left with the committee to adopt or not as they may please, but if the general plan & outline of the building sh*[oul]*d not meet their appreciation, you will confer a favour on me to return the same by first opportunity.*

I have the honour to be Sir
Y[ou]*rs most respectfully*

John Kutts
No. 31 Court St.
Boston.

PS The room & gallery intended in this plan as a "Circuit room" contains 200 ft superficial measure more than the one now used in this city [Boston] *for the same purpose.*

J.K[3]

Another communication, from Woodstock Farm at Albany, was dated 20 July.

"Sir

*"Having been prevented by severe indisposition from prosecuting the duties of my profession—I now find it impossible to complete my drawings of the New City Hall by the time allotted in the Advertisement—viz—*this day:—*I have therefore written to entreat your kind intercession in my behalf with the other members of the Building Committee—in getting them to suspend their decission for a few days when my plan will be furnished—I am sorry to be compelled to ask any infringement of their laws, but sickness is a thing over which we can have no control—*

"Either of the Committee (should they feel disposed to side this way) may see the plan as far as it goes—and I believe it is sufficiently finished for them to judge partially of its effect—

Waiting your reply

I am

Sir

Your most ob[edian]*t Ser*[van]*t*

Geo[rge]. *Vernon*" [4]

The plans received by the mayor were exhibited publicly,[5] and on 23 July 1829 were reviewed by the common council.

"The Building Committee reported to the Board that they had received Plans & Elevations with specifications for the City Hall, from the following persons—which they submitted to the board viz

from Messrs		*Toron* [I. Town] *&* [A. J.] *Davis*	*of New York*
"	*Mr*	[Minard] *Le Fevre* [Lafever]	" "
"	"	[Isaiah] *Rogers*	" *Boston*
"	"	*Edward Shaw*	" "
"	"	*Peter Banner*	" "
"	"	*George Rich*	*of WaterVliet*
"	"	*H*[enry]. *Rector*	" *Albany*
"	"	*Ph*[ilip]. *Hooker*	" "
"	"	*R*[obert]. *Higham*	" "
"	"	*W. M. Brown*	" "
"	"	*Scobè*	" *Montreal*

which several plans were taken into consideration by the Board, & the following resolution was offered by the Recorder & adopted viz

"*'Resolved that each member propose anyone or more of the plans submitted to the Board, which plans so proposed shall be submitted to a Committee to select & report at a future meeting of the Board out of such number such one as they are of opinion ought to be adopted & any plan which no member shall propose to be referred to such Committee shall be deemed to be rejected. Whereupon the plans proposed by the following Gentlemen were referred according to foregoing Resolution to wit. Messrs Le Fevre's, Rogers, Rector's, Hooker's, Higham's and Scobè's.*

"*'Resolved that the said plans be referred to the Building Committee to report an estimate or estimates of the expense of the same and their opinion thereon.'*" [6]

A twelfth entry was received by 25 July from a Mr. Ryder.[7] On 27 July, entries from John Kutts and George Vernon were added to those referred to the building committee.[8] The next day, the committee reported to the common council.

"The City Hall Building Committee reported for the sanction of the Board, Hooker's plan of elevation, with Kutt's Cupola for the City Hall, upon which the following resolution was offered by the Recorder and passed.

"*'Resolved that the report of the Building Committee be accepted, to adopt Hooker's elevation with the alteration of the upper windows with Kutt's plan of Cupola and that the premium offered by the Board be divided between the two Architects.'*" [9]

The plans and the council's decision, which was publicized on 30 July, were the source of much discussion.[10] Of particular concern was the intent to combine two designs in the execution of the building. One local critic, his pseudonym displaying a taste for English architecture and considerable presumption, addressed the editors and readers of the *Albany Daily Advertiser.*

Gentlemen— Having read the paragraph in your paper, stating that the corporation had adopted the plan of Mr. Kutts, of Boston, for the cupola and attic windows of our new City Hall, and for the remainder of the building, the plan of Mr. Hooker, and that the premium had been divided between them, I was induced to look at the two designs.

Without saying anything of the division of the premium, (which has the recommendation, certainly, of novelty,) I must ask the liberty to say a word or two as to the appearance of the building, under the effect of the joint plans.

There is no part of our city so prominent, or in which a building of any magnitude can be seen at so great distance or to better advantage. Northward, when approaching from Troy, or south, several miles down the river, the edifice on this high ground, properly constructed, will be seen with a striking effect. It was with pleasure, therefore, that I heard it suggested, when the proposals for plans were given out, that this elevation would be crowned with a dome that would give a stately appearance, and a peculiar and striking character to the building, and an air of grandeur to the city, that we look for in vain in the other public erections.—It was under such impressions, probably, that Mr. Hooker designed what he may call a dome, which, however, I believe was only an enlarged cupola, but which was large, and therefore preferable to any thing except a dome of the extent of the noble and classic plan of Mr. Rogers of Boston. What was my surprise, on seeing the selection, that the notion of a dome, had been altogether discarded: that even the large cupola had been rejected, and that a sort of balcony, or if you please lightning rod, had been adopted in their stead!

Now, I wish to speak with deference of the taste and opinions of others; but I should fail to discharge a duty to the city, if I allowed the occasion to pass without uttering at least one protest against a design that will appear diminutive, and will not satisfy our citizens, who, since this building has been so much talked about, and got such notoriety, have expected that it would be worthy of our city, and of the improved architecture of the age. If they are not disappointed in this respect, it will be owing to the expression of our citizens, to and [i.e., and to] *the potent aid of the press.*

CHRISTOPHER WREN[11]

Similar but more extensive discussions were published in the *Albany Argus.*

THE CITY HALL.— The article on this subject, which we publish to-day, is entitled to consideration as coming from a highly respectable source and from a citizen of good taste. Without expressing an opinion at this time upon the objections of the writer to the proposed union of the two plans for the Hall, which he considers incompatible with each other, we can have no objection to a free discussion through our columns of a subject of such interest to our citizens.— Upon the second branch of the subject,—the dome or cupola— we concur in the probable opinion of this writer, and in that of a writer in the Daily Advertiser, that a dome of reasonable magnitude, would, of all things, give a striking appearance to the edifice, visible as it would be for many miles north and south which would be wholly lost in a comparatively diminutive cupola.[12]

1. Root, p. 178, from Albany City Hall, Manuscript Minutes of the Building Committee, 12 June 1829.
2. Ibid., p. 179, from Albany City Hall, Manuscript Minutes of the Building Committee, 26 June 1829.
3. Townsend Papers, DC 10441, Box 1, Folder 1, MSC NYSL.
4. Root, p. 180, from the document.
5. *Daily Albany Argus,* 21 July 1829.
6. Root, pp. 179–80, from Albany Common Council, Manuscript Minutes, 23 July 1829.
7. *Daily Albany Argus,* 25 July 1829.
8. Root, p. 180.
9. Ibid., p. 181, from Albany Common Council, Manuscript Minutes, 28 July 1829.
10. *Daily Albany Argus,* 30 July 1829. A lively exchange of letters in the *Microscope* of 21 November, 12 December, and 26 December 1829 was centered on the building but was more concerned with the personalities and practices of the authors, who were apparently two of the unsuccessful competitors for the commission, Henry Rector and George Vernon.
11. *Albany Daily Advertiser,* 3 August 1829.
12. *Albany Argus,* 11 August 1829.

To the Editor of the Albany Argus—

Sir— I perceive by some publications in the Daily Advertiser, that the attention of our citizens has been specially directed to the decision of our corporation upon the plan for the new city hall; and from the opinions I have heard expressed by individuals in private conversation, I am well convinced that the dissatisfaction produced by that decision is much stronger and more general, and rests upon better and more serious grounds, than from the tenor and character of the articles attended to, would, in the first instance, be supposed.

The attempt of the author of the last of those communications to attach ridicule to the committee or to the common council, for adopting part of two distinct designs, I consider, however, unjust as well as ungenerous; because it is not to be presumed, on the one hand, that those gentlemen were so ignorant as to intend to unite incongruous portions of different designs—nor, on the other, that they were either so well versed in the principles of architecture, or so skilful in the practical applications of the rules of good taste, as to be aware of the almost insuperable objections to the amalgamation of any two plans, even the most apparently reconcilable, and capable of coalition in one and the same general design. I conceive, therefore, that the corporation, intend no more nor less by the determination at which they have arrived, than to adopt, as the foundation of their plan, the design of Mr. Hooker, and to engraft upon it a part of the elevation furnished by Mr. Cutts;—substituting in the place of the attic story and dome of the former, the exterior of the upper story and cupola of the latter, and leaving it to the skill and ingenuity of one of these architects, or of some other, to render the parts thus superinduced, conformable to the principal design, in regard both to the order of the architecture and the proportions of the edifice.

But from some little knowledge of the theory of the art, derived from books, and the contemplation of some of the best models of ancient and modern architecture, and more from the opinions of others whom I have consulted, and who possess greater skill in matters of taste and a more scientific acquaintance with the works of art; most of whom, also, from not residing here, are entirely free from all local or personal bias; I am induced, after much inquiry and reflection, to believe that it will be found impossible to blend the two plans, even in the manner supposed, without offending the principles of good taste, violating the rules of architectural unity, destroying the harmony of proportion between different members of the same design, and thus producing, in lieu of a chaste and classic specimen of an elegant and useful art, an illegitimate and monstrous abortion; disjoined, unproportioned and deformed; disowned by both of its putative fathers, and destined to become, I fear, the lasting opprobrium of its adoptive parent.

This, I am aware Mr. Editor, is strong language—but I mean nothing offensive by it; neither do I use it as a mere figure of speech; and with all due deference to the opinions of others, and especially to the judgment of the common council and its committee, I beg leave respectfully to suggest the reasons for my own; trusting to them to vindicate the expressions, in which, not less in kindness than in sincerity, I have indulged.

It will be recollected by all who have seen the plans and given any attention to the subject, that the design of Mr. Hooker was distinguished from all the rest (except from one, I believe by Mr. Ryder), by its high basement, which is elevated entirely above the level of the ground platform, and contains the exterior entrances, each having an ascent to it of several steps. This story is judiciously appropriated to the public offices of the city, and county. The principal or second story: or rather the first floor, as it is termed with greater propriety, having more lofty ceilings, contains, by an arrangement equally obvious and proper, all the larger rooms, besides a central saloon lighted from the dome, viz: the circuit court room occupying the whole depth of the edifice and one third of its front and rear, to the south of the saloon, and on the north side of the saloon the corresponding space being divided between the mayor's court room and common council chamber, whilst the space between the saloon and portico in front contains anti-chambers attached to each of the court rooms, for the accommodation of the judges. The space between the rear of the circular saloon and the rear of the building, is appropriated to the stair cases, and the whole floor is ventilated as well as lighted inwards from the dome, as well as each apartment outwards by its own windows. The jury rooms, and other smaller apartments for the use of some of our literary or municipal institutions, are disposed above into an attick or third story. This attic story, neither from its purposes requiring, nor by the rules of proportion admitting, of the same height of ceiling as the others, does not of course require or admit of so large windows; accordingly, a peculiar order or style of windows, denominated by artists attic windows, is appropriate to it; the height of which is also reduced by the necessity of setting them lower on the exterior of the edifice, in order to give room for the entablature of the proper order under the cornice, which surmounts the walls.

Now, the plan of Mr. Cutts consisted of a sunken basement; of a first story or ground floor, and of a second floor, which, according to his arrangement of the interior, as well as from the external elevation, is the principal story of his edifice; and his design neither needs nor comprizes an attic story. It seems, therefore, very clear that the corporation never meant to adopt this second story of Mr. Cutts in toto, and place it with every thing standing within or without, above Mr. Hooker's principal story instead of an attic; because this would be making the edifice to consist of a basement and two principal stories, instead of a basement, principal and attic. It would not only destroy the proportion of the exterior elevation, but the symmetry of the saloon, and of the interior dome or cupola, (whichever be adopted,) within and in the place of the requisite jury rooms, &c. in the third story, it would afford the superfluous accommodation of a second large court room and common council chamber, with jury rooms and antichambers attached. This, upon the face of it, is too absurd to believe. It is unfair then, as I have already intimated in reference to the incongruity of the architectural orders, and different dimensions of the two plans, to impute to the common council the intention of adopting any more of Mr. Cutt's upper story, than the style and proportions of his windows. But even this cannot be done without producing the anomalous results I have mentioned. For the windows of Mr. Cutts are still windows adapted and proportioned for the principal floor, and the plan of Mr. Hooker is already furnished in their proper places with windows of that style and those proportions; and in order to enlarge the windows of his attic story, either the height of the walls must be increased, or the enlarged windows must encroach either upon the entablature above, or upon the architraves of the second story windows below; and if Mr. Cutts' windows be adopted at their full size, they would encroach upon both. In the first case, that of increasing the height of the walls, not only the whole general proportions of the edifice, i.e. its height in relation to its length and breadth, will be destroyed; but the proportions of an important and conspicuous part of the front elevation, (I mean the portico and its columns,) utterly ruined. Whilst in the case of enlarging the windows without increasing the height of the attic, the relative distances and proportions between the windows of the two upper stories, and between the attic windows and the cornice above, would be affected in an equal degree and with equally injurious effects. Besides which, the approved and established rules of a pure and classic style of architecture would be infringed by varying the relative proportions between the dimensions of the two upper stories. This I apprehend is sought, and all indeed that is sought by those who have been strenuous for this alteration. The size of the attic windows strikes their eyes as diminutive; or rather, they appear to want height in proportion to their width. This objection, however, is not only unfounded in principle, but arises, I suspect, altogether from the persons in question not being in the habit of seeing the rules of proportion exemplified in the combination of windows in works of regular architecture. To common eyes, indeed, attic windows may seem strange; but it does not thence follow that they are disproportioned. The truth is, that we are much more accustomed to the irregular size of our domestic architecture than to any other, and hence it is natural enough that our ideas of architectural effects should be drawn from that source. This is unfortunate as well as erroneous; for it is evident that in private edifices, especially in town houses, we habitually, designedly, and from necessity, disregard many of the rules of architecture; and particularly of late years, this relative proportion between the windows of different stories; yet many of us may remember when the latter was in a great measure observed, and specimens of it may now be seen in some of the streets of this city. But a modern work, of more regular design, (the front of the Theatre in South Pearl-street), will exemplify the rule and its effects more clearly. Let any man of the slightest pretensions to intelligence and taste, look at this edifice, and say whether its attic windows seem disproportioned to the others, or too diminutive in themselves: Let him examine in our print-shops the representations of the best ancient and modern works of architecture, corresponding in design and style to the plan in question, and he will soon cease to think that there is anything even strange in the size or proportions of these windows.

In regard to the substitution of Mr. Cutts's cupola for that of Mr. Hooker, many of the same general principles and observations apply. Lest, however, I should destroy the symmetry of your columns, and violate those rules of fair proportion which ought to limit the dimensions of this article, in reference to more important matter, I shall defer my remarks on that subject to some future day—in the mean time, remain, yours respectfully. PETRONIUS.[13]

To the editor of the Albany Argus—

Sir—After allowing to you and your readers, as well as to myself, something of a breathing spell, I resume the subject of the new City Hall, and proceed to that part of the project which purports to supercede the dome of Mr. Hooker and adopt that of Mr. Cutts; and I think it will be apparent before I have done, that the union of the two plans in this particular is quite as unnatural as the anomalous conjunction of the second story of Mr. Cutts' design with the basement and principal of Mr. Hooker's.

The committee of the corporation seem duly to have appreciated the advantages of the scite selected for the new City Hall, and very judiciously resolved to avail themselves of the means and opportunity it afforded of erecting a dome of large dimensions, as an ornament, not only to the edifice itself, but to the city at large. Indeed, it seems impossible to conceive a situation in which a lofty building, surmounted by such a superstructure, could be placed with greater effect—as, from the descent of the ground towards the river, and to the eastern, northern and southern quarters of the city, a dome of the enlarged dimensions of which the edifice forming its base, admits, would crown the city as with an appropriate diadem, and furnish a most conspicuous and magnificent object to arrest and gratify the eye from every point of approach and view;—But these effects cannot, surely, be expected from a comparatively diminutive and disproportioned structure; and the first objection to Mr. Cutts' dome is, that it is neither of sufficient size to produce the effect intended, nor duly proportioned to its base. However well adapted to the edifice from which it was taken, it cannot, certainly, bear a corresponding relation to the one on which it is to be placed, as the size and proportions of the two are different. If, therefore, it be adopted in its present dimensions, not only will it be less conspicuous as an architectural ornament to the city, but the symmetry of the whole edifice will be destroyed; and that within, as well as without. For in regard to the interior, it is to be observed, that the dome forms a roof to the saloon and galleries of Mr. Hooker's plan, and must, consequently, bear its relative proportion to them as well as to the exterior of the edifice. But suppose it were possible to obviate this objection by an enlargement of this dome to the dimensions of Mr. Hooker's, then another no less formidable difficulty occurs, viz: that Mr. Cutts' dome is not of an order corresponding with Mr. Hooker's edifice, and therefore not proper to be united with it. It is not in fact conformable to any regular order of architecture; but a fanciful composition of an oriental character, and consequently the most incongruous imaginable to a pure Grecian style. To say that this objection also may be obviated by altering its order as well as its size, is to give up Mr. Cutt's dome entirely as well as Mr. Hooker's, and either to leave the building destitute of this crowning ornament, or to adopt some possible combination to be produced by the taste and fancy of the common council or its committee.—Neither of these expedients, Mr. Editor, I suspect, will be agreeable to our citizens. Public opinion, in a manner highly creditable to the public taste, has decided loudly in favour of a large and conspicuous dome; and I believe that both would be equally decisive in preferring the work of a scientific and skilful artist, to the joint production of a committee even of amateurs.

After all, what is the objection to Mr. Hooker's dome? It is in due proportion to the edifice which it surmounts—grand in its proper dimensions, simple in its structure and ornaments, and admirably calculated to produce the imposing effects intended by its erection. It is called indeed by one of the correspondents of the Daily Advertiser, "an enlarged cupola," and said not to be so chaste and original in its design as that of Mr. Rogers, another of the competitors. Now strictly speaking, every dome not exactly semicircular in its swell, and not springing immediately from the roof of the edifice it surmounts, but having its perpendicular diameter prolonged and supported intermediately by a gallery or basement of its own, is "an enlarged cupola." So are St. Peter's at Rome, and St. Paul's in London. They both spring from galleries below them. The perpendicular height of the former above its base, is five of its own diameters, and that of the latter four and a half; whilst that of Mr. Hooker's (purvis [i.e., parvis] *componere magna) is but three. The judgment and skill of the architect in all such cases are evinced by regulating the size and proportions of the structure, in reference to its locality, and the purposes, whether of use or embellishment, or both, intended to be accomplished. And these considerations ought also to be regarded in deciding upon the respective merits of different plans; for one may be absolutely superior to another, although in reference to the use and purpose for which the building is designed, and the situation in which it is to be placed, it ought not to be preferred. This I apprehend to be the case in the present instance; and although I agree with the writer in the Daily* [Advertiser], *as to the simple and classic elegance of Mr. Rogers' design, I am nevertheless of opinion that the plan of Mr. Hooker ought to have been adopted. Who should have had the premium? is another and subordinate question; but in strict justice it seems to me it ought to have been awarded to Mr. Rogers, as having produced the best plan according to the specification set forth in the advertisement by the mayor. But from the descent of the ground, the ediface designed by him, would be completely overlooked from the corner of Washington Street and the material which he proposed for it, and on which much of the effect of the plan would depend, would be much more expensive than that of Mr. Hooker. The great merit of Mr. Hooker's plan consists in its better adaptation to the situation and to the use for which the edifice is designed; and arises from the superior elevation he has given it by his high basement and attic story; in both of which particulars, he has departed from the specification. His plan, however, is not without merit in other respects; and all circumstances considered, was unquestionably the best offered.—The Corporation, therefore, were wise in adopting it, and in my humble judgment, have only erred in attempting to improve it. But it is by no means too late to correct the mistake; and I trust that long before the walls of this splendid edifice are reared to their summits, or its lofty canopy lifts its majestic form above them, the conscript fathers of our ancient city will evince their candour, as well as their discretion, and return to regular order and attic windows—to good taste and a DOME, grand from its simplicity as well as from its size. Your's, though not perhaps till then,*

PETRONIUS.[14]

Petronius remains unidentified, though his self-assurance in matters of taste is clear, having adopted the name of a first century Roman satirist known as *Arbiter Elegantiae* or *Judge of Elegance.* It is tempting to attribute these two letters to Hooker himself.

In keeping with the common council's decision, Kutts was sent half the premium, or $50.[15] However, from the descriptions of the Hooker and Kutts proposals in these letters, it seems that the Kutts design for the attic was abandoned in the execution of the building.

As originally contemplated by the committee, sandstone was to be employed for the facades of the basement and marble for the decorative trim on the building. On 23 July 1829, it was decided to construct the basement of marble,[16] probably at Hooker's suggestion. The remainder of the building was likely intended to be of brick with a marbledust stucco scored in imitation of stone.

Root discovered a *"Rough Sketch of a Bill of Marble wanted for the intended City Hall. (City of Albany),"* prepared by Hooker and unfortunately since lost.

> *"Plain ashler below the first floor in heavy courses from 12 to 1300 feet sup: with a sufficient number of headers to bind the work the upper edge of the last course—to have a wash of 2 to 2 1/2 inches by way of watertable—Above which will be 12 Courses of Chamfered Rustic—on three sides of the building. 14 inches high of suitable thickness. if built without headers, the courses should [be] 5 & 10 inches alternately—if with headers from 5 to 6 inches—this method has more strenght but does not appear quite so well—*
>
> *"A belt course all around the building—20 by 15 inches—having a fillet underneath of 3 inches thick—a wash of 15 inches on the upper part—of—belt course, raised with a curve to the face of the wall thus"*
>
> *[Hooker here includes a small section sketch of the belt course.]*
>
> *"Bases to six Columns.*
>
> *6 plinths—5 feet square. 7 1/2 inches thick—moulding, 5 feet diameter 15 inches thick—*
may be made in two thicknesses }
>
> *24 Bases to pilasters 4 feet 4 inches 22 by 18 inches may be made in thicknesses if prefered*
>
> *6 Capitals to Columns 5 feet 6 by 4 feet 3 in & 2 feet thick*
>
> *24* [Capitals] *to pilasters 4 feet 6* [inches]*—24 by 18 inches wrought with an Ovolo. fillets, abacus &c.*
>
> *Ovolo cut in egg & tongue—*
>
> *"Sundry window dressings* [and] *pannels under windows, not settled on untill drawing shall be made and approved—*
>
> *"N. B. working plans accurately figured will be necessary for the person who shall prepare the work—"*[17]

During August 1829, negotiations were commenced with Elam Lynds, superintendent of Sing Sing state prison, to supply the marble for the building.

Albany 21 August 1829

Sir

Mr. Wayson returned yesterday with your letter stating on what tearms you would furnish the marble for the City Hall. At a meeting of the Building Committee, your communication was laid before the Committee and [a] *resolution was passed, agreeing to accept your proposition to furnish the marble. I will send you the plans in a day or two, by which the stone are to be got out. I should like to be informed how soon we may direct to call at your docks for said* [stone] *or such parts as may be ready. From time to time,* [we] *also should like some infermation, as to the number feet estimated to the ton, on acc*[oun]*t of paying fr*[ei]*g*[h]*t.*

Respectfully yours
John Townsend
Mayor of Albany[18]

Sing Sing had been opened to take advantage of the demand for marble and the cheapness of prison labor. This was the cause of much public concern.

Messrs Editors—I have just learned, to my very great surprise, that our common council have concluded to use the Sing Sing stone in the erection of our City Hall. Until last week, I had never seen a specimen of that stone, and no one could be more disappointed. It has the appearance of loose sand stone, many of the edges and corners were broken off—and several pieces which had been cut off in dressing, were readily rubbed to powder in my hand, and I cannot help thinking that a prudent man might reasonably feel apprehensive for his personal safety in a building of that stone, when crowded, as such public places frequently are. I think if our common council should visit Troy [The Rensselaer County Court House, built of Sing Sing marble, was under construction at this time.] *and see the stone on the ground, and find the chips dressed off crumbling to powder under their feet, they would think of reconsideration.*

Another consideration, and which goes almost to make up the difference of the expense, is that the stone from Stockbridge [Massachusetts] *would be wrought by our own mechanics, who now are idle for want of employment, and deserting the city to avoid starvation. And most of the money paid for the stone would probably be expended among our own merchants and traders.*

It is hoped that our citizens, as well as common council, will be alive on this subject, while a remedy remains.

A CITIZEN[19]

The latter concern persisted, and would be the cause of protests and riots during the 1830s.

The laying of the cornerstone of the new building on 31 August 1829 was proudly reported in the local press.

CITY HALL

The cornerstone of this edifice was laid yesterday, by John Townsend, esq. the Mayor, in the presence of the Common Council and a large concourse of citizens who had assembled to witness this ceremony.

The deep interest and the public spirited feeling which seem to pervade all classes of our inhabitants, in regard to the erection of this noble building, is highly creditable, and augers well for the future prosperity of our ancient city.

The Mayor, Recorder, and members of the Common Council having met at the Capitol, proceeded with the architect, builder, and workmen and a number of citizens in procession to the site of the building. A large stone having been exca-

vated by the workmen and placed at the North East corner, according to established usage, a heavy leaden box was let into the opening, in which was placed the following as deposited for the benefit of future ages:

Inscription on a massive plate of copper.

"CITY HALL,
ERECTED FOR PUBLIC PURPOSES
This stone was laid by the Mayor, on the 31st day of August, A.D. 1829"

Also, having engraved upon it the names of the Mayor, Recorder, members of the Common Council, with the names of the Architect and Master Builders.

. . . The leaden box containing the deposits, was then closed and a heavy stone let down upon it. The Mayor, according to custom, then applied the plumb, square and level, and declared the whole "well laid, true and trusty." [20]

In his address to the assembled dignitaries and citizens, Mayor Townsend set forth the benefits of the new building.

This Hall will be of such dimensions, and constructed on such a plan, as to afford the most ample facilities for the administration of public justice both for our city and county; and at the same time it will contain all necessary accommodations for various departments of our city government. Its style of architecture will be such as will, it is hoped, secure the approbation of those for whose special use it is designed; and if the opinion which other[s] *may entertain of our taste and public spirit, shall be influenced by the style of our public buildings, we hope and trust that the architecture of this Hall may hereafter be referred to as creditable to our city. . . .*

The reasons which suggested the erection of this edifice at the present time, are generally well known. The inconvenience experienced, both by the state, and by the city and county, in the joint use and interest of the capitol, induced the city authorities, together with the county, to release their rights to the state in that building for a small amount compared to their expenditures upon it. The desire felt at all times by our citizens to afford every accommodation to the legislature and officers of the state government, and the belief that the seat of government in this city accommodated the state generally, has induced a willingness on the part of our inhabitants to submit to the expenditures which will be necessarily incurred. . . . [21]

Work progressed on the city hall through the winter of 1829–30. Encouraged by the quality and speed with which the stone was being fabricated in Sing Sing, it was resolved on 27 February 1830 to make the front and side elevations of marble. A Building Committee Minute of 4 October 1830 indicated that the rear facade was to be marbleized.[22]

Hooker went to the prison to give consultation at least once.

N York Tuesday Ev[enin]*g 9 o'clock* [c. spring 1830]

Just arrived from Sing Sing, have the stone we are in want of, on the bankers; have full assurance that they will be ready for delivery tomorrow evening. I shall endeavor in the morning to engage some vessil to touch there on Thursday, to ship them. A number have been shipped this day. I calculate to be in Albany on Thursday morning. I am desirous to be at home to attend to the duties of my office. If there has [been] *as much rain fall in Albany as we have had here, I could not have done much out door business, had I been there, untill this afternoon.*

Yours respectfully,
P. Hooker

Hon. J. Townsend [23]

Progress in constructing the building's portico, however, would be thwarted by difficulties at the quarry, as chronicled in correspondence between the new prison agent, Robert Wiltsie, and Albany mayors Townsend and Francis Bloodgood. Wiltsie's 7 December 1830 letter to Mayor Townsend introduces the problem:

> "... *we shall find it very difficult to get your Columns out in longer pieces than 2 1/2 or 3 feet except the bottom pieces which we think we can give you about 7 or 8 feet long—we will give them all to you in as long pieces as possible but in order to make the completion of the Job early in the Spring more certain it may be necessary to get out shorter stone than we otherwise would do.* ..."[24]

A March 1831 exchange of letters between Mayor Bloodgood and Wiltsie identifies problems with quality and timeliness, and acknowledges the frustration of local stonecutters with the situation.

> *[Bloodgood to Wiltsie, March 26, 1831.]*
>
> "... *I am requested to inform you, that the Base*[s] *to the columns* [that were] *sent up, lack in diameter of the lower torus six inches—and that they will not answer—others must be got out as soon as possible and sent up with the least delay.* ..."

> *[Wiltsie to Bloodgood, March 29, 1831.]*
>
> "*Yours of 26th Inst*[ant] *is befor*[e] *me we where aware that the lower part of the bases sent was a trifle deficient of the plans but it can make no possible difference wether that part of the base was a few inches longer or smaller as the top of the base whire the column commences is exactly right—These Stone where very difficult to get to work any larger than those sent. Mr Joy (our master stone Cutter) will shortly be at Albany and satisfy you that the dificiency will not materially Injure them—I also understand from Mr Joy that Mr Hooker himself was at one time disposed to think the variation not material. but of late Mr Hooker is rather disposed to be captious where our Prison is concerned—I should very much regret to have any difficulty in the finishing the City Hall. but I am aware of the opposition of a certain class in Albany to all our operations and if they are listened to much difficulty may be expected.* ..."[25]

It was apparently at this point that Wiltsie "*submitted* ... *two propositions—*

> "*1st To work out the columns in pieces of two and an half or three feet long and proposed thickness—or*
>
> "*2nd To reduce the size of the columns from a diameter of Three feet eight inches (as now required by the Contract) to Three feet two inches and receive them in lengths of Five feet.*"

The building committee responded to Wiltsie's proposals.

> *[Bloodgood to Wiltsie, May 18, 1831.]*
>
> "... *The building Committee of the Albany City Hall cannot consent to reducing the dimensions of the blocks for the columns in front of said building, the architect has proposed an expedient, which it is considered will obviate the difficulties mentioned by Mr. Wiltsie which is this—let the whole length of the shaft of each column be in 5—or not to exceed 6 pieces and each course subdivided*

13. Ibid.
14. *Albany Argus*, 13 August 1829.
15. Townsend Papers, DC 10441, Box 1, Folder 1.
16. Root, p. 183.
17. Ibid., pp. 183–84, from the document.
18. Townsend Papers, DC 10441, Box 1, Folder 1.
19. *Albany Gazette*, 25 August 1829.
20. *Albany Argus*, 1 September 1829.
21. Ibid.
22. Root, p. 184.
23. Townsend Papers, DC 10441, Box 1, Folder 1. The term *bankers* refers to the benches on which stonecutters dress and prepare blocks of stone.
24. Root, p. 185, from the document. For some of the original letters quoted by Root and recently rediscovered, see ACHR.
25. Root, pp. 185–86, from the documents.

into 3 pieces as above represented [Hooker included a sketch plan of a shaft.] *let the shafts be plated and the joints in the centre of the plate, they will be put together in the building and cramped with Iron & lead, in this way they will be easier handled & quarried—the Committee will receive the Columns in the form proposed by Mr. Hooker provided they are wrought in the manner designated in the above diagram and correctly fluted and diminished with a swell according to the drawing sent down with the model of the capitol they are to hold the diameter of 3 feet 8 inches 1/3rd of their height, from thence fall off in a regular parabolic curve to 3 feet 2 inches at the capitol—Instead of six weeks as proposed by Mr. Wiltsie the committee propose that he have seven weeks for the delivery of the whole*

"The Bases sent up will not answer they may do for some other building—let others be got out immediately & sent up together with the plinths which are 4 feet 10 inches Square and 7 inches thick. . . . "

[Wiltsie to Bloodgood, May 23, 1831.]

" . . . *Yours of 18th Inst*[ant] *is before me proposing a plan for cutting the columns which from the difficulty of cutting flutes in 3 pieces and having them come together with any degree of exactness renders it Impossible for us to undertake the Job—At present I cannot suggest any other plan by which you can have the Columns Immediately than by making them of smaller size or put them up of rough stone and make them of Imitation ma*[r]*ble—having the baise and cap of marble—or another plan. put them as you propose each length in 3 pieces and flute them when up—The fluting never was considered as any part of our Job—I have stated to you before that every exertion has been made use of to get the stone required—but from the difficulty of getting large stone from our quarries have not been able to succeed—*

"At same time I must confess that the course which has been pursued by your Committee and Architect of late has had an effect rather to discourage any further attempts in succeeding. now we all know that the baises for Instance was not exactly according to plan. at the same time they can be so altered by taking off the lower member and working that part on the plinth as never to be noticed by any other person than those who are determined to find fault. . . . "

[Bloodgood to Wiltsie, May 25, 1831.]

" . . . *yours of the 23d instant is received*

It was the intention of the Building Committee in making the last communication to relieve you from the difficulty in quarrying the stone of the size contemplated in the Contract. Your answer this morning received informs us that you cannot supply the stone in the manner suggested by our architect—

"Inasmuch therefore as the Architect refuses to reduce the size of the pillars the only alternative is to adopt the proposal made by you to Messrs Lansing & Wasson to procure the pillars in pieces of 2 1/2 or 3 feet long on the required diameter.

"We will therefore speak definitely to you on this subject and submit this proposition—

"You to furnish us with the pillars of the required length & diameter prepared according to contract in every respect except as to length which may be reduced to pieces not less than 3 or 2 1/2 feet long—provided the whole are finished & furnished within eight weeks from this date. . . . "

[Wiltsie to Bloodgood, June 3, 1831.]

" . . . *yours of the 24th ult. was received during my absence—in which you proposed taking the pieces for Columns of shorter dimensions than originally agreed on—You also request a definite reply on my part, as this reply must depend entirely on circumstances that cannot be contrauld or changed in any way I can only say that every exertion on my part shall be made use of to get the stone as you require them and within the time. . . .* " [26]

▶
Fig. 160. Albany City Hall (1829–32), west facade, c. 1875. Collection Douglas G. Bucher.

While problems plagued the construction of the portico, the remainder of the work progressed sufficiently for the city hall to be occupied in June 1831 (fig. 160).[27]

The remaining marble had not yet been quarried the next spring.

State Prison
Mt. Pleasant Jan 11 1832

Hon John Townsend
Dear Sir

I have your favour of 5th inst on the subject of the ballance of marble for your City Hall.

The prospect of procuring such stone is now some better than heretofore and, should our present success be continued for any length of time, we will undoubtedly be enabled to get all the pieces required to finish your City Hall in a few months.

I have had in hand 3 buildings similar to yours all done but such parts as require the ballance to be stone of the largest size and such as the quarries at this place would not produce in sufficient quantities.

To finish all these contracts as fast as stone could be procured has been my constant aim, as the large stone is the only difficulty in the way; and whenever

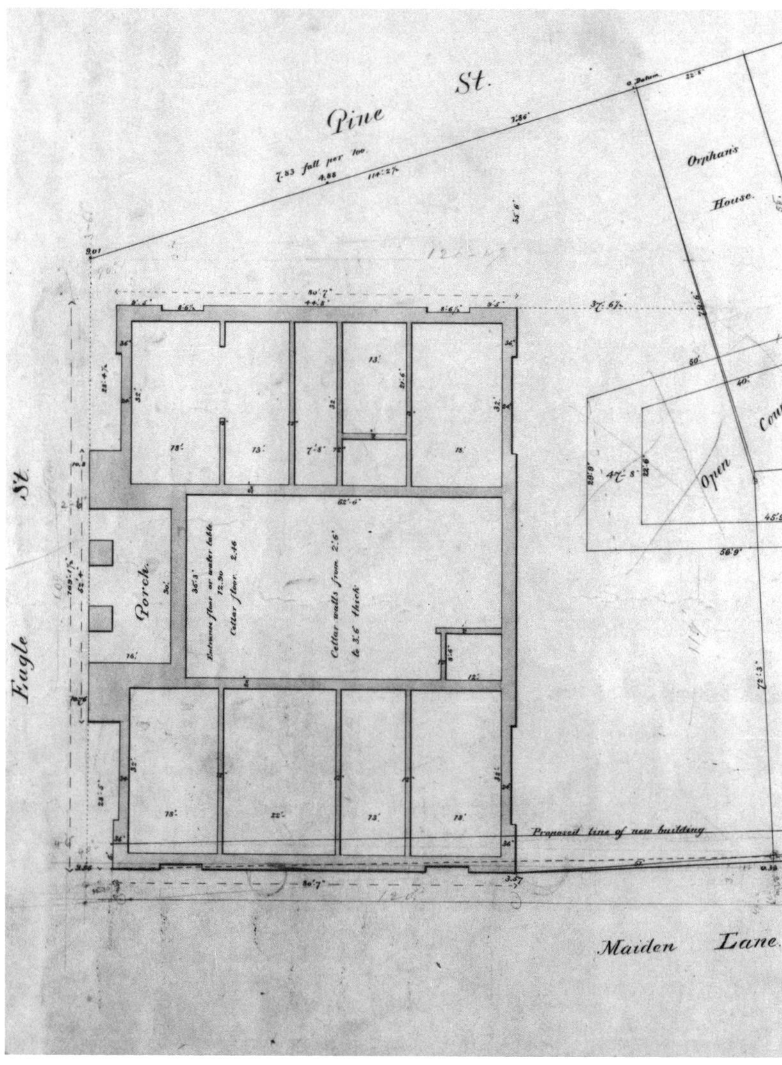

▶ Fig. 161. Albany City Hall (1829–32), plan of the sub-basement, c. 1880. Ink on paper with canvas backing. Albany County Hall of Records, Albany.

they can be procured rest assured, my dear sir, that no exertion of mine shall be wanting to complete your building early in the spring.

Very respectfully yours
Rob[er]*t Wiltsie*
agent[28]

The stone for the columns was not sent until June of 1832.[29]

About this time Hooker was requested to design the inscription of the date stone in the portico. He included diagrams of his proposals in his letter.

Being requested by his Hon, the Mayor to make a design for a tablet to be placed in front of the City Hall. (in the recess of the Colonade)

I should be pleased to know the Recorders opinion, with respect to the subject matter to be engraved, and how to be arranged

& he will oblidge
his hum[ble] *serv*[ant]
P. Hooker
11th Nov[embe]*r* [1832][30]

26. Ibid., pp. 185–89, from the documents.
27. Root, p. 189.
28. Townsend Papers, DC 10441, Box 2, Folder 4.
29. Root, p. 189.
30. Townsend Papers, DC 10441, Box 1, Folder 1. The date stone, as executed, is preserved in the basement of the current city hall.
31. Root, p. 189.
32. *Albany Daily Evening Times*, 10 February 1880.
33. Root, p. 189.

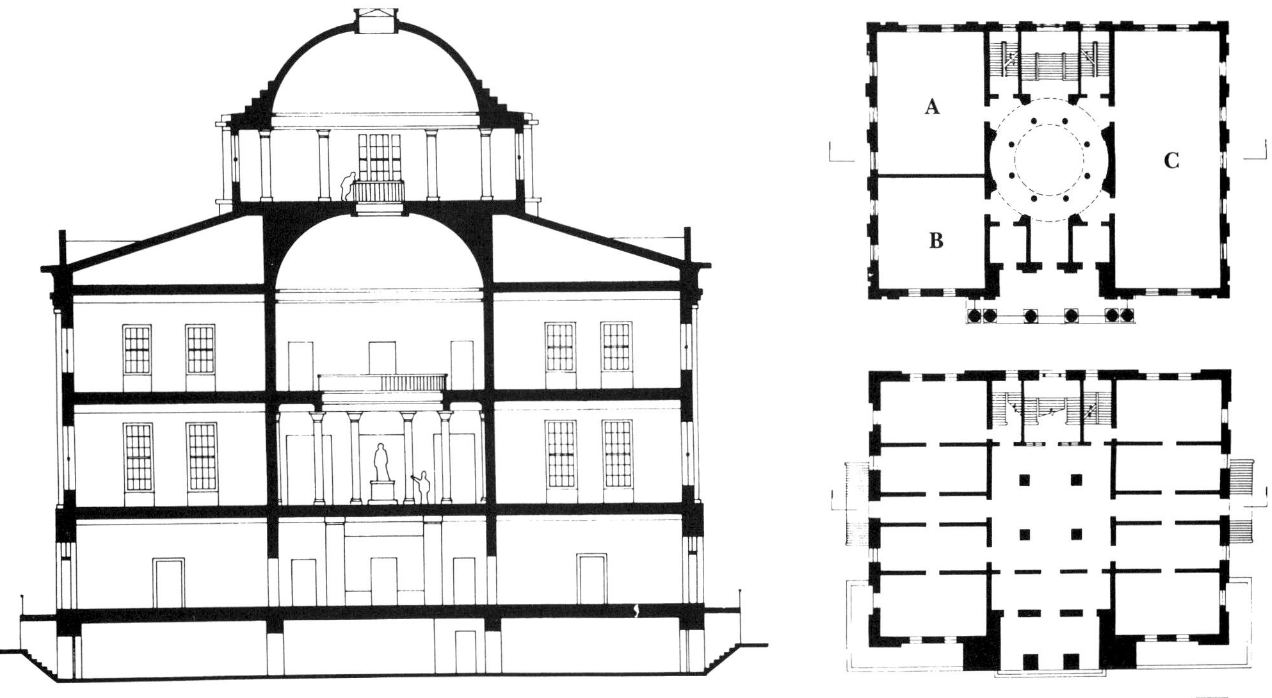

▲
Fig. 162. Albany City Hall (1829–32), section and plans of the basement, or ground, floor and the principal story, including A. Common Council Chamber, B. Mayor's Court Room, and C. Circuit Court Room, reconstructed by W. R. Wheeler, 1991.

Hooker was paid $341.75 for his services which included plans, expenses, and specifications up to 17 August 1832.[31] The total cost of the building as of 27 December 1832 was $92,836.91.[32] The state contributed $17,500, the county $15,000, and the remainder was provided by the city.[33]

According to Wilson's *Albany City Guide* of 1844, the building consisted of a sub-basement, basement, principal story, and third floor. The front elevation was 109 feet and the sides 80 feet; the walls were 60 feet high, and above the roof the belvedere measured 50 by 40 feet, surmounted by a hemispherical gilded dome 40 feet in diameter.[34] A recently discovered plan of the sub-basement suggests refinements to Wilson's dimensions (fig. 161). These sources, together with contemporary newspaper articles and illustrative material, have provided the basis for the reconstructed section of the building and plans of its basement, or ground floor, and the principal story above (fig. 162).

Howell and Tenney described the interior of the city hall in their bicentennial history of Albany.

> *There was but little of ornamentation to the interior of the building, yet the artistic was not wholly wanting. A full-length statue of Alexander Hamilton* [by Hewes; life-sized and on a four-foot-high pedestal] *stood in the center of the* [round] *upper hall, between the Court-room and the Common Council Chamber. Upon one side of this hall was a bas-relief of Dewitt Clinton* [by William J. Coffee], *with a view of the primitive canal-boat in the distance; and on the opposite wall a similar figure of Sir Walter Scott* [also by Coffee], *in like style of art.*[35]

34. S. Wilson, comp., *Albany City Guide, 1844* (Albany: Printed by C. Wendell, 1844), p. 31.

35. [George R.] Howell and [Jonathan] Tenney, eds., *Bi-Centennial History of Albany. History of the County of Albany, N.Y., from 1609 to 1886* (New York: W. W. Munsell & Co., 1886), p. 677.

▶
Fig. 163. Albany City Hall, A. J. Davis's competition entry (1829), with later revisions.
Ink and wash on paper with pencil revisions. The New-York Historical Society, New York, N.Y.

A newspaper article published after the structure had been razed (following the fire of 10 February 1880) indicates that vaults were constructed in the rear of the building underground (probably for cisterns) and that the foundation was laid on wood pilings.[36]

Knowledge of the various competition entries is limited. Letters published in the newspapers praised the classical character of Isaiah Rogers's scheme, especially its dome, but criticized the *want of height* in its basement and the expense its construction would have entailed.[37] The submission by A. J. Davis, which received little contemporary notice, has been identified by Jane B. Davies (fig. 163).[38] Davis's proposal made no provisions for windows on the front, seemingly an attempt to create a sense of monumentality. Davis returned to the drawing late in life and added windows in pencil.

It has been proposed by Jacob Landy that Plate 59 of Minard Lafever's *Young Builder's General Instructor* of 1829 (fig. 164) may depict Lafever's entry to the competition, an entry whose stylistic tendency may have been too *progressive* to be accepted by the building committee.[39] A more probable reason for the project's rejection is its omission of a dome and the fact that it is remarkably similar to the New York State Capitol (cat. 15), a building which it would have faced.

Hooker's design for the Albany City Hall combines various Neoclassical and specifically Greek Revival elements (fig. 16). The use of marble throughout gives the building a massive and monolithic character; the

36. *Albany Daily Evening Times*, undated clipping, Pruyn Room, Albany Public Library, Albany, N.Y.
37. See, e.g., *Daily Albany Argus*, 1 August 1829.
38. Jane B. Davies, conversation with the author, November 1990.
39. Jacob Landy, *The Architecture of Minard Lafever* (New York: Columbia University Press, 1970), pp. 12, 17–19.

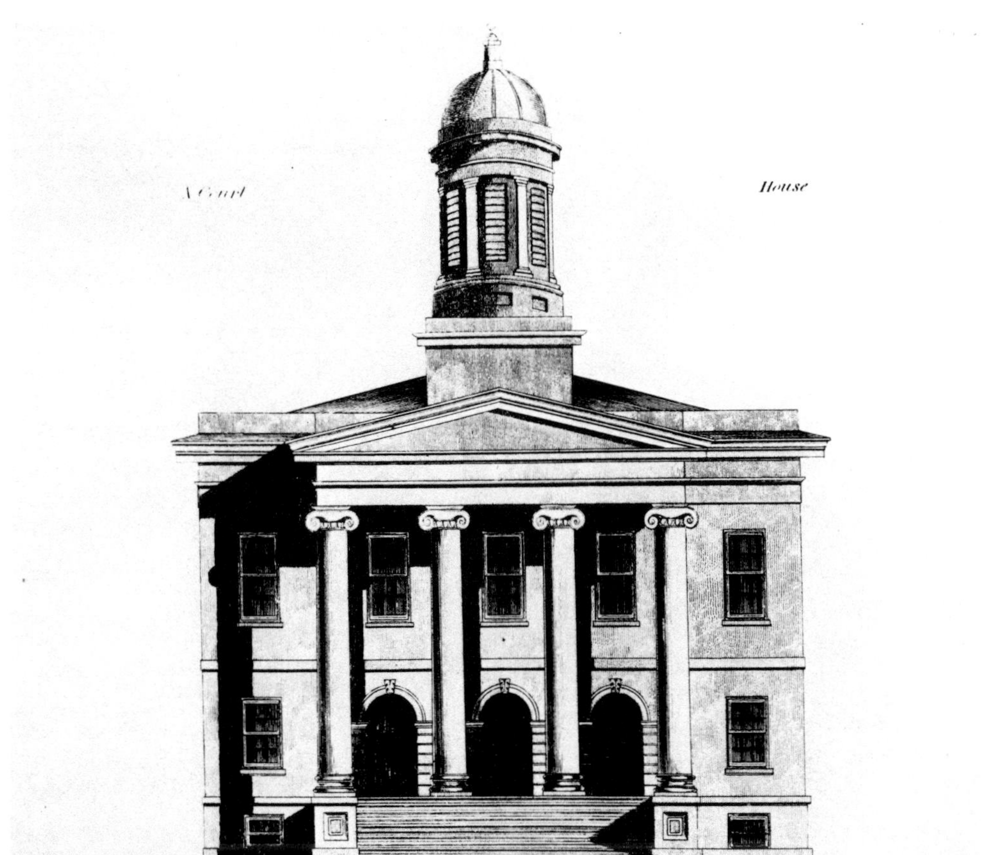

Fig. 164. Minard Lafever's elevation of a court house, Plate 59 in *The Young Builder's General Instructor* (1829), possibly his entry in the Albany City Hall competition. Courtesy New York State Library, Albany.

elements of the cupola have been abstracted to form a wonderful sculptural mass atop the building—one which is, unfortunately, poorly reconciled with the classically detailed building below. The difference between the treatment of the cupola and the remainder of the building gives it an awkward feeling, which some might attribute to the possible hybrid nature of the design. The cupola is typical of the best work of Hooker's later period, and used the same repetition of forms as the Fourth Presbyterian Church steeple (fig. 155) and the second design for the *Great House* at Hyde Hall (fig. 141). ✤

88. GARDENER'S HOUSE, VAN RENSSELAER MANOR

Head of Market Street (now Broadway), Albany, N.Y.
Designed by 22 January 1830.
Built spring 1830; razed.
Builder unknown.

On 22 January 1830, Hooker billed Stephen Van Rensselaer III $10.00 for *plans & estimate for a gardeners house.* He billed an additional $2.00 on 11 February for specifications and charged $1.00 on 20 April for *attendance at* [the] *building to direct workmen.* Construction of the gardener's house was presumably complete by 3 May 1830, on which date Hooker charged $5.00 for *drawings for finishing* [the building] *and attendance* [at] *sundry times.*[1] ✜

1. Van Rensselaer Manor Papers, SC 7079, MSC NYSL.

89. PROPOSAL FOR FRENCH ASYLUM (WITH ROBERT HIGHAM)

Unknown location.
Designed before 4 March 1831.
Unbuilt.

90. PROPOSAL FOR WAKEFIELD ASYLUM (WITH ROBERT HIGHAM)

Unknown location.
Designed before 4 March 1831.
Unbuilt.

91. PROPOSAL FOR GLASGOW ASYLUM FOR MANIACS (WITH ROBERT HIGHAM)

Unknown location.
Designed before 6 March 1831.
Unbuilt.

During the legislative session of 1830 a committee consisting of A. C. Paige, Eli Savage, and Peter Gansevoort was appointed *to inquire into the propriety or necessity of erecting new* [asylums], . . . *to ascertain the proper site for such new erection . . . and to prepare a plan of the same, together with an estimate of the probable expense.*[1]

On 10 March 1831 the committee members published their findings in an extensive report. Their concerns about the care of patients shaped their suggestions for the arrangement of the buildings, which in turn shaped the designs prepared by Hooker and Higham. The report reads in part:

> *These plans differ from each other in the shape and arrangement of the buildings, and also in the expense of their construction. The French plan exceeds the other in expense. The expense upon the plan of the Wakefield Asylum, of a building for the accommodation of 350 patients, being about $88,500, and that of a building upon the French plan, for the same number of patients, being about $99,000. An estimate of the expense of a building upon each of these plans, and also upon the plan of the Glasgow Asylum, made by Mr. Hooker, of Albany, an architect of reputation, is herewith submitted. It will be seen, by a reference to these plans, and to Tuke's Practical Hints upon the construction of Lunatic Asylums, that the great desideratum is, such an arrangement of the building as to be able to effect an entire separation of the sexes; and also the seclusion and separation of the patients of either sex in proper numbers, and in distinct apartments, according to the state of their minds; the separation to be according to the degree, rather than the species or duration of the disease, and not to exceed fifteen in number; the violent and noisy to be separated from those who are quiet, and those who are capable of some degree of rational enjoyment, and also from each other.*

The wards, galleries, day-rooms, and airing yards of the two sexes, and these different classes, should be totally distinct, and admit of no communication with each other; and they should be so arranged as to render it impossible for the patients to have any view of each other from their respective apartments and yards.

The building should be so constructed as to produce a system of easy inspection and superintendence, over the patients, by their attendants, and over both by the superior officers. The accommodations for the patients should be cheerful, and afford as much opportunity for voluntary change of place, and variety of scene, as is compatible with security. There should be rooms for the occasional seclusion of the noisy and violent patients, and means of easy transmission of the patients from one class to another, should be provided. The day-rooms should be so arranged as to present to the patient the strongest incentives to orderly conduct. And to facilitate inspection, the airing yards should be overlooked by the day-rooms, where the attendants generally are stationed, and the galleries, should be contiguous to the day-rooms, and the sleeping rooms to the galleries.

To aid the inspection by the superintendent, the day rooms should not be above the second story. The day rooms, galleries and airing yards of each class should easily communicate with each other. They should have a cheerful appearance; iron grating to the windows should be abolished, and frames of cast-iron, having the appearance of wooden ones, substituted.

To give the galleries a cheerful appearance, the lodging rooms should be placed only on one side; and on the other side windows should be constructed looking into the courts, and should afford a prospect to the patient. The patient, as far as is practicable, should be the master of his own actions, and have the privilege of going into his airing yard at all proper times for exercise, recreation or amusement, without interference or control. And the building should be so constructed, that in his passage down he will continue constantly under the eye of his attendant. The building itself should have an imposing appearance, so as to excite in the bosom of its inmates a feeling of grandeur. This will prevent a sense of degradation and consequent depression of mind. And to the building should be attached work-shops and spacious grounds for the employment of the patients. The improved mode of moral treatment cannot be carried into effect without a proper arrangement of the building. And without such arrangement, it is impossible to prevent abuses, or to render comfort compatible with security.

Water should be carried to every story by forcing pumps, and each gallery should be furnished with wash-rooms, baths, &c.

The building should be warmed with heated air conducted to each story, by means of air flues, which in summer will answer the purposes of ventilation; and all the improvements lately discovered in culinary operations, and in washing and drying linen, &c. heating water, &c. should be introduced into the building.[2]

Plans of three different asylums, with estimates, were submitted by Hooker and Higham and published with the report. Each asylum was to accommodate 350 persons.

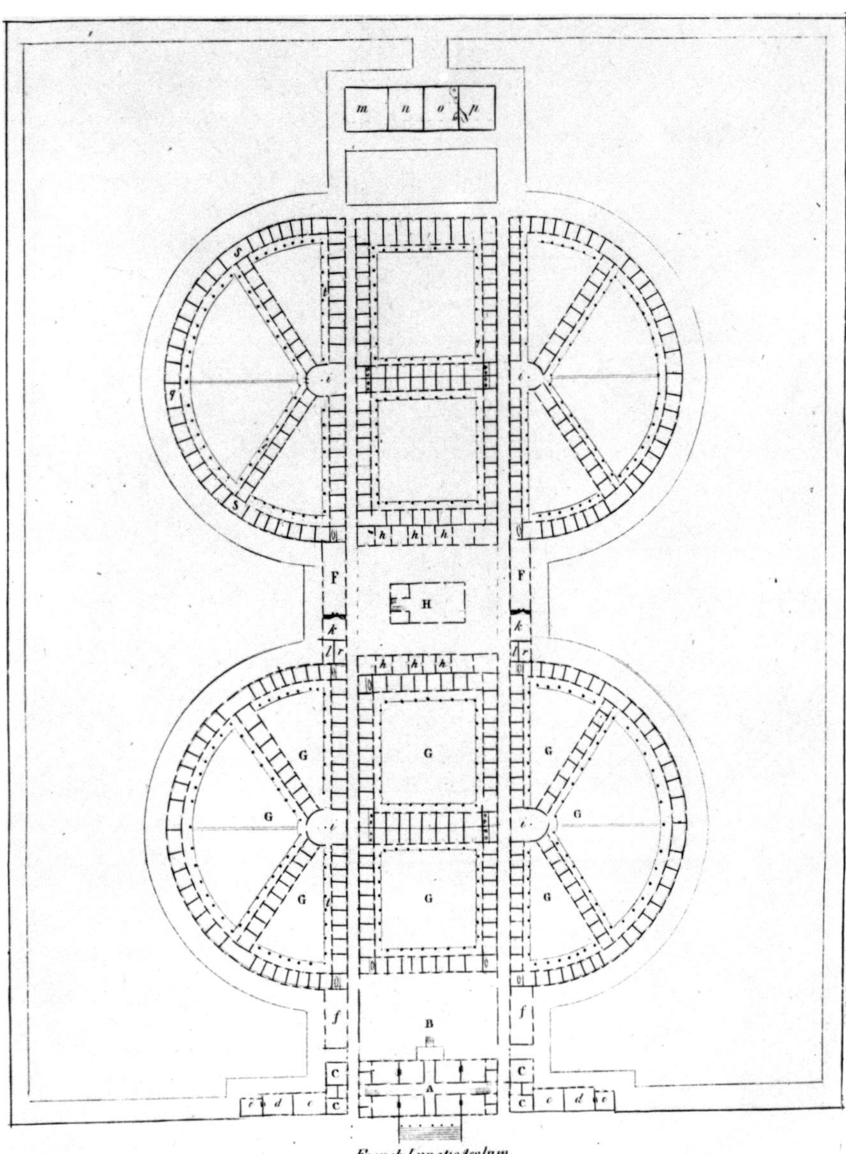

▶
Fig. 165. Plan of the proposed French Asylum, published in 1831.
Engraving. New York State Library, Albany.

PLANS,

And Estimates of Expense of erecting Lunatic Asylums.

References to the Plan of the French Asylum [fig. 165]

A,	*Centre building, 115 by 45 feet, a basement, principal and attic story.*
B,	*Court or garden, 115 by 66.*
C,	*Apartments for those having charge of the patients.*
ff,	*Infirmaries, 40 by 18 feet, one story high.*
dd,	*Dissecting rooms.*
ee,	*Dead rooms.*
G G,	*Wards and cells, baths, water closets, &c. for the different classifications of male and female patients.*

H,	*Chapel, situate in an area of 115 by 85 feet.*
hh,	*Chambers for convalescents.*
ii,	*Keepers' rooms, overlooking the several wards.*
FF,	*Dining rooms, 60 by 20 feet.*
kk,	*Kitchens, 25 by 20 feet.*
ll,	*Sculleries.*
rr,	*Pantries.*
mnop,	*Bakery, brewery, carriage and stable buildings, woodhouse, &c.*
qq,	*Refectories.*
ss,	*Halls of union.*
tt,	*Piazzas, paved walks.*

The principal building to have a basement of stone, superstructure of brick, to be finished in a plain and substantial manner, inside and out.

The interior arrangement for the accommodation of the insane, is calculated to be built with brick, on stone foundation; one story high, the walls made flush inside and out, and whitewashed.

The surrounding wall of stone, 12 feet above the surface, coped with hewn stone, two feet average thickness, having projecting piers at suitable distances for strengthening it.

Suitable drains are to be laid, having sufficient descent, from the kitchens, baths, water closets, &c.

Proper furnaces, or boilers, are to be constructed to generate heat, or steam, to be conveyed in pipes, for heating the establishment, as occasion may require.

The nearest calculation we can make of the expense, allowing the wall to inclose 12 acres of ground, is from $98,000 to $100,000.

HOOKER & HIGHAM.

March 4th, 1831.

WAKEFIELD ASYLUM [fig. 166]

Principal building, a high basement, principal and attic story, finished plain and substantial. The walls of the basement, stone; superstructure, brick. The length is estimated at 125 feet, width 55 feet.

Two wings, each 300 feet in length, 34 feet in width, three moderate stories in height; constructed with brick, laid flush inside and out, and whitewashed. Stone foundation, or cellar walls; furnaces, stone [sic], *and wood rooms in the cellars; the windows to have iron sashes, placed above a man's height, towards the centre courts. Each cell to have a ventilator wrought in the walls, to receive the foul air, immediately below the ceiling; and each cell is to be heated, when necessary, by pipes passing through the same; the doors are to be made strong, but not "prison-like"; furniture, simple and commodious.*

Two wings extended in a line with the principal building, will serve for dining rooms, kitchens, larders, sculleries, &c., over which may be infirmaries, or other apartments, being two stories in height, 86 feet in length, and 26 feet in width.

Other buildings will be required, such as bakery, brewery, stables, carriage-houses, sheds, &c. &c., which will be located as the form of the ground shall best suit; drains, baths, water closets, furnaces, boilers, and a variety of other appendages, which cannot all be comprehended in a brief sketch.

Supposing the surrounding wall to encompass eight acres of ground, the expense of this establishment is estimated, exclusive of ground, from eighty-seven to ninety thousand dollars.

HOOKER & HIGHAM.

March 4th, 1831.

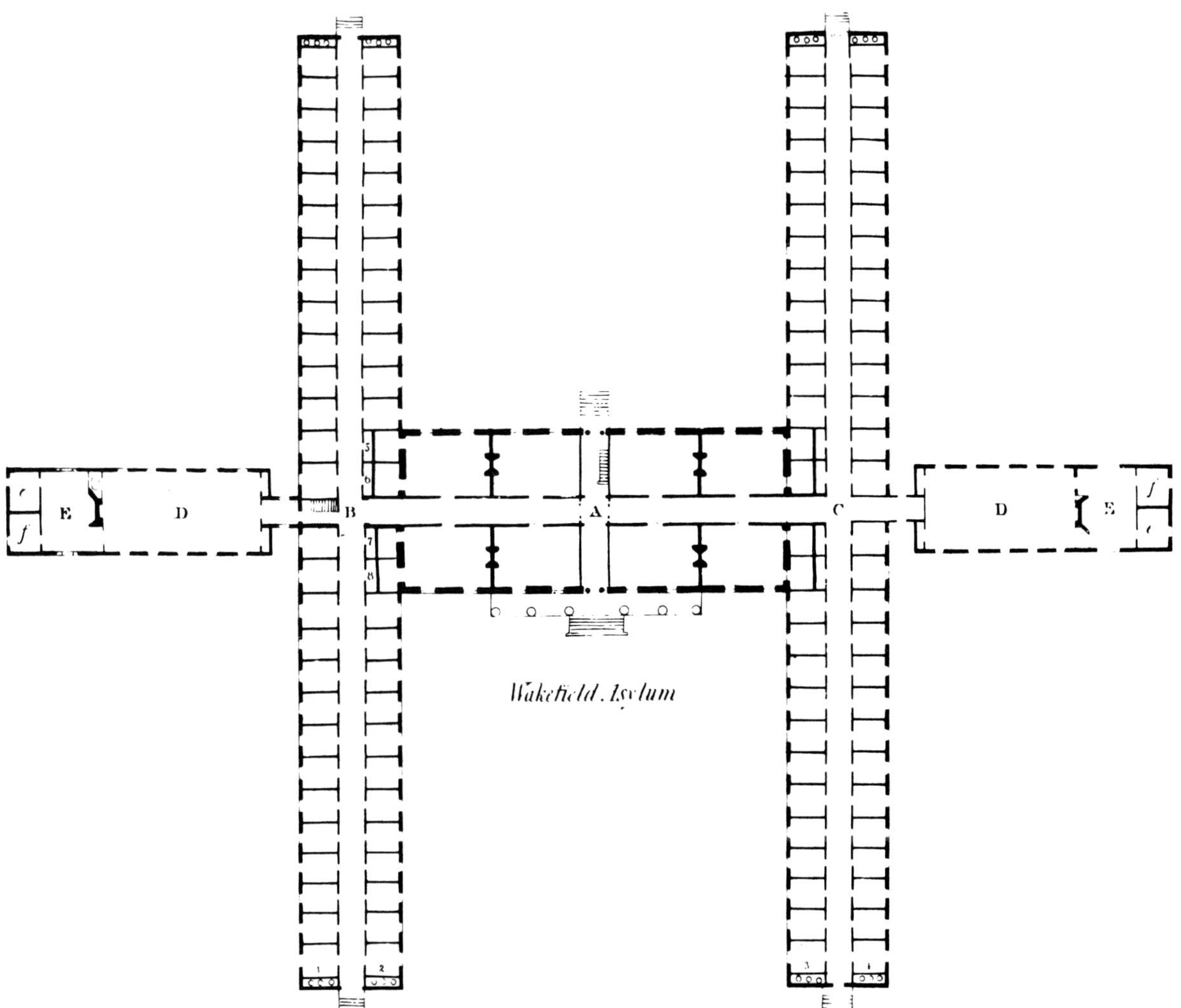

▲
Fig. 166. Plan of the proposed Wakefield Asylum, published in 1831.
Engraving. New York State Library, Albany.

References to the Plan of the Wakefield Asylum

A, *Centre building, 125 by 55 feet, containing a basement, principal, and attic story.*

B, *Wing for males, 300 by 34 feet, containing three stories of cells, baths, and water closets.*

C, *The same as B, for females, each containing 144 cells, 10 by 12 feet.*

D, *Dining rooms, 50 by 24 feet.*

d, *Closets two stories, infirmaries above.*

E, *Kitchens.* e, *Larders.* f, *Sculleries.*

1, 2, 3, 4, Baths, privies. *5, 6, 7, 8, Closets.*

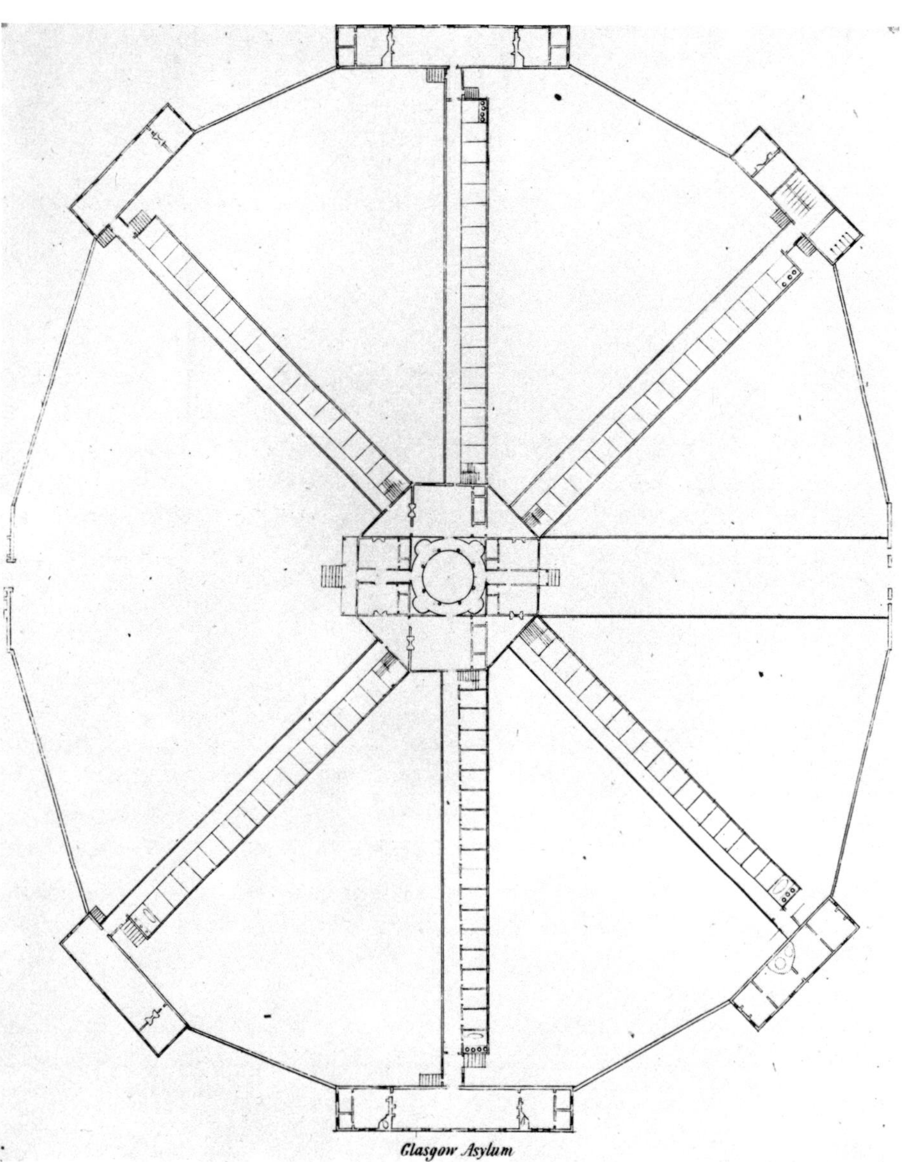

▶
Fig. 167. Plan of the proposed Glasgow Asylum for Maniacs, published in 1831. Engraving. New York State Library, Albany.

GLASGOW ASYLUM FOR MANIACS [fig. 167]
Altered and Improved, having Six, instead of Four Wings.

This establishment consists of an Octagonal centre building, 90 feet diameter, three stories high, with a circular belvidere above the roof, 40 feet diameter, overlooking the enclosure, and surrounding country; having a basement story, partly under ground.

Connected, and extending from the centre building, six wings are projected, 183 feet in length, by 21 feet in width, and three stories in height. Each floor of each wing containing 17 cells, stairs, water closets, baths, &c. [sic], *and spacious corridors.*

At the extreme ends of the two centre wings, which form a right angle with the direct line of entrance to the principal front, are transverse wings, containing dining halls, kitchens, and bakeries; each wing 116 by 22 feet, one and a half stories high.

Connected at the extreme ends of the two front wings, are infirmaries, and rooms for nurses. These are 66 by 22 feet; and the same height as the last mentioned.

And at the extreme ends of the two back wings, are similar buildings, for brewery, washing, stabling, &c. The surrounding wall to encompass an area of from eight to ten acres; having a well proportioned entrance, and porters' lodges; the surrounding grounds tastefully laid out, and planted with ornamental trees and flowering shrubs, gravelled walks, &c.

The expense of this establishment, may be at least estimated (including every appendage) at one hundred thousand dollars.

HOOKER & HIGHAM.

March 6th, 1831.[3]

The architects' statement about the Glasgow plan addresses the concerns of the committee while drawing on Hooker's approach in earlier institutional projects (cats. 23, 56).

In their execution, the three engravings bear little resemblance to each other. The French plan shows a tentativeness, almost sketchiness. The Wakefield plan is rendered boldly and expertly. These differences can be attributed to the sources from which the engravings were copied.[4] That none of the three plates is signed suggests that they were prepared by the engraver as incomplete drawings to be modified by the architects. In fact, the published plate depicting the Glasgow plan bears indications of reworking, and it is possible that an engraver copied the plan from a book and then turned the plate over to the architect, who made the alterations directly on the copperplate. This plan was submitted last.

No action was taken on this report by the legislature for several years, and the plans submitted by Hooker and Higham were abandoned. Construction of the state asylum at Utica in 1838–43 finally brought to fruition the work started by the legislative committee in 1830. ✣

1. *Documents of the Assembly of the State of New-York, Fifty-fourth Session, 1831,* Vol. III (Albany: Printed by E. Croswell, 1831), no. 263, p. 5.
2. Ibid., pp. 38–39.
3. Ibid., pp. 77–79. The *References to the Plan of the Wakefield Asylum* follows the description of the Glasgow Asylum in the original.
4. The specific sources have not been identified, but they probably included published works on institutional buildings.

92. PROPOSAL FOR THE REMODELING OF THE GANSEVOORT FAMILY BUILDING

Southeast corner of Maiden Lane and North Market Street (now Broadway), Albany, N.Y.
Designed before 1 July 1831.
Unbuilt.

Among the Gansevoort-Lansing papers is a voucher signed by J. P. Morange for Philip Hooker for a *sketch for buildings, corner Market Street and Maiden Lane and for examining buildings on the same lot.* These services date to 1 July and 29 July 1831, respectively.[1] Hooker was paid $2.00 for his sketch, which probably represented a remodeling of the Gansevoort family's ancestral home then on the site. The house burned in 1832, and was replaced by Stanwix Hall, designed by James Dakin of the New York City firm of Town, Davis & Dakin.[2] ✣

1. Gansevoort-Lansing Collection, Box 173, Folder 8, NYPL.
2. Gansevoort-Lansing Collection.

93. FENCE DESIGN AND SITE PLAN FOR ACADEMY PARK

Albany, N.Y.
Designed before 28 November 1831.
Built c. 1832.
Builder: Bailey G. Hathaway.

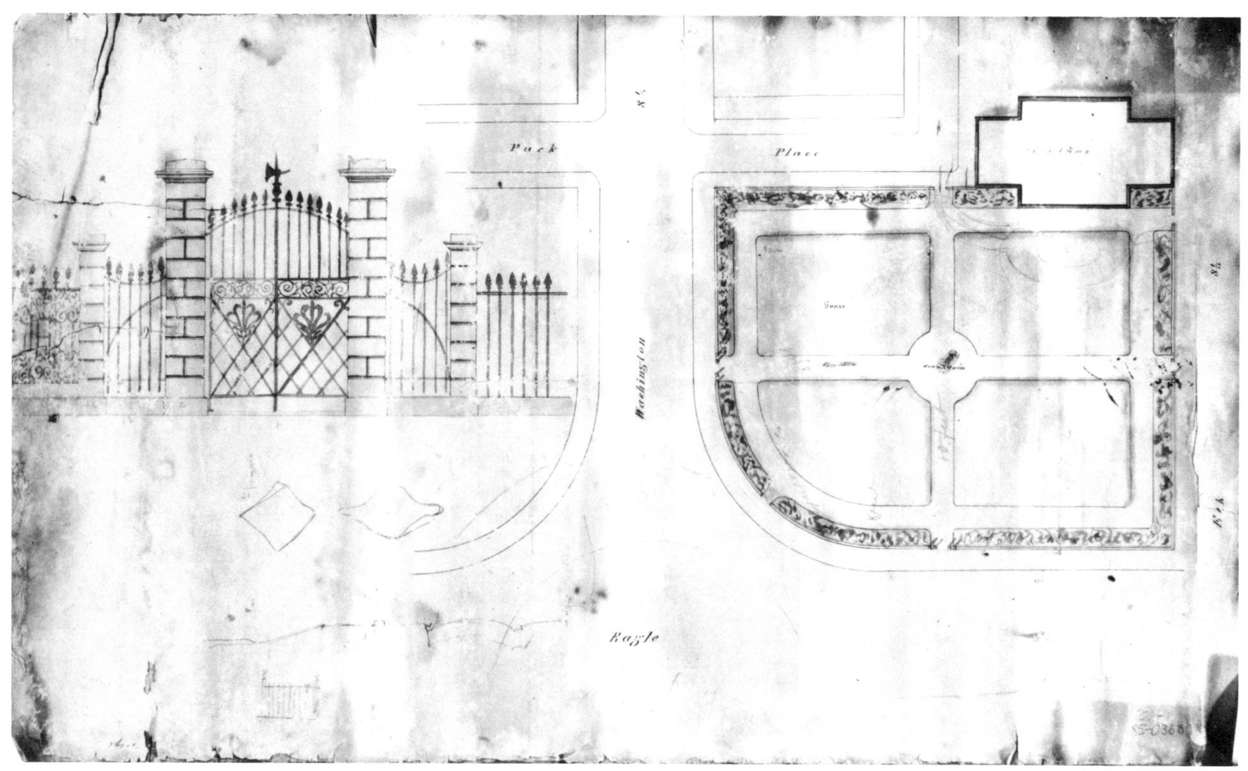

▲
Fig. 168. Fence Design and Site Plan for Academy Park, Albany, Hooker's drawing, 1831. Ink and watercolor on paper with canvas backing. Albany County Hall of Records, Albany.

The bold design of this fence demonstrated Hooker's full commitment to the Greek Revival. The decorative detail was probably intended to be of cast iron and, indeed, a bill for services rendered by Hooker records that in May 1832 he provided *the committee for improving the Academy Park* with a *design for a cast iron post for* [the] *park fence* and charged them $1.00 for his work.[1] The balusters and rail of the fence were probably constructed of wrought iron.

Hooker had billed the same committee $4.00 for his *new plans & design for iron railing, gates &c.* on 28 November 1831 (fig. 168). The *new plans* may be an oblique reference to an earlier proposal for the landscaping of the area in front of the academy, apparently from Hooker's hand (A24). In the later drawing, Hooker's design of straightforward walkways and lawns superseded the previous suggestions for a series of small triangular beds. Pencil emendations to the drawing, possibly by Hooker, suggest that an elliptical lawn was placed in front of the academy building in the project's executed form.[2] ✤

1. Albany Common Council, Laws Passed 1830, ACHR. For additional documents pertaining to the construction of this fence, including the contract, see Townsend Papers, DC 10441, Box 1, Folder 1, MSC NYSL.
2. Albany Common Council, Laws Passed 1830.

94. COTTAGE FOR ERASTUS CORNING I

Bethlehem, Albany County, N.Y.
Designed before 17 December 1833.
Unbuilt.

95. FARMHOUSE FOR ERASTUS CORNING I

Bethlehem, Albany County, N.Y.
Designed before 26 December 1833.
Built 1834–35, possibly from this design; razed.
Builder: Ruell Clapp.

96. COUNTRY SEAT FOR ERASTUS CORNING I

Bethlehem, Albany County, N.Y.
Designed before 8 January 1834.
Unbuilt.

97. BARN FOR ERASTUS CORNING I

Bethlehem, Albany County, N.Y.
Designed before 15 January 1834.
Built 1834–35, possibly from this design; razed.
Builder: Ruell Clapp.

Erastus Corning I (1794–1872) moved to Albany in 1814 and soon became a prominent iron manufacturer. He was one of the original organizers of the Utica and Schenectady Railroad and served as that company's president from 1833 until its merger with the New York Central in 1853. His involvement in the railroads and iron manufacture made him one of the wealthiest men in the state. Corning served as Albany's mayor from 1834–37, a position he had just been elected to when these buildings were commissioned. He also served in the state assembly and senate.[1]

A single receipt in the Corning Papers records that Hooker was paid from $1.50 to $5.00 for each of the four designs noted here.[2] The modest payments indicate that the schemes were probably not refined to any great degree, and were most likely meant to suggest the range of design possibilities that were at Corning's disposal.

Erastus Corning I did build a farmhouse and barn during 1834–35.[3] There is no indication whether or not Hooker was called upon to furnish a more complete set of drawings for either. Receipts identify architect Henry Rector as having some involvement in the project, and Ruell Clapp as the builder.[4] ✤

1. Erastus Corning I (1794–1872) Papers, 1801–1872, MK AIHA.
2. Ibid.
3. Ibid.
4. Ibid., AP 166.

98. FOUR SPECULATIVE TOWN HOUSES FOR LUTHERAN EBENEZER CHURCH

North side of Lancaster Street at Capitol (now Park) Street, Albany, N.Y.
Designed between 2 May and 26 May 1834.
Built July 1834–May 1835; razed c. 1960.
Builders: James A. Morse, and Woodruff and Kingsley.

On 2 May 1834 the Lutheran Ebenezer Church Council resolved that *the money received by the church from the sale of lands to the state should be expended in buildings* [speculative houses] *to be erected on vacant lots lying in Capital & Lancaster Sts and the president of* [the] *board* [of trustees] *is authorised to employ Philip Hooker to draw a plan of said buildings.*[1] Hooker had performed architectural services for the church at various times over the past eighteen years (cats. 37, 45, 57), and he remained their designer of choice. By 26 May the drawings were complete and had been submitted to the church council. On that day *the trustees agreed to give the plans & specifications for the . . . buildings . . . to some responsible persons to estimate thereon, viz Jas. A. Morse, Boardman & Van Vorst, Lawrence Hallenbake and John Goodrich Carpenters. The carpenters and masons to give in their estimates separately, to be given to the lowest estimate.*[2] The estimates were received by 19 June 1834, when they were opened.

> *The lowest sum was $3150.00 from Ja*[me]*s A. Morse carpenter, and the lowest mason was M. Kingsley, being $2900.00, amounting to $6050.00. Whereupon it was agreed that G. H. Kerker & W*[illia]*m Hosch be a committee to employ P*[hilip] *Hooker to draw the contracts and necessary securities between the parties for the performance of said buildings and that the said P. Hooker shall be superintendant of said buildings until compleated according to the plan & specifications. To be completed on or before the 15th of March 1835.*[3]

Work probably continued until May 1835. The bills of Woodruff and Kingsley and James A. Morse totalled $6,263.72, including *extras.* Hooker was paid $64.00 for *superintending & setera* on 12 May 1835.[4]

No visual documentation of these four houses[5] has been located. ✤

1. First Lutheran Church Council Minutes, 2 May 1834, Archives, First Lutheran Church, Albany, N.Y. (hereafter A FLC).
2. Ibid., 26 May 1834. *Boardman & Van Vorst* [sic] was undoubtedly the firm of William Boardman and Albert Van Voast, identified in Edmund B. Child, comp., *Child's Albany Directory, and City Register, for the years 1833–4* (Albany: Printed by E. B. Child, 1833), p. 74; and G. J. Loomis and T. G. Wait, comps., *Albany Citizens' Advertiser and General Directory, for 1834–5* (Albany: G. J. Loomis, 1834), p. 213.
3. First Lutheran Church Council Minutes, 19 June 1834. *M. Kingsley* may refer to mason Nathan Kingsley, who is listed in Child, *Child's Albany Directory for 1833–4,* p. 137; and Loomis and Wait, *Albany Citizens' Advertiser for 1834–5,* p. 279.
4. Treasurers Book, A FLC.
5. Ibid. A note of 24 October 1834 records that *22.00* was *spent for insurance on 4 houses in Lancaster St.* From the knowledge of their general location and photographs of the area, it is likely that they were razed about 1960.

99. CONSISTORY ROOM AND DWELLING FOR LUTHERAN EBENEZER CHURCH (WITH JAMES T. KELLY)

Chapel Street, Albany, N.Y.
Designed between 4 August and 3 September 1835.
Built 1835–July 1836; razed spring 1869.
Builder: Lawrence Hallenbake.
Mason: Adam Todd.

On 30 May 1834, the Trustees of the Lutheran Ebenezer Church received a letter from the minister, elders, and deacons of the church requesting the *building* [of] *a suitable lecture room* with the monies received from the sale of land to the state.[1] Nothing was done on this matter until 4 August 1835, when it was recorded that *the trustees have appointed a committee consisting of Henry Newman & John C. Feltman to engage two persons to draw a plan for the purpose of building a lecture room and other buildings in the rear of the church fronting on Stueben St.*[2]

It is unclear whether the *two persons* were to work together or to produce alternate proposals. Bills indicate that Hooker was working with James T. Kelly at the time and that they were paid $28.50 *for plans, specifications & cetera.* Henry Rector was paid $35.00 *for plan and specifications* during this same period, but the records are silent regarding the nature of Rector's work.[3]

Hooker and Kelly's plans and specifications were ready by 3 September 1835, at which time the trustees agreed to receive bids from Lawrence Hallenbake, Boardman and Van Vorst,[4] Fish and Hawley, and John Boardman. These carpenters were to select masons who submitted their estimates separately, with the job given to the lowest bidder.

The proposals were opened on 18 September 1835, and the job went to Lawrence Hallenbake *to do all the carpenters work for the sum of $1915.00.* The lowest mason's estimate was submitted by Adam Todd, who agreed *to do all the mason work according to plan and specification drawn by Philip Hooker for the sum of $1975.00.* Hooker was engaged to produce the contracts for the buildings, and Anthony Van Santford was appointed building superintendent. The whole project was to be completed by 15 April 1836.[5]

The mason work appears to have been finished by 26 November 1835, as Adam Todd charged $106.65 for extra work on that date. Lawrence Hallenbake was joined by a Mr. Mehar during the course of construction. Their work appears to have been completed by 22 July 1836. The cost of the building, including extras performed by *Hallenbake & Co.*, totaled $4,027.45.[6] ✜

1. First Lutheran Church (hereafter FLC) Council Minutes, 30 May 1834, Archives, First Lutheran Church, Albany, N.Y. (hereafter A FLC).
2. Ibid., 4 August 1835.
3. Ibid., 3 September 1835. For Kelly, see pp. 45, 50 n. 80.
4. This was undoubtedly Boardman and Van Voast; see cat. 98, n. 2.
5. FLC Council Minutes, 18 September 1835.
6. Treasurers Book, A FLC. Only a small portion of this building is visible in a photograph of the church published in Henry H. Heins, *Swan of Albany: A History of the Oldest Congregation of the Lutheran Church in America* (Albany: First Lutheran Church, 1976), p. 77.

100. COTTAGE FOR RUELL CLAPP (WITH JAMES T. KELLY)

Unknown location, probably Albany, N.Y.
Designed by 8 October 1835.
Probably unbuilt.

Among the papers discovered during the renovation of 93 Herkimer Street in Albany is a bill *to plans and elevation for a cottage $6* addressed to *Mr. R. Clapp* and dated 8 October 1835.[1] Payment was received on 28 November 1835 by a Mr. Hastings for *Hooker and Kelly.* That the bill is addressed to Ruell Clapp does not necessarily indicate that he was the client for the project, although this is possible.

This bill provides further documentation of Hooker's working relationship with James T. Kelly, which appears to have started at some date between June 1834 and July 1835 and lasted until Hooker's death in January 1836.[2] ✤

1. Ruell Clapp Papers, Collection, Don Carpentier; photocopies of the majority of these papers on file at the New York Historical Association Library, Cooperstown, N.Y.
2. For Kelly, see pp. 45, 50 n. 80.

ATTRIBUTIONS

W. Richard Wheeler

About the Attributions:

In identifying designs that may be attributed to Philip Hooker, the author has considered various factors—the architect's documented involvement with a project in a role other than as a designer (providing estimates, superintending construction), the architect's known association with a client, and stylistic similarities to works known to have been from Hooker's hand. Ed.

A1. COUNTRY HOUSE FOR ABRAHAM TEN BROECK

Arbor Hill, Albany, N.Y.
Built 1797–98; remodeled c. 1830s; extant.
Builder unknown.

Hooker became acquainted with Abraham Ten Broeck in his work on the North Dutch Reformed Church. Although the interior of the house was extensively remodeled in the Greek Revival style during the first half of the nineteenth century, surviving original features include what may be the first semicircular stairway in the city as well as a handsome fireplace mantel, now located in a second floor chamber but formerly situated in one of the first floor rooms.[1] The use of false balustrades in recesses below the sills of the second-story windows also occurs at the Stafford-Yates house, a somewhat later dwelling whose design has also been attributed to Hooker (A10). ✣

1. Mendel · Mesick · Cohen, *Ten Broeck Mansion: A Historic Structure Report* (Albany: Mendel · Mesick · Cohen, 1975).

A2. EAGLE TAVERN

Court Street (now Broadway), Albany, N.Y.
Built by 1806; enlarged 1819; burned 1848.
Builder unknown.

▶
Fig. 169. Eagle Tavern, Albany, engraving from a drawing by Hooker. Collection Douglas G. Bucher.

An engraving of the hotel, evidently executed for its proprietor Matthew Gregory as early as 1806 and definitely by 1814, identifies Hooker as the draftsman of the original view (fig. 169).[1] Hooker's drawing of the building, as well as his later design of an addition to it (cat. 46), suggest that he might have been involved in its initial construction. ✣

1. Gorham A. Worth, *Random Recollections of Albany, From 1800 to 1808*, 3d ed. (Albany: J. Munsell, 1866), p. 82.

A3. REMODELING OF THE SECRETARY OF STATE'S HOUSE

Unknown location, Albany, N.Y.
Designed before 12 March 1806.
Built between 12 March and 22 April 1806; probably razed.
Builders: John Fraser and Samuel Hooker.

In a 1956 article Harley McKee documented Hooker's part in the 1806 remodeling of the Secretary of State's house.

> *The house occupied by the state secretary was purchased by the state, in a deal involving the sale of his former residence in New York City, on Broadway. This brought in $16,800, which left the treasury a surplus after the purchase and repairing of the house in Albany for $13,597.74 1/2. These repairs, costing $586.78, were chiefly carpentry, painting and decorating. . . . Philip Hooker . . . for an 8% fee superintended carpentry and finish woodwork. . . . The two men working under his direction, John Fraser and Samuel Hooker* [Philip's father], *received 11 shillings ($1.37 1/2) per day; this is shown on an itemized bill signed by Philip Hooker, covering the period between March 12 and April 22, 1806. His duties included* [the] *purchase of materials and payment of the workmen; he apparently advanced the money for his part of the job. Overall direction of repairs to the house was given by the secretary himself, Thomas Tillotson, whose signature appears on several bills.*[1]

Unfortunately, the author has been unable to locate McKee's original source material.[2] Based on the lack of drawings or written specifications, McKee doubted that Hooker had designed these renovations, but it seems unlikely that Hooker would have superintended work that was not to his design. ✜

1. Harley J. McKee, "Building for the State of New York, 1790–1890," *Empire State Architect*, XVI, 3 (May–June 1956), 23.
2. It has not been located at the Onondaga Historical Association which, according to McKee, *rescued* the government papers from a Canadian paper mill.

A4. GOVERNOR DANIEL TOMPKINS HOUSE

Washington Avenue, Albany, N.Y.
Built c. 1807; razed c. 1975.
Builder unknown.

The use of a pediment over the central three bays of the facade and of a Palladian window in a blind arch have correlations in Hooker's documented works.[1] Daniel Tompkins resided here during his term as governor but the original owner has not been determined. ✜

1. For a photograph of the house, see Collection, AIHA.

A5. STEEPLE FOR FIRST PRESBYTERIAN CHURCH

East side of South Pearl Street, between Norton and Beaver streets, Albany, N.Y.
Church built by Elisha Putnam, 1795–96.
Steeple built 1808; building razed c. 1890.
Builder: John Boardman.

▶ Fig. 170. First Presbyterian Church, Albany, erected by Elisha Putnam (1795–96), with the design of the steeple (1808) attributed to Hooker, exterior, c. 1880s. Courtesy W. R. Wheeler, Troy, N.Y.

The design of this steeple (fig. 170) bears numerous similarities to that of the cupola on the Union College building (fig. 28). It was one of two schemes provided by John Boardman, who is not otherwise known as an architect. ✥

A6. DOUBLE TOWN HOUSE FOR THOMAS GOULD

58–60 Division Street, Albany, N.Y.
Built c. 1809–10; altered; extant.
Builder unknown.

The plan of these dwellings for Thomas Gould (fig. 171)[1] is closely related to that of a double house drafted by Elisha Putnam in 1797, probably under Hooker's supervision (fig. 172).[2] One unit of each pair has a square staircase and the other has a semicircular one. A central arched opening in the Flemish bond brick facade of the Gould double house gives access to a one-story passage extending between the two units to a rear yard.[3] ✥

1. Information on the origins of this structure has been obtained from the research of Douglas Sinclair.
2. Gansevoort-Lansing Collection, NYPL.
3. The double town house formerly at 100–102 North Pearl Street had a similar arrangement, but its facade featured a recessed oval panel above the arched opening.

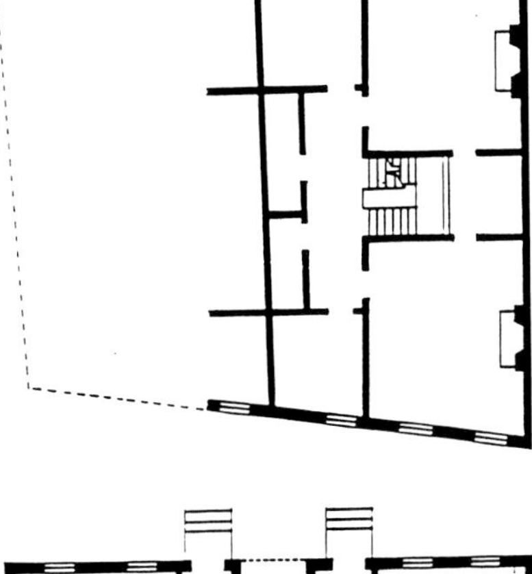

Fig. 171. Double Town House for Thomas Gould, Albany (c. 1809–10), design attributed to Hooker, first and second floor plans reconstructed from on-site measurements by Douglas G. Bucher and W. R. Wheeler, 1991.

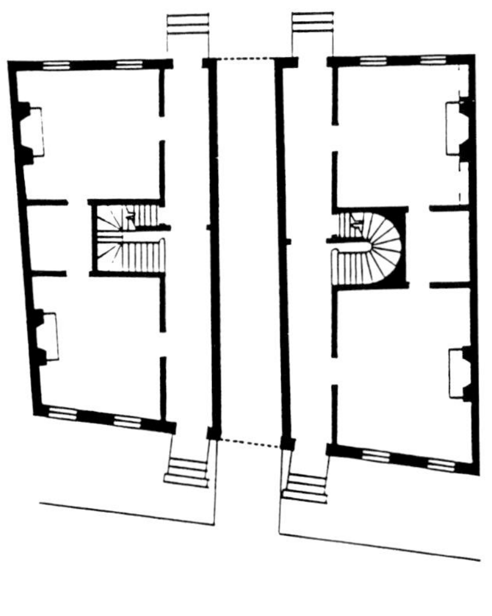

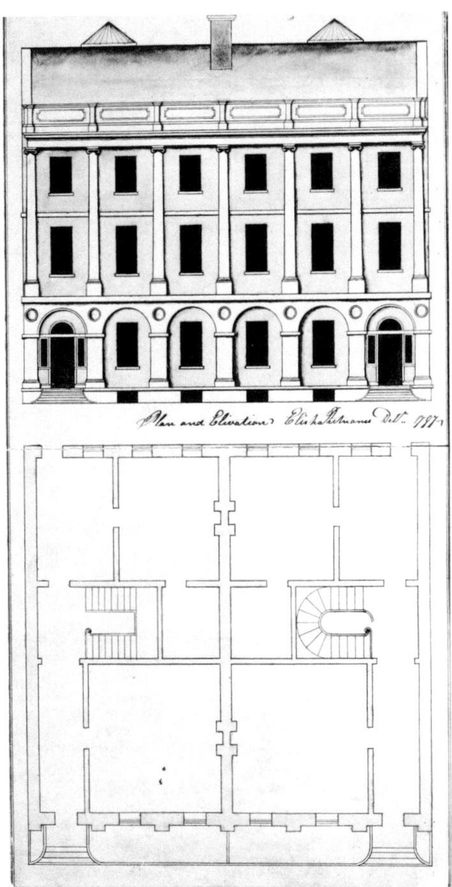

Fig. 172. (Far right) Elisha Putnam's drawing of a pair of town houses for the Gansevoort family, 1797.
Ink on paper. New York Public Library, New York, N.Y., Gansevoort-Lansing Collection, Manuscripts and Archives Section.

A7. TOWN HOUSE FOR SAMUEL HILL

110 Washington Avenue, Albany, N.Y.
Built c. 1810; altered c. 1835, c. 1880, and c. 1925;
extant as part of the Fort Orange Club.
Builder unknown.

Hooker had become acquainted with Hill as early as 1802 through the latter's position as Trustee of St. Peter's Church (cat. 6), and his association with this project is suggested by its similarities to his documented work. The round-headed recessed arches of the facade recall those of the William Alexander house in Little Falls (fig. 44). The plan, featuring a wide center entrance hall beyond which two parlors extend across the rear of the house, is like that of the contemporary New York State Capitol (fig. 47).[1] ✥

1. Other plans of the type are to be found at Wyebrook, in nearby Loudonville, New York, and in several of the Livingston family houses along the east side of the Hudson River, particularly Montgomery Place (1804) near Rhinebeck.

A8. MECHANICS AND FARMERS BANK

Northeast corner of North Market Street (now Broadway)
and Mark Lane, Albany, N.Y.
Built c. 1811–12; razed c. 1875.
Builder: Mr. Smith.
Stonemason: Peter McNab.

▶ Fig. 173. Mechanics and Farmers Bank, Albany (c. 1811–12), design attributed to Hooker, exterior. Albany Institute of History & Art, McKinney Library, Photograph Collection.

The employment of the Palladian motif within a blind arch and of circular panels call to mind Hooker's earlier New York State Bank facade (fig. 38), while the treatment of the fenestration and the landing of the entrance stairs are similar to his slightly later Albany Academy (fig. 73). The small glazed dome, a prominent feature of this elegant building, was unique for its time (fig. 173).

A9. GENERAL JOHN E. WOOL HOUSE

First Street, Troy, N.Y.
Built c. 1812; altered c. 1890; extant.
Builder unknown.

▶ Fig. 174. General John E. Wool House, Troy, N.Y. (c. 1812), design attributed to Hooker, exterior, 1991.

It seems likely that Hooker designed this house (fig. 174), which features a facade treatment identical to the one he planned for the North Dutch Reformed Church Consistory House (fig. 65).[1] The surviving original interior woodwork of the Wool house incorporates carved detailing of fine quality.

1. Other buildings in Troy—the Bank of Troy, the Bank of Lansingburgh, and the Dickenson-Warren House—share an arcaded treatment on either their first or second floors.

A10. HOUSE FOR JOHN STAFFORD (STAFFORD-YATES HOUSE)

96 Madison Avenue, Albany, N.Y.
Built c. 1812; altered c. 1823 for Governor Yates; altered 1890; extant.
Builder unknown.

▶ Fig. 175. House for John Stafford, Albany (c. 1812), design attributed to Hooker, exterior, 1988.

The treatment of the side of this house, with oval windows placed in the center of the elevation at the first floor and attic levels (fig. 175) is similar to that of the house and store Hooker planned for Josephus Bradner Stuart (fig. 110) and of the Stephen Van Rensselaer IV town house, an attributed work (fig. 181). Oval windows were also originally located at each of the stair landings, creating an interesting fenestration pattern on the rear elevation. In its detailing, the entrance doorway resembles that of the Wool house in Troy (A9). The ornament on the arch which spans the interior stair hall of the Stafford house was probably inspired by Plate 30 of Asher Benjamin's *The American Builder's Companion* (1806).

Upon its completion, the Stafford town house was considered one of the most elegant in the city. In 1824 the Marquis de Lafayette was entertained by Governor Yates at the recently remodeled house. ✤

A11. COUNTRY SEAT FOR CATHERINE DUANE (FEATHERSTONHAUGH HOUSE)

Mansion Road, Duanesburgh (now Duanesburg), N.Y.
Built 1812, possibly begun as early as 1796; extant.
Builder unknown.

The plan of this house, with its two elegant parlors arranged across the full length of the rear elevation, bears close relation to the Hill house, an attributed work (A7). The interior woodwork includes details similar to those used by Hooker at the Albany Academy (cat. 33).

A two-story columned porch wraps across the back and sides of the building, a feature that is practically unique in the Northeast. J.-J. Ramée laid out the grounds for this estate in 1813, and may have been responsible for the design of its stables.[1] ✤

1. Roger G. Kennedy, *Orders from France: The Americans and the French in a Revolutionary World, 1780–1820* (New York: Alfred A. Knopf, 1989), p. 226.

A12. SECOND PRESBYTERIAN CHURCH

Chapel Street, Albany, N.Y.
Built 1813; altered c. 1927; razed c. 1960.
Builder: Elisha Putnam.

▶ Fig. 176. Second Presbyterian Church, Albany (1813), design attributed to Hooker, exterior, c. 1900. Collection Douglas G. Bucher.

Nineteenth century tradition attributes this project to Hooker (fig. 176).[1] It was constructed by Elisha Putnam, Hooker's former partner, who is not known to have been active as a designer during this period. The building's tower bears resemblance in its details to those of other Hooker-designed churches. References to this building in the contract written by Hooker for the Lutheran Ebenezer Church (cat. 37) add substantial weight to this attribution. In its final years of existence the building was remodeled for use as a theater.[2] ✜

1. Root, p. 201.
2. Ibid., p. 205.

A13. BANK OF UTICA

North side of Whitesboro Street, near Hotel Street, Utica, N.Y.
Built 1813; altered 1850s and c. 1900; extant.
Builder: John Hooker?

The gabled three-bay center pavilion here is reminiscent of Hooker's work. This, together with the fact that the facade was originally ornamented with the obverse and reverse of a coin, a decorative device used by Hooker in his New York State Bank in 1803 (fig. 38), suggest his involvement in the structure's design. His brother, John, is recorded as having received rather substantial payments from the bank at the time construction of its building would have been under way.[1] ✜

1. Bank of Utica Accounts Book, Oneida County Historical Society, Utica, N.Y.

A14. ALTERATIONS TO JOHN BRYAN'S HOUSE (SCHUYLER MANSION)

Clinton Street, Albany, N.Y.
Built c. 1815; extant.
Builder unknown.

▶ Fig. 177. Hooker's *View of Bryans Place*, Albany, showing the newly constructed vestibule and outbuildings, c. 1818. Watercolor on paper. The New-York Historical Society, New York, N.Y.

A report and small watercolor painting by Hooker document his connection to this project (fig. 177). Created to record and provide a valuation of recent repairs to the dwelling of 1761, the report indicates familiarity with the extent of the work recently completed.

> *The above Sketch, is a representation of the Mansion house, of the late Gen. Philip Schuyler, at whose demise the grounds were laid out into streets & lots, it is a part of the second ward, of the City of Albany—*
>
> *The lot on which the mansion & out buildings are situate, (and which is now the property of Mr. John Bryan) is 112 feet front & rear, & 396 feet in depth from front to rear.*
>
> *It is a handsome piece of table land, considerably elevated above the lower part of the City toward the river and commands a good prospect of part of the City & River, for eight or ten miles up & down, & the Country on the opposite shore—which renders it an inviting place of residence for a Gentleman who prefers living a little retired from the cares & bustle of business.*
>
> *This building is in front 60 feet & in depth 48 feet, two stories of 12 & 10 feet, with complete cellars under the whole, from the north west angle, extends a wing. Containing a kitchen and housekeeping room, a large barn and stables on the rear of the lot, of excellent frame work—it is about 80 by 50 feet—*
>
> *The walls of the Mansion house are of the most substantial kind, the basement, stone, & those of the superstructure, of bricks.*
>
> *Mr. Bryan has at the expense of about $8,000 put these buildings into a complete state of repair, new modled the interior, in the modern style, new sashed the windows with the best crown glass of a large size—& added an hexagonal vestibule to the front, of singular beauty, with an elegant flight of stone steps & ornamental iron railing to the entrance, to some stately elms of antient growth, he has added some evergreens, & other ornamental trees, a piazza in the rear, well, well house, cistern, & other conveniences, all in good order.*

Bounded as follows, East Church Street, in front, North Catharine Street, West Elizabeth Street 5 vacant lots of 33 feet between, South J. Bryans vacant lot, Schuyler Street, extends from the front of said Building to Hudsons River 60 ft. wide, the other streets are all 60 feet—

The Mansion house is estimated at		*$13,000*
Kitchen & out Buildings		*3,500*
Lot at present low value of property	*4,500*	
		$21,000

Surveyed & valued Jany. 20th 1818
P. Hooker City Surv.[1]

The remodeling mentioned by Hooker included the construction of the hexagonal vestibule and the outbuildings. It is possible that they were built under his supervision. Hooker may also have added the delicate fretwork balustrade to the roof line of the house. Similar railings are illustrated in *The Carpenters Complete Instructor* by Abraham Swan, a copy of which was acquired by Hooker in 1797.[2] ✥

1. P[hilip] Hooker, "View of Bryan's Place," Museum Department, Acc. 1961.13, Collection, NYHS.
2. See p. 29.

A15. REMODELING OF HOUSE FOR JAMES KANE (YATES HOUSE)

Broad Street, Albany, N.Y.
Built c. 1815; razed 1864.
Builder unknown.

The flanking single-story wings that were added to the Yates-Kane house about 1815 were similar to those designed by Hooker for the Van Rensselaer Manor House (cat. 44). These additions were to a house formerly owned by Peter Waldron Yates and built c. 1785, possibly to Hooker's design. This fine mansion, perhaps the first to be constructed in the city immediately following the Revolution, featured a pedimented center entrance bay with a large Palladian window in the second story. A delicate fretwork balustrade extended across the facade above the eaves.[1] The added wings had similar balustrades and were fenestrated with newly fashionable tripartite windows.[2]

The house and its grounds were later known as Ash Grove. ✥

1. For an early, probably original, elevation drawing of the house, see Collection, AIHA.
2. For a view that included the additions, see Gorham A. Worth, *Random Recollections of Albany, From 1800 to 1808*, 3d ed. (Albany: J. Munsell, 1866), opp. p. 53.

A16. MOHAWK BANK

1 North Church Street, Schenectady, N.Y.
Built 1816; altered c. 1875; extant.
Builder unknown.

The massing of this building recalls that of Hooker's Albany Jail (cat. 23) of 1810, though without the cupola of that example.[1] ✥

1. For an early illustration of the bank building, see George S. Roberts, *Old Schenectady* (Schenectady: Robson & Adee, [1904]), p. 248.

A17. ZION LUTHERAN CHURCH

West Sand Lake, N.Y.
Built 1816; burned August 1944.
Builder: Christopher Slouter.

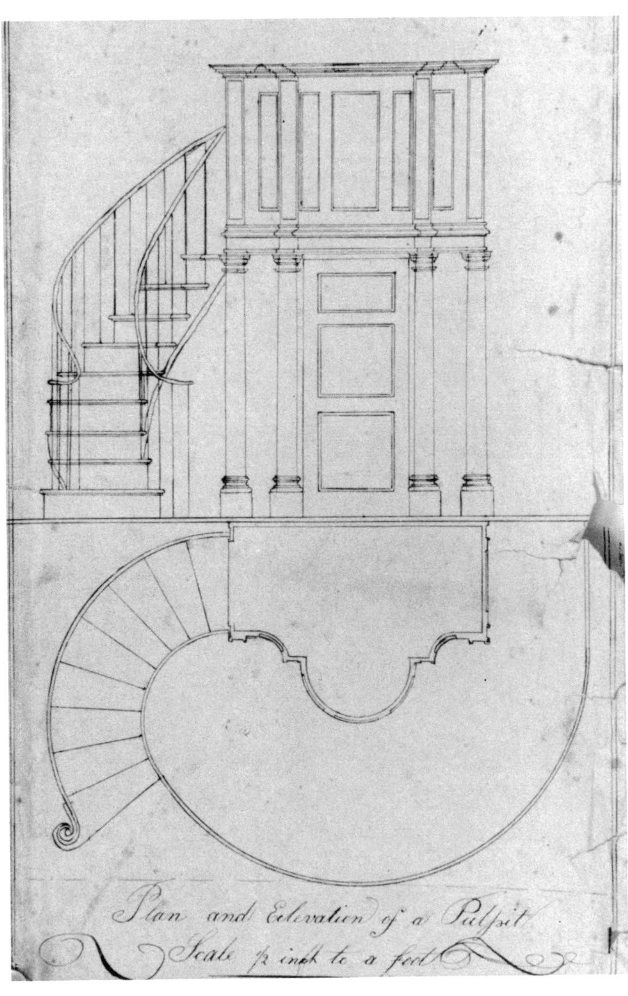

▲
Fig. 178. Zion Lutheran Church, West Sand Lake, N.Y. (1816), plan and elevation of the pulpit, possibly by Hooker. Ink on paper.

▶
Fig. 179. Elevation of the spire, possibly by Hooker. Ink and watercolor on paper. Rensselaer County Historical Society, Troy, N.Y.

The papers of Christopher Slouter, preserved at the Rensselaer County Historical Society, include drawings for this building. Two of these, one of the pulpit (fig. 178) and another of the spire (fig. 179) utilize drafting techniques and exhibit stylistic features common to Hooker's work.[1] Other drawings in the collection do not share these features and are possibly by Slouter. ✤

1. The spire bears similarities to that of St. Peter's Episcopal Church at Sherrill (fig. 115).

A18. TOWN HOUSE FOR STEPHEN VAN RENSSELAER IV

North Market (now Broadway) and North Ferry streets, Albany, N.Y.
Designed before July 1816.
Built 1816–18; altered c. 1860; razed c. 1960.
Builders: Seth Geer and John Boardman.

▶
Fig. 180. Stephen Van Rensselaer IV Town House, Albany (1816–18), design attributed to Hooker, exterior, published in 1848.
Courtesy W. R. Wheeler, Troy, N.Y.

This project was commissioned by Stephen Van Rensselaer III for his son, Stephen IV. Construction was near completion when Hooker submitted this estimate:

An Estimate of Extra work, done by John Boardman, in the principal Story of Stephen Van Rensselaers New house—

Finishing folding doors with Columns	*$70.—*
[Finishing]*—9 Setts door Cases, with pilasters*	*54.—*
[Finishing]*—5 doors with d*[ou]*bl*[e] *Architraves*	*17.50*
[Finishing], *arch in the Hall, both Sides*	*12.—*
[Finishing], *9 panneled front door, lock hinges bolts*	*25.—*
[Finishing] *1 back 6 panneled* [door], *lock hinges &c*	*12.50*
[Finishing] *6 windows, with pilasters & foot Caps*	*39.—*
[Finishing]*—2* [windows]*–Circular*	*20.—*
[Finishing]*—5* [windows] *with double architraves*	*20.—*
[Finishing]*—152 1/2 feet Best base*	*24.40*
[Finishing]*—14 1/2* [feet] *Circular* [base]	*4.64*
[Finishing] *67* [feet] *good common* [base]	*10.05*
[Finishing] *27 1/2 torus & Plinth*	*2.20*
[Finishing] *1 door & trimmings &c to Cellar Stairs*	*6.50*
	$317.79

Surveyed & Valued, Albany September 19th 1817

Ph. Hooker

Fees $10 *Seth Geer*[1]

Construction may have started around July 1816, a date suggested by Hooker's bill for the period July 1816 to October 1820 in which he *rendered . . . designs*, wrote up *sundry contracts*, obtained and made estimates, and superintended construction of the patroon's buildings.[2]

1. Van Rensselaer Manor Papers, SC 7079, MSC NYSL.
2. Ibid.
3. The front elevation of what was evidently this house is illustrated as the residence of L. S. Parsons in William Hunt, comp., *Hunt's Albany Commercial Directory, for 1848–9* (Albany: William Hunt, 1848), p. 6.
4. The curved rear wall is most clearly understood from Sanborn insurance maps of Albany, but is also visible in an engraving by Rawdon, Clark and Co. of Albany after a drawing by James Eights, in Amos Eaton's *A Geological and Agricultural Survey of the District Adjoining the Erie Canal in the State of New-York*, Pt. I (Albany, 1824), frontispiece.

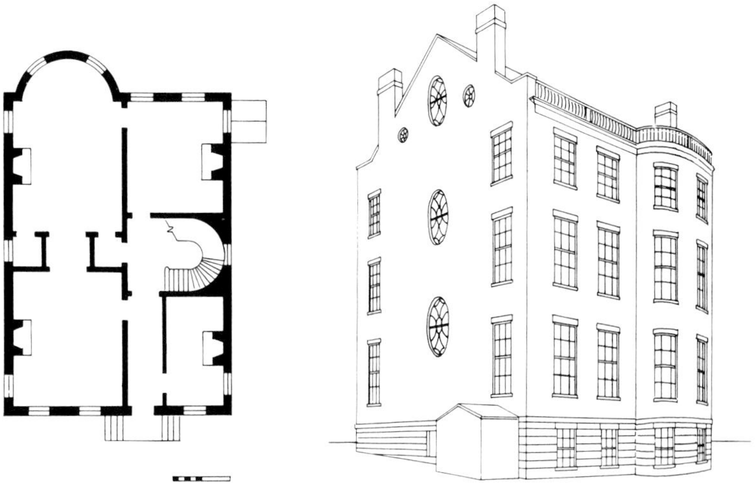

▶
Fig. 181. Stephen Van Rensselaer IV Town House, Albany (1816–18), design attributed to Hooker, first floor plan and view from the rear, reconstructed by Douglas G. Bucher, 1991.

The house was a four-bay-wide structure, with the door and hall in the second bay from the right (fig. 180).[3] The estimate above and published images of the house[4] suggest that a drawing room with a curved end wall occupied the rear half of the left side, a feature that would become popular in fine Albany houses during the 1820s. The placement of the oval openings in the side elevation likely indicate the location of the interior staircase in the center of the right side of the house (fig. 181). This arrangement, which probably included a small room in front and in back of the stair, represents a typical solution to the design of a four-bay house. ✣

A19. ISAAC DENNISTON HOUSE

Lydius Street (now Madison Avenue); later cited as Elm and Hawk streets, Albany, N.Y.
Built before 1818; razed before 1875.
Builder unknown.

In discussing the area of Albany bounded by Eagle, Elm, Myrtle, and Hawk streets, Isabelle K. Savell notes that

> *in the early 1800's, much of the land had belonged to Isaac Denniston. Isaac had acquired the hilltop and a fine colonial house built by Philip Hooker, and had surrounded it with extensive gardens filled with plum, peach and pear trees from France. Even the dry legal documents of the day referred to it as Isaac Denniston's mansion house and garden.*[1]

Savell gives no source for her reference to Hooker, and contemporary records seem to provide little assistance. City directories first list Denniston at this location in 1818, although deeds indicate that the land had been in the family at least ten and perhaps twenty years earlier. Savell indicates that the dwelling was demolished in the third quarter of the nineteenth century. ✣

1. Isabelle K. Savell, *The Executive Mansion in Albany: A Century of New York History* ([Albany]: New York State Office of General Services, 1982), p. 6.

A20. ALTERATIONS TO THE NEW YORK STATE CAPITOL

State Street at Public Square (now Capitol Park), Albany, N.Y.
Built 1818; razed 1883.
Builders: Geer and Duncan.

▶ Fig. 182. New York State Capitol, Albany (1806–9, altered 1818), Senate Chamber (originally Supreme Court Room), 1856. Courtesy Cornell University, Ithaca, N.Y., Olin Library.

In August 1817 the Supreme Court judges decided that the courtroom on the second floor of the capitol needed modifications, including the removal of the visitors' gallery and the relocation of the judges' bench from the east to the south side of the room. Perhaps because the windows of the room were immediately shaded by the building's portico (fig. 48), the judges also decided *"in order to afford sufficient light, to construct a Skylight."* This addition involved the installation of 270 panes of glass in a dome, with a final cost of $6,067.35 (fig. 182).[1]

Because Hooker was involved concurrently in other aspects of renovation work at the capitol he may also have been responsible for these alterations. On 6 January 1818, Hooker provided a *"Valuation of door Cases"* which builders Geer and Duncan were constructing there. These door surrounds, which featured fluted Ionic columns, drapery festoons, *"Raffle flowers,"* and *"open pediments"* containing *"Roman Vases,"* were estimated at $95.00 each. Their description matches in all details those which are still in place in the entrance hall of the Albany Academy (fig. 77).[2]

Hooker's last-known receipt from this period is dated 6 August 1818 and relates to the carving of Ionic capitals, perhaps destined for the Supreme Court Room.[3] ✤

1. Harley J. McKee, "Building for the State of New York, 1790–1890," *Empire State Architect*, XVI, 5 (September–October 1956), 52. This room later became the Senate Chamber.
2. Ibid.
3. Root, p. 112.

A21. TOWN HOUSE FOR WILLIAM AIKEN

Broadway and Aiken Avenue, Rensselaer, N.Y.
Built 1818; extant.
Builder: Ruell Clapp?

1. Several houses on Park Street in Albany, including that at No. 7 built for Lewis Benedict in 1828–29, also have the more formal second story.

This house incorporates oval windows identical to those used in another attributed work, the Stafford-Yates house (fig. 175). As was typical of the finer houses of the period, it features second-floor triple-hung windows with wrought iron balconies (now removed).[1] The second floor front room includes an impressive original mantel of fine detail. ✥

A22. PROPOSAL FOR A PUBLIC MARKET

South Pearl Street, between Howard and Beaver streets, Albany, N.Y.
Designed between 11 January and 29 March 1819.
Unbuilt.

On 30 November 1818 the Albany Common Council appointed *Mr Moody, Mr Hart and Mr Hooker* [to] *be a committee to devise means for the building* [of] *a general market . . . and report a place for the same.*[1] On 28 December the committee suggested that a public poll be taken to determine the best location for the proposed market.[2] Their recommendation was rejected by the common council, and a new committee was appointed on 11 January 1819 with Hooker the only member retained from the original group. They were directed *to prepare a plan and estimate of the probable expence* of the market.[3]

This committee reported on 29 March 1819 and made the suggestion *to site* [the] *Market on* [the] *former location of* [the] *Lutheran Church, on lands recently bought by the city.*[4] The proposal was not acted upon, however, and was eventually abandoned. Any accompanying design seems likely to have included the input of the committee's member with architectural credentials. ✥

1. Albany Common Council Minutes, 30 November 1818, ACHR.
2. Ibid., 28 December 1818.
3. Ibid., 11 January 1819.
4. Ibid., 29 March 1819.

A23. UNIDENTIFIED HOUSE

Unknown location.
Designed c. 1820.
Building history unknown.
Builder: Ruell Clapp.

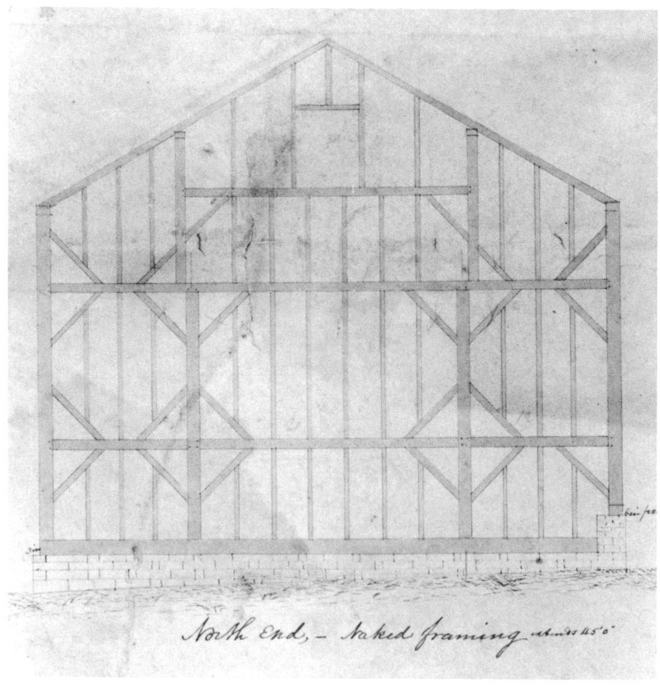

▶
Fig. 183. Framing drawing, attributed to Hooker, for an unidentified house, c. 1820. Ink and wash on paper. Collection Don Carpentier.

The attribution of this design to Hooker is based on an analysis of the drafting and handwriting techniques used in the drawing which documents this project (fig. 183). The fine lines and light washes together with elegant and restrained handwriting further indicate that the drawing dates from the middle of his career. Ruell Clapp, an Albany builder among whose papers this drawing was found, began the practice of his profession around 1818.[1]

The drawing is a framing elevation for the side of what appears to be a two-and-one-half-story dwelling. Its foundation, built into the side of a hill, is rendered as cut stone laid in a Flemish bond pattern. Three-inch shelves are shown on the front and rear, west and east elevations, presumably to carry a veneer wall of brick. If this was the case, the building as orginally planned shared this feature with later houses designed by Hooker (cats. 63, 65) and would have been located in an urban row. The rise of the foundation on the west elevation suggests that this was the intended street front.

If the cross beam heights are indicative of the location of floors, the first floor would have been seven feet high and the second, eleven feet. The house would have had its primary rooms on the second floor, with servant space, the kitchen, and the family dining room on the first floor.

The verso of this sheet preserves calculations of materials, possibly relating to the project. ✥

1. Ruell Clapp Papers, Collection, Don Carpentier; photocopies of the majority of these papers on file at the New York Historical Association Library, Cooperstown, N.Y.

A24. PROPOSAL FOR THE DESIGN OF THE PUBLIC SQUARE

Public Square (now Capitol Park and Academy Park), Albany, N.Y.
Designed c. 1821.
Unexecuted.

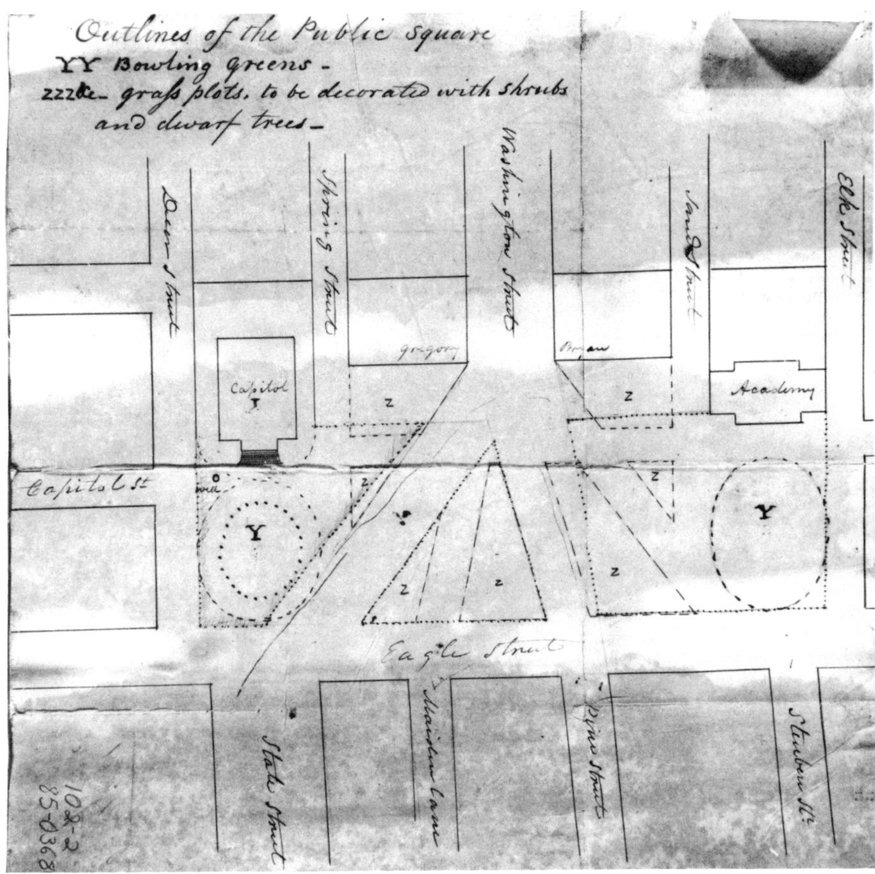

▶ Fig. 184. Proposal for the Public Square, Albany, drawing attributed to Hooker, c. 1821. Ink on paper with canvas backing. Albany County Hall of Records, Albany.

With the construction of the New York State Capitol (cat. 15) and the Albany Academy (cat. 33) on the west side of the Public Square, a formal plan for its landscaping became increasingly important. Regrading had begun in 1817 with the completion of the academy, the plan being for the *embellishing* [of] *the . . . square by planting trees and making walks and in enclosing the same in* [a] *fence.*[1] It was proposed *to use for that purpose the fencing materials which are now deposited* [at] *the Capitol,*[2] which might have been the leftover materials from Hooker's fence of 1812 (cat. 26).

Because of insufficient funds the proposal was not immediately realized and on 25 September 1820, the Public Square Committee was authorized to proceed with the work if they could raise the funds through public donations.[3] On 30 October, however, the city superintendent was *authorised to declare levels & assess people for the expenses of* [the] *public square improvements.*[4]

1. Albany Common Council Minutes, 11 August 1817, ACHR.
2. Ibid.
3. Ibid., 25 September 1820.
4. Ibid., 30 October 1820.
5. Ibid., 11 June 1821.
6. City Engineer's Maps, 102-2, ACHR.

On 11 June 1821 the Public Square Committee was authorized to proceed on improvements to the public square *upon such a plan as shall be aggreed upon by them.*[5] Although unsigned, the drawing which documents the proposal (fig. 184) can be attributed to Hooker by an analysis of the handwriting and drafting techniques. It can be dated to the years 1817–29 because of the inclusion of the academy building and the omission of the city hall.

This proposal included the re-routing of roads, the insertion of bowling greens in front of the capitol and the academy, and the creation of *seven grass plots, to be decorated with shrubs and dwarf trees.*[6] Apparently taxes were not assessed and due to lack of funds the project was delayed and was eventually superseded.[7] ✥

7. For the Capitol Park fence designed by Henry Rector and erected in 1832–33, see *Documents of the Assembly of the State of New-York, Fifty-sixth Session, 1833,* Vol. III (Albany: Printed by E. Croswell, 1833), no. 150. For Hooker's c. 1831 site plan and fence for Academy Park, see cat. 93.

A25. MORTUARY VAULT FOR THE VAN RENSSELAER FAMILY

Swan Street, Albany, N.Y.
Designed before November 1823.
Built c. 1823–24; razed c. 1850.
Builder unknown.

A bill dated 14 November 1823 indicates that Hooker was involved in the construction of the Van Rensselaer Family Vault located in the family cemetery on Swan Street.[1] Although there is no record of payment for design work, Hooker's supervision of construction and the fact that during this period he was regularly paid for *sundry . . . designs,*[2] suggests that he may have planned the structure. Hooker is nowhere documented to have been involved in the construction of buildings not of his design.

The vault was destroyed around 1850, when the family remains were transferred to the Albany Rural Cemetery. ✥

1. Van Rensselaer Manor Papers, SC 7079, MSC NYSL.
2. Ibid.

A26. FIRST PRESBYTERIAN CHURCH

Division and Third streets, Waterford, N.Y.
Built 1825–26; remodeled 1866 and 1886; razed c. 1911.
Builder unknown.

▶ Fig. 185. First Presbyterian Church, Waterford, N.Y. (1825–26), shown during the flood which caused its destruction, c. 1911. Rensselaer County Historical Society, Troy, N.Y.

Hooker makes reference to this structure in his specification for the Dutch Reformed Church of Niskayuna (cat. 68), thus indicating his familiarity with the building.[1] The tall blind arches, barely visible in the photograph (fig. 185), recall those on the facades of the North Dutch Reformed Church (fig. 9). ✤

1. Reference to the church in Waterford had also (and initially) been made by the consistory of the Niskayuna church.

A27. THORP AND SPRAGUE'S MARBLE BUILDING

Broadway and State Street, Albany, N.Y.
Built 1827; altered c. 1875; razed c. 1910.
Builder unknown.

Hooker's authorship of this design (fig. 18) is suggested by the distinctive Federal-style quality of its Greek Revival details, comparable to those of the Albany City Hall (fig. 160).[1] ✤

1. For an earlier view of the building, identified as the Albany Museum, see the copperprint engraving in G. J. Loomis and T. G. Wait, comps., *Albany Citizens' Advertiser and General Directory, for 1834–5* (Albany: G. J. Loomis, 1834), frontispiece.

A28. CONSISTORY HOUSE AND DWELLING FOR SOUTH DUTCH REFORMED CHURCH

Beaver Street, Albany, N.Y.
Designed between 17 January and 13 March 1828.
Built March–December 1828; razed c. 1893.
Builders: Jonathan Brooks, joiner; James Denniston, carpenter.
Mason: Jacob Goewey.

At a consistory meeting on 4 September 1827, church officials resolved to sell some of the land around the South Dutch Reformed Church, retaining enough for the siting of a contemplated consistory house. They hoped that the revenues from the sale of the lots would facilitate the construction. A building committee was formed on 17 January 1828 and was *authorised to procure a plan and estimate of a consistory house in the basement and a dwelling house above.* The contract for $4,746.00 was signed with the builders on 13 March 1828.[1] Hooker's name appears among the *bills to be allowed and paid* for work on the building on 2 December and he was paid $15.00 for his services, which may have included his superintendence.

As executed, the building featured a consistory room on the second level and an apartment for the church sexton below. This organization allowed the attic area to be used for a great arched ceiling in the consistory room, a feature common to other Hooker-designed consistories. The exterior, visible in photographs of the South Dutch Church (figs. 54, 55),[2] bore a remarkable similarity to that of the consistory house designed by Hooker in the same year for the North Dutch Reformed Church (cat. 73). ✣

1. Consistory minutes, South Dutch Reformed Church, passim, A FCA.
2. For a more complete view of the consistory house, see Joel Munsell, ed., *Annals of Albany*, Vol. X (Albany: Munsell & Rowland, Printers, 1859), frontispiece.

A29. SPECULATIVE TOWN HOUSES FOR STEPHEN VAN RENSSELAER III

1–5 Elk Street, Albany, N.Y.
Designed before 24 October 1828.
Built c. 1828–29; altered c. 1890, c. 1910, and c. 1970. No. 1 and portions of Nos. 2–5 razed c. 1970; portions of Nos. 2–5 extant.
Builder unknown.

Documents in the Van Rensselaer Manor Papers note Hooker as being on site and laying out the foundations for these dwellings.[1] Unfortunately, further records connecting him with this project have been lost. The four houses that still exist in this row have been extensively altered over the years. ✣

1. Van Rensselaer Manor Papers, SC 7079, MSC NYSL.

A30. SPECULATIVE TOWN HOUSES FOR WILLIAM JAMES

128–138 Green Street, Albany, N.Y.
Built c. 1829; Nos. 128 and 130 destroyed; others extant but altered.
Builder unknown.

William James was Hooker's landlord when the architect died at No. 130 in this row on 31 January 1836. These dwellings (fig. 186) are typical of speculative rows for middle class housing of the period, although their innovative window lintels mark the earliest use of cast-iron architectural elements in Albany. ✥

▶ Fig. 186. Speculative town houses for William James, Albany (c. 1829); design attributed to Hooker; photograph 1993.

A31. TOWN HOUSE FOR JOHN MEADS

99 Columbia Street, Albany, N.Y.
Built 1829 –30; altered c. 1855; extant.
Builder unknown.

Hooker and Meads, a well-known Albany cabinetmaker, were in professional contact over the course of many years. Meads furnished mahogany and a *venitian* window for the South Dutch Reformed Church (cat. 18), and joined with Hooker to assess construction work on the North Dutch Reformed Church Consistory House (cat. 73). He also provided a number of pieces of furniture for George Clarke's Hyde Hall.[1] Meads probably was responsible for the distinctive detailing of the interior of his house and perhaps also in part for its unique inset entrance way, with a curved door and fan light.[2] Although the present third story is a later addition, the front elevation of the house retains its original surface treatment—stucco scored in imitation of stone. ✥

1. Douglas R. Kent, "History in houses: Hyde Hall, Otsego County, New York," *Antiques*, XCII, 2 (August 1967), 188–89; and Jeane Newbold Miller, *John Meads (1777–1859): An Albany Cabinetmaker Furnishes Hyde Hall* (N.p., [1989]).
2. For a photograph, see Root, fig. 98. For a photostat of J. L. Dykeman's measured drawing of the entrance, see photograph collection, MK AIHA. For the doorway itself, see Collection, AIHA.

A32. VESTRY HOUSE FOR ST. PETER'S EPISCOPAL CHURCH (WITH ROBERT HIGHAM)

Unknown location, Albany, N.Y.
Designed before 9 November 1830.
Built 1830–31; razed.
Builders: Brooks and Platto.

Vouchers preserved in the New York State Library document construction on this project between 9 November 1830 and 6 June 1831, with recorded expenses totaling $2,050.[1] The full cost of the structure is unknown. The vouchers were authorized by Robert Higham on all but one occasion. Hooker is mentioned only when he made estimates of work necessary to complete the project in May 1831.[2] These facts suggest that while Hooker may have designed the building, Higham was chiefly responsible for overseeing its execution.

This seems to be the earliest documented project from the office of Hooker and Higham, whose partnership lasted until 1832 when Higham relocated to New York City.[3] ✤

1. St. Peter's Episcopal Church Papers, Albany, N.Y., Records, 1790–1900, SC 19680, MSC NYSL.
2. Ibid.
3. For Higham, see pp. 44, 50 n. 76.

A33. TWIN HOUSES

29–31 Elk Street, Albany, N.Y.
Built c. 1830; No. 31 destroyed c. 1970; No. 29 extant.
Builder unknown.

The treatment of the details on the facades of this unusual pair of houses, together with their interior trim, which is remarkably similar to that found in the Albany Academy (cat. 33) and other Hooker projects, suggest authorship by Hooker. ✤

A34. COUNTRY HOUSE FOR ROBERT DUNLOP

(500s) Broadway, Menands, N.Y.
Built c. 1831–32; razed c. 1970.
Builder unknown.

The use of tripartite windows and the similarity of the Doric portico and entrance door to the contemporary *Great House* (fig. 141) at Hyde Hall suggest Hooker's connection to this project. Hooker had met Dunlop by 1828, when he was directed by him (on behalf of the North Dutch Church) to provide a design for a consistory house and iron fence.[1] ✤

1. Doc. 139-8, Dutch Reformed Church Collection, A FCA.

APPENDIX

PRELIMINARY CATALOGUE of SURVEY MAPS by PHILIP HOOKER

This list has been compiled from records of maps submitted by Hooker to the Albany County Clerk and to the City of Albany,* and from references found in private collections. Despite representing a substantial body of Hooker's survey work, this remains a preliminary catalogue. A thorough examination of the deeds executed for Albany properties between 1800 and 1836 would furnish additional references to the architect's drawings, while a systematic reading of the Albany Common Council minutes for the same period would provide a complete listing of work required of Hooker as City Surveyor. Furthermore, this list includes only those maps signed by Hooker. No attempt has been made to attribute any of the many unsigned maps in the Albany County Clerk's and City Engineer's map collections. Topographic profiles drawn by Hooker during his tenure as City Surveyor, noted by Edward W. Root in his monograph on the architect, are not indexed anywhere and are not included here.

Albany's first City Surveyor, Abraham Oake, who was appointed in 1800, is a strong contender for Hooker's teacher in the science of surveying. Simeon De Witt and Pierre Pharoux are also possible candidates. The presence of the names of Robert Higham and James T. Kelly on some of the maps along with Hooker's provides valuable information about their association with their mentor.

Not all of the drawings listed here are extant. Many of Albany's early nineteenth century records were lost in the 1880 fire that destroyed Hooker's City Hall and in subsequent fires as recent as the 1970s. Thus some of the citations which follow the individual entries refer only to the prior existence of the respective maps. For a key to collection abbreviations, see p. 51. No concerted attempt has been made to modernize street names.

---

*The former are indexed under *Maps* in the city *Grantors* deed books at the Albany County Hall of Records, while the latter are filed in the City Engineer's map collection, also at the Hall of Records.

1810
Survey of Wolf, Hawk, Otter, and Eagle streets, Albany. (City Engineer's Maps, ACHR)

1 April 1811
Survey of John J. Van Rensselaer's *mansion house and store house.* (Van Rensselaer Papers, AA2, MK AIHA) (Hooker refers to this document as a survey. It is similar in content to the assessment he did for John Bryan; see A14.)

23 November 1813
Map of the premises at the point of Lion Street and the Great Western Turnpike, Albany. For the estate of Solomon Southwick. (*Grantors,* ACHR)

16 May 1814
Property of James Gourlay on the Great Western Turnpike, Lion and Perry streets, Albany. (*Grantors,* ACHR)

c. 1815
Map of property south of the Second Presbyterian Church on Chapel and Lodge streets, Albany. (Second Presbyterian Church Papers, Doc. 52, MK AIHA)

8 November 1815
Division Map, apportioning the properties of the Dutch Reformed Church to the North and South Dutch churches, Albany. (Doc. 136-8, A FCA)

1 May 1818
Map of the area between Hallenbake and South Pearl streets, Albany. (Lush Papers, Collection, Paul Huey)

1820
Survey of proposed location of the Erie Canal between Albany and German Flatts. (Doc. 16667, MSC NYSL)

6 March 1823
Map of property on South Market and Quay streets, Albany, for the estate of Stephen Van Schaick. (*Grantors,* ACHR)

18 August 1824
Church Burying Ground in State Street, including Capitol and Eagle streets, Albany. (Doc. 136-8, A FCA)

10 December 1824
Map of the southwest corner of Montgomery and Quackenbush streets, Albany. (*Grantors,* ACHR)

c. 1825
Map of area lying between Montgomery and North Market streets, Albany. Land owned by heirs of Christopher Beekman. (Gansevoort-Lansing Collection, NYPL)

1 January 1825
Map of the block bounded by Lodge Street, Maiden Lane, Eagle and Pine streets, Albany. (MSC NYSL)

5 January 1825
A map of a gore of land . . . formerly occupied as a street called oak street at the intersection of Columbia and Chapel streets, Albany. (City Engineer's Maps #433, ACHR)

1826
Sketch of plan of extending Spencer Street west of Montgomery Street, Albany. (Gansevoort-Lansing Collection, NYPL)

20 April 1827
A map of the Fly Market laid out into building lots. The Market to be erected along & Fronting South Pearl Street [Albany] . . . features a schematic plan of the Centre Market and its outbuildings. (City Engineer's Maps #275, ACHR)

17 May 1827
Map of Montgomery and Water streets, Albany, for McNab & Kirk, owners. (*Grantors*, ACHR)

5 March 1828
Sketch map, southwest corner of Hallenbake and Lydius streets, Albany. (Albany Gallery of Fine Art Records, MK AIHA)

4 August 1828
Map of property on Quay Street from Lodge to John streets, Albany. Copied 5 June 1835. (City Engineer's Maps #286, ACHR)

4 August 1828
Opening of Quay Street from Ferry Street to the *old watering place*, Albany. (City Engineer's Maps #301, ACHR)

7 September 1828
Opening of Spruce Street between Eagle and Hawk streets, Albany. (*Grantors*, ACHR)

October 1828
Survey of Lot No. 2, Schuyler Farm. (Van Rensselaer Manor Papers, SC 7079, MSC NYSL)

20 December 1828
Map of *opening* of Herkimer Street between Church and South Pearl streets, Albany. (*Grantors*, ACHR)

20 December 1828
Map of *opening* of Johnson Street from Franklin to Pearl streets, Albany. (*Grantors*, ACHR)

1829
Survey of lots in Capitol Street owned by the Lutheran Ebenezer Church, Albany. (Philip Hooker Papers, Bills to Lutheran Church, Doc. 130, MK AIHA)

March 1829
Map of widening of Union Street from Hamilton to Lydius streets, Albany. (*Grantors*, ACHR)

14 March 1829
Map of Ground Situate on the east side of S [outh] *Market Street* [Albany] *formerly known as the watering place* . . . features a schematic plan of the South Market. (City Engineer's Maps #133, ACHR)

30 March 1829
Map of *opening and widening* of South Pearl Street from Hamilton to Howard streets, Albany. (*Grantors*, ACHR)

30 March 1829
Map of widening of Columbia Street between Chapel and Pearl streets, Albany. (*Grantors*, ACHR)

30 March 1829
Map of widening of Columbia Street from Pearl to Montgomery streets, Albany. (*Grantors*, ACHR)

30 March 1829
Widening of Columbia Street, Albany. Lots on north side of Columbia between Eagle and Chapel streets. (City Engineer's Maps, ACHR)

28 August 1829
Map of property on Knox Street between Washington and State streets, Albany. Subdivision of lots 11 and 12 of the Simeon De Witt Bloodgood Estate. (*Grantors*, ACHR)

7 September 1829
Map of Delaware Street, Albany. Subdivision of part of the Schuyler Farm showing property owned by Ebenezer Baldwin. (*Grantors*, ACHR)

15 September 1829
Map of *opening* and extension of South High Street from Lancaster Street to Hudson Avenue, Albany. (*Grantors*, ACHR)

3 October 1829
Map of opening of Jay Street from Hawk to Eagle streets, Albany. (*Grantors*, ACHR)

14 October 1829
Map of Gallows Hill, Albany. (City Engineer's Maps #380, ACHR)

3 November 1829
Survey of lots on Columbia Street, Albany. (Book of Deeds, ACHR)

17 November 1829
Widening of Colonie Street from North Market Street to the Basin, Albany. (*Grantors*, ACHR)

c. 1830
Map of the east side of North Market Street south of Quackenbush Street, Albany. (City Engineer's Maps #453, ACHR)

1830
Division of properties owned by the Gansevoort and Quackenbush families, Albany. (Gansevoort-Lansing Collection, NYPL)

1830
Survey of lots in Capitol Street owned by the Lutheran Ebenezer Church, Albany. (Philip Hooker Papers, Bills to Lutheran Church, Doc. 131, MK AIHA)

26 June 1830
Map of lots 9 and 10 at South Pearl, Schuyler, and Franklin streets, Albany. For the estate of J. V. Henry. (Maps, 74743, MSC NYSL)

4 September 1830
Map of Division, Market, Green, and Quay streets and Store Lane, Albany. For the estate of James Bleecker. (*Grantors*, ACHR)

5 October 1830
Survey map & boundaries of Eagle Tavern, Albany. (Van Rensselaer Manor Papers, SC 7079, MSC NYSL)

16 October 1830
Survey of lot No. 4 Lydius Street, Albany, by Hooker and Robert Higham. (Van Rensselaer Manor Papers, SC 7079, MSC NYSL)

November 1830
Map of *opening* of Jackson Street from Lumber to Colonie streets, Albany. (*Grantors*, ACHR)

1 November 1830
Widening of Market Street between Ferry and Johnson streets, Albany. (*Grantors*, ACHR)

4 December 1830
Survey & measurement of filling lots Corner of Ferry and Green Streets, Albany. By Hooker with Robert Higham. (Van Rensselaer Manor Papers, SC 7079, MSC NYSL)

1831
Map made for opening State Street [Albany] . . . *by Rob*[er]*t Higham for P* [hilip] *Hooker city Surveyor.* (City Engineer's Maps #144, ACHR)

1831
Map of ground taken for *opening* of Jackson Street, Albany. (Gansevoort-Lansing Collection, NYPL)

9 May 1831
Map of *opening* of Green Street, Albany, amended 3 June 1831. (*Grantors*, ACHR)

6 June 1831
Map for opening Dallius Street, Albany, from Mulberry to Lydius streets. (City Engineer's Maps #274, ACHR)

4 July 1831
Map of *opening* of Philip Street from Hudson Avenue to Lydius Street, Albany. (*Grantors*, ACHR)

28 July 1831
Map Made for opening a street between Howard and Beaver streets [Albany] . . . *by R*[obert] *Higham for P* [hilip] *Hooker city Surveyor.* (City Engineer's Maps #135, ACHR)

August 1831
Map of State lots on Lawrence and Dewitt Streets [Albany] *as surveyed by Philip Hooker, protracted by Robert Higham.* (MSC NYSL)

6 September 1831
Map of *opening* of Quay Street, Albany. (*Grantors*, ACHR) (A later copy of this map is in the City Engineer's Maps #165, ACHR.)

16 September 1831
Map of property on North Market, Jackson, and Colonie streets, Albany. Drawn by Robert Higham for Hooker. (*Grantors*, ACHR)

14 October 1831
Map of widening of State Street from Dean to Quay Street [Albany] *surveyed by Robert Higham for Philip Hooker.* (City Engineer's Maps #143, ACHR)

2 December 1831
Map of *opening of Jackson Street and continuing said street from Lumber to Spencer Streets*, Albany. (*Grantors*, ACHR) (A copy of this map is in the City Engineer's Maps, ACHR.)

3 December 1831
Map made for opening an alley between Howard & Beaver streets, Albany. (*Grantors*, ACHR)

3 December 1831
Map made for opening Market Street near Lumber Street, Albany. (City Engineer's Maps #328, ACHR)

3 December 1831
Widening of North Market Street (east side) between Wilson and Lumber streets, Albany. (*Grantors*, ACHR)

3 December 1831
Widening of North Market Street near Wilson Street, Albany. (*Grantors*, ACHR) (A copy of this map by Cushman & Carpenter dated 2 May 1832 is in the City Engineer's Maps #134, ACHR.)

5 December 1831
Map of *opening* of Spencer Street, Albany. (*Grantors*, ACHR) (A copy of this map is in the City Engineer's Maps #173, ACHR.)

5 December 1831
Map of *opening* of Spencer Street, between the Erie Canal and Montgomery Street, Albany. (*Grantors*, ACHR)

1832
Property between Hamilton and Beaver streets, Albany. (ACHR)

4 February 1832
Map of State Street [Albany] *by P. Hooker pro*[tracted] *by Robt. Higham, examined and corrected.* (City Engineer's Maps #311, ACHR)

12 August 1832
Map of Isaac Denniston's lots through which Embargo Alley is intended to be laid, Albany. (ACHR)

5 September 1832
. . . *the Property of Isaac Denniston through which Embargo Alley is to be laid,* Albany. (City Engineer's Maps #331, ACHR)

9 November 1832
Map of Hallenbake Street, Albany. (City Engineer's Maps #296, ACHR) (A later copy of this map is in the City Engineer's Maps #387, ACHR.)

6 February 1833
Map of Hallenbake Street, north of Hudson Avenue, Albany. Property of Henry & Emott. (*Grantors,* ACHR)

9 May 1833
Map of Herkimer (now Jefferson), Wolf, Westerlo, and Swan streets, Albany. (*Grantors,* ACHR)

4 June 1833
Map of Fox Street. (City Engineer's Maps #473, ACHR)

22 August 1833
Map for extending embankment on Fox Street. . . . (City Engineer's Maps #315, ACHR)

14 January 1834
Map of property belonging to the heirs of G. W. Van Schaick [Albany]. (Gansevoort-Lansing Collection, NYPL)

10 April 1834
Survey of Lot on Fox Street, Albany. (Philip Hooker Papers, Certification of survey of lot on Fox Street, Doc. 81-18.2, MK AIHA)

March 1835
Survey of lots to be auctioned by Townsend. By Hooker and James T. Kelly (lithograph). (Maps, 74743, MSC NYSL)

1 May 1835
Map of Hallenbake Street, Albany. Subdivision of Robinson's Hill, extends from Lydius to Hudson streets and between Eagle and Grand streets. (*Grantors,* ACHR)

18 June 1835
Map of the property of Abraham Varick, Albany. By Hooker & Kelly. (*Grantors,* ACHR)

December 1835
Map of *opening* of High Street from Hudson to Lancaster streets, Albany. (*Grantors,* ACHR)

December 1835
Survey of Lots to be auctioned by Townsend. By Hooker and Abraham Oake (lithograph). (MSC NYSL)

SELECTED BIBLIOGRAPHY

PUBLISHED WORKS

BOOKS AND PAMPHLETS

Adam, Robert. *The Works in Architecture of Robert and James Adam.* Edited by Robert Oresko. London: Academy Editions, and New York: St. Martin's Press, 1975.

Albany City Directories, 1813 to 1841.

Albany's Historic Street. 1918. Reprint. Schenectady: Papp Historical Publications, 1976.

Alexander, Robert S. *Albany's First Church and its Role in the Growth of the City, 1642–1942.* Albany: First Church in Albany, 1988.

Andriot, John L., comp. and ed. *Population Abstract of the United States.* Vol. I: *Tables.* McLean, Va.: Andriot Associates, 1983.

Architects' Emergency Committee. *Great Georgian Houses of America.* 2 vols. 1933, 1937. Reprint. New York: Dover Publications, Inc., 1970.

Bagg, M. M., ed. *Memorial History of Utica, N.Y.* Syracuse: D. Mason & Co., 1892.

————. *The Pioneers of Utica.* Utica, N.Y.: Curtiss & Childs, 1877.

Beach, Allen C. *The Centennial Celebrations of the State of New York.* Albany: Weed, Parsons & Co., Printers, 1879.

Beebe, Richard T. *Albany Medical College and Albany Hospital. A History: 1839–1982.* [Albany], 1983.

Benjamin, Asher. *The American Builder's Companion.* 1st ed. 1806. Reprint. New York: Da Capo Press, 1972.

————. *The American Builder's Companion.* 6th ed. 1827. Reprint. New York: Dover Publications, Inc., 1969.

————. *The Rudiments of Architecture.* 1st ed. Boston: Printed for the author by Munroe and Francis, 1814.

Bennett, Allison P. *The People's Choice: A History of Albany County in Art and Architecture.* Albany: Lane Press, 1980.

Bentham, Jeremy. *Complete Works.* Vol. IV. Edited by John Bowring. Edinburgh, 1843.

Blackburn, Roderic H., and Piwonka, Ruth. *Remembrance of Patria: Dutch Arts and Culture in Colonial America, 1609–1776.* Albany: Albany Institute of History and Art, 1988.

Boos, John E. *Ramblin' With Jerry, 1931.* Landmarks of the Capitol District, vol. I. Albany: Morris Gerber, 1972.

————. *Roaming Near the Fireplace, 1944.* Landmarks of the Capitol District, vol. II. Albany: Morris Gerber, 1972.

Boyd, Sterling. *The Adam Style in America, 1770–1820.* 2 vols. in 1. Outstanding Dissertations in the Fine Arts. New York and London: Garland Publishing, Inc., 1985.

Brown, William. *The Carpenter's Assistant.* Worcester, Mass.: Edward Livermore, 1848.

Child, Edmund B., comp. *Child's Albany Directory, and City Register, for the years 1833–4.* Albany: Printed by E. B. Child, 1833.

————, comp. *Child's Albany Directory, and City Register, for the years 1835–6.* Albany: Printed by E. B. Child, 1835.

Cowdrey, Mary Bartlett. *American Academy of Fine Arts and American Art-Union.* 2 vols. New York: The New-York Historical Society, 1953.

Curtis, Gates, ed. *Our County and Its People: A Memorial Record of St. Lawrence County, New York.* Syracuse: D. Mason & Company, 1894.

da Costa Nunes, Jadviga M. *Baroness Hyde de Neuville: Sketches of America, 1807–1822.* New Brunswick, N. J.: Jane Voorhees Zimmerli Art Museum, Rutgers, The State University of New Jersey, and New York: The New-York Historical Society, 1984.

Documents of the Assembly of the State of New-York, Fifty-fourth Session, 1831. Vol. III. Albany: Printed by E. Croswell, 1831.

Documents of the Assembly of the State of New-York, Fifty-sixth Session, 1833. Vol. III. Albany: Printed by E. Croswell, 1833.

Donoghue, John. *Alexander Jackson Davis: A Romantic Architect, 1803–1892.* New York: Arno Press, 1982.

Duncan, William, [ed.] *The New-York Directory, and Register, for 1792.* New-York: Printed for the editor, 1792.

———. *The New-York Directory, and Register, for 1792* [sic; i.e., 1793]. New-York, 1793.

Eaton, Amos. *A Geological and Agricultural Survey of the District Adjoining the Erie Canal in the State of New-York.* Pt. I. Albany, 1824.

Eddy, Thomas. *An Account of the State Prison or Penitentiary House in the City of New-York.* New York: Printed by Isaac Collins and son, 1801.

Ellis, David Maldwyn. *The Upper Mohawk Country: An Illustrated History of Greater Utica.* Woodland Hills, Calif.: Windsor Publications, Inc., 1982.

Ellis, Franklin. *History of Columbia County, New York.* Philadelphia: Everts & Ensign, 1878.

Enys, John. *The American Journals of Lt. John Enys.* Edited by Elizabeth Cometti. Syracuse: Syracuse University Press, and [Blue Mountain Lake, N.Y.]: Adirondack Museum, 1976.

Federation of Historical Services. *Historic Resources of the Upper Hudson, Champlain and Mohawk Valleys.* 2d ed. Albany: Fort Orange Press, 1987.

Fry, J., comp. *Albany Directory, for the Year 1814.* Albany: Printed by H. C. Southwick, and Packard & Van Benthuysen, 1814.

[Gerber, Morris, comp.] *Old Albany.* 4 vols. Albany: Morris Gerber, 1961–79.

[Gerber, Morris, comp.] *Old Albany.* Vol. V. Albany: Price Chopper Books, Inc., 1989.

Gilder, Cornelia Brooke, ed. *Albany Architects. The Present Looks at the Past.* Albany: Historic Albany Foundation, 1978.

Grills, Russell A. *Cazenovia: The Story of an Upland Community.* Cazenovia, N.Y.: Cazenovia Preservation Foundation, Inc., 1977.

Groft, Tammis Kane. *The Folk Spirit of Albany.* Albany: Albany Institute of History and Art, 1978.

Hamlin, Talbot. *Benjamin Henry Latrobe.* New York: Oxford University Press, 1955.

———. *Greek Revival Architecture in America.* 1944. Reprint. New York: Dover Publications, Inc., 1964.

Harding, John R., ed. *One Hundred Years of Trinity Church, Utica, N.Y.* Utica, N.Y.: Thomas J. Griffiths, 1898.

Harrington, Elisha. *The Utica Directory. No. 5–1834.* Utica, N.Y.: E. A. Maynard, Printer, 1834.

Harris, Eileen. *British Architectural Books and Writers 1556–1785.* Cambridge, Eng.: Cambridge University Press, 1990.

Harris, Neil. *The Artist in American Society.* New York: George Braziller Inc., 1966.

Hart, Larry. *Tales of Old Schenectady.* 2 vols. Scotia, N.Y.: Old Dorp Books, 1975.

Haydon, Roger. *Upstate Travels: British Views of Nineteenth Century New York.* Syracuse: Syracuse University Press, 1982.

Hazen, Edward. *Popular Technology, or Professions and Trades.* New York: Harper & Brothers, 1841.

Heads of Families at the First Census of the United States Taken in the Year 1790: New York. 1908. Reprint. Baltimore: Genealogical Publishing Company, 1966.

Heins, Henry H. *Swan of Albany: A History of the Oldest Congregation of the Lutheran Church in America.* Albany: First Lutheran Church, 1976.

Hislop, Codman. *Albany: Dutch, English, and American.* Albany: The Argus Press, 1936.

———, and Larrabee, Harold A. *Joseph Jacques Ramée and the Building of North and South Colleges.* Reprinted from the *Union Alumni Monthly* XXVII, 4. [Schenectady, 1937.]

The History of Oneida County. [Utica, N.Y.]: Oneida County, 1977.

Hobart, John Henry. "Address." In *Journal of the Proceedings of the Annual Convention of the Protestant Episcopal Church in the State of New-York . . . 1819,* pp. 12–23. New York: Printed by T. and J. Swords, 1819.

Hough, Franklin B. *History of Lewis County, . . . New York.* Albany: Munsell & Rowland, 1860.

———. *History of Lewis County, New York, 1805–1883.* Syracuse: D. Mason & Co., 1883.

———. *Lowville Academy Semi-Centennial Anniversary.* Lowville, N.Y.: The Home Committee, 1859.

Howard, John. *An Account of the Principal Lazarettos in Europe.* Warrington, Eng.: Printed by W. Eyres, 1789.

Howell, [George R.], and Munsell, [John H.], eds. *History of the County of Schenectady, N.Y., from 1662 to 1886.* New York: W. W. Munsell & Co., 1886.

———, and Tenney, [Jonathan], eds. *Bi-Centennial History of Albany. History of the County of Albany, N.Y., from 1609 to 1886.* New York: W. W. Munsell & Co., 1886.

Hunt, William, comp. *Hunt's Albany Commercial Directory, for 1848–9.* Albany: William Hunt, 1848.

Jones, Pomroy. *Annals and Recollections of Oneida County.* Rome, N.Y.: Pomroy Jones, 1851.

Journal of the Assembly of the State of New-York at their Fifty-second Session. Albany: Printed by E. Croswell, 1829.

Kennedy, Roger G. *Architecture, Men, Women and Money in America, 1600–1860.* New York: Random House, 1985.

———. *Orders from France: The Americans and the French in a Revolutionary World, 1780–1820.* New York: Alfred A. Knopf, 1989.

———. *Rediscovering America.* Boston: Houghton Mifflin Company, 1990.

Kenney, Alice P. *The Gansevoorts of Albany.* Syracuse: Syracuse University Press, 1969.

Kirker, Harold. *The Architecture of Charles Bulfinch.* Cambridge, Mass.: Harvard University Press, 1969.

———, and Kirker, James. *Bulfinch's Boston, 1787–1817.* New York: Oxford University Press, 1964.

Kouwenhoven, John A. *Made in America.* New York: Farrar, Straus & Giroux, 1975.

Lafever, Minard. *The Young Builder's General Instructor.* Newark, N. J.: Printed by W. Tuttle & Co., 1829.

Landy, Jacob. *The Architecture of Minard Lafever.* New York: Columbia University Press, 1970.

Lassiter, William Lawrence. *Philip Hooker and the Old Albany Academy.* Albany, n.d.

Letters about the Hudson River and its Vicinity. New York: Freeman Hunt & Co., 1837.

Loomis, G. J., and Wait, T. G., comps. *Albany Citizens' Advertiser and General Directory, for 1834–5.* Albany: G. J. Loomis, 1834.

Lord, Jane S., et al. *Lansingburgh, New York, 1771–1971.* Lansingburgh, N.Y.: [Lansingburgh Historical Society], 1971.

Luckey, John. *Life in Sing-Sing State Prison.* New York: N. Tibbals & Co., 1860.
McEneny, John J. *Albany, Capital City on the Hudson.* Woodland Hills, Calif.: Windsor Publications, 1981.
McIntyre, A. McVoy. *Beacon Hill: A Walking Tour.* Boston and Toronto: Little, Brown & Company, 1975.
Mendel · Mesick · Cohen. *Ten Broeck Mansion: A Historic Structure Report.* Albany: Mendel · Mesick · Cohen, 1975.
Mendel · Mesick · Cohen · Waite · Hall · Architects. *Hyde Hall: A Restoration Feasibility Study and Master Plan.* Albany: Prepared for the Friends of Hyde Hall, Inc., 1986.
Miller, Blandina Dudley. *A Sketch of Old Utica.* Edited by Helen Lincklaen Miller. N.p., 1909.
Miller, Jeane Newbold. *John Meads (1777–1859): An Albany Cabinetmaker Furnishes Hyde Hall.* N.p., [1989].
Morris, Robert. *Select Architecture.* 2d ed. 1757. Reprint. New York: Da Capo Press, 1973.
Munsell, Joel, comp. *Annals of Albany.* 10 vols. Albany: J. Munsell, 1850–59. (Munsell, Joel or J., variously identified as compiler, editor, author, and publisher.)
———, comp. *Annals of Albany.* 2d ed. 4 vols. Albany: Joel Munsell, 1869–71.
[Munsell, Joel, comp.] *Collections on the History of Albany.* 4 vols. Albany: J. Munsell, 1865–71.
Myers, James T., comp. *History of the City of Watervliet, N.Y., 1630 to 1910.* Troy, N.Y.: H. Stowell and Son, [1910?].
New York State, Bureau of Historic Sites. *Schuyler Mansion: A Historic Structure Report.* [Albany]: State of New York, Office of Parks and Recreation, 1977.
Opitz, Glenn B., ed. *Mantle Fielding's Dictionary of American Painters, Sculptors & Engravers.* 2d ed., rev. and enl. Poughkeepsie: Apollo Book, 1986.
Pain, William. *The Builder's Pocket-Treasure.* London: W. Owen, 1785.
———. *The Practical House Carpenter, or Youth's Instructor.* 6th ed., corrected. London: J. Taylor, 1799.
Patterson, Ferne Kitson. *Pioneers of Vernon, Oneida County, New York, and the Root Family.* Interlaken, N.Y.: Ferne K. Patterson, 1985.
Phelps, H. P. *Players of the Century.* Albany: Joseph McDonough, 1880.
Pierson, William H., Jr. *American Buildings and Their Architects.* Vol. I: *The Colonial and Neoclassical Styles.* Garden City, N.Y.: Doubleday & Company, Inc., 1970.
———. *American Buildings and Their Architects.* Vol. II, [pt. 1]: *Technology and the Picturesque. The Corporate and the Early Gothic Styles.* Garden City, N.Y.: Doubleday & Company, Inc., 1978.
Pilcher, Edith. *Castorland: French Refugees in the Western Adirondacks, 1793–1814.* Harrison, N.Y.: Harbor Hill Books, 1985.
Pilkington, Walter. *Hamilton College 1812/1962.* Clinton, N.Y.: Hamilton College, 1962.
Plaw, John. *Ferme Ornée; or, Rural Improvements.* London: I. and J. Taylor, 1795.
———. *Rural Architecture.* [London: John Plaw], 1785.
———. *Sketches for Country Houses, Villas, and Rural Dwellings.* London: J. Taylor, 1800.
Przybycien, Frank E. *Utica: A City Worth Saving.* Utica, N.Y.: Dodge-Graphic Press, 1976.
Reynolds, Cuyler, comp. *Albany Chronicles.* Albany: J. B. Lyon Company, Printers, 1906.
Rice, Norman S. *New York Furniture Before 1840 in the Collection of the Albany Institute of History and Art.* Albany: Albany Institute of History and Art, 1962.

Rink, Oliver A. *Holland on the Hudson: An Economic and Social History of Dutch New York.* Ithaca, N.Y.: Cornell University Press, 1986.
Roberts, George S. *Old Schenectady.* Schenectady: Robson & Adee, [1904].
Rogers, E. P. *A Historical Discourse on the Reformed Prot. Dutch Church of Albany.* New York: Board of Publication of the Reformed Protestant Dutch Church, 1858.
Root, Edward W. *Philip Hooker: A Contribution to the Study of the Renaissance in America.* New York: Charles Scribner's Sons, 1929.
Roseberry, C. R. *Capitol Story.* 2d ed. [Albany]: New York State Office of General Services, 1982.
Saunders, Silvia. *Isaac Williams, Deacon and Master Carpenter of Clinton, New York.* Herkimer, N.Y.: Printed for The Clinton Historical Society, Herkimer Print Shop, 1985.
Savell, Isabelle K. *The Executive Mansion in Albany: A Century of New York History.* [Albany]: New York State Office of General Services, 1982.
Schimmelman, Janice G. *Architectural Treatises and Building Handbooks available in American Libraries and Bookstores through 1800.* Worcester, Mass.: American Antiquarian Society, 1986.
Shaw, Edward. *Civil Architecture.* Boston: Edward Shaw and William F. Stratton, 1830.
Small, Verna. *Nineteenth Century Dwelling Houses of Greenwich Village.* [New York]: Association of Village Homeowners Landmarks Committee, 1968.
Smith, Helen. *The Historic Pastures, A Walking Tour.* Albany, 1987.
Spafford, Horatio Gates. *A Gazetteer of the State of New-York.* Albany: H. C. Southwick, 1813.
Springer, A. O. *Albany's Bi-Centennial.* 2d ed. Albany, 1886.
Summerson, John. *Georgian London.* Rev. ed. Baltimore: Penguin Books, Inc., 1962.
Swan, Abraham. *The Carpenters Complete Instructor.* London: Robert Sayer, 1768.
Sylvester, Nathaniel Bartlett. *History of Rensselaer Co., New York.* Philadelphia: Everts & Peck, 1880.
Tenney, Jonathan. *New England in Albany.* Boston: Crocker & Co., 1883.
Transactions of the Albany Institute. Vol. I. Albany: Webster [sic] and Skinners, 1830.
Transactions of the Albany Institute. Vol. VI. Albany: J. Munsell, 1870.
Transactions of the Society for the Promotion of Useful Arts, in the State of New-York. [Vol. II.] Albany: Printed by John Barber, 1807.
Transactions of the Society for the Promotion of Useful Arts, in the State of New-York. Vol. III. Albany: Printed by Websters and Skinners, 1814.
Transactions of the Society for the Promotion of Useful Arts, in the State of New-York. Vol. IV, pts. 1, 2. Albany: Printed by Websters and Skinners, 1816, 1819.
Troy City Directories, 1829 to 1841.
Utica City Directories, 1828 to 1834.
The Utica Directory. Utica, N.Y.: Elisha Harrington, 1828.
von Weich, Valerie, ed. *A Resourceful People.* Norfolk, Va.: The Donning Co., 1987.
Waite, Diana S. *Nineteenth Century Tin Roofing and Its Use at Hyde Hall.* 2d ed. [Albany]: New York State Parks and Recreation, Division for Historic Preservation, 1974.
———. *Ornamental Ironwork: Two Centuries of Craftsmanship in Albany and Troy, New York.* Albany: Mount Ida Press, 1990.
Waite, John G. *The Architecture of Lansingburgh, New York.* Lansingburgh, N.Y.: Lansingburgh Historical Society, 1976.
Walsh, John J. *Vignettes of Old Utica.* Utica, N.Y.: Utica Public Library, 1982.
Watson, Winslow C., ed. *Men and Times of the Revolution; or, Memoirs of Elkanah Watson.* New York: Dana and Company, 1856.

Weise, A[rthur] J[ames]. *History of the City of Troy.* Troy, N.Y.: William H. Young, 1876.
Weise, Arthur James. *Troy's One Hundred Years, 1789–1889.* Troy, N.Y.: William H. Young, 1891.
Wilcoxen, Charlotte. *Seventeenth Century Albany: A Dutch Profile.* 2d ed. Albany: Albany Institute of History and Art, 1984.
Wilson, S., comp. *Albany City Guide, 1844.* Albany: Printed by C. Wendell, 1844.
Worth, Gorham A. *Random Recollections of Albany, From 1800 to 1808.* 3d ed. Albany: J. Munsell, 1866.

MAPS AND ATLASES

Hoffman, Pease & Tolley. *Map of the City of Albany.* N.p.: Sprague & Co., 1857.
Insurance Maps of Albany, New York. New York: Sanborn-Perris Map Co. Limited, 1892.
Sanborn Insurance Maps of Albany, New York. Vol. I. New York: Sanborn Map Company, 1934.

JOURNAL ARTICLES

"Albany Female Academy." *The Zodiac* I, 8 (February 1836), 116–17.
"Albany Fifty Years Ago." *Harper's New Monthly Magazine* XIV, 82 (March 1857), 451–63.
Bucher, Douglas G. "Philip Hooker: Upstate Federal Period Architect." *Newsletter: Preservation League of New York State* X, 1 (January–February 1984), 4–5.
Cobb, Henry Ives, Jr. "1803 Facade moved as a Unit." *American Architect* CXXXVII, 2580 (February 1930), 60–61, 84.
Cogswell, Ledyard, Jr. "Some Albany Views." *Antiques* LX, 1 (July 1951), 39–41.
"Columbia County Court House." *Rural Repository* XVII, 1 (20 June 1840), 1.
Columbian Magazine II (April 1788), 178.
Cooper, Henry S. F., Jr. "Hyde Hall." *Historic Preservation* XVII, 5 (September–October 1965), 172–75.
Cutler, C. B. "The Albany Academy." *Architectural Record* XXXIX, 1 (January 1916), 132–43.
———. "Albany Academy." *Architectural Record* XXXIX, 3 (March 1916), 247–64.
"Description of the New State Hall." *The Zodiac* I, 9 (March 1836), 137–38.
Dykeman, J. L. "The Lancaster School, Albany, N.Y., Philip Hooker, Architect." *Architecture* XXXVI, 6 (December 1917), 245–46, pls. CCXIII–CCXVI.
Dykeman, John L. "The Three Hooker Churches." *Architecture* XXXIX, 5 (May 1919), 123–25, pls. Frontispiece, LXIX–LXXIV.
"First Reformed Church, Albany, N.Y." *Architecture* XXXIX, 6 (June 1919), pls. XCI–XCIII.
Grills, Russ. "Lorenzo: In Search of an Architect." *John Lincklaen Journals* (The Friends of Lorenzo), No. 6 (October 1983), n.p.
Kennedy, Roger G. "A New Discovery Enhances the Architectural Legacy of Pierre Pharoux." *Architectural Digest* CXXXIX, 2 (February 1991), 27, 30, 34, 38, 40.
Kent, Douglas R. "History in houses: Hyde Hall, Otsego County, New York." *Antiques* XCII, 2 (August 1967), 187–93.
———. "Hyde Hall: America's Greatest Country House." *Newsletter: Preservation League of New York State* XII, 4 (Fall 1986), 4–5.
Lassiter, William L. "James Eights and His Albany Views." *Antiques* LIII, 5 (May 1948), 360–61.

McKee, Harley J. "Building for the State of New York, 1790–1890." *Empire State Architect* XVI, 3 (May–June 1956), 23; 4 (July–August 1956), 19; 5 (September–October 1956), 51–52; 6 (November–December 1956), 33–34.
Mather, Frederic G. "The Old Capitol in Albany." *Harper's Weekly* XXVII, 1395 (15 September 1883), 587–88.
"Meeting House in Hollis Street." *Massachusetts Magazine* V (December 1793), 707.
"Mount Hope." *The Cultivator* [n.s. II, 2] (February 1845), 43–44.
"New York State National Bank, Albany, N.Y." *Architecture* XXXIV, 6 (December 1916), 272, pls. CXCI–CXCII.
Reynolds, Marcus T. "The Colonial Buildings of Rensselaerswyck." *Architectural Record* IV, 4 (April–June 1895), 415–38.
Schuyler, Montgomery. "A History of Old Colonial Architecture." *Architectural Record* IV, 3 (January–March 1895), 312–66.
"Scientific Convention. The Section of Mathematics, Physics and Astronomy, Senate Chamber." *Frank Leslie's Illustrated Newspaper* II, 39 (6 September 1856), 193–95.
"Second Presbyterian Church, Albany, N.Y." *Architecture* XL, 3 (September 1919), pls. CXLII–CXLVI.
Sinclair, Douglas. "The Dissolving of Division & Green." *Albany Preservation Report* VIII, 1 (February–March 1989), 1, 5–8.
Wheeler, Walter Richard. "The architecture of Philip Hooker in New York State." *Antiques* CXLI, 3 (March 1992), 472–79.
Wiencek, Henry. "Dark Shadows." *Connoisseur* CCXXII, 960 (January 1992), 64–71, 115.

NEWSPAPERS

Albany Argus
Albany Daily Advertiser
Albany Daily Evening Times
Albany Gazette
Albany Register
Daily Albany Argus
Microscope (Albany)
Utica Daily Gazette

UNPUBLISHED PAPERS AND MANUSCRIPTS

UNPUBLISHED THESES AND DISSERTATIONS

Gotsch, Charles Edward. "The Albany Workingmen's Party and the Rise of Popular Politics." Ph.D. dissertation, State University of New York at Albany, 1976.
Horst, Susan. "The Watson Manor: A Preliminary Historic Structure Report." Master's thesis, Columbia University, 1980.
Miller, Jean Newbold. "John Meads of Albany, Cabinetmaker (1777–1859)." Senior project, Bard College Continuing Studies Program, 1987.
O'Donnell, Wilson E. "John Meads, Albany Cabinetmaker." Master's thesis, Cooperstown Graduate Program, State University of New York College at Oneonta, 1981.
Rowley, William Esmond. "Albany: A Tale of Two Cities 1820–1880." Ph.D. dissertation, Harvard University, 1967.

MANUSCRIPT COLLECTIONS

Albany County Hall of Records, Albany, N.Y.
- Albany Academy Building Committee Minutes
- Albany Academy Papers
- Albany Common Council, Laws Passed 1830
- Albany Common Council Minutes
- City Engineer's Maps
- Bob Cohen. "37–39 South Ferry Street." 1981 (typescript)
- [Steve McArdle?] "No. 59 South Ferry Street." n.d. (typescript)
- Edward C. McCulloch. "No. 83 Columbia Street." 1977 (typescript)
- "Nos. 60, 62, 64 and 66 Westerlo Street." n.d. (typescript)
- Philip Hooker, Historian's File
- State Archives Records Administration (SARA)

Albany Institute of History & Art, McKinney Library, Albany, N.Y.
- Erastus Corning I (1794–1872) Papers, 1801–1872
- George W. Featherstonhaugh Papers, 1771–1856
- Philip Hooker Papers
- Lush Family Papers
- Peter McNab Account Book (photocopy)
- Photograph collection

Albany Public Library, Pruyn Room, Albany, N.Y.
- Vertical file

Douglas G. Bucher

Don Carpentier
- Ruell Clapp Papers

Cornell University, Department of Manuscripts and University Archives, Olin Library, Ithaca, N.Y.
- George Hyde Clarke Papers

First Church in Albany, Archives, Albany, N.Y.
- Consistory Minutes, South Dutch Reformed Church
- Dutch Reformed Church Collection
- Dutch Reformed Church Consistory Minutes
- Dutch Reformed Church Consistory Notes
- "1814 Consistory House Erected"
- Miscellaneous documents

First Lutheran Church, Archives, Albany, N.Y.
- Building Costs Account Book
- First Lutheran Church Council Minutes
- Miscellaneous items
- Treasurers Book

First Presbyterian Church, Archives, Albany, N.Y.

First Presbyterian Church, Archives, Cazenovia, N.Y.
- Construction contract

Friends of Hyde Hall, Inc., Springfield, N.Y.

Hamilton College, Archives, Clinton, N.Y.
- Edward Root. "The Architecture of Philip Hooker: Its Place in History." [c. 1930] (typescript)
- Edward Root. "Old Albany Architecture of Philip Hooker." [c. 1925] (typescript)

Herkimer County Historical Society, Herkimer, N.Y.

Library of Congress, Division of Prints and Photographs, Washington, D.C.
- "The First Dutch Church in Albany, N.Y.," Historic American Building Survey drawings. 1939–41 (submitted but not approved)

Lorenzo State Historic Site, New York State Office of Parks, Recreation and Historic Preservation, Cazenovia, N.Y.
  Lincklaen/Ledyard Papers
New York Historical Association Library, Cooperstown, N.Y.
  Ruell Clapp Papers (photocopies)
The New-York Historical Society, Manuscripts Division, New York, N.Y.
  Utica, Misc.
The New-York Historical Society, Museum Department, New York, N.Y.
  P[hilip] Hooker, "View of Bryan's Place"
New York Public Library, New York, N.Y.
  Gansevoort-Lansing Collection
New York State Library, Manuscripts and Special Collections, Albany, N.Y.
  John V. A. Lansing Papers
  "Mixed Medley," Memoirs. 1821 (Elkanah Watson)
  Pierre Pharoux. "Journal of Castorland," English translation
  Phelps Family Papers, 1781–1919
  St. Peter's Episcopal Church Papers, Albany, N.Y., Records, 1790–1900
  Townsend Papers
  Van Rensselaer Manor House, 1766–1836
  Van Rensselaer Manor Papers
  Van Schaick Family Papers
  Elkanah Watson Papers
New York State Library, New York State Archives, Albany, N.Y.
  Office of the State Comptroller, Archives
Niskayuna Reformed Church, Archives, Niskayuna, N.Y.
  Consistory Minutes
  Miscellaneous items
Oneida County Historical Society, Utica, N.Y.
  Bank of Utica Accounts Book
  Susan Fitchett. "The Eames, Sanger Home." 1980 (typescript)
  Photograph collection
  John J. Walsh. "From Frontier Post to Modern City: A History of Utica 1784–1920." 1978 (typescript)
  John J. Walsh. "Vignettes of Old Utica, Persons, Places and Events." 1975 (typescript)
Kenneth G. Reynolds
  Marcus T. Reynolds Papers
Rensselaer County Historical Society, Troy, N.Y.
  Christopher Slouter Papers
St. Paul's Church, Albany, N.Y.
  Scrapbooks
St. Peter's Episcopal Church, Archives, Albany, N.Y.
Dorothy Sutherland
  Peter McNab Account Book
Trinity Episcopal Church, Archives, Lansingburgh, N.Y.
  Miscellaneous items
  Protestant Episcopal Church Vestry Minutes
University of Michigan, William L. Clements Library, Ann Arbor, Mich.
  Josephus Bradner Stuart Papers
Utica Public Library, Utica, N.Y.
  Photograph collection
Walter Richard Wheeler, Troy, N.Y.
  Walter Richard Wheeler. "Philip Hooker: Rediscovered." 1983 (manuscript)

INDEX OF CATALOGUE RAISONNÉ ENTRIES AND ATTRIBUTIONS

Churches
Civic Buildings
Commercial Buildings
Country Houses
Educational Buildings
Miscellaneous
Urban Houses

CHURCHES

Catalogue Entry

CIVIC BUILDINGS

Catalogue Entry

COMMERCIAL BUILDINGS

Catalogue Entry

COUNTRY HOUSES

EDUCATIONAL BUILDINGS

MISCELLANEOUS

URBAN HOUSES

Catalogue Entry